AN EXPLORER'S GUIDE

Arizona

AN EXPLORER'S GUIDE

Arizona

Christine Maxa

Photographs by David A. James

SECOND EDITION

The Countryman Press ✱ Woodstock, Vermont

We welcome your comments and suggestions. Please contact Explorer's Guide Editor, The Countryman Press, P.O. Box 748, Woodstock, VT 05091, or e-mail countrymanpress@wwnorton.com.

Second Edition

Arizona: An Explorer's Guide

ISBN: 978-0-88150-894-9

Cover and text design by Bodenweber Design
Interior photographs: © David A. James unless otherwise noted
Maps by Paul Woodward, and Erin Greb Cartography© The Countryman Press
Text composition by Eugenie S. Delaney

Published by The Countryman Press, P.O. Box 748, Woodstock, Vermont 05091

Distributed by W. W. Norton & Company, Inc., 500 Fifth Avenue, New York, NY 10110

Printed in the United States of America

10 9 8 7 6 5 4 3 2 1

EXPLORE WITH US

Arizona: An Explorer's Guide is broken down into sections representing different areas of the state, then into chapters focusing on an individual city or town. Each chapter opens with a general or historical introduction to the city or town, and then continues with information on destinations, accommodations, and restaurants that, largely, are quintessential Arizona.

We've tried to list independent venues as much as possible, for two reasons. Most readers, first of all, will know what to expect with the franchises. More important, independent businesses are a perfect example of the spirit of Arizona. We've also done our best to interweave history and fun facts into every aspect of the book, not just the introductions. This, we feel, is invaluable in getting to know a place.

WILDER PLACES

lists backcountry destinations of unique interest and/or scenic beauty.

LODGING

will give you ideas of where to find unique and/or consistently good places to stay. In almost every case, if we haven't stayed there, we've paid a visit and checked it out. Often these lodgings come with some great history attached. Sometimes our listings are slim because a town offers mostly franchises.

WHERE TO EAT

lists venues that serve dependably good food. We've divided them into two categories—*Dining Out* (better restaurants) and *Eating Out* (casual ones). Sometimes restaurants have off nights or suddenly change hands and morph into something totally unacceptable. Please do not blame us—but do inform us.

THE ARTS

are featured not only because art and art walks are becoming popular and valuable sources of revenue for towns but also because these forms of self-expression often reveal the personality of the residents and a place. We tell you where to find galleries and art-centered shops, murals, or museums.

KEY TO SYMBOLS

- **Special value.** The blue-ribbon symbol appears at restaurants and lodging that have a consistently good product available at a moderate or low price.
- **Pets.** The dog-paw symbol signals accommodations that allow pets and other venues that are unusually pet-friendly. Any stipulations appear in the review.
- **Child-friendly.** The crayon symbol appears next to lodgings, restaurants, and activities that are welcoming to youngsters.
- ♿ **Handicapped access.** The wheelchair symbol appears beside lodgings and attractions that offer handicapped access.
- **WiFi access.**
- **Hosts weddings/civil unions.**
- **Eco-friendly establishment.**
- ♥ **Romantic.**

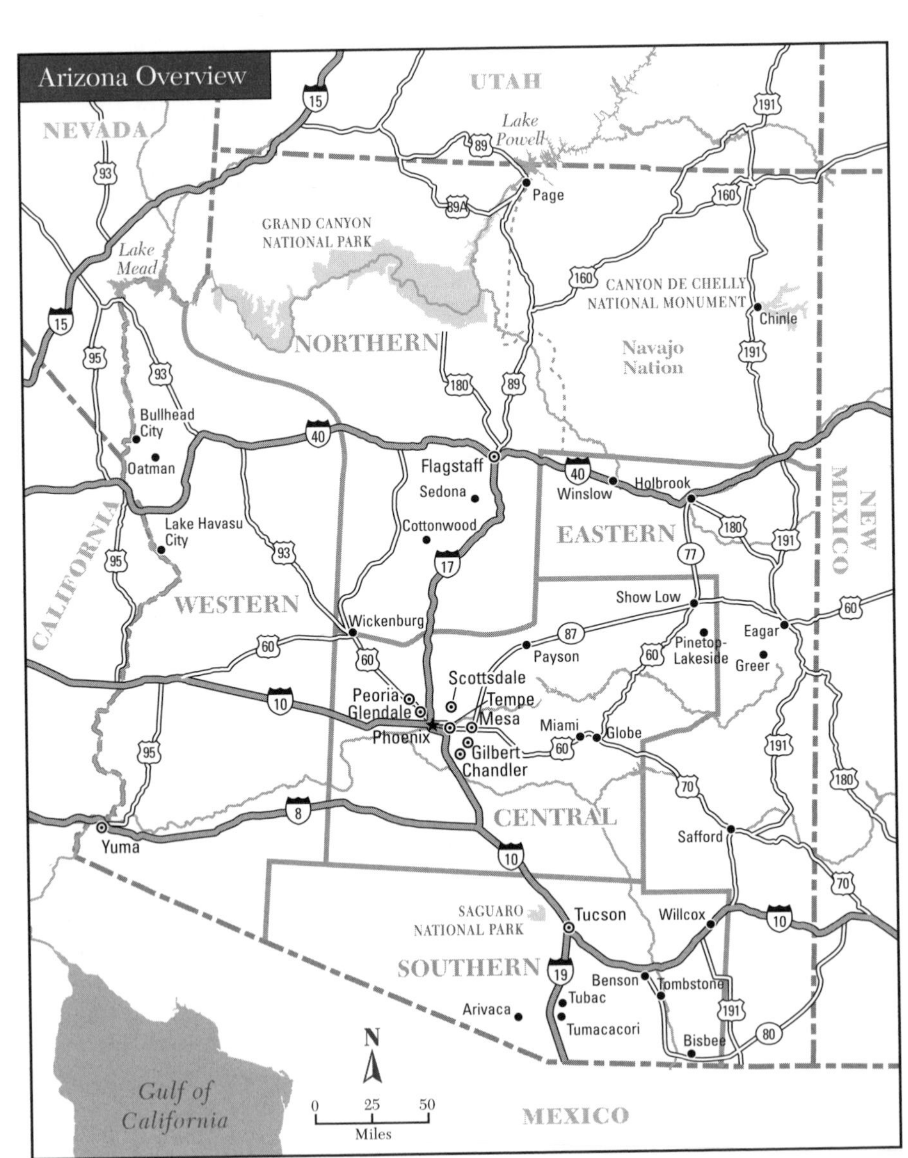

Arizona Overview
UTAH
NEVADA
Lake Powell
Page
GRAND CANYON NATIONAL PARK
Lake Mead
CANYON DE CHELLY NATIONAL MONUMENT
Chinle
NORTHERN
Navajo Nation
Bullhead City
Oatman
Flagstaff
Sedona
Winslow
Holbrook
Lake Havasu City
Cottonwood
EASTERN
NEW MEXICO
CALIFORNIA
WESTERN
Show Low
Wickenburg
Eagar
Payson
Pinetop-Lakeside
Greer
Scottsdale
Peoria
Glendale
Tempe
Mesa
Phoenix
Miami
Globe
Gilbert
Chandler
CENTRAL
Safford
Yuma
SAGUARO NATIONAL PARK
Tucson
Willcox
SOUTHERN
Benson
Tombstone
Tubac
Arivaca
Tumacacori
Bisbee
Gulf of California
0 25 50
Miles
MEXICO

CONTENTS

5 Western Arizona / 315

MAPS

INTRODUCTION

For many native and long-term residents of Arizona, the state has come a long way in the last 50 years. For decades the state lumbered along as a cowboy's workplace and a sunshine winter haven where snowbirds moved with the seasons from points north. Movie stars, politicos, and upper crusters who needed a breather from the masses nestled in the resorts clearly meant for a standard of living much higher than the locals'.

In the 1980s development happened. Populations doubled, and the slower, cowtown ways of life wobbled in the wake of city living. By the 1990s sophistication was seeping into every corner of the state. Corporate-weary professionals brought their tastes, and money, to Arizona, the nation's promised land, where jobs and opportunities prevailed.

YOU WON'T SEE MANY COWBOYS ALONG ARIZONA HIGHWAYS; YOU'LL HAVE TO GO ON A BACKCOUNTRY ADVENTURE.

By the turn of the millennium, the scale had tipped. Gone were the tracts of open space around the bigger cities. The small towns took their turn in the cultural shift. If you haven't taken a ride around Arizona for a few years, or dismissed it because accommodations and services didn't have what you needed in the way of comfort, it's time to take another look.

Small towns with crumbling historic architecture and services that hadn't progressed since Historic Route 66 gave way to I-40 have been practically born again. Buildings are getting repaired and remodeled. Businesses have quality products with touches of luxury. And chambers and visitor bureaus actually have information on not just the major draws that everyone knows about, but also the unique and interesting aspects of the community that people really want to discover.

In the bigger cities things are changing so quickly, you don't want to stay away more than a few months if you have any hopes of keeping current. Phoenix has resuscitated its downtown section so valiantly, people (this includes business people) living in the trendy Valley outskirts have moved to the city's interior "where all their friends are." Some say the heat (as in what's cool) has moved from Scottsdale to Phoenix. Let's just say you can be anyone you want and still feel comfortable in Phoenix. Tucson, second only to the West Coast in cool meccas for the hippie gypsy in the 1960s and '70s, has actually held on to its cultural mien while developing to the hilt. Flagstaff—always the quiet genius that shunned the limelight its neighbor Sedona adored, and content with the world coming through its doors on the way to the Grand Canyon—can't stay out of the nation's marketing limelight for too long.

It won't matter where you travel in the state: you will find exceptionally good food, and in the oddest places. Big cities here are approaching the same culinary level as New York City, Chicago, and Los Angeles. Yes, things have evolved that much. Every one of the larger cities should be on every locavore's list. More surprising, you are apt to find some of the best food experiences in the tiny towns. Remember the world-weary professionals who moved to small towns? They merely continued their genius where they plopped down.

This is one of the best times to live in and visit Arizona. Admittedly, some residents are reeling from all the rocking. Others are enjoying the ride. This goes the same for visitors. With that in mind, we've endeavored in this guidebook to seek out not only places that are consistently good in services and products but also destinations, accommodations, and restaurants that have historic and/or cultural ties or personify the state's personality.

Personality? The conservative, don't fix-it-if-it's-not-broken state has a personality? Actually, yes. Arizona is strongly independent, stubborn sometimes to its own hurt, and an utter romantic with a passion for legends and lore. The state has embraced some of the most colorful, creative, poetic, infamous, and, at times, nefarious characters in the history of the nation . . . many of whom would have been (or were) run out of town in other states. From this colorful brew, as any chaos theory expert will tell you, comes deep beauty and awesome creativity.

A VIEW FROM THE GRAND CANYON'S SOUTH RIM

And while Arizona has had its messy moments in history, it always comes out smelling like a rose. With characteristics like that, no wonder Arizona's been so misunderstood.

We would like to thank Kermit Hummel for the opportunity to write this guide, Lisa Sacks for editing it, and all the people who graciously helped in our gathering of information for it, especially Dwayne Cassidy.

WHAT'S WHERE IN ARIZONA

AGRICULTURE Farming in Arizona goes back to the days before the birth of Christ when native peoples farmed washes, terraces and the fertile land wherever a river or creek flowed throughout the state. After the Chinese came to "Gold Mountain" (California) in the 1840s, they followed the minerals into Arizona in the late 1860s, they farmed along rivers and had gardens in cities to feed the miners. In the early 1900s, Mexicans from Sonora made their way into the state and established *rancheritas* along the Gila, San Pedro, Santa Cruz, and Hassayampa rivers. The Salt River Valley (Phoenix), once overlaid with farms in the 20th century, has turned into a metropolis with a few farms, mostly on the outskirts. Foodies might want to visit several organic ones—**Duncan Family Farms, McClendon's, Maya's Farm**, and **Singh Farms**. The Tucson Basin's **River Road Farms**, located in an area with farming history, has a roadside stand every Saturday. South of Willcox, the Sulphur Springs Valley (especially **Fort Grant Road**) has fruit and nut orchards and roadside stands, such as **Brigg's & Egger**, which grows quality organic fruit. And don't hesitate to head to Yuma (the iceberg lettuce capital of the world) for those wonderful world-class Bard dates.

AIRPORTS Commercial airlines fly in and out of Phoenix's **Sky Harbor International Airport** and **Tucson International Airport** daily. Airports in smaller cities and towns are listed in *Getting There*. Also, the Arizona Office of Tourism refers travelers to www.azdot.gov/aviation/airports/airports.asp to find the more than 80 other airports in the state that accommodate private and public flights.

AMTRAK The Southwest Chief travels through Winslow and Flagstaff, and the Sunset Limited through Benson and Tucson in southern Arizona. Log

onto www.amtrak.com/servlet/Content Server?pagename=Amtrak/HomePage for more information.

ANTIQUES Although still relatively young, Arizona has a nice cache of antiques and collectible shops you can peruse. The Arizona Antiques Merchant Directory at www.azbonline.com /scripts/Merchant_Listing.asp?Category=553 is a good source.

AREA CODES The state's original area code, 602, is assigned only to central Phoenix. Outside Phoenix, generally, dial 480 for Scottsdale and the east Valley and 623 for the west Valley, 520 when in Tucson and most points inside Pima, Pinal, and Cochise counties, everywhere else, dial 928; for more specific information, log onto www.all areacodes.com/arizona_area_codes .htm.

ARIZONA TRAIL Described as remote and a challenge by the agencies that manage the land through which it passes, the currently 830-mile-long (and growing) Arizona Trail offers one of the most diverse and wild experiences a hiker can find on a relatively well-marked (and sometimes primitive) route. Divided into 43 passages and just over 90 percent completed, the Arizona Trail begins at the Coronado National Memorial on the U.S.-Mexico border and ends within the Bureau of Land Management's Arizona Strip District at the Utah border. In between, the Trail brushes through pine-oak grasslands, sweats through quintessential Sonoran Desert landscapes, struggles across razorback ridgelines, grinds up sub-alpine mountains, and scrambles through the grandest of canyons. The Arizona Trail's layout epitomizes the wide range of geological and ecological diversity in the state and some of the most spectacular scenery in

Western America. For more information, log onto www.aztrail.org.

AUTUMN COLOR Unlike the two- to three-week span of color most states in the country experience, Arizona enjoys three full months of arboreal color, starting in the high country aspen forests from the end of September to mid-October, moving into high desert canyons filled with hardwoods from October into November, and then finishing in the desert canyons' riparian forests of willows and cottonwoods from mid-November into very early December. Find the best color in the backcountry in Christine Maxa's *Arizona's Best Autumn Color—50 Great Hikes* (Jamax Publishers Press, 2001). Mountain roads, such as **Arizona 67** to the North Rim of the Grand Canyon (early October), **Snow Bowl Road** up Mt. Humphreys in Flagstaff (early October), **Arizona 89A** over Mingus Mountain by Jerome and into Oak Creek Canyon north of Sedona (mid-to late-October), the **Control Road (FR 300**, high clearance) on the Mogollon Rim (mid-October), the northern portion of **US 191** between Alpine and Hannagan Meadows (early October), and **General Hitchcock Highway** up Mt. Lemmon near Tucson (early October), have great shows of color.

BICYCLING Whether you mountain-bike or prefer skinny tires, you'll find plenty of places to ride. Cosmic Ray's *Arizona Mountain Bike Trail Guide: Fat Tire Tales &Trails* (Cosmic Ray Publications, 2009) is a fat tire favorite; Christine Maxa's *Cycling Arizona: The Statewide Road Biking Guide* (Westcliffe Publishers, 2007) is the state's only skinny tire guide and covers routes in the whole state. Also check the *To Do* section in each chapter.

BIRD-WATCHING The state bird, the cactus wren, is only one of 541 birds sighted in Arizona. Head to any waterway or forest (including saguaro cactus forests) and you'll find birds. Log onto http://azfo.org/index.html for Arizona birding details. Also check the *To Do* or *Wilder Places* in each chapter for birding hotspots.

BOATING With the Bureau of Reclamation's penchant for impounding river water, Arizona has gotten itself some respectable lakes on which to boat—**Lake Powell** near Page being the most alluring; the desert lakes along the Salt River: **Saguaro**, **Apache, Canyon, Roosevelt,** and **Horseshoe** and **Bartlett** along the Verde River nearby **Lake Pleasant** on the Agua Fria River; the Lower Colorado River and its pooled lakes: **Havasu, Mojave**, and **Mead** (and neighboring **Alamo Lake** on the Bill Williams River); southern Arizona's **Patagonia** and **Parker lakes**. The Mogollon Rim, Flagstaff (southeast), Williams, and White Mountains have some great tucked away natural lakes for nonmotorized boats. These and other lakes will be listed under the *To Do* or *Wilder Places* section in each chapter.

BUREAU OF LAND MANAGEMENT (BLM) LANDS Those looking for a wilder experience know BLM lands have less structure (and less people), as well as (usually) no user fees. They are listed in the *Wilder Places* section of each chapter with contact information in the *Guidance* section. Just be sure you have good route-finding skills and tell someone where you're going and when you'll be back. Some of these lands are out-there.

BUTTERFLIES As one of the prime butterfly spots in the United States, Arizona attracts around 180 species of butterflies, including the state's official (and rare) two-tailed swallowtail. Basically, head for where the flowers grow (see **WILDFLOWERS**). Some of the best butterfly spotting sights are **Desert Botanical Gardens** in Phoenix, **Boyce Thompson Arboretum** in Superior, **Garden Canyon** in Sierra Vista, and **Page Springs Fish Hatchery** in Page Springs just west of Sedona. **Boyce Thompson Arboretum** coordinates monarch butterfly taggings in September.

BYWAYS To really understand how diverse Arizona is, do some road tours on its 26 byways (www.byways.org/explore/states/AZ). While **Historic Route 66** and **Old Route 66-Oatman Road, Sedona-Oak Creek Canyon Scenic Road**, and **Kaibab Plateau-North Rim Parkway** draws the world to their pavements, you might want to make time for **Apache Trail Historic Road** just east of Phoenix, the high country along the

Coronado Trail Scenic Byway, and the Navajo Nation's **Naat' tsis' aan—Navajo Mountain Scenic Road.**

CAMPING Generally speaking, you can camp most anywhere (unless marked) off the road on Arizona's public lands. If you're looking for a campground, every national forest (see **NATIONAL FORESTS**) has a number of recreation sites, and most national parks and monuments have campgrounds. Campgrounds are listed in destinations throughout the guide. You can find more information on the national forests' websites or log onto www.camparizona.com.

CITIES Arizona's capital, Phoenix, is also the state's largest city. Tucson comes in second. Flagstaff is the largest city in northern Arizona.

CLIMATE You'll experience all kinds of climates if you do any traveling around the state. Check out the *When to Come* listings in this guide for more information on specific places. But if you just want warm to hot, stick to the Lower Sonora Desert in cities like Phoenix, Tucson, and Yuma. Bring a sweater for air-conditioned buildings in the summer. The high desert climes, such as Sedona, Prescott, Jerome, Sonoita, and Bisbee, will see some snow in the winter and 90-degree days with cool nights in the summer. The high country (7,000 feet and above) has the mildest (70s and 80s) weather in the summer, but snow happens anytime. Wherever and whenever you go, remember the temperatures will rise until late afternoon and then drop 20 to 30 degrees at night. (See also **MONSOON SEASON**.)

COFFEE You can find a Starbucks in just about any Safeway grocery store. Some of the more distinctive coffee spots around the state are listed in the *Eating Out* sections of the book. Circle K convenience stores usually offer a pretty darn good (and cheap) cup of Joe. Check out www.arizona-coffee.com/coffee-roasters-arizona for coffee roasters around the state.

COWBOYS Yep, Arizona still has cowboys, those spin-offs of the Mexican *vaqueros*. You may not see them, especially if you're hangin' around one of the big cities. But head out on Arizona 89 between **Prescott** and **Peeples Valley** and the dirt roads in the area; or out on the ranchlands in southern Arizona near **Sonoita** and **Patagonia**, and you may have a cowboy encounter. Or, just go to **Mormon Lake Lodge** near Flagstaff (owned by area rancher-businessman Rex Maughan) on the right weekend where the cowboys are havin' themselves a real good time during cowboy contests and you can purchase a T-shirt that says, I SURVIVED MORMON LAKE.

DOGS Most of Arizona's bigger hotels are dog friendly. This guide lists Fido-friendly places with a 🐾 icon, and mentions *Dog Parks* in most towns. However, national parks, most national monuments, and bighorn sheep areas do not allow dogs. This includes many trails around Tucson. Never, ever leave your dog unattended in the car. The hot sun, even in the lower elevations during winter, can heat the interior to unsafe levels. Remember to keep your dog hydrated. Always keep your canine on a leash on hiking trails. Owners who don't leash their pets in city parks may get a ticket if a park ranger sees them. Besides keeping dog owners out of trouble, leashes (no longer than 6 feet) will help keep dogs out of trouble, too. Coyotes, which see Fifi as food, will stay away because the leash will keep her too close to her human. During the summer, dogs should be off desert trails by 9 AM. During any time of the year, owners shouldn't hike any trail for which their pets aren't conditioned. A dog's paws must get conditioned before hitting the trail or hot pavement. Finally, dog owners who pooh-pooh packing out their dog's waste in city parks may be packing out a ticket for breaking local ordinances.

EMERGENCIES Dial 911 statewide in case of emergency. Contact information for regional medical facilities are provided under *Medical Emergencies* in each chapter.

EVENTS You can find out what events are happening, and when, in the *Special Events* sections.

FARMERS' MARKETS Arizona chefs have gotten on the farm-to-table bandwagon, with some changing their menus every day or so. So farmers' markets have become big events. The best are **Downtown Phoenix Public Market**, Scottsdale's **Old Town Farmers' Market**, and **Santa Cruz River Farmers' Market** in Tucson. Also check out the Saturday markets in Flagstaff and Prescott. Bring a bag with handles and cash in the form of small bills, put on sunscreen and bring plenty of water, and have fun talking with the desert farmers.

FISHING Fishing is big in Arizona. All of the state's lakes (see **BOATING**) make great places to catch *the big one.* **Lake Powell** is famous for small mouth bass. Huge northern pike lurk in **Lake Mary**. **Lake Pleasant** has great top-fishing in the hot months. Mountain streams flow with rainbow and Apache trout (the state's official fish), and fly fishermen favor the **upper Colorado River**, especially **Less Ferry**, **Silver** and **Canyon creeks** on the Mogollon Rim, and **Thompson Creek** in the White Mountains, and **Pacheta Creek** on the White Mountain Apache Reservation. Phoenix, Tucson, and Payson have urban lakes right in town. Game and Fish stocks lakes and ponds (one big fish for every 20) with **rainbow trout** from November through March, **channel catfish** March through July and September to November, and **sunfish** three times a year. Bass, crappie, blue gill, white amur, talapia, and carp roam the waters as well. Wherever you fish, a license is required, along with a trout stamp if you're casting for trout. Log onto www.azgfd.gov for more information.

GARDENS Botanicals go beyond cactus gardens here in Arizona. The **Rose Garden** at Mesa Community College

is one of 26 AARS test sites. The **Japanese Friendship Garden** in Phoenix is an authentic Japanese garden. However, if you're looking to learn about the Sonora Desert's native plants, check out the **Boyce Thompson Arboretum** in Superior, **Desert Botanical Gardens** in Phoenix, and **Tucson Botanical Gardens** and **Tohono Chul Park** in Tucson. To learn about the high country plants, visit the **Arboretum at Flagstaff**. More information on most all of these gardens is found in the *To Do* sections.

GEOGRAPHY Several distinctive geographical features make up the diverse Arizonan topography. The charismatic **Colorado Plateau** with its red-rock formations, slot canyons, hoodoos, and natural bridges, spans an area just north of the Mogollon Rim into Utah and New Mexico. Several mountain ranges make up the **Central Mountains**, where Jerome, Prescott, and Sedona are located. The **Mogollon Rim**, which has the largest stand of Ponderosa pine in the world, stretches just east of I-17 into New Mexico. The state's major cities of Phoenix and Tucson lie in the **Lower Sonora Desert**, an area roughly from just north of Phoenix down to the Mexican border. The **Lower Colorado River** country in western Arizona nudges the Mojave Desert and records the least amount of rainfall, lowest elevations, and highest temperatures in the state. The **Grasslands** of southeastern Arizona have sky island mountain ranges that jut several thousand feet from their high desert floor.

GEOLOGY Petrified sand dunes, ancient sea beds, massive uplifting, millennial erosion—all this geologic action helped create the colorful, stratified, dramatic and often awesome landscapes of Arizona. For the in-depth story, check out Halka Chronic's *Roadside Geology of Arizona* (Mountain Press Publishing Company, 1993).

GOLF Three hundred sunny days, more than 300 golf courses . . . what to do, what to do. **THIS** book presents some distinguished and/or popular courses in the *To Do* section. For more, check out www.arizonagolfcourses.com.

GREYHOUND BUS You can get to most towns along major highways in Arizona on the bus. Log onto http://www.greyhound.com/home for more information.

GUEST RANCHES You'll get a chance to test your new chaps or just laze around the ramada and take in the open-space views at guest ranches in several different areas around the state. Check out the *Accommodations* section in each chapter or log onto www.arizonaguide.com/hotels-lodging/guest-ranches.

HAUNTED HOTELS Some people call them spirits, some ghosts. Whatever they are, they're all over the place in Arizona. Or so they say. Most innkeepers of old historic hotels or buildings converted into bed & breakfasts, especially in the more raucous former mining towns, have a story or two to tell. If you're looking for an encounter, you might have an experience, especially at **Hotel Vendome** in Prescott, **Hotel Monte Vista** in Flagstaff, **Red Garter Inn** in Williams, **Copper Queen** in Bisbee, and just about everywhere in Jerome. Otherwise you can probably count on a good night's sleep.

HIGHWAYS Four interstates run through Arizona—latitudinal **I-40** travels across northern Arizona, **I-10** across the south, and **I-17** running north–south in between. **Interstate-19** continues south from I-17 to Mexico. **Arizona 89** travels a mostly rural route from Utah to Mexico, though it goes under different numbers as it nears Phoenix and heads south. Several sections of **US 66** parallel I-40.

HIGHWAY SHRINES Since the state has so many two-lane roads wending through some gnarly mountainous terrain, memorial shrines appear along many roads. Some will grab your attention, and make interesting reminders to slow down and enjoy your ride. There are several developed shrines not necessarily linked to highway fatalities that have become a traditional place to make requests to the Powers That Be. Some are listed under *Scenic Drives* or *To See*.

HIKING From the desert in the winter to the high country in the summer and the high desert in the seasons in-between; if you could, you could hike every day of the year in Arizona. Since more than 80 percent of the state is public land, hikers will never lack for trails. Trails you don't want to miss are listed in the *To Do* section under *Hiking* or in *Wilder Places*. Christine Maxa's informative *Hiking Arizona* (HumanKinetics, 2002) includes some of the best trails in the whole state.

HUNTING The Arizona Game and Fish Department (www.azgf.gov) has all the information about what, when, where and how much you can hunt. Tips, some from the grapevine, are: **white tail deer** (Galiuro Mountains), **elk** (White Mountains and San Carlos Apache Nation), **mountain lion** (Weaver and Santa Teresa mountains), **bighorn sheep** (Aravaipa Canyon area), **turkey** (White Mountains and Kaibab Plateau), **quail** (San Simon Valley), and **javelina** (just about everywhere in the high desert). If you're into hiking and not hunting, take care on high country trails during the fall months.

KAYAKING You can paddle all of the lakes (but watch for motorboats) and many of the rivers in Arizona. Places to kayak are listed in the *To Do* sections. Try **Watson Lake** in Prescott, the **Gila River** after heavy precipitation, and the **Verde River** from fall through spring.

LEAVE NO TRACE In the 1970s, the forest service developed a list of guidelines on how to experience the backcountry—plan ahead and prepare, travel and camp on durable surfaces,

dispose of waste properly, leave what you find, minimize campfire impacts, respect wildlife, be considerate of other visitors—and called them Leave No Trace (LNT). At the time of its inception, millions of hikers and backpackers were enjoying, the nation's backcountry and the guidelines were meant to help lessen the impact. In the desert, where the land can require decades to process impacts, LNT becomes a requirement. But LNT is much more than just minimum-impact guidelines for hiking and camping. It's an awareness: an understanding of one's responsibility and connection to our natural environment. For more information log onto www.lnt.org.

LIGHTNING Thanks to its summertime monsoon storms, Arizona has the reputation as the place of choice for storm chasers. The awesome streaks and flashes of lightning produced by the storms have between 100 million and 1 billion volts with temps of over 50,000 degrees F. Unless you're a Warren Faidley devotee, when lightning strikes, seek cover immediately, avoid tall trees, and don't touch your metal automobile.

LODGING Since most people know what to expect from the popular franchised accommodations, this book focuses on independent accommodations. Franchises are listed if they have a unique feature or personality.

MAPS The Arizona Office of Tourism (www.azot.com) has printed a great map of the state available for free at their tourism offices around the state. If you're heading into the backcountry, you can purchase topographical and agency maps at **Wild World of Maps** (stores in Phoenix, and Mesa or www.maps4u.com) or most forest service offices.

MONSOON SEASON During the summer, starting sometime around July 4 and ending mid-September, Arizona gets monsoon storms. The term *monsoon* comes from an Arabic word that means *season* or *wind shift*. Arizona "monsoons" happen during the summer season because of a wind shift. Arizona's prevailing winds flow from the west/northwest in winter. In summer, the winds shift to south/southeast. The wind shift occurs because of an upper-air subtropical high pressure called the Bermuda High. This wind shift brings moisture from points south (either the Pacific Ocean or Gulf of Mexico). The monsoon season officially begins when the dew point (the point at which condensation occurs) hovers around 55 degrees F or more for three days in a row. When the monsoon thunderstorms start, they blast the high country first, from late morning to early afternoon. Then the storm cells head southward into the desert. Rain may not hit Phoenix until late afternoon. Around Tucson, storms form atop the surrounding mountains, then head right into the city from different directions, The storms, often daily events in the high country, ebb and flow with weather systems south of the border, especially during *chubasco*, Mexico's storm season in August and September, when the extra load of moisture can produce a string of days with heavy rains. If you plan to do any outside recreation in the high country, get it done in the morning or bring raingear. Watch for lightning on the Mogollon Rim and mountain peaks.

NATIONAL FORESTS The state's five national forests cover 9,810,512 acres of land and a diversity of biomes. **Apache-Sitgreaves NF**, located in eastern Arizona, has the water—lakes, streams, rivers and creeks. It also gets less use. You can go for days, in the right spots, without seeing anyone. During a prolific monsoon season, its high country can look like a coastal rainforest. **Coconino National Forest** in north-central Arizona has the popular red-rock country, dramatic canyons, and the highest country (12,633-foot Mt. Humphreys in the San Francisco Peaks). The **Coronado National Forest** in southeast Arizona has the greatest diversity in flora and fauna because of its sky island mountain ranges. At elevations ranging from 3,000 to 10,720 feet, you can experience landscape you'd see traveling from Mexico to Canada in a few hour's time. The sky islands also dictate the forest's five districts, each separated by grasslands, The Grand Canyon cuts through the **Kaibab National Forest** in northern Arizona. If you want untrammeled open space, head for its northern ranger district on the Kaibab Plateau. Ponderosa pines and granite boulders make up the landscape of the **Prescott National Forest** in central Arizona. The largest, and most popular, **Tonto National Forest** is located just north of Phoenix. The landscape ranges from quintessential Sonora Desert to pine forests. Highpoints in each forest is listed in *Wilder Places.*

NATIONAL PARKS AND MONUMENTS There are 28 national parks and monuments to visit in the state and each are listed in *Wilder Places.*

NATIVE PEOPLES Twenty-two federally recognized tribes reside in Arizona (this includes the Pueblo Zuni, who have a land base in Arizona). Their communities and nations, located all over the state, are signed and you will need permission to travel anywhere off the main highway on these lands. For more information, log onto www.arizonaguide.com/things-to-do/native-cultures/tribes.

POISONOUS CRITTERS AND PUNCTURING THINGS Arizona has an impressive collection of poisonous, stinging and puncturing things—a dozen species of poisonous snakes (which includes the state's official reptile, the ridge-nosed rattlesnake); one poisonous species of scorpion; Gila monsters; tarantula, black widow, and brown recluse spiders; centipedes; and cactus all over the lower and high desert. Your best defense to prevent an event is to watch where you put your hands and feet. Also remember snakes and Gila monsters coincide nicely with humanity; it's usually when people provoke them that they will bite. Shake out your shoes before wearing to avoid scorpions, when staying in remote places. If you do get bitten by any poisonous reptiles or insects, head directly to a hospital. *Always* watch your kids and keep your dogs on a leash to prevent accidental bites and cactus encounters. (See **DOGS**.)

ROAD REPORTS You can get information about road conditions and construction by dialing 5-1-1. Or you can log onto www.az511.gov/home.php to learn more about travel time and restrictions.

SUNSHINE Depending where you are in Arizona, you can see more than

300 days of sunshine. In the summer, as little as 12 minutes of exposure at noon can burn unprotected skin. So you can understand how Arizonans have the highest rate of skin cancer in the United States and second highest in the world. Protect yourself by (1) spending as little time as possible in the sun between 10 AM and 3 PM; (2) wearing a wide-brimmed hat, long-sleeved shirt, and long pants; and (3) wearing a sunscreen with a sun protection factor (SPF) of at least 15.

TAXES The sales tax on items you purchase will vary, and includes a number of taxes. Rates start with the state sales tax at 6.6 percent. The counties and/or cities will add their figurative two-cents worth. Some examples at the time of this writing—Tucson at 8.6 percent, Flagstaff at 9.91 percent (10.91 for restaurants), Phoenix at 9.3 percent, Prescott at 9.35 percent, Scottsdale at 9.95 percent, Sedona at 10.725 percent, and Wickenburg at 11.5 percent.

UNIVERSITIES Arizona's public universities include **Arizona State University** (Tempe, Phoenix, Mesa), **Northern Arizona University** (Flagstaff), and **University of Arizona** (Tucson). Private universities include: **Argosy University** (Phoenix), **Embry-Riddle Aeronautical University** (Prescott), **Grand Canyon University** (Phoenix), **Midwestern University** (Glendale), **Northcentral University** (Prescott), **University of Phoenix** (multiple campuses), and **Western International University** (Phoenix).

VINEYARDS Arizona vintners have been turning the heads of experts for a couple decades, especially with **Callaghan Vineyard's** award-winning wines getting consistently high points in Parker reviews and appearing in the White House. Lately the scene has gotten lively with vintners bringing a little Hollywood glam (**Pillsbury Wines**) and rock-star sparkle (**Arizona Stronghold Vineyard**). Oregon pinot master **Dick Erath** has even planted some vines here. It all started in southern Arizona around **Elgin** and **Sonoita**, when University of Arizona soil specialist Dr. Gordon Dutt discovered the soil in the area was almost identical to that in Burgundy, France, and planted **Sonoita Vineyards**. The rolling hills rising to 5,000 feet get doused with sunshine but experience cool nights. More vineyards cluster farther east off I-40 and **south of Willcox**. **Page Springs**, west of Sedona, has become another successful growing area.

WATCHABLE WILDLIFE Since more than 80 percent of the land is public, chances are good you'll encounter wildlife as you tool around the state. You can see the state's official animal, the ringtail, in the lower desert, from city parks to backcountry washes. In the high country, you may see mountain lion, bear, elk, deer, javelina, and coatimundi. To find out

where the wildlife hangs out, log onto Arizona Game and Fish Department's Web site at www.azgfd.gov/outdoor_recreation/watchable_wildlife.shtml.

WHITEWATER RAFTING For some white-knuckle whitewater fun, the **Colorado River's** run through the Grand Canyon is a must. But don't forget the **Salt River** gets pretty feisty during snowmelt after a wet winter.

WILDFLOWERS People travel from all over the world to see the spectacular show of spring wildflowers in the Lower Sonora Desert after a wet winter. Flowers appear from late February into April, depending on nature's whim. The official state flower, saguaro cactus blossom, opens from May into June. If you visit in the summertime, head for the high country, where monsoon storms coax dozens of different species. Christine Maxa's *Arizona's Best Wildflower Hikes—The High Country* (Jamax Publishers Press, 2002) features the best trails to find flowers.

WINTER SPORTS When it's raining in the desert during the winter, snow lovers head for Arizona's higher mountaintops. For downhill skiing, **Arizona Snowbowl** in Flagstaff has the black diamond runs for speed seekers. **Sunrise Park Resort** in McNary in the White Mountains has long, moderate runs great for beginners and families. **Mt. Lemmon Ski Resort** near Tucson has everything from powder to mashed potatoes, and the early skier gets the best runs. The **Nordic Ski Center** in Flagstaff and **Pole Knoll Trail System** near Greer in the White Mountains has paths to wander upon with your skis or snowshoes. Sledders can head to the **Wing Mountain Sledding and Snow Play Area** in Flagstaff and **Mingus Snow Play** area just west of Jerome.

Northern Arizona

1

PAGE AND LAKE POWELL

NAVAJO NATION

GRAND CANYON NATIONAL PARK—NORTH RIM

GRAND CANYON NATIONAL PARK—SOUTH RIM

FLAGSTAFF

WILLIAMS

PRESCOTT

VERDE VALLEY
(Cottonwood, Camp Verde, Clarkdale, Cornville, Page Springs, Rimrock)

JEROME

SEDONA/OAK CREEK CANYON

PAGE AND LAKE POWELL

If it weren't for Lake Powell, Page might not exist. The child of the Colorado River formed with the construction of Glen Canyon Dam in 1957. However, the mesa-top town doesn't necessarily exist for the lake. The landscape, dramatic and highly attractive on its own, comes with a fascinating geological history. Once an expanse of ancient seas and freshwater lakes, the area endured the creation of mountains and plateau uplifting, resulting in a gorgeous landscape of sandstone cliffs carved by wind and water from the Colorado and the Escalante rivers. Only the most adventurous explored this beautiful but rugged area. Labyrinthine canyons were treasure chests that cached hanging gardens, dainty cascades, and relics from Native peoples out of sight from the masses.

Then things changed in the 1950s. The esoteric high-desert hideaway became a world-class water world when the dam came on the scene. Built to meet western energy demands, the dam pooled the volatile Colorado River waters into Lake Powell. Canyons were submerged; a new environment supported a different set of mammals and fish; and aesthetically, the place turned surreal. The lake brought a bit of Venetian enchantment to the harsh, but beautiful western landscape. The elegance of the lakeshore scenery tends to have the same overwhelming effect as any other international city that captivates its visitors' hearts and souls. People come to check out this exquisite setting, thinking they can sum it up with a *veni vidi vici* notch on their travel belt. Rather than being an *I came I saw I conquered* experience, the lake usually always ends up the conqueror, ever luring visitors back to its side for a continuing journal of adventure and discovery.

GUIDANCE **Page–Lake Powell Tourism Bureau** (888-261-7243, 647-A Elm St., offers information on things going on in town, on the lake, and around the Grand Circle area (northern Arizona and southern Utah). The **North Kaibab Ranger District** (928-643-7395), 430 S. Main St., Fredonia, can tell you more about trails in the national forest on the Arizona Strip. The **Bureau of Land Management** (435-688-3200), Arizona Strip Field Office, 345 E. Riverside Dr., St. George, Utah, is your source for exploring the national monuments in the area.

GETTING THERE *By car:* From points south, take US 89 out of Flagstaff. From Utah, head south and east on US 89. From the Navajo Nation, take AZ 98. *By air:* **Page Municipal Airport** (928-645-4337), 238 10th Ave., has a 5,500-foot asphalt concrete runway and service to Phoenix and Denver through Great Lakes Airlines.

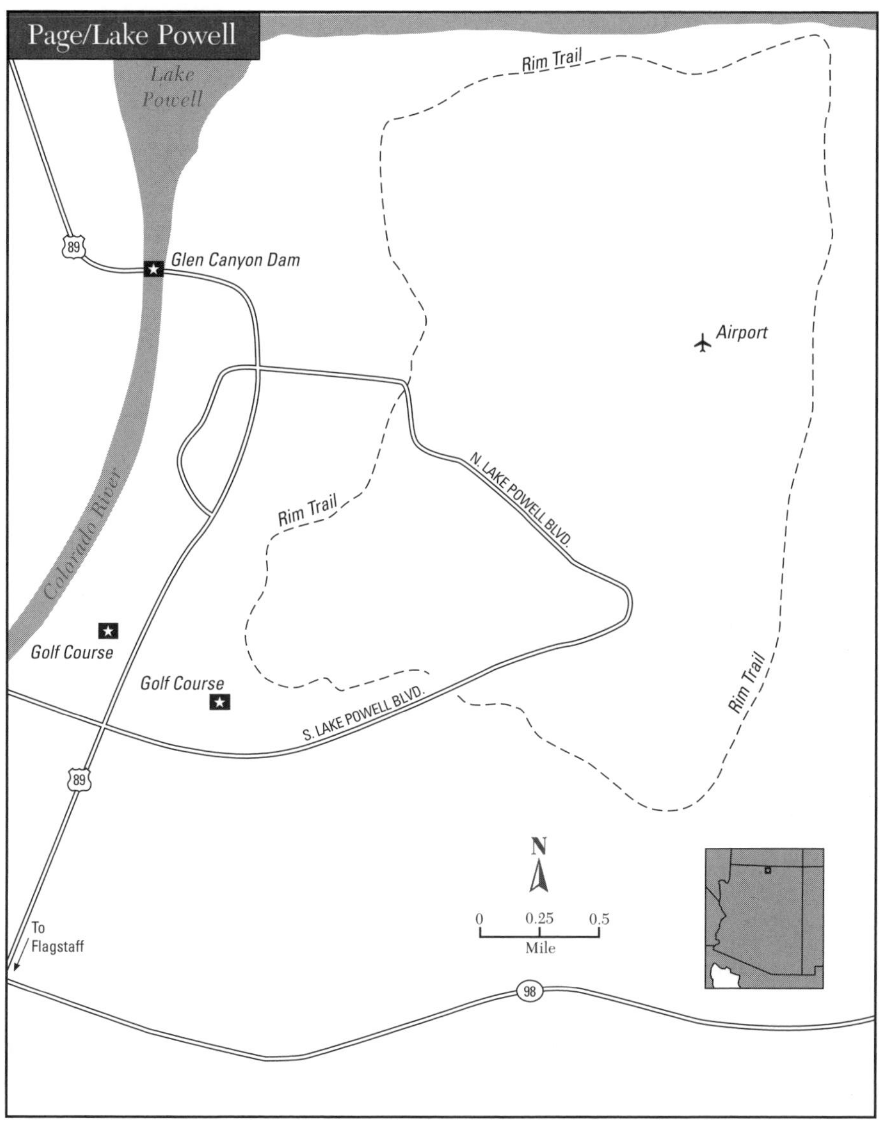

WHEN TO COME Summertime is high season for lake activities. If you're looking for a bargain, plan your trip for Nov.–March. Hikers, mountain bikers, and road bicyclists should visit during fall, winter, and early spring. Deer flies become merciless in late spring.

MEDICAL EMERGENCY Page Hospital (928-645-2424), 501 N. Navajo.

✷ To See

Carl Hayden Visitors Center at Glen Canyon Dam (928-608-6404). Open daily 8–5, except for summer (call for days) 8–6 and Nov.–Feb. 8:30–4:30; closed

Thanksgiving, Christmas, and New Year's Day. The facility has exhibits about the construction of the dam and tours through the dam and Glen Canyon Powerplant. The dam, finished in the 1960s, was built to supply electricity to western states—enough to power 400,000 households for a year. But all has not been rosy in the Colorado River since the completion of the dam. The resulting cold waters, perfect for rainbow trout, compromise the existence of the native fish, including the dour humpback chub. An aquarium lets you take a look at the endangered native fish that lurk in the Colorado River. Security check required to tour the dam.

John Wesley Powell Memorial Museum (928-645-9496), 6 N. Lake Powell Blvd. Open Mon.–Fri. 9–5. The museum has a number of interesting things packed into it—from dinosaurs and Anasazi artifacts to present-day finds from recent Colorado River explorations—and of course a display memorializing Powell's epic journey down the Colorado River 1869–1871. $5 adults, $3 age 62-plus, $1 ages 5–12.

✷ To Do

BOAT RENTALS The most comfortable way to experience elegant Lake Powell is by renting a houseboat. That way you can go where you like, exploring the captivating landscape by day and sleeping in a bed (or on the upper deck under the stars) at night. The portly vessels gulp about 10 to 15 gallons of gas per hour. This translates, on average, to a $500 to $700 gas bill for the week. If you like camping out, you can rent a 19- or 26-foot motorboat and spend a quarter of that in gas and rental fees per week. **Antelope Point Marina** (928-645-5900) rents 59- and 70-foot houseboats for three ($3,895) to seven ($7,995) days; 75-foot houseboats for five ($9,395) to seven ($12,995) days (all boats are replaced every three years). The fee runs $970–2,114 for a day's rental during peak season. **Aramark** (928-645-1067) rents 44- to 75-foot boats for three ($2,200) to seven ($12,492) days during peak season. Rates drop as much as 40 percent off-season.

FISHING The hottest fly-fishing in the state happens at **Lees Ferry** (at the community of Marble Canyon, just beyond the Navajo Bridge, turn right onto the signed turnoff for Lees Ferry and go 5 miles) in the Colorado River. It's world class in both fishing and scenery. You can employ a guide to help you land that lunker. Savvy Terry Gunn, owner of **Lees Ferry Anglers** at Cliff Dwellers (928-355-2261), says the fishing here is the best in the Lower 48.

GOLF **Lake Powell National Golf Course** (928-645-2023), US 89 and Lake Powell Blvd. One of golf's hidden gems, this championship-quality public course is a tricky one thanks to its 300-foot elevation change and undulations that hide traps. It's one of the toughest par-4s in the nation. The signature 15th hole has you teeing from the top of the course to the hole on its lowlands. Add to the exciting golf game the exquisite scenery of azure blue Lake Powell surrounded by sanguine sandstone cliffs, and you can understand why golfers around the nation have this on their list of must-play courses. 9 holes $40, 18 holes $69.

HOT-AIR BALLOONING **Page-Lake Powell Balloons, LLC** (928-640-0144). Page has hosted one of the most popular balloon regattas in the Southwest for several years (see *Events*) Now you can lift off any time of the year in Page-Lake

NAVAJO BRIDGE

Go south 25 miles on US 89, turn right onto US 89A and go 14 miles. Before the original Navajo Bridge was built in 1929, the only access between Utah and Arizona was the undependable river crossing at Lees Ferry. When floods flowed during storms, the ferry stopped, and so did traffic. The bridge presented cutting-edge technology, and was the highest steel-arch bridge in the country, rising 470 feet above the Colorado River. Grand Canyon National Park and Glen Canyon National Recreation Area meet on one side of the river, the Navajo Nation lies on the other.

As snazzy as this steel-frame structure was, it soon became outdated when load limits paled compared to what was needed for the heavier modern-day vehicles. Further, the original bridge was too narrow. The new bridge proved more an engineering marvel than the old because the project builders, Cannon and Associates, had to follow stringent environmental regulations and deal with intense public concern.

The mechanically inclined will be interested to know Cannon used a method called cantilevering to building the bridge. A tieback device held up the bridge as it was built, piece by piece, from both sides of the canyon. The tieback had to accommodate the wind, temporary decking, netting for debris, a crane, and the vehicle that transported materials to the site. For each of the 20 ribs on the bridge, workers drilled 55 feet into the rock to place a rock anchor, then post-tensioned them. Taking all that into consideration, when you cross either one of these steel-arch spans, know you are walking on some very special structures.

Powell's Basket Case balloon. The three-hour adventure includes an hour of airtime where the scenery is exquisite. The tradition landing ceremony includes a toast of champagne and fruit juices, and other surprises. Call for information and prices.

KAYAKING When drought conditions in the early 2000s dropped the lake water to half its pool capacity, houseboats and yachts encountered sandbar obstacles, and kayaks became de rigueur. They're also among the best vessels for up-close exploration. **Kayak Powell** (888-854-7862) takes you out on half-day to multinight tours Apr.–Oct. that include a guide (Kyle Walker, a state-certified guide and Coast Guard–certified captain with more than 10 years' lake experience), gear, and meals. You can join a scheduled trip or customize your own for three to eight people. Call for rates.

LAKE POWELL MARINAS Several marinas dot the thousands of miles of lakefront. The most accessible are **Wahweap Marina** (928-645-2433), 6 miles north of Page, and **Antelope Point** (928-645-5900), the largest floating concrete structure in the world, just east of Page on AZ 98. Both require $15 admission by the National Park Service. **Bullfrog Resort & Marina** (435-684-3000) is located in Utah, near midlake; **Halls Crossing Marina** (435-684-7460), also midlake, is across from Bullfrog Marina (435-684-7400); **Hite Marina** (435-684-2273) is on the east end of the lake, off UT 95; and **Dangling Rope** (928-645-2969) is 40 miles uplake from Wahweap, near the canyon to Rainbow Bridge.

LAKE TOURS **Lake Powell Resort** offers a number of Lake Powell tours: 90-minute-long Antelope Canyon Tour ($40 adults, $25 ages 3–12); 3-hour Navajo Tapestry Tour ($76 adults, $45 ages 3–12, includes lunch); and 7-hour tours to Rainbow Bridge ($172 adults, $102 ages 3–12, includes lunch).

MOUNTAIN BIKING Page has been called the next Moab, with its slickrock surfaces and stunning red sandstone scenery. The best time to bike is fall through spring. Contact Vance at **Lakeside Bikes** (928-645-2266), 118 6th Ave., for information on routes. Watch for a new bike trail in Glen Canyon National Recreation Area.

NAVAJO CULTURE With the Navajo Nation right next door, you don't have to go far to experience the vibrant landscape and culture of the Diné. **The Navajo Heritage Center** (928-660-0304), located at Coppermine Rd. and AZ 98 behind the Big Lake Trading Post, preserves and accurately portrays the culture and traditions of the Navajo people in a captivating presentation called **An Evening with the Navajo**. Diné artisans demonstrate rug weaving, jewelry making, and dances and offer insight into why they do things the way they do; Navajo food is included. $50 adults, $30 ages 6–13.

SLOT CANYON TOURS While the Colorado Plateau often flaunts its attractive geology in places such as the Glen Canyon National Recreation Center, Grand Canyon and Monument Valley, it has its secrets. Hidden away from the casual

ENTRANCE TO A SLOT CANYON NEAR LAKE POWELL

glance lay some of the most extraordinary natural features in the state, called slot canyons. Some of these canyons narrow to an arm span. Some have legends and lore. All have their own personality worth experiencing. Most tours companies travel into Antelope Canyon, the darling of slot canyons. Check out **Chief Tsosie** (928-645-5594), 55 S. Lake Powell Blvd., for a personable and insightful tour. Chief also leads exclusive tours into more rugged Cathedral Canyon, as well as photographic tours and a Star Gazing Adventure. $20–35 adults, $10 age 12 or under.

Overland Canyon Tours (928-608-4072), 695 N. Navajo, does exclusive tours into Canyon X. Named for the X formed by two intersecting canyons, this slot has less tour groups and a quieter atmosphere than Antelope Canyon. No noise. No crowds. Photographers love it. $100 adults, $35 kids.

Slot Canyon Hummer Adventures (928-645-2266), 12 N. Lake Powell Blvd. A unique three- to five-hour four-wheel drive experience in the leather-upholstered and air-conditioned comfort of a screaming yellow Hummer, which takes you over slickrock, steep roads, and sand dunes to a spectacular (and as of today) unnamed slot canyon upstream from famous Water Holes Canyon. Still pristine, visited by wildlife, and emoting a centering feeling; the twists, turns, and sinuous forms of the water shaped sandstone walls present an exclusive experience. $69–139.

SOFT-WATER FLOAT ON THE COLORADO RIVER **The Glen Canyon Float** is exclusively offered by Colorado River Discovery (928-645-9175 or 888-522-6644), 130 6th Ave., Mar.–Nov. The closest you'll get to river action on this smooth-water trip is gentle riffles. The big water comes after Lees Ferry, where this trip ends; you return to Page via bus. Still, the scenery is just as impressive as the classic whitewater river trip. Side trips to petroglyph sites make a nice diversion. $84 adults, $74 ages 4–12. For a more intimate float, reserve a spot on the full-day Rowing Trip ($161 adults, $151 ages 4–11). The boat seats only eight people and a guide.

✷ Wilder Places

ARIZONA STRIP Go south on US 89 for 25 miles, turn right onto US 89A, and continue 14 miles to Navajo Bridge at Marble Canyon. Detached from the rest of the state by the Colorado River, and left to its own devices, the Arizona Strip retains its wild and remote demeanor. If you like uncluttered wilderness where nature has the last word, you'll find it on the Strip. Most of the area remains undiscovered by the casual outdoors people. Check out **Cathedral Wash, Soap Creek Canyon** (contact the Bureau of Land Management), and **Kanab Creek Canyon** (contact the North Kaibab Ranger District).

NATIONAL PARKS AND MONUMENTS **Glen Canyon National Recreation Area** (928-608-6200). Because this multiarmed area ensconces the Colorado (Lake Powell), Escalante, and San Juan Rivers, people think backpacks are out and boats rule. This perpetuates one of the area's best-kept secrets: Lake Powell takes up only 13 percent of the recreation area. That means you have approximately 1,044,000 acres of high desert canyons, cliffs, and plateaus to explore on foot where lodes of petrified wood, dinosaur bones, seashells, and sharks' teeth await discovery. Get ready for some remote adventures. Check out their Web site for

A PANORAMA OF LAKE POWELL

hiking and mountain biking routes (www.nps.gov/glca/planyourvisit). $15/week per vehicles, $7/week per individual on foot or bicycle.

Grand Canyon-Parashant National Monument (contact the Bureau of Land Management). Talk about getting out there. This is where you go when you want to slip not only the crowds, but life in general. The land, located along the western reaches of the Grand Canyon, is big and the scenery beautiful. To the adventurous backcountry traveler, exploring the million-acre monument will be thrilling. If you're used to paved roads and signage, best you stick with the Grand Canyon's north or south rim. There are no paved roads here (high-clearance vehicle required), few signs, and only a handful of "semimaintained" trails. Canyon treks are awesome. For a soft adventure, check out the rock art at Nampaweap (go 46 miles on Toroweap Rd., turn west onto the signed turnoff for Mt. Trumbull, go 3.5 miles and turn south, go 1.1 miles to the parking area).

Grand Staircase–Escalante National Monument (contact the Bureau of Land Management). The cumbersome name comes from two of the monument's natural features: a geological stairway of different-colored cliffs—the Vermilion, White, Grey, and Pink Cliffs—that eventually rise 5,500 feet to the rim of Bryce Canyon in the west; and the Escalante River, which flows in the monument's eastern end. In between the monument's namesake features sprawls the 800,000-acre Kaiparowits Plateau, which you see on the north side of Lake Powell. The plateau's austere landscape, dotted by juniper trees sometimes well over 1,000 years old, hides an extravagant lode of fossils—one of the planet's best examples of continuous late Cretaceous terrestrial life. If you don't want to explore the monument, you can get an idea of the rich cache at the Bureau of Land Management's **Big Water Visitor Center** (435-675-3200), 100 Upper Revolution Way, Big Water, UT. Open daily Apr.–Oct. 9–6, Nov.–Mar. 8–5. The center has a stunning 30-foot mural depicting Late Cretaceous period and dinosaur fossils.

Paria Canyon-Vermillion Cliffs Wilderness/Vermilion Cliffs National Monument (Contact the Bureau of Land Management). A towering stature, sexy curves, and glamorous features. With looks so good, it's not surprising photographers flock to the Paria Canyon–Vermillion Cliffs Wilderness. From its colorful

crossbedded cliffs heaving and dipping like some kind of geological Tilt-a-Whirl in Coyote Buttes to 600-foot-high Navajo sandstone walls in the Narrows of Paria Canyon to the arm-span-wide slot canyon of Buckskin Gulch, the destinations in this wilderness not only show up on every serious outdoors person's life-lists, but science has taken an interest in it, too, since the Vermilion Cliffs has become the main reintroduction point for the California condor. Check out their tracking station along House Rock Valley Road off US 89A about 10 miles east of Jacob Lake.

Pipe Spring National Monument (Located 15 miles from Fredonia off Arizona 389). Located at one of the two main water sources in the area (the other is Moccasin Spring), the area drew Southern Paiute people, then Mormon settlers. The Mormons prevailed, and their homestead here makes an interesting tour. Situated on the Kaibab Indian Reservation, the park has a Kaibab cultural display in the visitor center museum explaining their lifestyles and traditions regarding Neung'we Tuvip, or Pipe Spring. $5 adults.

✷ Lodging

OLD QUARTER HISTORIC HOTELS **Bashful Bob's** (928-645-3919), 750 S. Navajo. Bashful Bob Wombacher has kept his rates the same for the 30-something years he's owned this historic property. Quiet, clean, and simple, each unit has a kitchen, private bathroom, large sitting area, complimentary WiFi, in-room telephones, BBQ grills, and free airport shuttle. The property is popular with European travelers, many of whom are repeat guests; reservations are recommended. $39 double occupancy.

Lulu's Sleep-Ezee (928-608-0273 or 800-553-6211), 105 8th Ave. Lulu Cannon completely overhauled the property into four pleasantly decorated units she keeps superclean. The common patio has a gas grill. Each room has a private bathroom, cable TV, microwave, coffeepot, and free Wi-Fi. Call for rates.

RESORTS AND INNS **Days Inn & Suites** (928-645-2800), 961 N. US 89. This franchise has pleasant rooms with great views. Double, queen, or king beds, along with free WiFi, refrigerator, coffeemaker, free local calls, and free continental breakfast. The property has a swimming pool, laundry facilities, and business center. Parking for boats, trailers, and RVs. Small pets are okay with a fee. $60–75.

Lake Powell Resort (800-528-6154), 100 Lake Shore Dr. A room at this resort is the closest you can come to sleeping on the lake without being waterborne. Ask for a lake-view room. The property has two pools and two restaurants, along with a recreational lawn area, walking path, lounge, gift shop, sports shop, fitness center, and boat tour reservation station. Each room has a mini fridge, cable TV, coffee, and patio or balcony. EcoRooms have Green Leaf certification from TerraChoice Audubon Green Leaf Eco-Rating Program. Pets $20 a night. Call for rates.

Quality Inn at Lake Powell (928-645-8851), 287 N. Lake Powell. Owned and operated by Navajo, the motel has little touches that reflect the traditions of the Navajo people. For instance, each room has a packet of cedar herb to assist you in achieving serenity. The Blue Corn restaurant serves traditional Navajo fare. The property includes a pool, guest laundry, and business center; rooms have complimentary high-speed Internet. A hot buffet breakfast is included with your room. $74–124.

BOAT HOTEL Antelope Point Marina (928-645-5900), Navajo Route 22B, Page. The curious or not-ready-for-prime-time-boaters can stay in a harbor-bound 59- or 70-foot houseboat. The boats are an upscale home away from home, including heat, A/C, electricity, potable water, full kitchen, up to six bedrooms, waterslide and Jacuzzi. All you need bring is the food. Checkout time can be as late as 5 PM, depending on availability. The marina has a floating restaurant that serves breakfast, lunch, and dinner. $300–500 per night.

ARIZONA STRIP LODGES

Lees Ferry Lodge (928-355-2230), HC67—Box 1, Marble Canyon. The old stonework building fits in perfectly with the remote landscape. Each of the 10 rooms opens up to a veranda. Furnished with the anglers who frequent the Colorado River in mind, the interiors are rustic but homey. You won't find a television in the rooms, but you will have a cozy Franklin stove to add a warm glow. Also, beds have down pillows. The Vermilion Cliffs Bar & Grille (see *Dining Out*) is on the premises. Reservations are advised, as rooms fill up quickly. $77.57–118.50.

Marble Canyon Lodge (928-355-2225 or 800-726-1789). If the Arizona Strip has a cosmopolitan area, it would be Marble Canyon. This historic hotel right by the Navajo Bridge gets busy with rafters awaiting, or decompressing from, their rafting trips. The property includes a gas station, restaurant, and laundry facilities. Rooms have TV but no phones. Lodge rates: summer $55–75, winter $50–65.

✷ Where to Eat

DINING OUT Blue Buddha Sushi Lounge (928-645-0007), 844 N. Navajo Dr., Page. The Buddha totally breaks Page's restaurant mold. In a town still under the influence of the bureaucracy that built it, not to mention the tendency toward unwavering tradition from the Navajo folk, this is a big thing. Sushi chef and owner Twist Thompson has thrown a curve ball of creativity into the town starting with the décor, which was designed by him and his wife, Jaime, as if it were their home. Masseuse Sheena Paulus will give you a neck and shoulder massage where you sit, for a few yen. As for the food, serving fresh sushi in the high desert is enough. But Twist adds his own twist to the dishes, with cream sauces (Holy Scallops Entrée and Baked Green Mussels), inventive rolls (such as the Buddha Roll with tempura asparagus, spicy lobster, mango, avocado, and eel sauce; and the LP Roll with salmon, mango, jalapeño, and avocado topped with sweet chile sauce) and fun desserts (Yum Yum Bombs made of tempura-fried Oreos topped with vanilla ice cream, chocolate drizzle and almond slices totally live up to its name). Tradition is not totally ignored, however. Twist can wield his sushi knife just like the old masters. The menu is extensive, and there's something for everyone. Japanese beer, a decent wine list, and flavored sake available. Entrées $14–28, sushi rolls $8–12.

Fiesta Mexicana (928-645-4082), 125 S. Powell. Open daily 11–9. This regional franchise serves classic Mexican fare that is reliably tasty. They are known for the best margaritas in town. Portions are large, so come hungry. Entrées $7.25–16.95.

Vermilion Cliffs Bar & Grille (928-355-2230). Located about 5 miles west of Navajo Bridge, and practically in the middle of nowhere. The eating place of choice for fly-fishers offers dependably good food in large portions, served up by attentive staff full of personality. An extensive selection of gourmet beer (about 100 different brands) is available. Servers are sometimes more colorful than the cliffs for which the restaurant was named. Entrées $5.95–15.95.

EATING OUT **LeChee Flea Market**. Located about 3 miles south of AZ 98 on about Coppermine Rd. Open Sat. 9–3, and sometimes Sun. As the saying goes, "You haven't lived until you've tasted a Rez Dog" (that being a hot dog, bratwurst, or Polish sausage wrapped in frybread dough, then deep-fried). You can get one at reservation flea markets, such as the one here at LeChee (pronounced le-chee-ee), as well as mutton and peppers on frybread, and tamales.

Ranch House Grille (928-645-1420), 819 N. Navajo Dr. Open daily 6–3. The best place in town for breakfast serves up tasty, freshly prepared egg dishes and pancakes all day, and they are (correctly) known for their huevos rancheros. Lunch (salads, sandwiches, and burgers) is decent. The Navajo love this place, from the hip-hop-loving kids to elders in traditional dress. Breakfast $6.25–11.75, lunch $6.25–7.75.

Slackers Quality Grub (928-645-5267), 635 Elm. Open Mon.–Sat. 11 AM–8 PM; from Memorial Day–Super Bowl Sunday, daily 10:30–9. Serving "world famous sandwiches" and "cheeseburgers that change your life," this local favorite gets voted best burgers and sandwiches again and again. Owner Chris Shores has installed TVs all around so you can have a beer or wine and watch the game. "We're not a sports bar," Chris said. "We're somewhere in the middle. We don't get as crazy." But they do get zany. The food, however, is seriously good. The pepper steak sub sure is a winner, as is the pastrami burger (hamburger with onions, pastrami, and melted provolone as well as a host of condiments). Old favorites, such as BLTs, charbroiled chicken, and hot dogs, are available as well. You can also get a full dinner (chicken, steak, ribs) Sandwiches: $3.50–7, dinners $12.50–19.50.

✷ Selective Shopping

Blair's Trading Post (928-645-3008 or 800-644-3008), 626 N. Navajo. The Blair family has traded with the Navajo for more than half a century, and their trading post presents some of the Navajo Nation's best, one-of-a-kind arts and crafts, such as jewelry, baskets, rugs, and kachinas. They'll even help you locate specific items. The founders' collection, displayed in a separate area of the trading post, can be seen upon request.

✷ Special Events

July: **Hometown Fourth of July Celebration** at City Memorial Park (928-645-2741) has vendors, food, and entertainment all day, then fireworks at night.

September: Learn all about the **Colorado Plateau at the Powell Symposium: Exploring the Colorado Plateau** (888-261-7243) through lectures, field trips, receptions, and Colorado River topics.

October: The **Pumpkin Festival** (928-660-3403) features the largest gathering of carved pumpkins in the whole state.

November: **Page Lake Powell Hot Air Balloon Regatta** (928-645-2431) has balloon liftoffs every day of the weekend celebration and features a street fair and balloon glow on Lake Powell Boulevard on Saturday.

December: **Festival of Lights Parade** (928-660-3403) has a parade of decorated floats and Christmas lights.

NAVAJO NATION

The Navajo Nation, full of long views and a wealth of open spaces, has one of the most charismatic landscapes in the state, and it inspires visits from people around the world. Its inhabitants, able to twist poetry with absurdity, are just as endearing, and famous for their sense of humor, artistry, and complex mythology. They call this high-desert country stretched between Four Sacred Mountains in three states (Arizona, Colorado, and New Mexico) the Glittering World or the Fourth Dimension. In Arizona this region stretches from Page eastward to the New Mexico border. On the south end, it curls just south of Cameron around the Coconino National Forest east of Flagstaff. It's a red-rock wonderland full of shifting sands, magnificent buttes and mesas, hues and shadows that change with the whim of the sun, and legends wonderful enough to celebrate humanity and dark enough to raise the hair on the back of your neck. Those who live on the Nation say all these legends are true. Once you travel the Nation, you'll have a chance to decide for yourself.

GUIDANCE Contact **Navajo Tourism**, (928-871-6436) for general information about the Navajo Nation. Obtain permits for hiking, camping, and backcountry travel from **Navajo Parks and Recreation Dept.** (928-871-6647) in Window Rock; **Cameron Visitor Center** (928-679-2303), located at the junction of US 89 and AZ 64; or **Antelope Canyon Tribal Park Office** (928-698-2808) in Page. For boating, fishing, or hunting permits, call **Navajo Fish and Wildlife** (928-871-6451). Tribal offices are open Mon.–Fri. 8–5.

GETTING THERE *By car:* You can approach the Nation, located in the northeastern corner of the state, via US 89 from Flagstaff from the south and Utah from the north. From Page, take AZ 98. From Colorado, take US 160; from New Mexico, US 64 to US 160.

WHEN TO COME Temperature-wise, the best times to visit are Apr.–May and Sept.–Oct. Summer and winter bring poetic moments with monsoon storms and snows that cover the red-rock cliffs. Spring, though mild, can be windy and fickle.

MEDICAL EMERGENCY Dial 911.

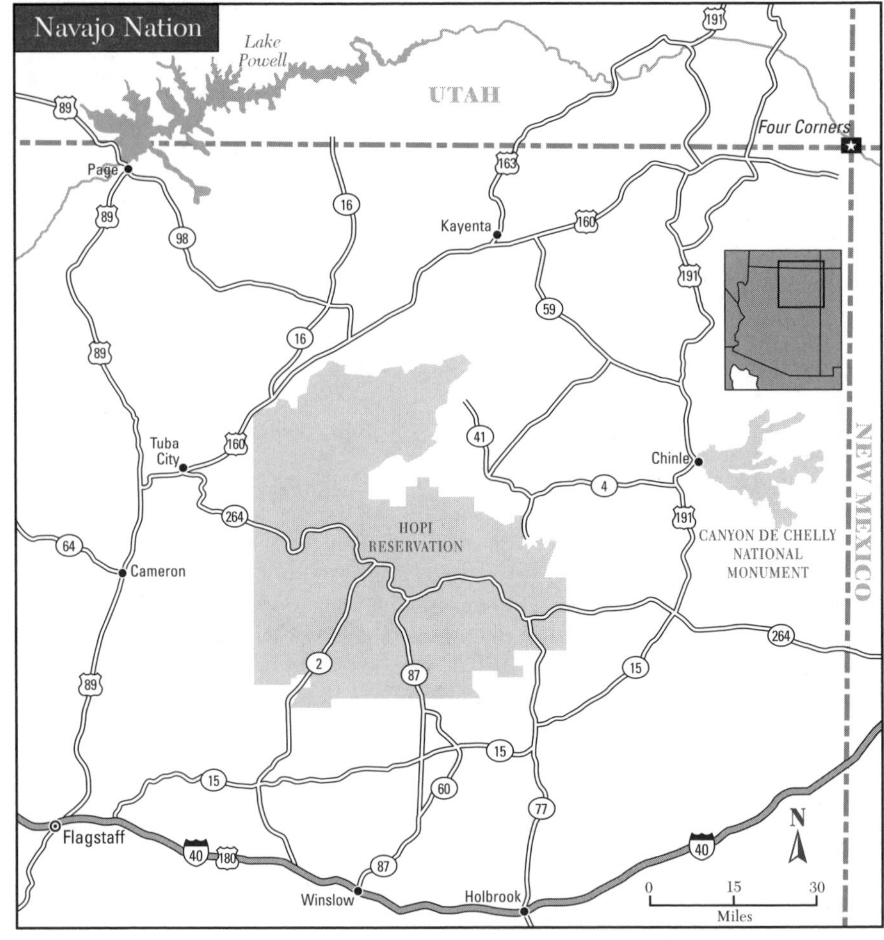

✷ To See

Code Talker Museum (928-697-3534). Located in the Burger King restaurant in Kayenta. An unusual museum in an unlikely location, this collection of memorabilia pays homage to the Navajo marines who created a radio code from their Navajo language (which, traditionally, was spoken, never written) for the U.S. military during World War II. The code was never broken, and historians credit the Navajo Code Talkers for helping to win World War II. Outside, the fast-food spot has historic exhibits and a hogan used by early inhabitants. Free.

Diné College (928-724-6600), 1 Circle Dr., Tsaile. The country's first Native American–owned community college has a curriculum that honors the philosophy of Sá'ah Naagháí Bik'eh Hózhóón—the Diné tradition in which humanity lives in harmony with the natural world and the universe. Of particular interest is the six-story hogan-shaped Ned Hatathli Cultural Center. This structure houses the Hatathli Museum and Gallery, with exhibits of Native American culture as well as a retail store of authentic Navajo arts and crafts, and the Diné College Bookstore. The drive to the college is a scenic adventure in itself. Free.

CULTURAL DIFFERENCES AT THE NAVAJO NATION

To avoid committing a faux pas while traveling the Nation, be aware of the following culture differences.

- Among many Navajos, eye contact is considered impolite. Even though you have their full attention, courteous Navajos will often look down or away.
- Navajos are generally taught not to talk too much, be loud, or forward with strangers. Engaging in conversation is not their mode of operation with strangers.
- If talking is not encouraged, touching can be downright disrespectful to a Navajo. Even a strong handshake is offensive.
- Although Navajos do not own the land on which they live, they do have tribal rights. Exploring without permission off the pavement (on foot or in a vehicle) is not allowed without a Navajo escort or permit.
- Taking a photo of a Navajo is incorrect without their permission. And a small fee is expected.
- Offering to buy jewelry a Navajo is wearing is considered gauche.
- Alcohol is not permitted on the reservation.
- The Navajo Nation observes daylight-saving time Apr.–Oct.

Dinosaur Tracks. Located in Moenave, 5 miles west of Tuba City. This natural site contains many lower Jurassic theropod tracks left around 200 million years ago, along with eggs and fossilized bones. Free.

♿ **People of the Fourth World Museum** (928-283-4545), Quality Inn, Main and Monave Ave., Tuba City. Open Mon.–Sat. 8–6, Sun. noon–6. In 2002 the Navajo Nation presented the Discover Navajo People of the Fourth World Exhibit at the Winter Olympics in Salt Lake City. The tribe has now moved this exhibit to the Quality Inn complex in Tuba City. Displays venture into the Navajo past, present culture, and ceremonial life. Exhibits include the Emergence (the Navajo creation story); the Clan Wheel (the family ancestry lines of the Navajo); a full-size hogan and sweat lodge; and rugs from across the Navajo Nation, each depicting its region's unique pattern; Seasons of the Navajo, explaining the traditional life of a Navajo family; and the Navajo Code Talker Museum, complete with small theater, authentic memorabilia, and original photos from the National Archives in Washington DC. The museum also has interactive displays on topics such as local shepherds and weavers, and an explanation of the Diné clan systems. $9 adults, $7 seniors, $6 ages 6–12, under age 6 free.

Four Corners Navajo Tribal Park (928-871-6647). Located at the northeast tip of Arizona on US 160. Open daily June–Sep, 7 AM–8 PM, Oct.–May, 8–5. You can stand in Arizona, New Mexico, Utah, and Colorado at once here on the brass and granite marker where the corners of the four states meet. Navajo vendors sell handmade jewelry, crafts, and traditional foods around the monument. Inside the visitor center you can watch Navajo artisans work their crafts. $3 per person.

Little Colorado River Gorge. Located in a Navajo tribal park on AZ 64, about 10 miles west of US 89. The Little Colorado River travels all the way from Mount Baldy in eastern Arizona's White Mountains to the Colorado River. Here, the river leaves its meandering ways behind as it plunges 2,000 feet in just 30 miles. From the overlook, the gorge presents a spectacular scene of finely layered upper limestone cliffs contrasted with ruddy sandstone below. Free.

Mystery Valley. Located just south of Monument Valley and open only by tour (see the Monument Valley sidebar, page 42). This collection of swirling sandstone formations, arches, and Indian signs presents an intriguing tour. The House of Many Hands, where whitewashed hand imprints cover the lower walls of a ruin, gave the valley its name. No one knows why the prints are there. Also, Mystery Valley is said to be haunted. The U.S. government buried soldiers here; robbers dug up some of the graves before they were finally moved. In the night Mystery Valley is said to sometimes echo with howling from the horses of these dead soldiers.

Navajo Nation Administration Center (928-871-6417), Window Rock. You can slip into the meeting chambers and view a council meeting from special seating around the perimeter. A Plexiglas barrier just inside the double front doors shields noises when you enter the chambers, to prevent distraction. Call to check when the council meets or to schedule a tour of the chambers.

EXPLORING A SLOT CANYON ON THE NAVAJO NATION

Window Rock Tribal Park and Veteran's Memorial (928-871-6647), located near the Navajo Nation Administration Center. Open daily 8–5. You can view the mystical redstone arch for which the capital is named here, just behind the building that houses the Navajo Nation headquarters and other government offices. Recently a Veterans Memorial was added at the base of Window Rock to honor the many Navajo who served in the U.S. military. The park holds a number of symbolic features: a circular path outlining the four cardinal directions, 16 angled steel pillars with the names of war veterans, and a healing sanctuary—used for reflection and solitude—that features a fountain made of sandstone. Free.

Also see An Evening with the Navajo in "Page and Lake Powell."

PARKS AND MONUMENTS **Canyon de Chelly** (928-674-5500). Located 3 miles east of Chinle on Navajo 7. The second largest canyon on the Colorado Plateau, this deep, soulful gorge (pronounced *de SHAY*) in the northeast corner of Arizona lies almost at the center of the whole Navajo Nation. Ruins and rock art dating from AD 350 to 1300 appear in canyon crevices, and galleries of cottonwood trees line the stream that shimmers along the canyon floor. Some call the 26-mile-long canyon Arizona's other Grand Canyon because of its large size, but the comparison stops there. The canyon does not vaunt itself as a recreational area to the world like the Grand Canyon. Rather, it keeps a private profile. Outside the 1.25-mile-long maintained trail that travels from the rim down to White House Ruins, the canyon's interior is off-limits without a Navajo escort. Still, this canyon exudes enough of its rich atmosphere to inundate anyone peering from overlooks along its rim drives. And step below the dramatic 1,000-foot terra-cotta walls streaked with desert varnish to enter another world where tradition flourishes amid the flow of tourists and modern civilization. There are no telephone or electrical lines in the canyon; sheep tending and farming remain the resident Natives' principal means of support. A spindly monolith known as Spider Rock remains a favorite of Indian parents, who threaten to deposit unruly children there for the mythic Spider Woman to deal with. Free.

Motorized tours: Visitors, strictly forbidden to enter the canyon without a Navajo guide, have several options. Four- and six-wheel-drive jeep tours head daily into the canyon from the Thunderbird Lodge Full day $74 per person; half-day $46 adults, $35 age 12 or under. **Canyon De Chelly Tours** (928-674-5433) will take you in a Unimog group tour for $66 for three hours ($66 adults, $44 under age 12) or on private tours in your SUV ($44 per hour, 3-hour minimum) or theirs ($192.50 for three hours).

Horseback tours: **Twin Trails Tours** (928-674-8425), North Rim Dr., 8 miles north of the visitor center. Two-hour to multiday rides are available; call for prices. **Totsonii Ranch** (928-755-6209), located 1.5 miles past the Spider Rock viewpoint turnoff on South Rim Dr., takes you to the base of Spider Rock, 1,000 feet below the canyon's rim. Call for prices, reservations, and questions.

Hubbell Trading Post National Historic Site (928-755-3475). Usually located along major highways and near chapter houses (the Navajo equivalent of a town hall), trading posts run the gamut from loosely stocked grocery stores to bustling shops with groceries, dry goods, crafts, restaurants, and gasoline. The Hubbell Trading Post, founded in 1876, remains one of the significant trading posts on the reservation and a National Historic Site. Named for Indian trader John Hubbell, the post has changed little in the last century. Old wooden floors still creak vociferously; colorful rows of foodstuffs line the shelves; frying pans, saddles, and handwoven baskets hang from the ceiling; piles of handwoven rugs are carelessly stacked in a separate room. Weavers work on woolen rugs in yet another room, their wooden picks tapping each strand into place with several quick thuds. You can purchase items here, or just admire how little time and traditions have changed. Several special events take place during the year. Aug.–Oct., farmers from the Ganado community bring their produce to the Farmers' Market. Collectors should check out the two Native American Art Auctions take place each year here, featuring contemporary and antique Navajo textiles, Pueblo kachina dolls, pottery, paintings, carvings, and basketry from several tribes. The Artist in Residence program allows

THE NAVAJO ARE RENOWNED FOR THEIR WOVEN RUGS

artists to stay for one to two weeks in a fully furnished stone hogan and create art. Admission is $2 per person.

Navajo National Monument (928-672-2700). Located at the end of AZ 564 off US 160. Open daily 8–5, May 15–Labor Day 8–7. Most pueblo villages in Tsegi Canyon stood on its floor or mesa tops. This park's Betatakin and Keet Seel ruins, however, were built in alcoves and survived the seven centuries of erosion that reduced unprotected ruins to rubble. The canyon, filled with pine and aspen trees at its higher reaches and exposed to the sun at its lower, wider sections, makes a beautiful hike that may turn out to be one of the most awesome and memorable you take. The Hisatsinom, ancestors of the Hopi, built the two ruins. You can visit the ruins via two trails. The 2.5-mile hike to Betatakin Ruins is ranger-led and free. You must obtain a permit to hike the 8 miles to Keet Seel, the older settlement of the two ruins (from AD 900). These permits are coveted, and it may take a few phone calls to get through when the window of opportunity opens (Memorial Day–Labor Day). The visitor center has exhibits on ancient Pueblo Indians, video presentations, and books for sale. Free.

Rainbow Bridge National Monument. Sacred to the Navajo and the largest natural bridge in the world, Rainbow Bridge spans the teal-green waters at the confluence of Forbidding and Bridge Canyons off the Colorado River. Navajo legend says the bridge, actually a petrified rainbow, allowed a war god to cross the tumultuous, storm-racked canyon. Since the pooling of Lake Powell, most people access the national monument via a tour boat on Lake Powell. Two trails lead to the tiny monument (see *Hiking*).

RUINS Although ruins lie cached in alcoves all over the Nation, you must have a guide to approach them in most cases. You can travel without a guide to **White House Ruins** in Canyon de Chelly (south rim) and **Betatakin** and **Keet Seel**

ruins in Navajo National Monument. For an in-depth experience, **Crow Canyon Archaeological Park** (970-565-8975 or 800-422-8975) schedules several-day-guided tours on the Navajo Nation led by informed archaeologists.

SCENIC DRIVES Because the Navajo Nation contains some of the most scenic landscapes in the world just about every paved highway here constitutes a scenic drive. Notice the word *paved*—technically, nonresidents must have a permit to access roads not paved or numbered. The drive from Page to Kayenta on AZ 98 (**Navajo Mountain Scenic Road**) passes the cream of the canyonlands on the reservation, where the sienna cliffs of Kaibito show off an alluring canyon system and unique formations. Deep gorges twisted by the elements hold well-preserved Indian ruins along **US 160** between Tuba City and Kayenta. Every shade of red shows itself in the domes, mesas, and buttes on the way to Monument Valley on **US 163**. At the town of Cottonwood (8 miles west of US 191 on **Navajo 4**), an unmarked northern turnoff travels the exquisite rainbow colors of the Navajo backcountry via a rugged paved road riddled with potholes that presents a combination of multicolored cliffs, the sweet smell of piñon, and unabashed quiet. Paved **Navajo 64** and **Navajo 7** travel the north and south, respectively, rims of Canyon de Chelly. Scenic pull-offs provide good spots for photos.

✱ To Do

HIKING AND BACKPACKING The Navajo Nation's combination of remoteness and scenery sealed in an envelope of quiet is most inspiring. For easy to moderate day hikes, check out the **Wildcat Trail** in Monument Valley and **White House Trail** in the Canyon de Chelly. For an up-close experience with the canyon country, plan a backpack on the north and south **Rainbow Trail**, which travels the Rainbow Plateau to Rainbow Bridge National Monument. Hidden amid an intricate maze of canyons, a hike to the bridge presents a beautiful, but challenging, 2- to 4-day round-trip backpack for experienced hikers. Contact Navajo Parks and Recreation for the required $5-per-day backcountry permit and $5-per-night camping permit.

HORSEBACK TRAIL RIDES **Navajo Country Guided Trail Rides** (navajocountry@gmail.com), mile marker 403 on US 163, 7 miles north of Kayenta. Evelyn Yazzie Jensen and Gunnar Jensen offer a range of opportunities to experience the Nation on horseback, from hourly to several-day rides. You can bring your own horses or ride theirs. Overnight rides include satisfying and good meals. Call for rates.

✱ Lodging

❀ ♿ **Anasazi Inn—Tsegi Canyon** (928-697-3793), Kayenta. Located 11 miles east of US 163 in Tsegi. The scenery surrounding this turquoise-roofed hotel is spectacular. The rooms adjoining the lobby are your best bet; and many have views into Tsegi Canyon. Rooms have king or double beds, cable TV, and air-conditioning. The property includes grills and picnic tables at the rim of the canyon, which makes for a very special outdoor barbecue. $89–99.

🐾 ♿ **Gouldings Lodge** (435-727-3231), Monument Valley, Utah. It was Henry Goulding—owner of this property, once a trading post near

MONUMENT VALLEY

(435-727-5874, -5870, or -5875), located seven miles off US 160 at the Utah border. Open daily Apr.–Sept.7 AM–7 PM, Oct.–Mar. 8–5. Before the Navajos took residence on the land several generations ago, the San Juan Band of Paiutes that frequented the area in AD 1300 also considered it sacred. They called it "Valley Amid the Rocks" and attributed supernatural powers to the area.

Not a valley, as its current and former Ute names imply, the landscape more aptly fits the Navajo's nomenclature of Tse' Bii' Ndzisgaii, or "changing of the rock." From the time an ancient ocean covered Monument Valley millions of years ago, erosional forces of wind and water have shaped the land.

The soft shales, siltstones, and slabs of sandstone eroded over time into pinnacles, spires, and buttes unique to Monument Valley. Iron oxide colored the rocks with hues of red, and manganese oxide painted on precipitous walls black streaks called desert varnish. The distinctive formations create a kinetic atmosphere where monoliths point to a turquoise sky, arches hollow out rockwalls, and erosion-carved formations turn anthropomorphic.

Self-guided trails: The only opportunities to explore the landscape untethered open up on the 17-mile road, which you can mountain bike, and the 3.2-mile nonmotorized Wildcat Trail that loops around West Mitten Butte.

Tours: **Roy Black** (928-429-1959 or 0637) provides guided tours by 4X4 open-air, jeep, horseback, or hiking excursion. **Navajo Land Tours** (928-697-3524) will guide individuals, photographers, or groups into the Valley. Call for prices.

Monument Valley—who opened the door of this stunning area to the world. Dealing with the Indians on everyday matters from buying their goods to acting as liaison between them and the federal government, Goulding knew how hard the Depression hit the area. When he heard that director John Ford planned to film a classic western starring John Wayne on location, Goulding grew determined to make that location Monument Valley and set out for Hollywood in 1938. Ford's staff told Goulding he might wait days before he could meet with the busy director. "I've camped out in worse places," Goulding replied, hauling out his bedroll. "I've got something you want to see, and I'm not leaving until you look at it." Goulding's verve got him an immediate audience with Ford. The "something" he had to show Ford—a portfolio of photos of Monument Valley taken by Josef Muench—wowed Ford, who eventually filmed Stagecoach there. Ford returned to film eight more movies in the area.

The lodge, with its comfortable rooms and tasteful decorations, has a museum memorializing Hollywood's role in the area. All rooms have views of Monument Valley as well as private balcony, cable TV, heat and air-conditioning, coffeemaker, iron and ironing board, and mini fridge. The property has a year-round heated pool and fitness room. $73–180 includes tickets to the museum and Earth Spirit show. Family suites and houses are available for large families.

🐾 ♿ **Hampton Inn** (928-697-3170), US 160, Kayenta. Built adobe style with rustic earth-toned interiors and southwestern-style appointments to meld with the Navajo Nation, this property has a walking trail, outdoor pool, and park-and-fly amenities. Rooms have TV, air-conditioning, and coffeemaker. A continental breakfast bar is included with room. The Kayenta Trading Company Gift Shop has an excellent variety of fine Native American arts, jewelry, and crafts, and is worth the stop in itself. Pets up to 15 pounds are okay, $20 per night. $66–109.

♿ **Navajo Nation Quality Inn** (928-871-4108), 48 W. AZ 264, Window Rock; and (928-283-4545), 10 N. Main St., Tuba City. Owned and operated by the Navajo Nation. A franchise classic, but with Diné influences—both properties have restaurants featuring local native foods like Navajo taco and mutton stew, along with Mexican and American foods. The Tuba City version includes **The People of the Fourth World Museum** with exhibits first presented to the world at the 2002 Winter Olympics. Rooms have double beds, satellite TV, and high-speed Internet. Breakfast buffet included. $72–88.

Thunderbird Lodge (928-674-5841 or 800-679-2473), P.O. Box 548, Chinle. Located 0.5 mile from the Canyon de Chelly Visitor Center. This historic property stands on the grounds of an old trading post and has remarkable character. Sprawling cottonwood trees, planted by the Civilian Conservation Corps in the 1930s, provide shady spots to relax under. There's a cafeteria-style restaurant that serves some tasty Native American dishes, as well as basic continental cuisine, and a gift shop with a great assortment of Navajo rugs. The rooms feature rustic furniture, Navajo paintings, full private bath, air-conditioning/central heating, telephone, and cable TV. You can arrange tours into the monument from the lodge. Oct.–Mar. $70–95, Apr.–Sep. $112–155.

✱ Where to Eat

DINING OUT Amigo Café (928-697-8448), located on AZ 163, just north of AZ 160 in Kayenta. Open Mon.–Fri. 10:30–8, Sat. 8 AM–8 PM. For more than 25 years, the diminutive Amigo has served up simple, but dependably good, Mexican food. You may be one of the few non-natives in the local favorite. Check out the Navajo taco. Entrées $5.95–9.95.

Cameron Trading Post Restaurant (800-221-0690), located on AZ 89 in Cameron. Open from 6 AM–9 PM daily. When the trading post opened around 1911, the only clientele were the Hopi and Navajo, who came to trade wool, blankets, and livestock for food and sundry items. Today, people from all over the world stop to eat, shop, and sleep here. The restaurant is usually pretty busy come lunch- and dinnertime. You can get a decent meal here, especially if it's a Navajo taco. Hamburger or stew (green chili is a favorite) for lunch. Steaks are big dinner fare. Omelets are custom made for breakfast. Besides the generally good food, the historic building and Navajo paintings make for a special atmosphere. If you travel during winter, the fireplace will be lit. Breakfast $5.99–10.99, lunch $5.99–8.99, dinner $8.99–21.99.

Thunderbird Lodge Café (928-674-5844), Thunderbird Motel in Canyon de Chelly. Open daily 6:30 AM–8 PM. Don't let the cafeteria-style service put you off. The Navajo dish out some tasty food here, ranging from traditional favorites to Continental fare. Authentic artwork (available for sale) crafted by local Native peoples adorns the walls. Entrées $6.50–10.

EATING OUT Choohostso Indian Market. Located on the northwest corner of AZ 264 and Navajo 12 in Window Rock. There's a variety of vendors here with menus that include mutton stew, ribs, sandwiches, corn stew, dumpling stew, squash stew, frybread, Navajo tacos, and Navajo burgers.

"1" **Shepherd's Eyes Courtyard Coffee Shop**, 0.25 mile west of US 163 on US 160. Open Sun.–Thu. 7 AM–7 PM, Fri. and Sat.7 AM–2 AM). The doughnut-shaped building has several things going on at different times. Mostly, it's a coffee/ espresso lounge where you can hook up to the Internet via computers ($4 for 15 minutes) or WiFi ($5). During the day Navajo set up shop and sell crafts. On weekends you may hear country-western or rock bands, or run across a powwow. Finally, you can always get traveler's information on what's going on in the Nation. Free (entertainment $3–10).

✱ Special Events

May: **Native American Arts Auction** at Hubbell Trading Post National Historic Site (928-755-3475) presents a collection of historic and contemporary Native American arts for auction; food vendors on the grounds.

June: **Sheep Is Life Celebration** (505-406-7428) in Tsaile has precelebration workshops, Elder and Youth Day, hands-on demonstrations, a Churro sheep show, rug auction, and presentations. The **Navajo Nation Museum** Music Festival (928-871-7941) at Navajo Nation Museum in Window Rock presents traditional and contemporary Native American music, arts, and crafts, along with vendors, book signings, and other activities.

July: **Navajo Nation Fourth of July PRCA Rodeo and Youth Celebration** (928-871-6647) in Window Rock features the Professional Rodeo Cowboys Association (PRCA) Rodeo, a carnival, traditional Navajo song and dance, concerts, arts and crafts, and fireworks.

September: **Navajo Nation Fair** (928-871-6646). The world's largest American Indian fair and multisanctioned Indian rodeo with traditional Navajo song and dance, intertribal powwow, Navajo food, concerts, parade, children's day, Miss Navajo Pageant, a fine arts competition and exhibit, agricultural and commercial exhibits, a home arts competition and exhibit, amusement rides, and a free barbecue.

GRAND CANYON NATIONAL PARK—NORTH RIM

Of the 4.5 million visitors to Grand Canyon National Park each year, less than a quarter make it to the North Rim. When you take the extra few hours you need to visit this remote but altogether wonderful side of the canyon, you get a more personal experience. Like an island adrift from the rest of the state, separated 8 to 16 miles from the rest of Arizona by the Grand Canyon, the North Rim offers an outback feel and—especially in the North Kaibab National Forest—an outback experience.

Because it's about 1,000 feet higher than the South Rim, the North Rim is cooler in summer, more colorful when autumn leaves turn, and definitely snowier in winter. Spring might not happen until May, when this side of the national park opens each year.

The North Rim doesn't have as much flash or as many activities as the South, but you will find more hiking trails above the rim, more scenic drives, fewer people milling about, no congestion, and a number of primitive camping spots. If you really want to give humanity the slip, head into the North Kaibab National Forest via unpaved road. The farther west of AZ 67, the more remote life gets. Just make sure you have enough provisions. You may not see anyone for days in these parts away from the rim.

GUIDANCE On the way to the North Rim, the **North Kaibab Plateau Visitors Center and Grand Canyon Association Bookstore** (928-643-7298) in Jacob Lake can give you information on the canyon. Inside the national park, the **North Rim Visitor Center** (open 8–6), located near Grand Canyon Lodge, has park information, interpretive exhibits, and rangers to answer any questions you may have. You can call 928-638-7888 for general information. ***The Guide***, the park's newspaper, contains current information including schedules of tours, sunrise /sunset times, and seasonal points of interest.

Get permits and information on backcountry use at **North Rim Backcountry Office**, located 11.5 miles south of the north entrance (open 8–noon and 1–5); by writing **Backcountry Information Center**, P.O. Box 129, Grand Canyon, AZ 86023; or by logging onto www.nps.gov/grca (click on The Guide for seasonal information about the North Rim). Contact North Kaibab Ranger District (928-

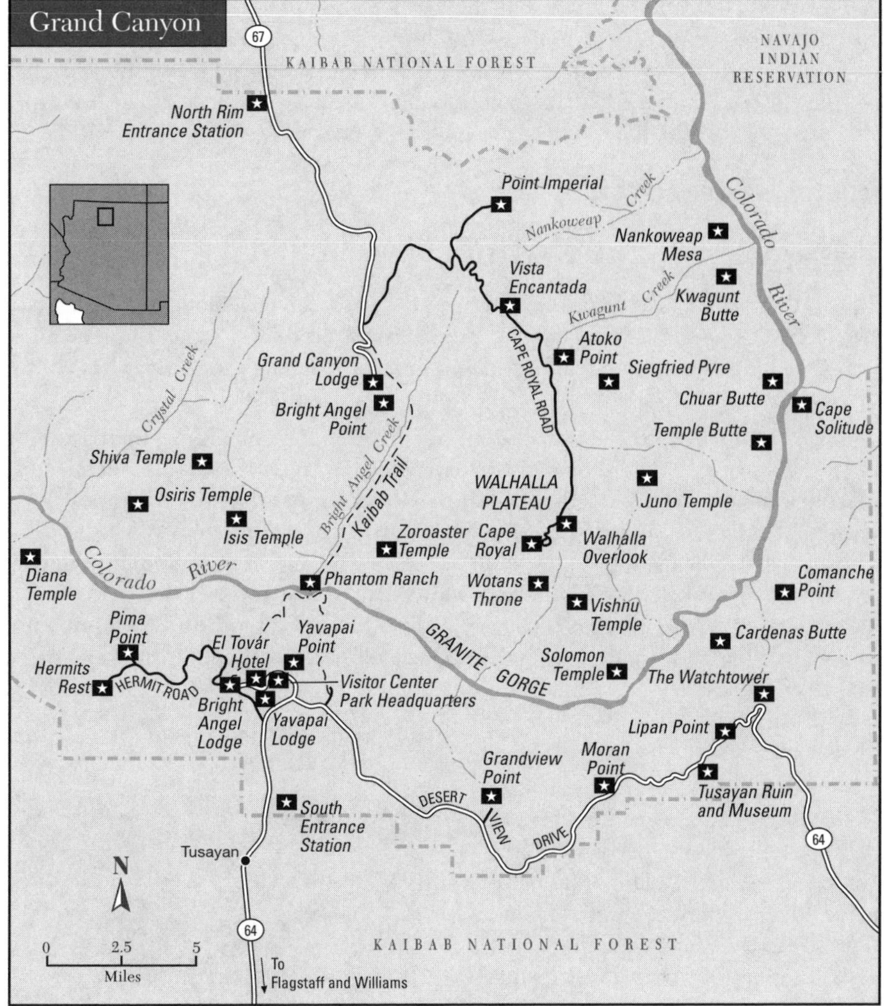

643-7395), 430 S. Main St., Fredonia, for information about hiking, camping, and back roads in the North Kaibab National Forest.

FEES The park entrance fee is $25 per private vehicle; $12 per individual on foot, bicycle, or motorcycle. This fee, good for seven days, includes both rims. The national forest does not charge user fees.

GETTING THERE Only one paved road leads to the Grand Canyon's North Rim: AZ 67.

GETTING AROUND You can take a shuttle from the lodge to the North Kaibab Trailhead for $8, $5 per extra person. From May 15–Oct. 15 **Transcanyon Shuttle** (928-638-2820) will take you to the South Rim for $80 one-way, $150 round-trip.

WHEN TO COME Because of its high elevation and propensity for snow, the North Rim season runs May 15–Oct. 15. The park remains open for day use only when the weather permits after October 16; however, visitor services and facilities remain closed. When AZ 67 (the road leading to the rim from Jacob Lake) closes (sometimes without notice) due to heavy snow, it does not reopen until mid-May.

MEDICAL EMERGENCY Dial 911.

✷ To See

SCENIC DRIVES The highway leading to the park (**AZ 67**), alone, makes a great scenic drive. The sprawling meadows and dense mixed conifer-aspen forests—the area's predominant natural feature—give a great sightseeing experience. But there's more.

The 11-mile drive to **Point Imperial**, the highest point on either rim, passes through a burn area to spectacular views of Mount Hayden, Saddle Mountain, and Marble Canyon. The 23-mile road to **Cape Royal** has a variety of landscapes, from open meadows full of watchable wildlife to cloistered old-growth forests. You can stop at several awesome viewpoints of the canyon along the way to the **Angel's Window overlook**, where California condors like to soar at road's end. If you have a four-wheel-drive vehicle, check out the 18-mile road to **Point Sublime** on the western end of the canyon, considered one of the most breathtaking panoramas anywhere.

✷ To Do

BICYCLING You can ride your bicycle on paved and unpaved roads in the park. Just outside the park, the Kaibab National Forest has a large number of unpaved roads perfect for mountain or tour bikes. The highway to the North Rim, AZ 67, is one of the best road biking routes in Arizona.

HIKING AND BACKPACKING You can hike a wide range of trails here. The 5-mile **Widforss Trail**, off the highway at the end of a dirt road, travels along the rim. Inside the park, the rimside **Transept Trail** is an easy trek of 1.5 miles from Grand Canyon Lodge to the North Rim Campground. Back on the main road in the park, the 14.2-mile **North Kaibab Trail** is the most traveled. You can make a reasonable dayhike on the 4.7 miles to Roaring Springs. Spending the night below the rim requires a backcountry permit: $10 per person and $5 per night.

A WISP OF A FIGURE, DISTORTED BY SPEED, SLIDES DOWN ELVES CHASM

The **Thunder River Trail** on the western rim is a favorite backcountry trail for experienced backpackers. For a remote hiking experience, check out trails on the Kaibab National Forest. The **Rainbow Rim Trail** follows along the rim for about 18 miles, through forests and meadows, giving glimpses of the Grand Canyon (for free). The **Jump-Up-Nail Trail** and **Snake Gulch Trail** each offers a wild and remote backpack in unusual canyon country.

HORSEBACK AND MULE RIDES **Grand Canyon Trail Rides** (435-679-8665). From 1-hour rides on the rim to half- or full-day rides on the rim or into the canyon. $40–165.

RANGER PROGRAMS A number of ranger-led talks take place almost every day in the park. Consult *The Guide* for a schedule.

✷ Lodging

Inside the Park

♿ **Grand Canyon Lodge** (888-297-2757; outside the U.S., 303-297-2757; same-day reservations, 928-638-2631). The only lodging in the park, this National Historic Landmark was designed to match its physical environment with limestone walls and timbered ceilings. The lodge has motel rooms and cabins, dining room, sunroom, café, saloon, gift shop, and laundry facilities. All rooms and cabins have double or queen beds, shower or bath, and telephone. Kids under age 15 can stay in the same room as an adult for free. Reservations recommended. $112–170.

CAMPGROUNDS North Rim Campground (800-365-2267; outside the U.S., 301-722-1257; www.reservations.nps.gov). No hookups or dumpsites. Stays are limited to 7 days. $18 per night.

Outside the Park

Jacob Lake Inn (928-643-7232), located 45 miles north of the North Rim. Open since 1923 by Harold and Nina Bowman, the inn has a rustic side to it. The property has motel rooms and cabins as well as a restaurant, grocery store, and gas station. Rooms have two double beds or one king, shower, heater, and sitting area; some units have cable television, phone, and Internet access. Cabins have a double, queen, or king bed; shower; heater; and a sitting area on a deck. Rooms $100–142, cabins $90–132.

✷ Where to Eat

DINING OUT **Grand Canyon Lodge Dining Room** (928-638-2611, ext. 160). Open daily May 15–Oct. 15 for breakfast 6:30–10, lunch 11:30–2:30, dinner 4:45–9:45. You get a unique dining experience here with Grand Canyon views. The menu features all natural beef and chicken, fresh and/or organic produce. Breakfast ranges from basic egg and griddle plates to a hot and cold buffet. Classics like Navajo Taco and Uncle Jim's Beef Stew are among the "old-time favorites" served at lunch. Fish, steaks and pasta dishes are among the lodge specialties and favorites at dinner. Reservations are required for dinner, and the park recommends you make them one to two months prior to arrival. Breakfast $5.95–9.95. lunch $6.95–10.35, dinner $15–23.

Jacob Lake Inn Dining Room (928-643-7323), Jacob Lake Inn. Open

May–Oct., 6 AM–9 PM; Nov.–Apr., 8 AM–8 PM. Meals are decent here, made with fresh ingredients. Their fresh-baked bread shows up on breakfast and lunch items. They serve a good hamburger, river trout, and *jager-schnitzel*; and the desserts (pies, specialty cakes, and cookies) are house-made. Entrées $5.95–12.95.

EATING OUT **Deli in the Pines**, Grand Canyon Lodge. Open daily 7 AM–9 PM. Grab a muffin or sandwich for the trail, snack on a hot dog, or order a whole pizza. The kind of convenience and comfort food you richly deserve after a day on the trail. $2–20.

* Selective Shopping

Jacob Lake Inn Gift Shop (928-643-7323), Jacob Lake Inn. You'll find some of the finest Native American arts here. The shop is packed with jewelry, Navajo rugs, fetishes, pottery, and basketry. The owners carry merchandise from nationally renowned artists, and you may even catch one selling his or her wares. You can also get information about the items sold at the shop.

GRAND CANYON NATIONAL PARK—SOUTH RIM

"There's this thing called *canyon magic*," a riverboat pilot named Okie said as he leaned back on his elbow and watched the Colorado River course peacefully around a distant bend. "Running the rapids is a hoot. But that's just part of the reason us boatmen keep coming back. It's the canyon magic. It gets into your blood."

No matter what your experience here—looking at distant panoramas from viewpoints on the rim, hiking down the wall of the canyon from the enchanting Supai Group into the shiny dark mounds of the ancient Vishnu Schist cradling the river, riding hair-raising rapids on a rafting trip—the Grand Canyon will captivate you, just as it does all its 4.5 million annual visitors.

Most of these folks never get any farther than the edge of the rim. The deeper, and longer, you go below the rim, the more the canyon gets into your blood. You don't necessarily have to travel to the heart of the canyon (the Colorado River) to know its soul. You can feel its heartbeat by hiking even a short distance on the routes between the rim and the river. Once you step below the rim, your whole perception of the grandest of canyons changes: Views become more detailed, smells more pungent; the weather varies; feelings of remoteness and isolation set in. The deeper and farther you go, the more exciting and wild your world gets. That's all part of the canyon's magic.

GUIDANCE **Grand Canyon Park Headquarters** (928-638-7888) will connect you to the right information source. The Web site www.nps.gov/grca has a wealth of information. *The Guide*, the park's newspaper, contains current information including schedules of tours, sunrise/sunset times, and seasonal points of interest. You can obtain permits and information on backcountry use at the **Backcountry Information Center** in the Maswik Transportation Center (open 8–noon and 1–5) or by writing Backcountry Information Center, P.O. Box 129, Grand Canyon, AZ 86023. When you get to the park, head to the bustling **Canyon View Information Center** near Mather Point. From the east entrance, go to **Desert View Park Information Center**, located at Desert View Point (this center has a passport stamp cancellation station). Contact the Kaibab National Forest's Tusayan Ranger District at 928-638-2443 for information about points outside the park in the national forest.

FEES The park entrance fee is $25 per private vehicle, and $12 for an individual on foot, bicycle, or motorcycle. This fee, good for 7 days, includes both the North and South rims.

GETTING THERE *By car:* The South Rim has two entrances: the main entrance, off AZ 64 from Williams (US 180 to AZ 64 from Flagstaff) and the east entrance, also off AZ 64 from Cameron (on US 89). *By bus:* You can take the **Greyhound Bus** (800-231-2222) to Flagstaff or Phoenix, then a shuttle via **Open Road Tours** (928-226-8060 or 877-226-8060). *By air:* The **Grand Canyon Airport** (928-638-2446) has service from Las Vegas. *By train:* From Williams, hop on the vintage **Grand Canyon Railway** (800-843-8724).

GETTING AROUND Free **shuttle buses** equipped with bicycle racks (pets not allowed) cover three routes indicated by different colors. The Hermits Rest Route (red) travels 8 miles from Village Route Transfer and Hermits Rest (stopping at overlooks). The utilitarian Village Route (blue) travels among the Canyon View Information Plaza, Yavapai Point, hotels, restaurants, campgrounds, and parking. The Kaibab Trail Route (green) heads from the Canyon View Information Plaza to South Kaibab Trailhead and Yaki Point.

Taxi service is available 24 hours a day from lodging to trailheads and the Grand Canyon Airport (928-638-2822 or 928-638-2631, ext. 6563).

May 15–Oct. 15, you can travel to the North Rim via the **Transcanyon Shuttle** (928-638-2820) for $80 one-way, $150 round-trip.

WHEN TO COME The busiest time in the national park is summer. Next are the spring and fall shoulder seasons (best for hiking). Winter offers a fine opportunity to miss the crowds and have a reasonably good chance to eat and sleep where you want without planning months in advance except for the week between Christmas and New Year's, when you may have to rely on luck rather than good planning.

MEDICAL EMERGENCY **The North Country Grand Canyon Clinic** (928-638-2551) is open June–Oct. 8–6, Nov.–May 8–5.

🐾 **KENNELS** (928-638-0534). Open daily 7:30–5. Pets are not allowed on shuttles or below the rim, and must be leashed at all times in the park.

✱ To See

Bright Angel History Room, Bright Angel Lodge. This compendium of memorabilia features the Fred Harvey legacy in old menus, a carriage, pictures, and plates. Check out the geological fireplace designed by architect Mary Colter, who also designed many of the public buildings on the rim. Free.

Desert View Information Center and Bookstore. Located at Desert View Point. Open daily 9–5. Just about everything you wanted to know about the Grand Canyon, but were afraid to ask during a ranger-led talk, is available in books here.

Kolb Studio. Located in the Village Historic District at the Bright Angel Trailhead. Open daily 8–6. The home and studio for Grand Canyon photographers Emory and Ellsworth Kolb goes five levels below the rim on the canyon wall. You can peruse free art exhibits and take a tour (free, but reservations are required) of the studio.

Tusayan Museum, 3 miles west of Desert View. Open daily 9–5; check winter schedule. A self-guided trail through the remains of an Ancestral Puebloan village gives you an idea of how Native Americans lived in the canyon about 800 years ago. The museum displays artifacts and art and has a gift shop.

Yavapai Observation Station Located at Yavapai Point. Built in 1928 with the goal of observing and understanding the canyon's bold geology, this station lives up to its mission. Panorama windows present unabashed views of the canyon, and a museum features geology and physiography.

SCENIC DRIVES Hermit Road allows only shuttles during most of the year (except Dec.–Feb.), but **Desert View Drive** (AZ 64) presents gorgeous canyon views all year round. The highway travels the canyon rim east of Grand Canyon Village for 26 miles.

✷ To Do

AIR TOURS They may infringe upon the sanctity of the landlubbers' experience in the national park (to the point that the Arizona legislature limited their flight space), but air tours over the stunning terrain sure are sensational. Tours originate from Grand Canyon Airport, Flagstaff, Sedona, Las Vegas, and Phoenix. **Air Grand Canyon** (928-638-2686 or 800-247-4726), located in Grand Canyon Airport, presents the most tours; they last 50–100 minutes. $109–189 adults, $75–169 under age 13. **Papillion Grand Canyon Helicopters** (702-736-6322) offers 45-minute helicopter tours from the Grand Canyon Airport. $168 adults, $148 kids.

BICYCLING You can ride your bicycle on paved and unpaved roads and the Rim Trail. You may not ride on any trail below the rim. If you plan to cycle Hermit Road, make sure you give the shuttle buses the right of way (pull off the road and dismount if need be). With the heavy shuttle traffic in summertime, best to avoid this road then.

HIKING AND BACKPACKING One of the most intimate ways to experience the canyon, foot travel requires adhering to a few guidelines for a successful venture: Drink enough water (at least a gallon a day in the summer), take electrolyte supplements, eat salty foods, wear a hat and sunscreen, and rest often. (Also note that pets are not allowed below the rim.) Although experienced hikers do it all the time, the National Park Service strongly advises against hiking from the rim to the river and back (or to the other rim) in one day. Hikers should not attempt such treks unless they can finish marathon-length hikes with 5,000-foot elevation loss and gain because an air-vac or rescue is expensive. Saner day hikes include a segment of the 12-mile (one-way, as are the rest of the mileages) **Rim Trail; Bright Angel Trail** to 1.5-Mile Resthouse or 3-Mile Resthouse; **South Kaibab Trail** to Ooh Aah Point (1.8 miles) or Cedar Ridge (3 miles); **Hermit Trail** to Waldron Basin (3 miles) or Santa Maria Spring (5 miles); and the **Grandview Trail** to Coconino Saddle (2.2 miles) or Horseshoe Mesa (3.2 miles).

Spending the night below the rim requires a backcountry permit: $10 per person and $5 per night. You can purchase the permit in person or by mail from the Backcountry Information Center.

MULE TRIPS (928-638-2631). As long as you're in average physical condition, over 4 foot 7, weigh less than 200 pounds, and speak fluent English, you can delve below the rim on a day ride to Plateau Point or 2-day overnight trip to Phantom Ranch (3-day trips are available in winter). $117.40–477.34.

RAFTING TRIPS A whitewater rafting trip, the quintessential canyon experience, usually requires a reservation made well in advance. Trips run from 3 to 21 days. Cancellations occur often, so take heart: It's not an impossible dream. **Wilderness River Adventures** (928-645-3296 or 800-992-8022); **O.A.R.S.** (800-386-6277).

RANGER PROGRAMS A number of ranger-led talks take place almost every day in the park. Consult *The Guide* for a schedule.

WALKING TOURS The **Grand Canyon Village Historical District** takes you back to the turn of the 20th century, when the Grand Canyon first got the world's attention. It includes structures ranging from the Santa Fe Railway Station (circa 1909) to the oldest standing structure on the rim: Buckey O'Neil Cabin, built in the 1890s. Get a map at one of the visitor centers. Take a stroll on the paved section of the **Rim Trail** between Pipe Creek Overlook and Kolb Studio for a look at one of the world's most awesome object lessons in natural history.

A RAFT NEGOTIATES CLASS 10 HERMIT RAPIDS

✷ Lodging

The Grand Canyon National Park has six lodges (operated by Xanterra Resorts & Lodges). To make reservations, call 888-297-2757 (outside the US, 303-297-2757; same day reservations, 928-638-2631) or contact Xanterra South Rim, LLC, 10 Albright, Grand Canyon 86023.

On the rim

BRIGHT ANGEL LODGE There's nothing more thrilling than walking into this rustic lodge when there's a cold enough bite in the air to warrant a fire in the lobby's great fireplace. Here backpackers and sightseers congregate, and a mélange of languages fills the air. This lodge, a National Historic Landmark, personifies the rugged essence of the canyon. Architect Mary Colter designed the lodge; her projects always emanate grace and inspiration. The property includes the Bright Angel and Arizona Room restaurants (see *Dining Out*), a gift shop, and the History Room. Lodge rooms have a telephone; some have private bath and/or fireplace. Historic cabins (try to snag a rim cabin) have television and private bath. Rooms $79–138, cabins $111–174.

♥ **EL TOVAR** This grand dame of the park's lodging, and a National Historic Landmark, got a remodel when it turned 100 in 2005. Elegant and popular, the rimside hotel stays booked, and you want to plan early if you simply must stay here during your visit to the park. There's a fine dining room (see *Dining Out*) and concierge. Rooms have double, queen, or king beds, cable television, telephone, full bath, and air-conditioning, as well as turndown and room service. $174–321.

♿ **KACHINA AND THUNDERBIRD LODGES** Located on the rim and more modern, these lodges' rooms work well for families. Some have canyon views. Rooms have two queen beds or one king bed, private bath, mini fridge, telephone, television, and safe. $170–180 double occupancy, $9 per extra person.

♿ **MASWICK LODGE** Located 0.25 mile from the rim in a ponderosa pine forest with several options: basic motel-style rooms (two queen beds, private bath, telephone, and television), more spacious rooms (two queen beds or one king, private bath, telephone, television, refrigerator, air-conditioning), and cabins (summer only—two single beds or one double bed, private bathroom with shower, telephone, and television). The lodge has a cafeteria, sports bar with widescreen TV, curio shop, and transportation/activities desk. $90–170 double occupancy, $9 per extra person.

♿ **YAVAPAI LODGE.** Located 0.5 mile from the rim in a townlike atmosphere next to the Market Plaza (which has a general store, bank, and U.S. post office) and near a laundry facility, this makes a perfect family base. The lodge also has a cafeteria, curio shop, and transportation/activities desk. Rooms have two queen beds or one king bed; all have private bath, telephone, and television. $107–173 double occupancy, $9 per extra person.

Below the rim

PHANTOM RANCH. Another Mary Colter design, the only accommodation below the rim resides beside Bright Angel Creek on the north side of the Colorado River. You can only approach Phantom Ranch via foot, mule, or rafting the Colorado River. If you can nab a reservation for Christmas week, consider it a prize. Dormitory space (men and women sleep separately) has heat in winter and evaporative cooling in summer, 10 bunk beds, a shower (bring your own soap), and restroom. Cabins have a set of bunk beds with bedding, cold-water sink, toilet, liquid soap, and towels. Showers in separate area. Remember to order a meal with your reservation if you don't bring your own food (breakfast; sack lunch; or a stew, steak, or veggie dinner $12–41). Dorm space $42.

CAMPING (800-365-2267; outside the U.S., 301-722-1257; http://reservations.nps.gov). Pets must be leashed and attended at all times.

Mather Campground. Open year-round for tent and RV camping (no hookups). Restrooms available. Wood and charcoal fires are permitted in provided campsite grills only. Laundry and showers nearby. Mar. 1–mid-Nov. (reservations recommended), $18 per site per night; mid-Nov.–Feb. 28, $18 per site per night on a first-come, first-served basis.

Desert View Campground. Located 26 miles east of Grand Canyon Village. Open mid-May–mid-Oct. No hookups; first come, first served. $12 per site per night.

✱ Where to Eat

The Arizona Room. Located in Bright Angel Lodge. Lunch 11:30–3 (closed Nov.–Feb.), dinner 4:30–10 (closed Jan.–Feb.); first come, first served; waits common during peak times. Popular because it's good, this restaurant gets busy, especially at dinnertime. The lunch menu offers salads, pasta, and sandwiches; at dinner it's aged, hand-cut steaks, BBQ ribs, chicken, and fish with Southwest accents. Signature margaritas and decent wine complement the meal. Lunch $7.75–13, dinner $15.65–25.80.

Bright Angel Restaurant. Located in Bright Angel Lodge. Open for breakfast 6:30–11:15, lunch 11:45–4, dinner 4–10. Get a good breakfast here, a salad or sandwich for lunch, and a decent meal for dinner. First come, first served. Ask, and you might get a window table. Breakfast $3.35–12.10, lunch $7.40–10.05, dinner $10.95–25.80.

♥ **El Tovar Dining Room** (928-638-2631) in El Tovar Hotel. Open for breakfast 6:30–11, lunch 11:30–2, dinner 5–10. Reservations recommended (up to 6 months in advance). This might be the only elegant restaurant in the state with a dress code casual enough that you can practically plop down right off the trail (providing this is not after a week-long backpack and/or your aroma doesn't overpower the food's) for a gourmet meal. The classic native stone and Oregon pine create a warm atmosphere. Request a window seat, and you might get it. The menu blends regional and classical flavors in a nice blend of meat, fish, and vegetarian dishes. Sources are environmentally friendly. Breakfast $5.80–9.80, lunch entrées $7.40–14.80, dinner entrées $22.25–33.40.

FLAGSTAFF

For centuries, travelers and cultures have considered Flagstaff a hub in the Southwest. Native peoples made seasonal camps in mountain meadows. Pioneers struggling through their westward journey considered the town a good place to camp. In the early days, scientists passed through or stayed in Flagstaff while studying the West's wonders—John Wesley Powell, the Colorado River; Clinton Hart Merriam, the life zones; Percival Lowell, the night sky; and Harold Colton, the archeological secrets of the surrounding Navajo and Hopi nations.

In the late 1800s, sheepherders, lured by lush meadows, set up ranches. The Atlantic and Pacific Railroad laid tracks through town, bringing with it workers bubbling with enough testosterone to give the young town the reputation as one of the wildest in the West. With the railroad came cattle ranching and the inevitable tussles between the sheepherders and cattle ranchers. Timber mills, fed by the gorgeous forests of ponderosa and yellow pines on the surrounding peaks, made the town prosper. Flagstaff had the biggest sawmill complex in the West by the turn of the 20th century.

Since those days, only the railroad remains, in Flagstaff. With ranching and timber pretty much passé, Northern Arizona University, the Grand Canyon, and the great outdoors took their place. Although it's considered the high desert, Flagstaff has several ecosystems: piñon-juniper plateau lands, mountain meadows, mixed-conifer subalpine forests, and barren tundra. It's one of the state's ultimate cool spots that still sports snowcapped peaks when temperatures start to hit novel numbers in the desert cities.

Flagstaff has the kind of cool, high-country hipness alluring to a variety of personalities—outdoor adventurers, artists, and Hollywood names. Its academia influences give it a sense of tolerance as the world and surrounding cultures gather to its side. Nevertheless, Flagstaff' still has its small-town insular tendencies, which make it quintessentially Arizona.

The historic section east of Route 66 has the most happening: buildings rumored to be haunted that have histories splashed with colorful anecdotes, restaurants, bars, and shopping. It's a mix of generations here, with students tipping the scale during the school year. It doesn't necessarily quiet down in summer., when residents from the lower desert arrive to escape triple-digit heat. The bars may be a bit less raucous, however. That is, if they're not one of the haunted spots . . .

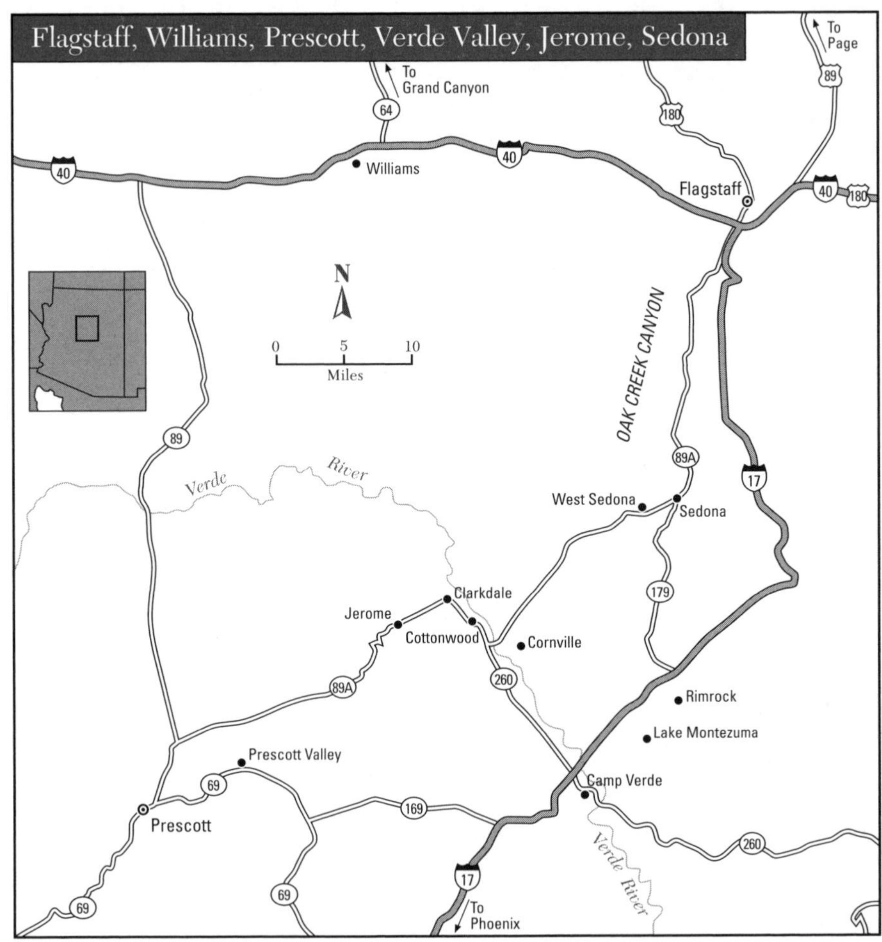

GUIDANCE Flagstaff Visitor Center (928-774-9541 or 800-842-7293), 1 E. Route 66 (in the historic train station), offers maps, brochures, up-to-date information on events, and a small gift shop. Open daily Mon.–Sat. 8–5, Sun. 9–4; closed Thanksgiving and Christmas days. If you plan to head out into the backcountry and need information on fishing, hiking, or mountain biking, call **Peaks Ranger District** (928-526-0866), 5057 N. US 89, or **Mormon Lake Ranger District** (928-774-1182), 4373 S. Lake Mary Rd. For information on the city's multiuse trail system, contact **City of Flagstaff** (928-779-7632).

GETTING THERE *By car:* Flagstaff is a hub for three major highways: I-17 runs south to Phoenix; I-40 runs east to Winslow and New Mexico and west to Williams and California; and US 89 runs north to Page and Utah. *By train:* **Amtrak** (928-774-8679), 1 E. Santa Fe Ave. *By bus:* **Greyhound Bus** (928-774-4573), 399 S. Malpais Lane. *By air:* **Flagstaff Pulliam Airport** (928-556-1234), 6200 S. Pulliam Dr., offers daily flights and service for Horizon Air, US Airways Express and corporate and private aircraft and has 400 free passenger parking spaces.

WHEN TO COME Sitting at the feet of Mount Humphreys, Arizona's tallest peak, Flagstaff enjoys mild summer days that finish off with cool nights; bring rain gear for daily thunderstorms. In autumn the aspens glow gold and draw residents from around the state into the high country to admire them. Also, during fall the town swells with the return of students to the university. If you plan a summer or fall visit, make sure you have a reservation. When the winter storms arrive, the mountain turns white—perfect for downhill skiing, cross-country skiing, and snowboarding.

MEDICAL EMERGENCY **Flagstaff Medical Center** (928-779-3366), 1200 N. Beaver St.; **Concentra Medical Center** (928-773-9695), 120 W. Fine Ave.; **Walk-in Clinic** (928-527-1920), 4215 N. US 89.

✷ To See

The Arboretum at Flagstaff (928-774-1442), 4001 Woody Mountain Rd. Open daily Apr.–Oct. 9–5. View the native wildflowers that appear in this area from the high desert to alpine meadows. The Arboretum is also the place of choice for birders around Flagstaff. Attracted to the avian necessities of life—a pond that gathers surface water, trees in which to roost or nest, and seeds and insects to feed upon—more than 100 different species of birds have made an appearance at the garden. Seasonal events include a Live Bug Zoo, wildflower walks, mushroom foraging, evening bat program, and Live Birds of Prey Demonstration Program. $6 adults, $3 ages 6–17, under age 6 free.

A SCENE FROM FLAGSTAFF'S HISTORIC DISTRICT

Lowell Observatory (928-774-3358), 1400 W. Mars Hill Rd. Open daily Nov.–Feb. noon–5, Mar.–Oct. 9–5. Open evenings: Sep.–May, Mon., Wed., Fri., and Sat. 5:30–9:30; June–Aug. Mon.–Sat. 5:30–10. One of the oldest observatories in the United States that has been on the cutting edge of astronomical discoveries since it opened. Scientists first noticed signs of an expanding universe here between 1912 and 1915, but the planetarium got its claim to fame when astronomers here discovered Pluto in 1930. Later, astronomers codiscovered the rings of Uranus in 1977. An anti-light-pollution campaign keeps Mars Hill and its five observatory telescopes sufficiently in the dark to let astronomers keep tabs on Pluto, Jupiter's moon Io, and asteroids and trans-Neptunian objects. Tours take you through the planetarium each hour. There's also nighttime telescopic viewing, weather permitting. $6 adults, $5 seniors and students, $3 ages 7–17.

Museum of Northern Arizona (928-774-5213), 3101 N. Fort Valley Rd. Open daily 9–5. Everything you wanted to know about the Colorado Plateau—and more—is found here. The plateau has the greatest diversity of geology, biology, and culture in the world, attracting scientists from across the globe. It's also a repository for several Native American tribes, and has about 600,000 artifacts. The museum displays fine arts, as well. Its collection includes easel art and sculpture. Displays present information on dinosaurs, volcanoes, fossils, and prehistoric people. Check out the museum founders' home, the Colton House. Keep in mind that you can rent it for an event. There's a museum shop and bookstore on site, too. $7 adults, $6 seniors, $5 students, $4 ages 7–17.

THE CLIFFS AT WALNUT CANYON HOSTED NATIVE AMERICANS FOR 200 YEARS

Walnut Canyon (928-526-3367). From Flagstaff, take I-40 east to exit 204, then continue 3 miles south. Open Dec.–Feb. 9–5, Mar.–Nov. 8–5;. Overcrowding at the nearby Wupatki site probably precipitated the move of some prehistoric Native peoples to this canyon just east of Flagstaff. More than 300 small cliff dwellings nestle in the 400-foot-deep canyon. With a dependable supply of water, good soil, and a protective environment that has a soothing and peaceful feeling, the canyon hosted Native Americans for 200 years, and then they disappeared suddenly. Several trails explore the canyon and its ruins. Call for information on ranger-escorted tours. $5 adults and age 17-plus, under age 16 free.

✷ To Do

BMX PARK **The Basin** (928-779-7690), corner of West and 6th Ave. Open 9 AM to dusk. This state-of-the-art 2.2-acre park has 900 tons of concrete and 8-foot-deep bike bowls. Free.

COOKING CLASS **The Cottage Place Restaurant** (see *Dining Out*) offers a cooking class every Sat. 11–2:30. This class, a huge hit, includes instruction, a packet of recipes, sampling of the featured creations, and wine tasting. $50 per person. Reservations required.

DOG PARKS 🐾 When Fido needs to stretch his legs and let off steam, head for the city's two off-leash areas: **Thorpe Park** at 600 N. Thorpe Rd. and **Bushmaster Park** at 3150 N. Alta Vista Rd. Water is available May–Oct.

FISHING Flagstaff's mountains don't have the trout streams that others of their size might, but there are a few area lakes in Mormon Lake Ranger District that get stocked by Arizona Department of Game and Fish, such as **Mormon Lake**, **Upper** and **Lower Lake Mary**, and tucked-away **Kinnickinnic Lake**. You can access these lakes by taking exit 337, Lake Mary, from I-17 and heading south.

GOLF **Continental Country Club** (928-527-7999), 2380 N. Oakmont Dr. Open May and Oct. at 8 AM, June–Sep. at 7 AM. Narrow fairways braced by ponderosa pines, open meadows, fresh air, and fast greens present an exciting but enjoyable golf game in the mountains. The 18-hole, 6,014-yard course presents what the management calls "fun-to-play" par-5s, along with demanding par-3s. Pro shop and driving range. PGA professional on hand for private lessons. $31–59.

HIKING (See also *Volcanoes*). The **San Francisco Peaks** have almost two-dozen trails—eight of which travel more than 8,000 feet inside the **Kachina Peaks Wilderness**. **Humphreys Trail** takes you to Arizona's citadel (but don't take this one unless you're in good physical health and not prone to altitude sickness). Several accesses to the **Arizona Trail** (www.aztrail.org) are located near the city. If you don't want to venture into the backcountry, try the **Flagstaff Urban Trail System** that meanders right around town, starting in **Buffalo Park**, 2400 N. Gemini Rd. You can get a map and more information from the City of Flagstaff.

MOUNTAIN BIKING This is the land of the fat tire. You'll see them on the street as well as the back roads and trails. You can ride anywhere that is not a designated wilderness area; the most popular trails travel around Mount Elden and Schultz Pass Road. Call Peaks Ranger District for information. Check out the **Flagstaff Urban Trail System** that meanders right around the town. You can get a map and more information from the City of Flagstaff. Stop at **Absolute Bikes** (928-779-5969), 202 E. US 66, if you need to rent a bike, acquire more gear, or find more information on area routes.

ROCK CLIMBING Experienced climbers gather at **The Pit** off St. Mary Rd., 2 miles south of the Mormon Lake Ranger Station. Beginners can start at the **Vertical Relief Climbing Center** (928-556-9909), 205 S. San Francisco St., where they don a hard hat and muster up a good dose of intestinal fortitude to climb the walls of the indoor gym. After they're comfortable with the indoor fun, they can graduate to an outdoor guided climb. Open Mon.–Fri. 10 AM–11 PM, Sat. and Sun. noon–8. Free.

SKIING Once the snow starts falling, the city's surrounding countryside gives you several ski options.

✐ ꝏ **Arizona Snowbowl** (928-779-1951), US 180 and Snowbowl Rd., is open for downhill skiing and snowboarding from mid-December through mid-April. Black-diamond runs are big here among its 32 trails, thanks to 2,300 feet of vertical drop. The average yearly snowfall measures up to 260 inches. Four chairlifts, full-service rental shop, repair shop, ski school.

Cross-country ski trails at **Flagstaff Nordic Center** (928-220-0550) traipse through more than 40 kilometers of groomed cross-country trails in the Coconino National Forest. Open Dec.–Apr.; rentals, lessons, snowshoeing, and group packages available.

SNOW PLAY

The old-time ranchers used to say the snow comes after Christmas to the high country. And when it does, it's playtime in Flagstaff. The San Francisco Peaks see about 120 inches in a normal year. When El Niño broods in the Pacific, the mountains will see much more. Lowlanders know when it rains in the desert, it's snowing on the Peaks. If you're traveling, call the Visitor's Center at 928-774-9541 or 800-842-7293 for a snow or log onto www.visitor center@flagstaffaz.gov to find areas open for winter play. Get there early during the weekends (or you may be turned away) or go during the week to beat the crowds.

SKY RIDES **Arizona Snowbowl** (928-779-1951, ext. 115), US 180 and Snowbowl Rd. Open end of May–Labor Day, 10–4. Hop on a chairlift and rise up to 11,500 feet while you take in eagle-eye views of northern Arizona. $12 adults, $8 seniors and ages 8–12, age 70-plus free.

VOLCANOES Flagstaff sits right atop the **San Francisco Lava Field**—which harbors more than 600 volcanoes. You can bet things weren't always cool, calm, and collected around town! These relics of volcanism create perfect venues for outdoor recreation. You can climb them, view them, and even enter chambers formed by them. Contact Peaks Ranger District for information on the following: Hikers who head for the 2-mile-long **Inner Basin Trail** in Lockett Meadow can stand in the palm of the caldera formed when Mount Humphreys blew its top. **Lava River Cave** gives you a subterranean view of volcanism via a lava tube about 0.75 mile long, with some places as big as a subway tunnel and others you have to crouch to pass through. With peaks and spires reminiscent of Bryce Canyon National Park, **Red Mountain**'s surreal amphitheater of orange-tinged volcanic stone has eroded fantasy forms that look as aesthetic as a volcano can get. **Strawberry Crater Wilderness** has a 1.5-mile-long loop trail that winds around a beautiful cindered area up to almost the top of a crater shaped like its name.

Sunset Crater National Monument (928-526-0502), 12 miles north of Flagstaff on US 89. Open Dec.–Feb. 9–5, Mar.–Nov. 8–5. You can see just how wild and beautiful a postvolcanism landscape can be at Sunset Crater, the San Francisco Volcanic Field's youngest volcano. Explorer Major John Wesley Powell explained that the "contrast in the colors is so great that on viewing the mountain from a distance the red cinders seem to be on fire. From this circumstance, the cone has been named Sunset Peak." The surrounding landscape along the monument's loop drive looks untouched from the time of its formation: Cinder hillsides slope casually like swells of the sea, their ruddy brown or jet black colors contrasting austerely with gaunt stands of ponderosa or red dots of wildflowers. Squeezeups, giant slabs of lava piercing sharply as serrated teeth of a shark, jut dramatically along the Lava Flow Nature Trail. Raspy rocks and boulders jumble pell-mell in the Bonito Flow. $5 per person age 17-plus, under age 16 free (Wupatki National Monument included).

Wupatki National Monument (928-679-2365), located about 22 miles north of Flagstaff off US 89, at the opposite end of horseshoe Sunset Crater–Wupatki Rd. Open Dec.–Feb. 9–5, Mar.–Nov. 8–5. The ancient Sinagua people—along with several other cultures—migrated here when the Sunset Crater volcano erupted. The largest set of ruins in the Flagstaff area lies just behind the visitor center. Basalt mesas, formed from older volcanic eruptions, rise from the ruddy Moenkopi sandstone formation. Some mesas have exquisitely mortared pueblos still standing upon them. $5 age 17-plus, age 16 and under free (Sunset National Monument included).

WALKING TOUR Memorial Day–Labor Day, Fri. 3 PM, Sat. and Sun. 10:30 AM. Join a historical walk around downtown Flagstaff. Reservations suggested (928-774-8800). Free.

✷ Wilder Places

Kachina Peaks Wilderness. The highest peaks in the state present subalpine forests, mountain meadows, and some of the earth's oldest trees. Ferns deck aspen forest floors, where Basque sheepherders carved their initials and names in the trees' argentine bark decades ago. Hikers who climb the highest peaks can see panoramas of the Grand Canyon, Painted Desert, and Sedona.

✷ Lodging

HOTELS AND HOSTELS

DuBeau Hostel (928-774-6731 or 800-398-7112), 19 W. Phoenix. One of the oldest hostels west of the Mississippi has Young Boomer Retro interiors. You get private and dormitory accommodations, with a bathroom in every room. The property boasts a large party room, complimentary pool and foosball tables, two kitchens, high-speed Internet, and complimentary breakfast; no lockout, curfew, or chores. Local calls are free. You can also sign up for a tour to the Grand Canyon and Sedona here. Dorms $18–20, private rooms $41–48.

Grand Canyon International Hostel (928-779-9421,888-442-2696), 19 S. San Francisco St. This homespun hostel with a quiet demeanor has a hotel feel with outside entrances. You'll find two kitchens, high-speed Internet, a TV lounge with video library, and complimentary breakfast. There's free shuttle transport to and from the Greyhound station, and you can walk to the Amtrak station only a block away. Sign up for a tour to the Grand Canyon and Sedona. Dorms $18–20, private rooms $38–45.

Hotel Monte Vista (928-779-6971), 100 N. San Francisco St. In its heyday this hotel attracted the likes of Zane Grey, Esther Williams, and Bing Crosby. The hotel gave locals a chance to rub shoulders with the world as it passed through the frontier town. Rooms of the famous are attractively restored to period furnishing. All rooms have cable TV and telephone. Like an aged relative who can get away with eccentric behavior, the hotel (more than 80 years old) has accumulated some quirky habits over the years: A rocking chair in Room 305 insists on facing out the window no matter how many times it's turned toward the room. A bar stool in the hotel's lounge sometimes whizzes past patrons across the room. And the hotel's whole second floor seems to give some people the creeps. The hotel is rife with spooky phenomena. $50–175 double occupancy; $10 per extra person; pets $25 deposit.

Little America Hotel (928-779-7900), 2515 East Butler Ave. Named for the base station built by Admiral Byrd in Antarctica, the hotel brings some Old World classiness into the rugged West. Stained-glass windows appear like so many gems around the lobby, restaurant and Tiffany Bar (which has a Tiffany stained-glass tree that canopies over the bar. A hearty hearth, so requisite for cozy moments in this mountain town, warms each of these public areas. The sunny oversize rooms and suites make great bases, especially if you plan to spend a few days in town. Leaning on the elegant side, with French provincial furniture, they also have mini fridge, large flat-screen plasma TV with movies and games on demand, free Internet access, coffeemaker, down pillows and comforters, big bathroom. It's totally civilized. The 500-acre property has a 9-foot-deep swimming pool, built when diving was in; a 2-mile hiking trail that winds around the Ponderosa pines, an outdoor hot tub, and a fitness center. What's with the Sinclair gas station on the grounds? The hotel's owner, the Holdings Family, also owns Sinclair Oil Corporation. $109–149.

BED & BREAKFASTS ♥ **England House Bed and Breakfast** (928-214-7350 or 877-214-7350), 614 W. Santa Fe Ave. As soon as you look at this house, built in 1909, you sense something special. Made from stones hewn for a stonemason, the craftsmanship is impeccable, down to the basalt fireplace and fireproof ceiling in the parlor. Owner-innkeepers Laurel and Richard Dunn put some elbow grease into the home and expertly finished the inside with period furnishings and décor they call "anti-doily" (mostly 1850–60 French antiques). Each room has its own bath; beds have ironed sheets and pillowcases, along with down feather beds or memory mattress. On arrival, guests can decompress with a complimentary shoulder massage and a glass of wine or ale. Fresh-baked treats and fruit are available all day; ice-cream bars are always available for late-night snacks. In the morning Laurel makes a very healthy, and very delicious, full breakfast (included with room). No pets, and no kids under age 10. $129–199.

♥ **Inn at 410 Bed & Breakfast** (928-774-0088 or 800-774-2008), 410 N. Leroux St. The historic building, listed on the National Register, is one of the oldest buildings in the city, located across from the Babbitt homestead. Built as a one-bedroom in 1894, the grand room has exquisite oak millwork. Owner-innkeeper Gordon Watkins comments that the home, like many others on the block, still has the former owners milling around, at times. Gordon does everything possible to make your stay a great one. Having had a successful career working in operations and development for some of the grander names in the hospitality industry, such as the Ritz Carlton, Hyatt, and InterContinental, he knows just what a weary traveler needs to make a great stay, Each of the themed nine rooms is spacious; they all have gas fireplaces, down pillows and comforters, TV and access to an 800+ movie library, Wi-Fi, microwaves, and mini fridges; three have Jacuzzi tubs. Rates include a full gourmet breakfast for two (served on the patio gushing with yellow columbine flowers when the temps hit 70) with afternoon snacks and refreshments. Children 5 years of age and over are welcome in Dakota Suite, Suite Nature, and The Observatory.

An additional charge of $25 per person per night shall apply. Pets are not allowed. $170–235.

♥ **Starlight Pines Bed and Breakfast** (928-527-1912 or 800-752-1912), 3380 E. Lockett Rd. Innkeeper-owners Richard and Michael are delightful hosts in this Victorian-style home decorated with period furniture and appointments. It's high romance here, with period colors, 12-foot ceilings, wood-burning fireplaces, clawfoot tubs, unique antiques (including a 650-pound china bathtub and a fainting couch), fresh flowers, Tiffany lamps, and original skeleton keys for every door. The hosts call it "Victorian with an Edge." You will call it very cool and utterly comfortable. Michael makes gourmet breakfasts (which appear in national magazines, for good reasons) while Richard makes sure everything is there at your disposal—including an amenities drawer that contains everything you might need but forgot. $169–179.

COTTAGES AND LODGES **Comfi Cottages of Flagstaff** (928-774-0731 or 888-774-0731), 1612 N. Aztec St. Pat and Ed Wiebe's collection of cottages all have a retro homey feel. Pat stocks each one like a doting mother, including a generous supply of fixings for breakfast, including bacon, eggs, bread, butter, muffins, cream cheese, milk, and OJ. It's everything that travelers who prefer to make their own meals or want a home base could want, as each home is a real one, with bedroom(s), kitchen, and bathroom. One cottage has a loft that kids will adore. The cottages are within walking distance of the historic section. All cottages have complimentary WiFi, cable TV, gas barbecue grill, and telephone. Bicycles, tennis rackets, and picnic baskets are provided on request. $120–260, under age 6 free.

Montezuma Lodge at Mormon Lake (928-354-2220). From Lake Mary Road, drive about 4 miles on Mormon Lake Road to the signed turnoff. You may remember staying at a classically retro cottage like one of these built in the 1930s and '40s. The property has several cottages clustered in a pine forest where herds of elk roam and raptors perch for their next meal. Just down the road pools Mormon Lake. $105–125 per night and $700 weekly. Two-night minimum stay.

Mormon Lake Lodge (928-354-2227), Main St., Mormon Lake. Situated in a pine forest next to a lake that draws wildlife, the lodge is one of the places of choice for Arizonans to cool off from the infamous desert heat. From its very start 80-plus years ago, it was popular: the true Wild West, where loggers, ranchers, and hunters hung out. Nowadays, team roping and rough stock cowboy events spice up the atmosphere. Cowboys come from all points in the Southwest to compete. And as their reputation goes, they work hard and play hard. The lodge sells T-shirts bragging "I survived a weekend at Mormon Lake Lodge." The property has a restaurant that serves excellent steaks from locally raised grass-fed Black Angus, a fishing pond, campsites, and horseback rides, a petting zoo, and buffalo. Cabins $134–249, rooms $59–109, campground and RV park $10–24 per night.

✷ Where to Eat

DINING OUT ♿ **Brix Restaurant & Wine Bar** (928-213-1021), 413 N. San Francisco St. Open daily from 5 PM. Located in the historic Carriage House, Brix is a casual fine dining restaurant that specializes in farm fresh, contemporary American cuisine. The seasonal menu includes regional organic produce from the northern

Arizona/Four Corners area. Dine inside or on the patio. The wine list has several dozen wines from which to choose. Reservations recommended. Entrées $25–31.

Dara Thai (928-774-0047), 413 S. San Francisco St. Open Mon.–Fri. 11–10, Sat. noon–6, Sun. noon–9. Red-orange walls, floral upholstered booths, and wooden floors and tables blend tastefully like the food's pungent and floral spice notes of chile pepper, kefir lime leaves, basil, lemongrass, ginger, mint, and fish sauce. The authentic meals are done well. The whole experience gives you a true taste of the graceful Thai culture. Entrées $11.95–16.95.

Granny's Closet (928-774-8331), 218 S. Milton Rd. Open daily 11 AM–midnight. Still going strong after 35 years, this Flagstaff favorite serves up big portions of decent homemade food. Nothing in the salad bar gets scooped from a can. The prime rib comes from a family recipe. The Italian food has the same roots and some zip in its sauce. The family's granny makes apple pie every morning. The place has two dining areas: one for Lumberjacks (a.k.a. Northern Arizona University students), which is where it's all happening, and one for those who like it quiet. You can choose. Entrées $9.99–18.99.

♥ **Josephine's Modern American Bistro** (928-779-3400), 503 N. Humphreys St. Open Mon.–Sat. (Sun. during summer); lunch 11–2:30 (closed in winter), dinner 5:30–9. The restaurant is named for owners' Jill and Tony Consentino's mother, who taught them all they know about food. They learned well enough to earn the restaurant awards over the years and the Award of Excellence from *Wine Spectator* magazine. The building, on the National Historic Register, was one of the first in the area constructed with volcanic rock. The utilitarian Craftsman bungalow design has battered rock columns on the porch, a sculpted rafter with diamond sash windows, coffered ceilings, and plenty of wainscot paneling. You'll find classic dishes here with creative twists. The Osso Buco comes with green chile demi-glace and Butternut Squash Mascarpone Risotto (you can order the latter on its own). Diablo Shrimp "Macaroni and Cheese" has seashell pasta in smoked Gouda cheese topped with sun-dried tomatoes and wild Mexican shrimp. The signature champagne vinaigrette salad features a perfect blend of sweet candied pecans, creamy goat cheese, and tart grapefruit with a tease of curry. Don't pass up the velvet-textured homemade ice cream. Entrées $19.50–27.50.

La Bellavia Restaurant (928-774-8301), 18 S. Beaver St. Open daily 6:30–2. A favorite breakfast spot for locals. If you do as the locals do, you'll order the wonderful Swedish oatcakes. Don't make the mistake of thinking they're like regular pancakes. These are *big*: in texture, taste, and size. You can also get eggs in a variety of special dishes of the eggs Benedict ilk. Bread is fresh baked—if you see cranberry and hazelnut French toast as a special, don't hesitate to order it. Espresso drinks and local art available. Entrées $4.75–7.75.

♥ **PASTO-Cucina Italiana** (928-779-1937), 19 E. Aspen. Open for lunch Mon.–Sat. 11–2 and dinner Mon.–Sat. 5–closing, daily Memorial Day–Labor Day. Chef Michael Long, thoughtful with his ingredients and presentations, makes everything in-house—from the pasta to the prosciutto. He knows how to use fresh herbs to add personality to some of the simpler dishes, like the frittata that occasionally appears on the menu or his Caprese Salad. Many of his ingredients are *denominación de* *origen controlada.* During the summer, he uses local produce, which adds variety to the menu as well as a little challenge for him. Staying true to the Italian palate, which prefers pork over beef, the menu has several dishes that are distinctively Italiano, such as Bagna Cauda (warm anchovy garlic dip with vegetables and breads), Minestrone Genovese, and Truffled Maccheroni. Where you sit can be just as special as the food. There are the coveted window seats (reservations essential) and the red brick patio filled with Gambel oak trees, aspens, and forest meadow flowers; the sacred datura gets the most attention. Pasta dishes come in two sizes and prices, course ($8–9) and meal ($15–17); entrées $17–27.

Salsa Brava (928-779-5293), 2220 E. Route 66. Open daily 11–9. Perennially on the local favorite list, appearing on TV foodie channel spots and usually busy no matter what time you go there, this color-saturated venue doles out some basically good and fresh Mexican food. Every meal is made-to-order, has no lard or MSG, and contains real Wisconsin cheese, which may be the reason why you won't get the heartburn that often comes with this fare. The large menu offers basics like enchiladas, burritos, and tacos; several vegetarian dishes; and specialties like blackened salmon, Lobster Enchiladas with cilantro cream sauce, and the signature Stuffed Sopapilla (like a Navajo taco, which they also serve, but stuffed instead of topped with ingredients). The salsa bar displays seven house-made salsas for which they hand-cut 700 pounds of tomatoes each week. They serve some of the best tequilas, several beers, and house wine. Entrées $8.95–16.95.

Tinderbox Kitchen (928-226-8400), 34 S. San Francisco St. Open Mon.–Sat., lunch 11–2, dinner 5–9. Chef Scott is known for his bold comfort-food creations. He developed a following at the former venue at which he worked in town. So when he opened this one with his cousin, Kevin, who manages it, the places was rockin' from day one. "We didn't run out of food," Scott recalls some of those early weekends, "but almost." The moral of the story is, get there early and be prepared to enjoy. Chef Scott changes his menu often to keep it fun and fresh for people that come in three or four times a week, and Tinderbox has many patrons who do just that. It's approachable food with a modern twist— The BBQ Berkshire Pork Chop has blue cheese, twice-baked potato and fig-blackberry mustard. Jalapeño Mac-N-Cheese, one of the diners' favorites, comes with duck leg confit, garlic bread crumbs, and white truffle oil. The chef's Nightly Fin Fish Preparation is always well received because the fish, like everything else, is fresh. Chef Scott makes his own charcuteries and "a darn good dessert," thanks to classes in Napa. The recipe for his Earl Grey Truffles appeared in *Bon Appétit* magazine. Entrées $16–28.

♥ **Western Gold Restaurant** (928-779-7979), Little America Hotel. Open 6 AM–9 PM. *The* restaurant of choice for the locals who like dependably good food with an upper-crust touch. Think the Dresden Restaurant or a more moderately priced Pump Room. So loyal are the locals, Chef David said he sees the same 100 people seated for lunch throughout the week. The Lunch Buffet for $10 may explain the loyalty. And they like to order their favorite foods. So much so, they will raise a ruckus if Chef David wants to get creative and tries to replace a favorite dish with a new entrée. This is why the Roast Turkey Dinner (with all the Thanksgiving trimmings) has remained on the menu for more than 30 years.

The recent addition, Grilled Chipotle Chicken, however, is a hit. You don't want to miss their special-occasion buffets on holidays, laden with delicacies, or the Saturday Prime Rib Dinner. As staid as it may seem, Western Gold serves some excellent food. The Belgian Waffle will melt in your mouth, the salads are garden-fresh, and the meats are quality. Not only menu items have a following. Server Eleanor Gardner, who's worked the dining room for more than 30 years, has a number of loyal patrons. She's even received a governor's service award. But be prepared to wait up to 2 hours (!) for her. Breakfast $6.50–10.95, lunch/dinner $7.95–22.95.

EATING OUT **Diablo Burger** (928-774-3274), 120 N. Leroux St. Open Mon.–Wed. 11–9, Thu.–Sat. 11 AM–11 PM. Derrick Widmark opened this hamburger spot with a mission—to showcase the grass-fed beef raised on the environmentally progressive Diablo Trust land in northern Arizona for which he does PR. The ecological overtones take a backseat as soon as you bite into the juicy and tasty burgers served on toasted English muffins with the "db" logo seared into the top (with a real branding iron). This is serious comfort food that is seriously good for you—the beef comes from open range-raised cattle that's antibiotic- and growth-hormone free, the hormone-free milk for the milkshakes comes from the Straus Family Creamery, beer hails from North Coast Brewing in Fort Bragg, and wine is from family-owned vineyards around the West. Frites, not Fries, are freshly made Belgian style and sprinkled with herbs. Because the good-guy food is so fresh and local, Widmark said several vegetarians have jumped off the wagon. One vegetarian regular rationalized in the comment book, "The karma is worth it." Burgers $7–9.25. Kids' menu available.

Fratelli Pizza (928-774-9200), 119 W. Phoenix Ave. Open daily 11–10. Perennially voted Best of Flagstaff since 2002. You can count on a great piece of pie—for several reasons. The dough is house-made and hand-tossed, the sauce balanced and very tasty, and the pizzas are made in a stone deck oven. Plus, the slices are *big* and cheap ($2.72). They serve some good brews and feature a good, reasonably priced wines each week. Pizzas $7.25–11.50 plus toppings.

Macy's European Coffee House (928-774-2243), 14 S. Beaver St. Open daily 6 AM–10 PM. True international cities always have a restaurant like this one, where you'll find an eclectic crowd that spans the social and cultural strata. The shop has a coffeehouse feel but serves excellent vegetarian fare that can be altered to vegan. Besides enjoying an excellent variety of coffees and teas, you can get healthy and delicious breakfast and lunch, too. Entrées $6.25–7.

New Jersey Pizza Company (928-774-5000), 2224 E. Cedar. Open daily 11–10. The best pizzeria in town serves an incredible variety of pizzas made from fresh and/or local foods. Their claim to fame is serving "thousands upon thousands of pizza combinations over the years." With more than 30 veggie toppings, a variety of meats, and rich cheeses, you can understand the possibilities. Desserts (including the gelato and cannoli shells) are house-made, and all ingredients are fresh and local, such as Sedona apples, Camp Verde peaches, pumpkins, and pecans, and local organic farm eggs. Pizzas $7.47–18.67.

Tacos Los Altos (928-714-1012), 3650 E. Route 66. Open daily 10 AM–8 PM. If you don't mind the taquería set-

MACY'S EUROPEAN COFFEE HOUSE, THE PLACE WHERE EVERYONE WHO'S ANYONE CONGREGATES IN FLAGSTAFF

ting of a generic fast-food eatery or you plan to take away, this is the place for some Jalisco food. The portions are big, the ingredients fresh (including the seafood: *camarónes*, *mojarra*, and *ostiones*), and the taste good. *Menudo* is served on the weekend. $4.75–10.99.

✷ The Arts

First Friday Art Walk at the Artists Gallery (928-773-0958), 17 N. San Francisco St. Monthly art walks (held 6:30–9 PM) give visitors a chance to see why Flagstaff is listed in art critic and author John Vallani's book *100 Art Towns in the U.S.* The free art walk is ongoing year-round.

Bruce Aiken Fine Art Studio (928-226-2882), 113 N. San Francisco St., Suite 209. There is a lot of good, affordable art in Flagstaff, but not many artists come with Bruce's story. The Grand Canyon artist known internationally used to live along the North Kaibab Trail at Roaring Spring in the Grand Canyon. He manned the pumphouse that provided water to the buildings in the national park. Having such an intimate life in the canyon has given him a unique interpretation of it. You can view his collectable works and talk canyon with him in his studio. His giclée prints are more affordable than you might think.

✷ Selective Shopping

There are a number of antique shops around the city. Stop by the Visitor's Center for a brochure.

You'll also find a number of boutique and specialty shops in the historic section of the city. One of the more fascinating ones is **Fire on the Mountain** (928-774-9025), 324 W. Birch St. Every Saturday and first Friday evening you can watch Georg Averbeck create his famous Fire on the Mountain glassware. Entertaining, as he is talented, George will expound about glassblowing ("It's like sex, you have good glass days and bad glass days.") and watch how he creates his trademark glassware from the dip of the stick into the 2,000-degree oven to the 900-degree cooler.

✷ Special Events

April: **Northern Arizona Book Festival** (928-774-9541). Acclaimed authors participate in readings, panel discussions, and workshops. **Soar into Spring Kite Festival** (928-213-2300). Spring is one windy season in northern Arizona. Head to Foxglen Park to launch your kite and have fun; non-kite-fliers can check out the carnival games and amusements, view arts and crafts, and eat fun foods.

May: May 2 is National Astronomy Day, and **Lowell Observatory and Coconino Astronomical Society** celebrate with telescope viewing and prize giveaways. Run for the Mountain 2K, 5K and 10K races. **Zuni Festival of Arts and Culture** (928-774-5213). Zuni artists share their art, music, and dance all day at the Museum of Northern Arizona. **Movies on the Square** (928-637-6192). Free family-oriented movies every Friday night in Heritage Square through mid-Sep.

June: **Route 66 Regional Chili Cook-off** (928-774-9541. The annual world championship qualifying event happens at Thorpe Park. **Annual Gran Fiesta Del Barrio and Fajita Cook-off** (928-774-9541) celebrates Hispanic culture and food at San Francisco de Asís Catholic School. **Annual Flagstaff Music Festival** (928-774-9541) promotes local music in Heritage Square.

July: **Museum of Northern Arizona Heritage Program** (928-774-5213). Hopi and Navajo festivals of arts and culture celebrate Native American culture.

September: **Coconino County Fair** (928-679-8000). Exhibits, livestock, rides, food, and entertainment. Route 66 Days (928-774-9541). Live music, vintage and hot-rod car show, and a parade all celebrate the Mother Road. **Annual Flagstaff Open Studios** (928-779-2300) gives you a chance to visit more than 80 top artists in their studios. **Flagstaff Festival of Science** (www.scifest.org) launches you into the scientific strata with 10 days of field trips, exhibits, star parties, talks, hikes, and scientific open houses. **Annual Navajo Festival of Arts and Culture** (928-774-5213) presents more than 60 of the best-known Diné artists who share their work at Northern Arizona Museum along with music, dancing, storytelling and art demonstrations.

December: **New Year's Eve Pinecone Drop** (928-779-1919, ext. 430). Who needs a glittering ball when you have a giant pinecone?

WILLIAMS

Located at the foot of Bill Williams Mountain and named for the colorful fur-trading mountain man Bill Williams, the city of Williams couldn't help but enjoy the same rugged individualism and love of the backcountry the mountain man displayed. Known for his creative thinking and unconventional wisdom, Bill Williams eluded demise several times while traipsing the wilds.

The tall, slim redhead for whom the city is named had some colorful characteristics. Some pages of Old Bill's personal history have him teetering between itinerant preacher and whiskey aficionado. Regardless, Old Bill was a master in the backcountry, and he earned the respect and friendship of some of history's more famous mountain men, such as Antoine Leroux and Zebulon Pike. Old Bill's independent personality and sense of adventure have trickled down into the city of Williams.

Williams prospered in its early days via the railroad and lumber, then took a cosmopolitan turn when the Santa Fe Railway built a spur line to the Grand Canyon at the beginning of the 20th century, bringing the world to Williams's doorstep. The town became downright rowdy trying to entertain humanity with saloons, bordellos, gambling houses, and opium dens. It took awhile for some of these eyebrow-raising vices to wane, even by 1936 when Route 66 put Williams on the Main Street of America. When I-40 bypassed the city in 1984, Williams held tightly to its Grand Canyon connection by registering its trademarked claim, The Gateway to the Grand Canyon.

The city endured a tired spell in the 1990s—to the point that some old buildings felt the breeze from the swing of the demolition ball. Old Bill's creative spirit came through, however, and innovative business people took the initiative to dust off the business section's marvelous old architecture (listed on the National Register of Historic Places), renovate with pleasant upscale interiors, and offer quality accommodations.

Today Williams has become an attractive destination in itself by blending its colorful history with today's comforts. Especially in the summertime, when live music fills the air from outdoor cafés and people from all corners of the world chatter in many different languages as they stroll the sidewalks and browse the stores along Route 66. Plus, Williams still has the only train to the Grand Canyon, the longest segment (2 miles) of Historic Route 66, and that marvelous backcountry where Old Bill Williams once roamed. Once? His spirit has never really left.

GUIDANCE Pick up a map of the historic buildings and information about the town and surrounding area, including the Grand Canyon, at the **Williams–U.S. Forest Service Visitor Center** (928-635-4061 or 800-863-0546), 200 W. Railroad Ave. Open daily 9–5. You can also get information on, and maps of, the South Kaibab National Forest backcountry surrounding the town.

GETTING THERE *By car:* Take I-40 right to Williams, located between Flagstaff to the east and Ash Fork to the west. *By air:* **H. A. Clark Memorial Field** (928-635-1280), 3501 N. Airport Rd., has a 6,000-foot runway and 16 transient tie-downs.

WHEN TO COME High season happens from Memorial Day to Labor Day, when temperatures range from the 80s in the day to the 50s at night; then once again from Thanksgiving to mid-Jan., when you should dress for winter's 40-degree days and freezing nights.

MEDICAL EMERGENCY **Flagstaff Medical Center** (928-779-3366), 1200 N. Beaver St., Flagstaff.

✱ To See

Cataract Creek Gang Gunfight. Every day in summer, around sundown, someone gets killed on Main Street (Route 66). The same ne'er-do-wells who rob the Grand Canyon Railway (see *To Do*) come back into town to raise a ruckus around 7 PM.

✐ **Grand Canyon Deer Farm** (928-635-4073), 6769 E. Deer Farm Rd. (I-40, exit 171). Open daily Oct. 16–Mar. 15, 10–5; Mar. 16–Oct. 16, 9–6. This petting zoo has a fun variety of animals. Several kinds are in perfect proportion to pint-size kids, such as pygmy goats and miniature donkeys, monkeys, mini cattle, baby bison, and a baby camel. They also have llamas, peacocks, several species of deer (including reindeer), talking birds, wallabies, coatimundi, and marmosets. Here kids can learn up close and personal all about the animals and how to approach them. $8.50 adults, $5 ages 3–13, $7.50 age 62-plus, under age 2 free.

✱ To Do

CROSS-COUNTRY SKIING Located off Spring Valley Rd. north of I-40. Contact Kaibab National Forest. The **Chalender X-Country Trails** feature a network of three trails totaling 21.9 miles created especially for cross-country skiing. The trails range from easy **RS Hill Trail**, to intermediate **Spring Valley Trail**, to difficult **Eagle Rock Trail**.

GOLF **Elephant Rocks Golf Course** (928-635-4935), 2200 Country Club Dr. Named for the pachyderm-size lava boulders situated along the road into the course, the city golf course rates as one of the most scenic in the state. The course, built in the 1920s, developed problems such as fairways without grass and oil-sand greens. In 1989 the city took over the 9-hole course and had Gary Panks redesign it; in 2000, another 9 holes were added to make it into an 18-hole beauty. Driving range, practice greens, pro shop, and clubhouse. $26–54 includes cart.

FISHING Several area lakes (**White Horse**, **Dogtown**, **Cataract**, and **Kaibab**) get stocked with trout. Nonmotorized boats only in **Cataract** and **Kaibab**; electric motors one horsepower or less on **White Horse** and **Dogtown**. Contact the Williams–U.S. Forest Service Visitor Center for more information.

HIKING There are almost three-dozen dayhikes in the national forest around Williams, including the Grand Canyon. Check out the **Bill Williams**, **Sycamore Rim**, and **Bixler Saddle** trails. Also, you can access the **Arizona Trail** from nearby trailheads. Contact the Williams–U.S. Forest Service Visitor Center for more information.

HORSEBACK RIDES **Stables in the Pines** (928-635-0706), 1000 Circle Pine Rd. Open May–Sep. Saddle up for a half-hour or all-day trail ride through the Kaibab National Forest. You can make reservations for night rides and cookouts, as well.

MOUNTAIN BIKING Kaibab National Forest has created several official mountain bike routes, including 6-mile-long **Ash Fork Hill Route**, the 6.9-mile **Devil Dog Bike Tour**, **Old Perkinsville Road** (9.3 miles), **Round Mountain Loop** (18.3 miles), and 15.9-mile **Stage Station Loop**. Contact the Williams–U.S. Forest Service Visitor Center for more information.

RAILROAD **Grand Canyon Railway** (800-843-8724). Vintage trains with restored 1923 Harriman coaches leave the historic 1908 depot every day (except Dec. 24–25), climbing hills and winding around valleys for just over two hours up to the Grand Canyon. Along the way stowaway musicians play old tunes and bandits wait along the tracks in an attempt to rob the train. Once you're at the Grand Canyon, you have almost four hours to take in the sights. Packages available for several-day trips. $70–190 adults, $40–110 kids.

ROCK CLIMBING Some of the country's choicest climbing routes scale the walls of Sycamore Canyon, especially at **Sycamore Falls**—where you can often see climbers just about any day all summer. Contact the Williams–U.S. Forest Service Visitor Center for more information.

SKIING **Elk Ridge Ski Area** (928-814-5038), 418 W. Franklin (Bill Williams Mountain). Open Thu.–Sun. in season, when snow permits. It's a small area, but it works well for beginners or advanced skiers who need a downhill run in a pinch. The focus here is on families and it has a snow play and snow tubing slope.

✷ Wilder Places

The **Grand Canyon**, only an hour's drive away, makes a spectacular destination.

Sycamore Canyon Wilderness. Contact the Williams–U.S. Forest Service Visitor Center. One of the wilder canyons in northern Arizona lies just south of Williams. Its premier multiuse trail, the **Sycamore Rim Trail**, is one of the state's most diversified. Check out the Rocky Mountain iris spread in spring. In summer, wildflowers dot meadows, and boggy areas have water lilies. You get views of the dramatic red-rock canyon walls, mountain climbers at Sycamore Falls, and the historic Overland Trail. No mechanized equipment allowed.

Bill Williams Mountain. Contact the Williams–U.S. Forest Service Visitor Center. The 9,264-foot-high peak has a network of multiuse trails with pine-oak to aspen-fir forests. The most popular is the Bill Williams Trail, as rough-and-tumble as Old Bill himself.

✱ Lodging

Grand Canyon Hotel (928-635-1419 or 877-635-1419), 145 W. US 66. Closed Dec. 1–Mar. 15. One of the state's oldest hotels has had a global list of guests since it opened in 1891, from the king of Siam to General Pershing to John Muir. The European-style hotel still attracts people from all over the planet, with pieces of paper money from 67 countries tacked up around the front desk to show for it. It's a friendly place with clean, vintage rooms at a great price that exude character. Owner Oscar Fredrickson explained the hotel is a comfort zone for Europeans. Accommodations may run small and have a bathroom down the hall, but this is nothing new to anyone but Americans, who relish large rooms and private bathrooms. A Dane checking in for the night confirmed Oscar's statement by saying, "This is perfect." A lobby bar serves beer and wine. $50–145. Hostel bed (six in a room) $23.

Grand Canyon Railway Hotel (800-843-8724), 233 N. Grand Canyon Blvd. Large rooms decorated in classical French Revival with a Southwest flair have queen beds and cable TV. Southwestern suites have a sleeper couch, chair, TV, and kitchenette with microwave, mini fridge, coffeemaker, and wet bar. The property has a lounge, an indoor swimming pool and Jacuzzi, basketball and volleyball courts, and a small children's playground. $98–200; call for specials.

♥ **The Lodge** (928-635-4534 or 877-563-4366), 200 E. Route 66. The old adobe-style building is an attractive blend of cheeky exteriors full of kitsch and recently remodeled interiors leaning toward luxury. Single rooms and suites have wood and travertine flooring, solid wood furniture, and ultra-comfortable bedding. Rooms have queen or king beds, cable flat-screen TV, radio, and complimentary continental breakfast. Suites have upgraded flat-screen TV and video, microwave, refrigerator, and dining table; some have fireplace. Continental breakfast is included. $99–199.

BED & BREAKFASTS **Canyon Country Inn** (928-635-2349), 442 W. Route 66. The inn's homey country décor features quilts and stuffed bears. The rooms are quiet, clean, and have their own bathroom. Continental breakfast is included. No pets. $59–94.

Red Garter Bed and Bakery (928-635-1484 or 800-328-1484), 137 W. Railroad Ave. The two-story Victorian Romanesque–style bed & breakfast, once considered the rowdiest abode on Williams's Saloon Row, was constructed in 1897 as a saloon and bordello that remained in service until the 1940s. A steep flight of steps known as the "Cowboy's Endurance Test" led to the girls upstairs. Owner-innkeeper John Holst transformed the seamy saloon into a classy B&B now listed on the National Register of Historic Places that, unlike the girls that did business there decades ago, gets better looking as years go by. Holst has doted on the interiors and designed period woodwork in the lobby. Breakfast consists of homemade pastries (scones, cinnamon rolls, croissants, and Danish), fruit, juice, and gourmet coffee (included with the room) in the bakery downstairs. No pets. $120–145.

✷ Where to Eat

DINING OUT Dara Thai Café (928-635-2201), 145 W. U.S. 66, Suite C. Open Mon.–Sat; lunch 11–2, dinner 5–9. The spin-off of the Flagstaff restaurant serves good Thai and vegetarian food in the small but breezy and inviting restaurant. Nationalism runs high here, with posters of the homeland, as well as pictures of their royalty. The ingredients sometimes veer to the inventive side, but flavors remain close enough to traditional Thai. Lunch $7.95, dinner entrées $9.95–14.95.

Old Smoky's Restaurant and Pancake House (928-635-1915), 624 W. Route 66. Open 6 AM–1 PM; closed Wed. and Thu. in winter. One of the area's classic diners opened in 1946 as a 24-hour-a-day café. Over the years, the diner evolved into a BBQ eatery and currently into a country-style breakfast venue, and a darn good one. The rustic exterior reminds you of an old cozy cabin; inside its old diner style feels like the good ol' days. The food is burly breakfast at its best, including all-you-can-eat biscuits and gravy or pancakes for under $5. You can build your own omelet, or order a health-conscious meal, too. At lunchtime, the main fare is sandwiches. Entrées $4.99–7.99.

THE RED GARTER BED & BAKERY, IN HISTORIC WILLIAMS ALONG FAMOUS ROUTE 66, SERVES FRESH-MADE BAKED GOODS EACH MORNING

Pine Country Restaurant (928-635-9718), 107 N. Grand Canyon Blvd. Open daily 5:30 AM–9 PM. You can get a great breakfast and decent lunch and dinner here, with fried chicken, chicken-fried steak, and steak being the customer favorites. What makes the venue truly special is its showcase of homemade pies—banana coconut cream, lemon meringue, and apple (à la mode) are the pies of choice. Meals are "very, very big," so you have to plan to save room for the grand finale. Entrées $8.99–21.99

♥ **Red Raven Restaurant** (928-635-4980), W. Route 66. Open Tue.–Sun.; lunch 11–2, dinner 5–9. The Raven, which opened around 2005 with immediate rave reviews, continues gaining kudos. Owner David Haynes attributes his success "to good, fresh ingredients, and some of the best steaks around." The Raven's remodeled building has fresh and balanced interiors with tables dressed in linens and fresh flowers. The fine-dining menu lists about a dozen thoughtfully prepared items featuring pasta, fish, steaks, and wraps. Tempura pops up around the menu. The wine and beer list matches the fine dining. Lunch $6–10, dinner $10–22.

EATING OUT **Twisters** (928-635-0266), 417 E. Route 66. Open daily 8 AM–8 PM (till 10 PM in summer). Pure Route 66, from the malt-shop fare to the 1950s music to the Route 66 Place gift shop. The food—hamburgers, hot dogs, onion rings, fries, milk shakes, and phosphates—makes this one of the best comfort-food joints around. And for $5, you can get a sandwich and one of seven sides (fries, potato salad, coleslaw, and more).

✷ Special Events

May: **Rendezvous Days** (928-635-4061) celebrates the town's western heritage with buckskinners, a black powder shoot, a parade, and family activities.

June: **Renaissance in the Pines** (928-635-4061) reenacts a more romantic era; come in costume or as you are to watch jousting, entertainment, and fair maidens and handsome knights.

July: **Cowpuncher's Reunion Rodeo** (928-635-4061). Working cowboys in the area get together and rodeo.

August: **Cool Country Cruise-In and Route 66 Festival** (928-635-4061). This celebration of Route 66 features a variety of activities such as an open car and bike show, a poker run, a '50s dance, and a battle of the bands.

September: **Labor Day PRCA Rodeo** (928-635-4061) brings the Professional Rodeo circuit to town with a parade and dances.

October: **Family Fun Fall Festival** (928-635-4061) features a carnival, major recording act, and live entertainment.

November–January: **Mountain Village Holiday** (928-635-4061) lasts from Thanksgiving to New Year's, with Christmas lights, hayrides, craft sales, art show, holiday activities, and shopping. **The Polar Express** (800-843-8724), through mid-Jan., is based on the classic children's book by Van Allsburg.

PRESCOTT

When Arizona's celebrated mountain man Joseph Walker led a group of prospectors up the Hassayampa River to prospect for gold, they finally hit paydirt when they started to explore the river's tributaries near Spruce Ridge. The prospectors, fueled with storied sayings—"If ya wash yer face in the Hassayampa River, you can pan four ounces of gold dust from yer whiskers," had placer claims that brought $50 to $100 a day. The group made camp near Granite Creek in 1863 close to the present-day Courthouse Square. Walker kept this gold camp rigidly disciplined—a feat that bordered on the miraculous as his wards were totally taken with gold fever—until reinforcements came.

Rustic and raucous, even by mining camp standards, this camp soon traded its generic name of Granite City for the more respectable Prescott, in honor of historian William Hickling Prescott. Shortly afterward, when the newly designated Arizona Territory needed a nonpartisan capital, Prescott fit the bill and became the only wilderness capital in U.S. history.

The ragamuffin capital quickly filled with the ilk so common to boomtowns—prospectors, cowboys, merchants, gamblers, shady ladies, and shysters. As the town grew, so did its caliber of citizens, whose names of Gurley, Groom, Goldwater, and Hall became memorialized in streets, buildings, and nature. Intertwining local color with class, ingenuity with personality, and wit with wisdom, Prescott endured to become one of Arizona's most endearing cities, coined "Everyone's Hometown."

The city also earned the title "One of America's Dozen Distinctive Destinations" from the National Trust for Historic Preservation. And for good reason: The town has more than 700 buildings on the National Historic Register, including Victorian homes, a huge courthouse square, and old-time saloons. A number of antiques shops allow you to take a piece of history home with you.

GUIDANCE Prescott Chamber of Commerce and Tourist Information Center (928-445-2000), 117 W. Goodwin St. Open Mon.–Fri. 9–5, Sat. and Sun. 10–2. You can get maps, a schedule of events, and answers to questions about the Prescott area. A walking tour pamphlet ($1) lists 34 different historic buildings. **Bradshaw Ranger District** (928-443-8000), 344 S. Cortez St., can give you information on backcountry use in the Prescott National Forest.

GETTING THERE *By car:* The majority of visitors enter Prescott by way of I-17: From the north, take exit no. 217 (AZ 169), drive 12 miles, turn right onto AZ 69,

WHISKEY ROW

and drive 19 miles. From the south, exit at AZ 69 and drive 34 miles. Heading from Sedona, take AZ 89A all the way, about 61 miles. From I-40, take AZ 89 (exit 144) south for 50 miles. *By air:* **Ernest A. Love Field** has three paved runways. **Prescott Airport Shuttle** (800-445-7978) makes 16 trips a day from Phoenix.

WHEN TO COME It's mild all the way around the calendar in Prescott: snow hardly lasts a day, and hot days evanesce into cool nights. The season starts in March, intensifies by June, peaks on the July Fourth weekend—when lodging is booked months ahead of time—then relaxes after Labor Day. December is a big month, since another of the town's nicknames is Arizona's Christmas City.

MEDICAL EMERGENCY **Yavapai Regional Medical Center Hospital** (928-445-2700), 1003 Willow Creek Rd.

✷ To See

Courthouse Plaza, located at Gurley and Montezuma sts. A timeline chiseled in the plaza concrete measures the county's history with events between 1581 and 1985. Readers following the timeline will end up at a bronze sculpture dedicated to the most glamorous fighters in the United States Calvary, the Rough Riders, designed by Solon Borglum—whose brother worked on Mount Rushmore. Every night in summer the plaza has some kind of entertainment.

The Phippen Museum (928-778-1385), 4701 AZ 89 N. Open Tue.–Sat. 10–4, Sun. 1–4. Named for the first president of the Cowboy Artists of America, George Phippen. The art museum correctly describes itself as the most beautifully located museum in Arizona, standing in the mist of the stunning outcroppings of Granite Dells. It features western and Native American art and has a marketplace of authentic Indian items. $5 adults, $4 seniors, age 12 and under free.

Sharlot Hall Museum (928-771-1130), 415 W. Gurley St. Open Mon.–Sat. 10–4, Sun. noon–4. The largest museum in the area is an educational adventure—much like its namesake founder's life. Prescott's poet and former state historian Sharlot

Hall traveled Arizona's mining camps to collect oral histories. With captivating exhibits that change frequently during the year, a research library, and historical plays enacted in the Blue Rose Theater, you get an entertaining dose of the area's lively past. The campus contains the territorial governor's mansion, a gazebo, a rose garden, and other buildings dating from the frontier days. $5 adults, under age 18 free.

♿ **The Smoki Museum** (928-445-1230), 147 N. Arizona St. Open Tue.–Sat. 10–4, Sun. 1–4. Perhaps one of the most unusual museums in America. Designed to resemble an Indian pueblo, and full of Native American artifacts, the museum was built in 1935. Native stone and thousands of pine logs were used to create the inside columns, window enclosures, slab doors, vigas, and latillas. Filled with priceless Native American artifacts, art, and a research library, the museum presents an overlook of Native American mystique, legends, and history. The name came from the Smoki People, a group of Prescottonians so captivated by the Hopi Indians, they took to enacting Hopi ceremonies and dances—including the controversial Hopi snake ceremony—as well as those of other southwestern tribes. The faux ceremonies and dances ended in 1990 when the Hopi people actively protested against the group in downtown Prescott. $5 adults, $4 seniors, $3 students, under age 12 free.

SCENIC DRIVES Take a look at surrounding ranch country on the 50-mile-long **Iron Springs Road Loop**. This is also a popular road biking route. From Gurley St., go north on Montezuma, and continue as it bends westward and turns into Iron Springs Rd. out of town and south to Skull Valley. At Thompson Valley Rd., turn left. Go about 4 miles to AZ 89 and turn north. This road will wind up into the Bradshaw Mountains and bring you back into Prescott. To tour the backcountry, take the **Bradshaw Mountains Motor Tour**—a 25-mile loop that takes you on a backcountry route (high clearance is required for some segments) into a historic world of mining deep in the national forest. Go east on AZ 69, turn south onto Mount Vernon St. (Senator Hwy.), continue south to FR 197, and turn left, back to AZ 69.

✷ To Do

DOG PARK 🐾 **Willow Creek Dog Park** (928-777-1122), 3181 Willow Creek Rd. Open daily 7 AM–10 PM. Open to dogs over 4 months old. Walking path, dog fountain, tables, benches, shade ramada, small-dog area.

GAMING **Bucky's Casino** (928-776-5695), 1500 E. AZ 69.The Yavapai-Prescott tribe's casino has 300 slots machines and live poker. Across the street is the **Yavapai Casino** (928-445-5767), 1505 E. AZ 69. The smaller of two Yavapai casinos, this one has 175 slot machines, including Wheel of Fortune and Jeopardy! progressives, and bingo. Free bus rides from Phoenix.

GOLF Prescott offers a number of courses, from affordable to state-of-the-art. Each gives you a challenge with its varying terrain of rolling hills, tree-lined fairways, and granite outcroppings balanced with tremendous views.

Antelope Hills Golf Courses (928-776-7888), 1 Perkins Dr. Among Arizona's best affordable courses, the two par-72 courses at Antelope Hills rank among the favorites. Not only are their views some of the most stunning golfers can set their eyes upon, looking toward the Granite Dells and Mogollon Rim, but they're both 18-hole championship courses. Lawrence Hughes designed the north course, and Gary Panks the south course. It's like having resort golf at public prices. The facility has a natural-turf driving range and full-service golf shop, **Manzanita Grille** (good food), and lounge. Dress code calls for a shirt with collar and no cutoffs. $30 with cart.

Prescott Golf & Country Club (928-772-8984), 1030 Prescott Country Club Blvd., Dewey. Located just down the road from Prescott, out in the countryside where the spaces are open and mountain views impressive, this course spreads in the valley between the Mingus and Bradshaw Mountains. The 7,200-yard, 18-hole course has a tree-lined fairway and fast bent greens. A double-sided practice facility has driving tees and chipping and putting greens. The country club has a golf shop, restaurant, and lounge. $24–40. Fees include golf and cart.

StoneRidge (928-772-6500), 1601 N. Buff Top Rd., Prescott Valley. This 18-hole championship golf course gets its name from its location among granite boulders and deeply carved washes—particularly around hole 12, where pockets of boulders, rocks, and ridges follow you. The par-72 course is listed among *Golf Digest*'s 2008/2009 Best Places to Play. The course runs 7,052 yards with 350 feet of elevation changes from lowest tee to highest green. $25–70. Rates include cart.

HIKING Right in town you have **Thumb Butte**, the locals' trail of choice for a short fitness hike, at the end of Thumb Butte Road, as well as the 4-mile-long barrier-free **Peavine Trail** at the Granite Dells. Get information from the visitor center. The trails in the Granite Mountain Wilderness travel through ponderosa forests, around weather-smoothed granite boulders. Lynx Lake has a network of short trails. Contact the Bradshaw Ranger District.

HISTORIC TOURS In a city whose motto is "Where History Lives On," you don't have to look too far to dip into the past. More than 700 Prescott buildings appear on the National Register of Historic Places. From May through Oct. at 10 each morning, the Prescott Chamber of Commerce (928-445-2000 or 800-266-7534), 117 W. Goodwin St., presents an hour-long docent-led **Historic Walking Tour of Downtown Prescott**. Prescottonian Melissa Ruffner—**Melissa Ruffner's Prescott Historical Tours** (928-445-4567)—takes you on a colorful spin through Everyone's Hometown, elucidating upon the town that created her family heritage since 1867. You'll see some of the best examples of Victorian-style homes on a self-guided tour down **Mount Vernon Street.** A stroll down the street will take about an hour to view beautifully restored buildings.

HORSEBACK RIDING **Smokin' Gun Adventures** (928-308-0911). Smokin' Dave Wrangler gives an entertaining trail ride in several areas around Prescott, ranging in length from an hour to all day. Smokin' Dave offers three-day vacations for cowpokes that don't want to leave the trail.

KAYAKING AND CANOEING There are several lakes in the area, and they all present perfect kayak conditions (see *Wilder Places*). **Prescott Outdoors, LLC,** runs concessions at Watson and Goldwater (canoe only) Lakes. All boats are rented on a first-come, first-served basis; no reservations. Apr.–Sep., weekends 10–4.

MOUNTAIN BIKING Prescott has hundreds of miles of trails to ride within minutes of the downtown area. The trails range from easy to technical, and from popular to the kind you won't see a soul upon all day. For information on trails, stop at the chamber of commerce for a bicycle map. For more information on more remote trails, contact the Bradshaw Ranger District. To rent a bicycle, go to **Ironclad Bicycles** (928-776-1755), 710 White Spar Rd.

ROCK CLIMBING The perpendicular granite walls of the Granite Mountain Wilderness are prime rock climbing haunts. **Rubicon Outdoors** (800-903-6987) leads half- and full-day ascents.

✷ Wilder Places

Goldwater Lake (928-777-1100), city of Prescott, 201 S. Cortez St. Go 4 miles south on Mount Vernon to the signed turnoff and turn right. This sweet little lake sits in a cozy of ponderosa pines. A trail with benches rings it; picnic sites overlook it. $2 parking fee. Boat rentals and fishing available.

Granite Mountain Wilderness. Contact the Bradshaw Ranger District for information. No mountain bikes or mechanized machinery are allowed in the wilderness. The golden granite boulders stack up to produce aesthetic moments with far-reaching panoramas. Higher up in the mountain, the piñon-juniper forest transitions into ponderosa pine. The wilderness has world-class rock climbing and favorite hiking trails. The Little Granite $5 per car; free every Wednesday.

Lynx Lake (928-777-1121). Go east about 3 miles on Gurley St., and turn right onto Walker Rd.; go 2 miles to the lake. Open mid-Apr.–mid-Oct. 6 AM–10PM, mid-Oct.–mid-Apr. 8 AM–sunset. Peaceful Lynx Lake has hiking trails, camping, and fishing. $2 day-use permit to park. Wednesdays are free.

Watson Lake/Granite Dells (928-777-1121), about 5 miles north on AZ 89. Open 7–sunset; Memorial Day–Labor Day 6 AM–10 PM. One of the most scenic spots in the area was a hiding place for the nefarious a century ago. Erosion-carved granite outcroppings make for an aesthetic scene amid sapphire-hued water. If you have a kayak, bring it to explore the lake and channels, or rent one at the lakeshore. Watch for rock climbers scaling granite walls. $2 parking fee.

Watson Woods Riparian Preserve (928-777-1121). Go east on Gurley St., and turn left onto AZ 89; go 2.2 miles, and turn right onto Prescott Lakes Pkwy.; turn left at Sun Dog Ranch Rd., then left again into the parking lot. This preserve gives you an opportunity to view watchable wildlife in a cottonwood-willow riparian forest on a very short trail, a premier bird-watching area. $2 donation.

✷ Lodging

BED & BREAKFASTS ✐ ⇴ ♥ **Gold Bar Ranch Bed & Breakfast** (928-427-3235). You can get a taste of the cowboy life at this working cattle ranch located along the Hassayampa River less than an hour south of Prescott. Or just come out to veg. Mike and Ella McCracken have fixed up the old ranch-hand bunkhouse located on a family ranch into a nice 800 sq. ft. house with two bedrooms, 2 bathrooms, and full kitchen. Ella will provide the ingredients for breakfast (such as fresh eggs from their chickens and fresh-made maple-flavored sausage "so good, it drives people crazy"), which you make yourself at your convenience. The Hassayampa River winds through the ranch, so bird-watching is a given (150 species sighted so far). You can also hike along the river or pan for gold along it the way the old-time prospectors did. Throw in a line in their stocked reservoir for large-mouth bass, bluegill, or catfish. Or go horseback riding to petroglyphs or Apache ruins on one of the ranch horses, which, Ella informed, have great ground manners and do what you tell them. If a roundup is happening during your stay, you can take part in it for $550 a day (food included). "You have to be a pretty good rider," Ella advised, "because we go into some pretty rough country." Whether you take part in a cattle drive or not, at the end of the day, when the sun turns the land golden and coyotes start to howl, you know you're standing in part of Arizona that hasn't changed since way back when. Bed & breakfast $120 double occupancy, $10 per extra person; camping $15 per person per night.

The Pleasant Street Inn Bed and Breakfast (928-445-4774), 142 S. Pleasant St. The century-plus-old Victorian home was moved from a location a few blocks away to the historic district in 1990, then remodeled. Modern interiors keep the feel of the place light, and sun-filled rooms add airiness. There's plenty of parking, and you can walk the three blocks to the downtown stores and Whiskey Row from here. Of the four available rooms, two are suites and two are large rooms. All have queen or king beds with pillow-top mattresses; three have in-room private bath and one offers private use of a hall bathroom. One is connected to an outside deck. Guests have use of a refrigerator on the main floor that has complimentary bottled water and soda; and books and a sitting area by the fireplace. Kids older than age 12 are welcome. No pets. Owner-innkeeper Jeanne Watkins will fix you a full breakfast with quality ingredients, or you can have a quick continental breakfast if you plan to eat and run early in the morning. $130–185.

THE PLEASANT STREET INN B&B

((ɪ)) **Prescott Pines Inn** (928-445-7270), 901 White Spar Rd. The inn, located on the southern edge of town away from Whiskey Row, comes with a historic lineage. It first came on the scene in 1863 as the Brookside Ranch. In the 1930s it became the Haymore Dairy. In 1987 it was remodeled and restored as a comfy, but not stuffy, Victorian inn. There are 11 guest rooms plus the three-bedroom chalet—a 1,300-square-foot A-frame house that sleeps 8 to 10—in the compound of buildings. Each room has its own entrance and bathroom; and some rooms have TV/DVD. In summer the air wafts with the smell of roses and peonies in the garden. Located closer to the national forest than downtown, the inn has a relaxed feeling in the surrounding pines. Rooms $79–89 (add $10 for breakfast for two), guest houses $100–150, chalet (self-service only) $320.

♥ **Rocamadour Bed and Breakfast** (928-771-1933), 3386 N. Hwy. 89. Located 4 miles north of the city, the Rocamadour—Old French for "rock lover"—takes its name from the enchanting rock formations of the Granite Dells in which it's located. The labyrinthine collection of granite formations, which attracted Hollywood stars such as Tom Mix and John Wayne, spreads around the property and creates some gorgeous views. Innkeepers Mike and Twila Coffey spent several years in Burgundy, France, which shows in the rooms' appointments, creating the appeal of a French country inn. Mike and Twila attend to every detail savvy travelers appreciate. The three rooms have a private entrance, private bath, cable TV, fireplace (some), and Internet. Gourmet breakfasts are included. The property is a favorite of national and world travelers. $149–219.

HOTELS AND INNS 🐾 ((ɪ)) ♥ **Hassayampa Inn** (928-778-9434 or 800-322-1927), 122 E. Gurley St. Like the river it's named for (the Apache word hassayampa means "the river that loses itself"), the hotel started out as a "first-class hostelry" and lost itself for a time before returning to its hotel roots and claiming an AAA Three Diamond rating. Built in 1927 as The Grand Hotel, the property hosted the upper crust and Hollywood. A child of the Jazz Age, Prohibition, and gangsters, it took its wayward turn in the 1970s and dallied as a boardinghouse, retirement home, and interim campus for Prescott College. It was born again when it found a place on the National Register of Historic Places and went through a multimillion-dollar renovation in 1985. Since then, the hotel has remained the classiest act in the town, with a gorgeous lobby full of original Castillian oak furnishings, a tiled fireplace, and a hand-operated original Chinese red elevator. Art deco has a strong say here, and it's well done. Rooms have central AC, WiFi, TV, private bathroom, and phone. $99–189 includes complimentary breakfast at the hotel restaurant, the Peacock Room (see *Dining Out*).

🏵 **Hotel St. Michael** (928-776-1999 or 800-678-3757), 205 W. Gurley St. Advertised as having "modern electricity" and being "the only absolutely fire proof building in Prescott" when it was first built in 1891 as the Hotel Burke, the building promptly burned to the ground during the Great Fire of 1900. Rebuilt a year later, the hotel was subsequently named Hotel St. Michael and continues as one of Prescott's most beloved properties. Check out the cartoon faces along the top of the building. They're said to be the architect's rendition of some of the city's local officials, presiding during the construction of the hotel. Situated on the north end of Whiskey Row and across the street from the Courthouse Square, it's right in the middle of all the action. You'll have some of the best views in town from these rooms. Rooms have double, queen, or king bed; cable TV; direct-dial phones with free local calls; and air-conditioning. Breakfast at the Bistro St. Michael (see *Dining Out*) is included in rates. \$59–119.

Hotel Vendome (928-776-0900), 230 S. Cortez St. Clara Worthen advertised her newly built hotel in 1918 as "a place where particular people will be satisfied." The hotel's parlorlike lobby and European style are particularly attractive. The hotel, restored to its horse-and-buggy days interior, has another particular point of interest: ghost Abby Byr, who died in Room 16, and her cat, Noble. Abby plays pranks and Noble mews. Abby, rumor has it, is a friendly ghost. Room have queen, king or twin beds. Four units have 2 bedrooms. Continental breakfast is included in rates. Beer, wine, coffee, and WiFi available in lobby. \$89–179.

✷ Where to Eat

DINING OUT 129½ An American Jazz Grille (928-443-9292), 129½ N. Cortez St. Open for dinner Mon.–Thu. 5–9, 10 Fri. and Sat. 5–10. This combination restaurant–jazz club has the cool warmth of an expatriate club in France with a menu that flirts with a different cultures—Trout Florentine, Prickly Pear BBQ Ribs, Harvest Scallops with Hominy Hash and Rosemary Cream, and their signatures: Balsamic Calves Liver & Onions and The Bad Boy (10 oz. pork chop filled with sage cornbread and sausage stuffing and wrapped in bacon, and covered with Rosemary Cream) Steaks are big and the pasta is fresh. It also has some of the best jazz in the city (Wed.–Sun. starting at 6 PM). You'll find an eclectic crowd here, from 20-somethings doing the social scene to baby boomers nodding their heads and cowboys tapping pointed toes to the music. The food is as good as the music and as decadent as the red-and-black décor. The fare tends toward hearty, with some lean dishes for lighter eaters. Entrées \$17.95–26.95.

Bistro St. Michael (928-776-1999), 205 W. Gurley St. Open Fri. and Sat. 7 AM–10 PM, Sun.–Thu. 7 AM–7 PM. Known for its plate-glass floor-to-ceiling windows, this restaurant has some of the best ground-level seats in town. The cognac wooden trim lavished all around and metal ceiling pull you back, with a friendly tug, to the turn of the 20th century when the building was constructed. You can get a decent meal here and order a good brew or glass of wine. Breakfasts lean toward bistro style, with eggs Benedict, Belgian waffles, and huevos rancheros. Lunch and dinner offer unusual sandwiches, burgers, and pastas. Special menu on holidays. Entrées \$9.95–16.95.

El Gato Azul (928-445-1070), 316 W. Goodwin St. Open Mon.–Thu. 11–9, Fri. and Sat. 11–10, Sun. 12–3 and 4–9. The chef here braids a bit of Mediterranean with a strand of Spanish and a dash of Southwest. You end up with a creative and tasty menu. Meals like prickly pear–stuffed toast, open-faced *rellenos*, vegan tamales with roasted vegetables, and blue corn pancakes make this restaurant as fun as its decidedly Latin décor. When the weather's right, outdoor dining places you right alongside the banks of Granite Creek. Tapas are served 3–5. Entrées \$14.95–23.95.

The Palace Restaurant and Saloon (928-541-1996), 120 S. Montezuma St. Open daily for lunch 11–3; dinner

Sun.–Thu. 4:30–9, Fri. and Sat. 4:30–11. Some of the West's most notorious characters stopped in for a drink here at the town's historic bar. In the late 1870s the famous trio of Wyatt Earp, Virgil Earp, and Doc Holliday showed up. The good doctor locked into a winning streak on Whiskey Row, rumor has it at The Palace, where he won $10,000 just before he left for Tombstone. Enough about the saloon, gamblers, and infamous patrons; you're interested in food, right? Steaks are big here: all hand-cut Angus beef—from a pound T-bone to cut-it-with-your-fork fillet—but balanced with fish from salmon to cat. Lunchtime serves gourmet sandwiches. Entrées $13.95–29.95.

♥ **Peacock Room** (928-778-9434), Hassayampa Inn, 122 E. Gurley St. Open daily for breakfast 7–11; lunch 11–2; and dinner Sun.–Thu. 6–9, Fri. and Sat. 6–9:30. Prescott's popular fine-dining establishment has the most consistently good meals in town; a claim made possible by Chef Pedro Sevilla. Chef Pedro has cooked in some of the best kitchens on the European continent and was a Tucson favorite for years before he moved to Prescott. Although his menu centers on fine dining basics, you'll see his favorite nouvelle cuisine creative touches in most every dish. Breakfast is labeled "A Gala Affair," which it certainly feels like with the piped-in classic music and sterling silver and crystal appearing here and there. The less elegant (but no less delicious) daily Hometown Dinner menu (served 4:30–6) will save you a couple dollars per entrée. Entrées $16–32.

Prescott Brewing Company (928-771-2795), 130 W. Gurley St., Suite A. Open Sun.–Thu. 11 AM–10 PM, Fri. and Sat. 11 AM–11 PM. This is where you'll find the best beer in town/Arizona/the nation/the world—depending on what kind of brew you order. Showing off a wall full of coveted first-place national and international beer awards, owner John Nielsen says this is the only brewpub in Yavapai County. Three award-winning brews remain on tap year-round; other winners appear seasonally. Whiskey aficionados should check out the lavish scotch menu. The food served with this celebrated beer is pub fare with a flair. Kids' menu available. After a meal here, you just might end up agreeing with Poor Richard when he said, "Beer is living proof that God loves us and wants to see us happy." Entrées $8–15.

EATING OUT ✿ **Annalina's** (928-776-1277), 126 S. Montezuma. Open Wed.–Mon. 11–8 (call after 6 PM on weekdays); closed Tue. The food at this colorfully decorated eatery is about as authentic as you can get, and it has some Mexico City influences. *Menudo* is a daily occurrence, tacos are delightfully soft shelled, and the beans are downright soulful. Corn tortillas are made fresh daily, and the chips fried throughout the day. Entrées $7.50–8.75.

✿ **Cattlemans Bar and Grill** (928-445-4300), 669 E. Sheldon St. Open daily 11–10. The bar and grill has been a part of Prescott for 100 years. The restaurant owners like to acknowledge its hole-in-the-wall legacy that just happened to evolve into one of the best places for a great steak—porterhouse, rib eye, top sirloin, or filet mignon—at a great price. Good enough to make local favorite. Lamb and pork chops are just as good. Popular items include the flat-iron steak sandwich, filet mignon, and 24-oz. porterhouse. Fish is flown in fresh daily. Lunch $7.75–11; dinner $11.50–23.50.

WORLD'S OLDEST RODEO

In Mexico and some points in Southern California, you'll hear the event pronounced "row-DAY-oh." Most everywhere else, it's "row-DEE-oh." But here in Prescott, it's not just a "row-DEE-oh," it's the World's Oldest Rodeo. Claiming one has the world's oldest rodeo (and continuous on top of that) is not easy, nor a trivial matter as the makers of the game Trivial Pursuit found out when rodeo town Pecos, Texas, challenged one of their question and answers that read: "What rough-and-tumble Western sport was first formalized in Prescott, Arizona?" Answer: "Rodeo." One must meet the following important criteria:

Have a committee to plan and stage the rodeo;
Invite cowboys to compete;
Charge admission;
Give prizes and trophies;
Have the contests documented.

Over the years, Prescott has gotten protests from other rodeo towns, namely its neighbor down the road, Payson. After careful scrutiny and the lack of the documented proof, Prescott can ante up, the title always lands back in Prescott's hand. So Prescott finally patented the event. They now have the government's blessings and hopefully, if not begrudgingly, Pecos's and Payson's.

Dinner Bell Café (928-445-9888), 321 W. Gurley St. Open Mon.–Fri. 6:30 AM–2 PM; Sat. and Sun. 7 AM–2 PM. No checks, credit or debit cards. accepted, but there is an ATM machine inside. This local favorite—where every stratum of society meets, from retro hippies to their suit-and-tie grandparents—has two sides. The front brings you back a step or two into time with its 1960s décor; the back room overlooks Granite Creek with floor-to-ceiling windows that open up like a garage door in warm weather. Both have fresh and natural ingredients, filtered water, and low prices. Breakfast (such as special waffles and omelets you build yourself with a boatload of ingredients from which to choose) is served all day. Lunch is home-cooked sandwiches and specials. Beverages range from specialty coffee drinks to frappe freezes, fresh fruit smoothies, and Italian sodas. Unlike the rest of the menu, choosing dessert remains simple—there's only one item, homemade apple pie, plain or à la mode. Entrées $5.95–7.50.

Pangaea Bakery & Café (928-778-2953), 220 W. Goodwin St., Suite 1. Open Mon.–Sat. 7 AM–4 PM. Nicole Marshall has been making artisan bread products here for more than a decade. Each day has its own schedule of breads. In the morning, she offers several breakfast dishes, and at lunch it's interesting but intensely good sandwiches, soups, and salads. She serves more than a dozen smoothies (with almost as many add-ins), as well as organic coffees and teas. Entrées $5.95–9.

The Raven Café (928-717-0009), 142 N. Cortez. Open Mon.–Wed. 7:30 AM–11 PM, Thu.–Sat. 7:30 AM–midnight, Sun. 8 AM–3 PM. One of the town's hottest meeting spots serves up politically correct coffee, gourmet teas, an incredible line of beers (30 on tap and more than 200 labels in total), and some nice wines. The breakfast, lunch, and dinner menus feature local and/or organic foods. They randomly hold special theme nights, but you can count on classic/cult movies every Tuesday night. All the interiors were designed and created by local artists and craftsmen. The place is as green as the owners can get. Entrées $7.95–12.

Scout's Gourmet Grub (928-442-3336), 1144 Iron Springs Rd. Mon.–Fri. 7–7, Sat. and Sun. 8–3. Scott Simmons, a former park ranger, has created a national park–themed restaurant with meals named for the outdoor greats—such as the Grand Canyon Grinder, rugged Rocky Mountain Meatball, Yummy Yosemite, and Canyonlands Classic. There's a nice variety of veggie sandwiches, too, as well as salads. Gourmet pizza comes in individual sizes. And for dessert, they are located in the same building as Baskin-Robbins. The local favorite gets perennially voted for best sandwiches. Entrées $5.69–7.99.

✷ Entertainment

JAZZ You can hear jazz nightly at **129½ An American Jazz Grille** and the **Peacock Lounge** at the Hassayampa Inn (see *Dining Out* for both).

The Palace Restaurant and Saloon has honky-tonk piano every Sun. 2–5, dinner theater every other Mon. (a play or musical group), country music on Fri. and Sat. nights. See Dining Out for more information on all three.

The Jersey Lilly Saloon (928-541-7854), 116 S. Montezuma St. has live music Thu.–Sun. The upstairs bar has a balcony that overlooks Whiskey Row and makes a stellar spot to enjoy a summer libation.

✷ The Arts

Prescott's ART the 4th connects people to the arts. Each month, their 4th Friday Weekend Long Art Walk presents Prescott's diverse art experience from Friday evening through Sunday afternoon. Currently, 19 galleries in the area take part in the walk.

✷ Selective Shopping

If you like to shop until you drop, head straight for **Cortez Street**, where you'll find antiques, collectibles, folk art, Indian jewelry, and funky fashions. After that, you can move on to the art galleries on **Montezuma Street** and **McCormick Arts District**, then the boutique shopping malls on Gurley Street and in the Hotel St. Michael.

✷ Special Events

Call 928-445-2000 for more information.

June: **Territorial Days** is an art and craft show on Courthouse Plaza.

DOWNTOWN PRESCOTT'S *ART FOR ALL* MURAL ON CORTEZ STREET

Tsunami on the Square, named for the least likely natural event to happen in the high desert, features a festival featuring performing arts and culture. **Folk Arts Festival**.

July: **Frontier Days** and **World's Oldest Rodeo** include the Frontier Days Parade. **Indian Art Market** (Sharlot Hall Museum) presents quality Native American art and crafts. **Old Town Square Arts and Crafts Festival** (Courthouse Plaza).

August: **Arizona Cowboy Poets Gathering** (Sharlot Hall Museum).

September: **Faire on the Square Art & Craft Show** (Courthouse Plaza). Yavapai County Fair has a rodeo, food, vendors.

December: **Christmas Parade and Courthouse Lighting**. During the **J. S. Acker Musical Showcase**, businesses provide caroling, music, hot beverages, and snacks.

VERDE VALLEY

(COTTONWOOD, CAMP VERDE, CLARKDALE, CORNVILLE, PAGE SPRINGS, RIMROCK)

"Cottonwood," one businessmen in the Verde Valley pragmatically explained, "and its next-door neighbor, Clarkdale, exist because of the mines at Jerome. The single miners who liked to party a lot lived right in Jerome. Clarkdale was built for the mine's executives, and the blue-collar workers lived in Cottonwood."

But the textbook history of these towns goes beyond copper mines to the beginning of the Arizona Territory in 1863, when Anglos started streaming into the Verde River Valley at its confluence with West Clear Creek. Trouble started because the valley already had inhabitants—the Apache. Within two years, Camp Verde (first known as Fort Lincoln) was established as a war outpost.

After a decade the army prevailed and impounded the tribes in the Rio Verde Reservation, near present-day Cottonwood. Two years later Tucson businessmen successfully demanded that the army uproot and transport the tribes to the San Carlos Agency near Globe. In another two years, miners and ranchers moved into the area.

The towns started to cater to Jerome mining during the teen years of the 20th century. Cottonwood supplied vegetables to the miners (as well as some pretty hot bootleg booze that brought imbibers from neighboring states), and Clarkdale became the oldest master-planned community when John Clark developed it into a residential community with state-of-the-art homes to house mining executives. In the 1930s and '40s, tiny Rimrock (next to Camp Verde) attracted a curious mix of ranchers, movie stars, and gangsters on the lam.

When Jerome went bust in the 1950s, Cottonwood prevailed and continued as the leading marketing center for the area. Clarkdale got caught in a retro pocket for several decades, and the smaller communities like Page, Cornville, and Rimrock slumbered. By the 1990s these towns started to get outside attention. Cornville became a renaissance area for artists of all types, Camp Verde wiped the sleep from its eyes and is on its way as a family and nature-lover's destination, and Page Springs captured the eye of vintners. Like many little Arizona towns, they have all attracted entrepreneurs with extraordinary talent who like open space and serenity.

GUIDANCE Camp Verde Chamber of Commerce (928-567-9294), 385 S. Main St., Camp Verde; **Cottonwood Chamber of Commerce** (928-634-7593), 1010 South Main St., Cottonwood; and **Clarkdale Chamber of Commerce** (928-634-9438), P.O. Box 308, Clarkdale. For information about backcountry use in the national forest, contact **Coconino National Forest** (928-527-3600) and **Verde River Ranger District** 928- 567-4121.

GETTING THERE Camp Verde (to the east) and Cottonwood (in the west) are located like bookends along the banks of the Verde River along AZ 260. Clarkdale lies just north of AZ 260, and Cornville and Page Springs are located just south of AZ 89A on Page Springs Rd. along Oak Creek.

WHEN TO COME Mild weather (60 degrees) draws visitors here in winter. The simmer of summer days (98 degrees) cools down comfortably by midnight (60s).

MEDICAL EMERGENCY Verde Valley Medical Center (928-634-2251), 269 S. Candy Ln., Cottonwood.

✷ To See

🐾 ♿ **Montezuma's Castle National Monument** (928-567-3322), 2800 Montezuma Castle Rd., Camp Verde. Located off I-17, exit 289. Open daily 8–5 (Jun.–Aug. 8–6); closed Christmas Day. It never had a visit from Montezuma. And it doesn't have a castle, either. But Montezuma's Castle National Monument does have one of the best-preserved cliff dwellings in the Southwest. The five-story, 20-room cliff dwelling, located along Beaver Creek in the Verde Valley, once housed about 50 Sinagua Indians between AD 1100 and 1400. You can reach it on a barrier-free ⅓-mile-long trail. Bring your (leashed) dog along for the stroll, rather than leave it in the car. Another ruin, called Castle A, lies just south of Montezuma Castle. A picnic area makes a shady respite right along Beaver Creek. $5 adults, under age 16 free.

🐾 ✐ ♿ **Montezuma's Well** (928-567-3322), located about 11 miles north of Montezuma Castle, I-17 exit 293. Open daily 8–5 (Jun.–Aug. 8–6), closed Christmas Day. Once you see Montezuma's Castle, take a walk down the half-mile barrier-free trail to a sinkhole (a collapsed underground limestone cavern) that, when it filled with water, was the main water source for the Native Americans who stayed in Montezuma Castle. The well at the "lake" pumps out 1.5 million gallons of 76-degree water daily. The well's carbon-dioxide-rich water sustains several forms of plant and animal life not found anywhere else in the world. Free.

Old Town Cottonwood. Located at the north end of town along historic AZ 89A, Old Town Cottonwood has a museum, unique shops, restaurants, and galleries. Most of the shopping area's buildings were constructed at the turn of the 20th century.

✐ ♿ **Tuzigoot National Monument** (928-634-5564). Open daily 8–5 (till 6 in summer). Located off old AZ 89A on Tuzigoot Rd. The red sandstone hilltop pueblo once housed more than 200 Signagua Indians in 110 rooms. You can explore the site on the loop trail, which also gives pretty panoramas of the Verde River. This trail, and the Tavashi Marsh Overlook Trail are both ¼ mile long and barrier-free. Archaeologists have stabilized the ruins to give an idea of what they might have looked like. The visitor center has a museum full of artifacts: ollas, pottery, tools, and shell/stone jewelry to peruse. $5 adults, age 16 and under free.

✱ To Do

BIRDING Although the Verde Valley has become an object of ardor among birders in the last several years, the area has always been a hot spot with birds. Since Dr. Edgar Mearns, who lived at Fort Verde, started cataloging the area's avian life in the area in 1889, 340 species have shown up. The hot spots are trails along the **Verde River**, **West Clear Creek**, and **Oak Creek**. Contact the national forests for trails. More than 100 species have been sighted in and immediately around the **Dead Horse Ranch State Park** (see *Wilder Places*). During winter, watch for bald eagles along the **Verde River**. The Audubon Society named Arizona Department of Game and Fish's **Page Springs Hatchery** (928-634-4805), 1600 N. Page Springs Rd., Cornville, an Important Bird Area. More than 100 birds have been sighted at the fish hatchery. At **Tavasci Marsh**, an old oxbow of the Verde River, the Audubon Society has cataloged 167 different species. Take Tuzigoot Rd. to Sycamore Canyon Rd. and veer right at the fork onto Pecks Lake Rd.

GAMING Cliff Castle Casino (800-381-7568), 55 Middle Verde Rd., Camp Verde. The Yavapai-Apache casino has a cosmic bowling alley (with fluorescent-colored lights), arcade, Kids Club for children 6 weeks to 12 years old, Dragonfly lounge for adults with nightly entertainment, and a lodge and restaurant just off the premises. The casino offers 570 slot machines, keno, live poker, blackjack, and bingo.

HIKING The high-desert countryside of the Verde Valley presents some intriguing trails that are best hiked from early fall through late spring. The most exciting trails travel the **Sycamore Canyon Wilderness** (Coconino National Forest), especially **Parsons Trail** or **Dogie Trail**; and the **Woodchute Trail** near Mingus Mountain (Prescott National Forest). More experienced hikers who have good route-finding skills should check out the historic **Mail Trail** that starts around Camp Verde and travels to Payson (Coconino National Forest).

HORSEBACK RIDING M Diamond Ranch (928-300-6466) is a 100-year-old working cattle ranch of cross-bred black Angus in Rimrock. You can take a 1- to 2-hour trail ride, cook out, or take part in a cattle drive. Call for reservation and prices.

KAYAKING With 18 miles of the Verde River flowing through Camp Verde, you can put in for a paddle that can range from a gentle float to a lively Class II ride from Feb. through May. Contact Verde Ranger District for a Verde River guide.

PETROGLYPHS ♿ **V-bar-V Heritage Site** (928-284-5323). Open daily Fri.–Mon. 9:30–3:30; closed Thanksgiving and Christmas days. From I-17, go south on AZ 179 past Beaver Creek Campground to the signed turnoff. The largest-known and best-preserved petroglyph site has more than 1,000 glyphs in 13 panels that show perfect examples of the Beaver Creek Style. No pets allowed. Red Rock Pass ($5) required.

RAILROAD Verde Canyon Railroad (928-639-0010 or 800-293-7245). Vintage FP7 engines pull cars along a historical route along the Verde River between Clarkdale and Perkinsville. Each season has its sensational features: Spring reveals wildflowers coloring the banks and waterfalls flowing (if the winter had enough rain); black hawks and night herons show up in summer; cottonwood and willow trees glow gold in fall; and bald and golden eagles migrate here in winter. Travel via coach, first class, and caboose with access to the open-air viewing car. Coach: $54.95–79.95 adults, $34.95–49.95 age 12 and under, $49.95 age 65-plus. Or rent the caboose for $600.

WINE TASTING Who would imagine Arizona, especially tucked-away Page Springs, could produce quality wines? People thought the same when Napa Valley settlers planted vineyards with cuttings snipped from Sonoma and San Rafael vines in 1861. **Page Springs Vineyards & Cellars** (928-639-3004), 1500 N. Page Springs Rd., Cornville, is producing award-winning wines. Winemaker Eric Glomski specializes in Rhône-style wines. Tasting room open daily 11–6 ($10). **Javelina Leap Vineyard & Winery** (928-649-2681), 1565 Page Springs Rd., Cornville, has several award winners. Tasting daily 11–5 ($12). **Alcantara Vineyards** (928-649-8463), 3445 S. Grapevine Way, Verde Valley, has a great wine-tasting area overlooking the Verde River. Contact the Cottonwood Chamber of Commerce for a **Northern Arizona Wine Trail** brochure. Tasting from 11–5 daily ($10).

✷ Wilder Places

Dead Horse Ranch State Park (928-634-5283), 675 Dead Horse Ranch Rd., Cottonwood. Open daily. One of the few remaining Fremont cottonwood/Goodding willow forests in the state runs along the Verde River. This state park includes a portion of this richly diverse riparian forest (the Verde River Greenway State Natural Area) that draws wildlife, especially birds. Several multiuse trails—including the 1.5-mile-long Verde River Greenway, which meanders along one of the state's best nesting habitats—network around the park. The Northern Arizona Audubon Society has sighted 240 species of birds. In winter the park's lagoon gets stocked with trout, a big draw for bald eagles that migrate to the river. $7 per vehicle, $3 per bicycle. Camping is $12 per night, $19 with electric hook-up, and $50 for a cabin (bring your own linens and walk to the shower down the way).

✷ Lodging

BED & BREAKFASTS AND INNS

Desert Rose Bed and Breakfast (928-646-0236), 4190 E. Bridle Path Rd. You get a choice of three different sizes—1 full-size with a king bed, full bath with Jacuzzi tub, quality sheets, and private phone with free long distance in the continental U.S.; 1 mid-size room with a ½ bath and private phone, and 1 compact room that shares a full bath. All have private entrance, cable TV, radio, and library. Everyone gets to use the BBQ grill, business center, and board games. A continental-plus breakfast is included. Innkeepers Betty and Sebastien Lauzon speak six different languages. You can board your horse at a neighbor's stable. Lunch is $25 extra. $89–149; two-night minimum stay with $20 charge for one night only.

🐾 ♿ ((ı)) ⚭ ♥ **Luna Vista Bed and Breakfast** (928-567-4788 or 800-611-4788), 1062 E. Reay Rd., Rimrock.

Innkeeper-owners Kala and Frank have warm personalities that match their home: a sophisticated yet safe haven. Themed suites are aesthetically balanced, roomy, and comfortable. The property has a heated pool and spa, game room, business center, library, complimentary WiFi, private patios, gardens, outside facilities for pets, and horse and trailer facilities. Area massage therapists are available to provide a number of different therapies on the premises. Nearby are private hiking trails with cultural interest. A generous happy hour with snacks welcomes you. Breakfasts (brunch on Sunday) are hearty and included in rates. Children age 8 or older preferred. $175–235.

HOTELS AND MOTELS

Cottonwood Hotel (928-634-9455), 930 N. Main St., Cottonwood. The oldest hotel in Cottonwood (built in 1925), and listed on the National Historic Register, has upper-level rooms that overlook the heart of Old Town. Rooms are neat, clean, and full of history. If the walls could talk, you might hear some details about ol' Duke; Gail Russell, his squeeze at the time he stayed here; or the antics of Mae West, who roomed here before her star rose in the Hollywood skies. Each apartment has its own unique décor. The rooms are small but have attractive amenities, such as beds with quality sheets and 4-inch memory-foam tops, private bath, (most) fully stocked kitchen with (all) refrigerator and microwave, TV, free Wi-Fi, (some) VCR, and views. The property includes a gift shop, coin-op laundry, common balcony, and TV/VCR area. $65–105.

Pines Motel (928-634-9975 or 800-483-9618), 920 S. Camino Real, Cottonwood. Clean and simple, and perfect as a casual base if you plan on tooling around. There's a heated pool (seasonal); rooms have cable TV, WiFi, microwave, mini fridge, in-room coffee, and free local calls. Pets $10. $49–89.

✷ Where to Eat

DINING OUT Mai Thai on Main (928-649-2999), 157 S. Main, Cottonwood. Open Mon.–Sat. for lunch 11:30–2:30, dinner 5–9. Noi Olson's wonderful, authentic restaurant serves traditional food from her Thai homeland. The food matches the distinctive harmony of flavors you would find in a restaurant in Chiang Mai. This is an enduring favorite. Entrées $9.95–13.25.

♥ **Piñon Bistro** (928-649-0234), 1075 S. AZ 260, Cottonwood. Open Thu.–Sun. at 5 PM. Closed during summer. From the location of this venue buried in the back of a strip mall among a variety of box franchises, you might think the name should be *diner*, rather than *bistro*. Just wait until you get inside; the name will make sense. Aesthetic with art hanging on the walls and fresh, local foods on the menu, this is a place foodies, especially oenophiles fresh from the vintners' tasting rooms, will enjoy. Owners Donna Fulton (in the kitchen) and Terri Clements (everywhere else) serve a creative menu (small, like the restaurant). The menu changes often, depending on what's seasonally available. These ladies hail from Maine, so you can understand why the seafood is excellent. The wine list is creative, with several AZ labels. Desserts the perfect pièce de résistance.

Su Casa (928-634-2771), 1000 Main, Clarkdale. Open daily 11–9. Located in Clarkdale's historic section where retro culture comes on thick. This friendly restaurant serves authentic Sonoran and Arizonan food that's fresh and well made. The menu has several vegetarian meals, and the *chiles rellenos* has a following. Entrées $6.95–10.95.

The Tavern Grille (928-634-6669). 914 N. Main St., Cottonwood. Open daily 11–9. Located in the historic Rialto Theater in Old Town Cottonwood. Attractive and loaded with history, the concrete building was designed by a Joseph Becchetti in answer to the fires that constantly raged in the area. Most buildings in Old Cottonwood, and northern Arizona, in general, were made of wood. In this dry climate, all one needed was a spark to set a devastating fire. The theater, the longest running single-screen theater in the nation, withstood its first test, a fire that destroyed several buildings in town. Merely scorched then, the Rialto withstood another fire in 1998. Restaurant owners Eric and Michelle Jurisin bought the theater, renovated it, and opened the grill in 2005. But not only the building has history, the grill does, too. The local favorite also lands on out-of-towners' lists of places to stop while in the area. The food is descent, the portions large, and the prices reasonable. The meat loaf (with ingredients that go way beyond comfort food) is a signature dish, and the steaks and pastas are popular. But don't forget this is a tavern. More than a dozen high-definition plasma TVs broadcast all kinds of sports events, from all-American to monster trucks jams and bull riding. $8–23.

✷ Special Events

February: **Wine and Pecan Festival** (928-567-0535) in Camp Verde features local wines, more than 3,000 pounds of pecans—the fruit of century-plus-old pecan trees—and jazz.

April: **Verde Valley Birding and Nature Festival** (928-282-2202). Spotlighting the birds of the Verde Valley and natural history through field trips, talks, and workshops at Dead Horse State Park.

May: **Verde Valley Fair** (928-634-3290) in Cottonwood features animals, artwork, baked goods, and more, with a carnival, rodeo, and entertainment.

June: **Arizona Crawdad Festival** (928-567-0535) at Camp Verde cooks crawdads in the most delicious ways with music, vendors, and fun.

July: **Cornfest** (928-567-0535) in Camp Verde cooks up a ton of sweet corn from Hauser & Hauser Farms with other foods, contests, vendors, and music.

September: **Verde River Days** (928-634-5283) at Dead Horse Ranch State Park in Cottonwood honors the preservation and care of the Verde River with exhibits and a lot of water fun.

October: **Fort Verde Days** (928-567-0535) in Camp Verde looks at the fort's past with cavalry drills, a carnival, a parade, and other events. **Fall Harvest Carnival** (928-639-3200) at the Old Town Ball Field. On **Bootleggers Days** (928-634-7593) merchants dress in period costumes and keep their shops open for evening shopping.

December: **Cottonwood Christmas Parade** (928-634-7593) on Main Street, Cottonwood, has floats, music, entertainment, candy, and Santa. Later that evening, head to Old Town for the **Chocolate Lovers' Walk**. **Parade of Lights** (928-567-0535) in Camp Verde beams with decorations, floats, music, and fun.

JEROME

Teetering atop Cleopatra Hill, the City in the Sky can be seen from miles away—especially at night, when the lights of its handful of streets twinkle. In the early-morning light it glows like burnished copper—the mineral that made it famous and earned its other nickname of Billion Dollar Copper Camp.

Jerome had two copper kings who kept thousands of miners busy: William Clark, who owned the United Verde Mine and created Clarkdale; and "Rawhide" Jimmy Douglas, who owned the Little Daisy Mine. At its height (1914–20), Jerome had 15,000 residents stuffed into enough mountainside shacks for only a third of them. They worked (and played) in shifts around the clock, so one room could house three miners, who took turns sleeping in it. Like every mining town, the miners played as hard as they worked. With one bar for every 100 people, you can imagine how the atmosphere rocked from more than mining equipment.

Over the years, mining took its toll on the mountain: Smelter smoke smothered the vegetation, dynamite rankled foundations, and raucous behavior attracted extra attention and stern laws. By 1953 the copper market had dropped too low for profits, and Jerome pretty much closed down. In the 1970s the counterculture took to the funky ghost town, and Jerome started to come to life again—this time with art as its mainstay. The town has tidied itself up over the last few decades, but the funkiness remains.

In this hilltop town where canyon wrens drop their glissando cry and agave blossoms, beaming like lemon lanterns, angle boldly from the rocky slopes, the gray hardship of the miners' lives gets overshadowed by color. Weird is wonderful in Jerome. WE ARE ALL HERE, signs appear around town, BECAUSE WE ARE NOT ALL THERE. JEROME, ARIZONA, another sign proclaims, POPULATION: STRANGE.

While the rest of the world rushes along in conformity and standards, Jerome backflips into its own state of mind. Some say it's just being high-spirited. Speaking of which, spirit sightings are rife. But let's be clear about this: Jerome is not haunted, nor does it have ghosts. Jerome has spirits. Hang around Cleopatra Hill long enough, and you just might have your own spirit-filled encounter.

GUIDANCE **Jerome Chamber of Commerce** (928-634-2900), 310 Hull. Run by volunteers, this trailer office usually opens by 10 AM, especially Thu.–Sun. Stop by to get info and a Jerome Historic Building and Business Map, which lists the original names of historic buildings and the businesses that currently reside in them. If the office isn't open, they usually leave maps in an outside bin. For

DOWNTOWN JEROME

information on backcountry use in Prescott National Forest, contact **Verde Ranger District** (928-567-4121), 300 E. Hwy 260, Camp Verde.

GETTING THERE Jerome lies right on AZ 89A, almost equidistant between Prescott and Sedona. From Phoenix, take I-17 north, exit at AZ 260, then head northeast to Cottonwood to link up with AZ 89A.

GETTING AROUND This tiny mountainside town has few parking opportunities along the streets—many as narrow as an old European village's. Best to park your vehicle in the public lots on the east end of town, put on a pair of walking shoes, and stroll.

WHEN TO COME The height of humanity gathers here in October when all things spooky are celebrated, Halloween being the main event. Aug. and Jan. are slow, and some shopkeepers go on vacation (that would be physically). All other months draw crowds on the weekends. With only about 60 rooms to accommodate everyone, it's best to make reservations if you plan to spend time here.

MEDICAL EMERGENCY **Verde Valley Medical Center Sedona Campus** (928 639-6000), 269 S. Candy Lane, Cottonwood.

✷ To See

Gold King Mine (928-634-0053), located off AZ 89A on Perkinsville Rd. (follow the signs). Open daily 9–5; closed Christmas Day. Looking for copper, the Haynes Copper Company dug 1,200 feet and struck—gold! The camp grew into the town of Haynes, with a population of just over 300. Now the 100-plus-year-old ghost town (population: 1) remains alive and well as a living museum with a collection of antique trucks, tractors, and construction and mining equipment dating back to the turn of the 20th century. $5 adults, $4 ages 62–74, $3 ages 6–12; under 5 and 75-plus free.

SCENIC DRIVES **AZ 89A**, traveling in either direction, makes a scenic paved drive. Heading south to Prescott takes you through the pass near Mingus Mountain; heading north, you go into the red rocks of Sedona. Go 43 miles north on **Perkinsville Road** to Williams (23 miles unpaved, but graded).

✷ To Do

HIKING There are a handful of trails in the Prescott National Forest just outside town along AZ 89A. The best time for hiking them is Mar. through Nov. Contact the Verde Ranger District. Check out the 5.5-mile-long North Mingus Trail on Mingus Mountain.

✷ Wilder Places

Mingus Mountain. One of the area's high points stands at just over 7,700 feet about 7 miles south off AZ 89A. Several trails take you around the mountain, through forests of Gambel oak trees up into ponderosa pines laced with bigtooth maple and aspen trees. This makes for some gorgeous autumn color hikes. Contact the Verde Ranger District.

Woodchute Wilderness. Another high point, Woodchute Mountain, at 7,800 feet, lies in a designated wilderness. Its popular Woodchute Trail takes you to its heights. It's a great place for wildflowers after a wet winter. Contact the Verde Ranger District.

✷ Lodging

HOTELS 🐾 **Conner Hotel** (928-634-5006 or 800-523-3554), 164 Main St. You can simply walk out the door into the hub of activity in Jerome when you stay here. The restored hotel has a balance of antiquity with some modern-day luxuries. Rooms have antiques, overstuffed furniture, and local artwork and photographs celebrating Jerome's history. Each room has a king or queen bed, private tiled bath, satellite TV, telephone, coffeemaker, microwave, and mini fridge. Rooms 1–4 are located above a bar; all others are quiet. $105–165.

Cottage Inn (928-634-0701), located on East Avenue. The town's oldest B&B has two suites. The Garden Suite has a living room and bathroom with an old clawfoot tub. The Patio Suite has two bedrooms, a living room, and bathroom with stellar views of the red rocks and San Francisco Peaks. Both suites have patios and include a hearty breakfast. $75–95.

♿ **Jerome Grand Hotel** (928-634-8200 or 888-817-6788), 200 Hill St. What used to be the ultramodern United Verde Hospital that opened in 1927 is now a restored hotel with the best views in town. The highest public structure in the Verde Valley stands solidly on a 50-degree slope, built to withstand mining blasts of up to 100,000 pounds of dynamite. A 1926 Otis elevator provides service to all five floors. The 50-horsepower Kewanee boiler provides steam heat to all 23 rooms. Each has queen or twin beds with Diamond Award mattresses and extra pillows, satellite TV and VCR, private bath, and telephone serviced by an antique switchboard. No pets. The views from the Balcony Rooms are worth the little extra they cost. $120–185.

BED & BREAKFASTS Ghost City Inn Bed and Breakfast (888-634-4678), 541 Main St. (AZ 89A). One of Jerome's most popular places to stay, for good reason, has the best of both worlds, blending history and comfort. Built as a boardinghouse around 1890 and remodeled in the 1990s, the building still has quirky lines and original bead board ceilings—not to mention gorgeous views of the Verde Valley. Six themed room interiors range from period to outdoor. Rooms have private bath, TV, VCR, ceiling fan, and air-conditioning; breakfast included. $95–145.

Mile High Inn (928-634-5094), 311 Main St. This over-the-restaurant inn gives you a perfect perch when things are happening on the ground. A couple rooms in the back have quiet and more privacy. A couple of rooms have their own bathrooms. All the rooms have great interiors—a blend of Southwest and Continental—with red appointments that add bit of sauce. Each room has its own character. And you get breakfast at the Mile High Grill (except if you're staying Mon., Tue., or Wed. nights in the winter), below. $85–120; $185 for the Apartment, which has a kitchen.

🐾 The Surgeon's House Bed and Breakfast (928-639-1452). This Hill Street home, built in 1916, was once owned by a doctor. The home has a décor akin to a kaleidoscope image, with colorful, curious, and creative items and artifacts. Owner-innkeeper Andrea Prince, as distinctive as her home, has a ready story about all the interesting things in her bed & breakfast and life in Jerome. Andrea has created a number of little niches on the property for you to enjoy, from a lively patio to a hidden garden. Breakfast is a real treat here because, not only is Andrea an excellent cook, but she also adds creative touches to produce a meal that's a meld of gourmet and yummy. Plus, the view from the dining room is awesome. Her gardens are Edenic, and offer contemplative and secretive nooks. Nonguests can join the breakfast hour for $15 and 12 hours' notice. Pets are okay with prior notice and a $35 fee. $175–265.

✷ Where to Eat

DINING OUT The Asylum (928-639-3197), 200 Hills St. (in the Jerome Grand Hotel). Open daily for lunch 11–3, dinner 5–9. The restaurant motto—"We're not just a restaurant, we're an adventure!"—fits. The wine red interiors set off by white tablecloths and black napkins celebrate the menu's bold elegance, which appears from the wine to the desserts. The restaurant often earns the Wine Spectator Award of Excellence for their selection of wines chosen by sommelier–co-owner Paula Woolsey. Professional wait staff tend gracefully to your needs. The prickly pear pork is perfect. The butternut squash soup, which lures people back for return visits along with the grilled sea bass, is silken good; the homemade bread, distinctively doughy; the brûlée cheesecake, exquisite. The menu is full of delicious dishes that have ingredients like "happy little mushrooms" on the mushroom bacon burger or "oh, so sumptuous chipotle apricot chutney" on the turkey sandwich, and "mouth dripping juicy seasonal fruit" with the cheeseburger.

THE SURGEON'S HOUSE B&B

Dinner has a bit more decorum with the descriptions, but the same level of delight with a classic blend of flavors in the Spinach Pasta, the rich Chicken Tenderlions Alfredo, and Rocky Point Shrimp. Lunch entrées $10–16, dinner entrées $16–29.

15.quince Grill & Cantina (928-634-7087), 363 Main St. Open Tue. and Wed. 8–5; Thu., Fri., and Mon. 8–7; and Sat. 8–9. Vlad Costa, owner and chef, and Jerome make a perfect fit. The old Safeway store (Arizona's first) has turquoise walls with red corral accents. Chef Vlad, who lived among Indians in New Mexico, said these Native American colors have significance—the coral is protective and turquoise was traded like diamonds by the native peoples. More than a dozen works from local artists deck the walls, and the place has become a hangout for artists and locals. Chef Vlad describes his food as "a communion between Native American, Mexican, and Spanish foods," Everything is house-made, from the sauces for the flat blue cornmeal enchiladas to the hamburger patties, to the green (made with Hatch chiles) and red chiles. Specials might feature lamb, buffalo, or elk. The house wine is a cab-merlot blend that people order for the taste, rather than the cost. The unusual name stands for the number 15 in *I Ching*, which signifies humility; *quince* is Spanish for 15. Breakfast $5.95–7.95, sandwiches and salads $5.95–10.95, entrées $8.95–12.95.

EATING OUT Haunted Hamburger (928-634-0554), 410 N. Clark St. Open daily 11–9. Everybody loves this place. You can get many different items here, from hamburger to ribs and steak, or you can choose French fries or a salad side. Everything is dependably good. Hamburgers, however, are the stars of the show, and the more oozing with trimmings, the better. The celebrated burgers draw people from all over the country. The only thing better than the hamburgers is the view from the porch. But you might have to wait for it. Entrées $6.95–17.99.

✷ The Arts

When Jerome turned ghost town, the ramshackle buildings looked good to the freethinkers who took up residence in the 1970s. Although the culture was creative, and especially expressive, they all weren't necessarily artists. Over the years the visual arts have maintained a role in the community. Lately the art has matured, and it is at the point collectors may find some great buys.

✷ Shopping

The whole town is a shopping fest, from the kitschy to the collectible.

✷ Special Events

May: The **Annual Home Tour and Biannual Jerome Garden Tour** gives you a look at some of the special homes and gorgeous gardens around town.

October: **Halloween Night** is the big bash that howls with fun and games all night long.

December: **Light Up the Mountain** shines with lights and luminarias on the mountainside homes, candles glow in shops, and hayrides add an old-fashioned touch.

SEDONA/OAK CREEK CANYON

They were warned not to stay, the legend about Palatkwapi says. Spirit guides sternly directed them not to indulge themselves in the idyllic atmosphere of Palatkwapi, the "place of the red rocks." But the early Hopi ignored the spiritual guidance of their deities and pursued their life of leisure with abandon. Finally, the story goes, a few virtuous Hopi entreated the deities to bring a flood.

Before the flood forced the early Hopi to higher ground, and their eventual settlement at First Mesa, legend says the people built Palatkwapi into a thriving cultural and religious center. Palatkwapi, now called Sedona, was a meeting and healing place for native peoples all over the Southwest 1,000 to 2,000 years ago. Now a town with more than 40 art galleries and 22 public art landmarks packed into 15 square miles—and enough seers, crystal shops, and New Age centers to wreak havoc at a séance—things haven't changed much. The red-rocked town has the world passing through its doorways, to the tune of around four million visitors a year. And for good reason: The city got the top slot on *USA Today*'s list of the 10 Most Beautiful Cities in the United States. It's also the main tourist stop on the way to the Grand Canyon.

Situated at the mouth of Oak Creek Canyon, where erosion has carved the Mogollon Rim into a jigsaw of colorful sandstone mesas and formations that stretch for several miles along the creek, Sedona is the area's hub—though Oak Creek Canyon, with its awesome riparian forest and slickrock formations, has also racked up some impressive accolades, ranking among the nation's most beautiful drives (AZ 89A). Residents claim the canyon has its own set of vortexes, and it will take you down a notch or two (to which visitors will testify) no matter how hectic your lifestyle.

Although its appearance has changed since its recent cowtown days, Sedona hasn't really hasn't strayed too far. You can still buy a pair of custom-made boots. The same characteristics of the cowboy founding fathers show up in modern-day residents: These are some independent, iconoclastic, community-minded, informal folks, not to mention some out-and-out characters. Neither has the town veered from its legendary Hopi spirituality. Beyond the vortexes and metaphysical hype, you can still feel a special inspiration when you visit. If it's not enough to change your life or heal you—it's certainly enough to get your attention.

GUIDANCE **Uptown Visitor Center** (928-282-7722 or 800-288-7336; www.visitsedona.com), 331 Forest Rd. Contact **Coconino National Forest Red Rock**

THE RED ROCK–SECRET CANYON WILDERNESS BORDERS SEDONA TO THE NORTH

Ranger District (928-203-7500), 8375 AZ 179, for information on trails, picnic areas, and back roads. Open daily 8–4:30.

GETTING THERE *By car:* Sedona is located at the intersection of AZ 89A and AZ 179. You can take the scenic route from Flagstaff via AZ 89A. From I-17, exit at AZ 179 to Sedona; or take AZ 260 to Cottonwood then AZ 89A east to Sedona. *By air:* **Sedona Airport** (928-282-4487), 235 Air Terminal Dr., has transient hangers. From **Phoenix Sky Harbor Airport**, you can take the **Sedona Phoenix Shuttle Service Inc.** (928-282-2066) or **White Tie Transportation** (928-203-4500).

GETTING AROUND **Sedona RoadRunner Transit System** (928-282-0938). This daily free city transit service runs every 10 minutes 9–6:30 on the 1.3-mile corridor between Hillside Galleries on AZ 179 and the north end of uptown Sedona on AZ 89A.

Sedona Trolley (928-282-4211), 276 N. AZ 89A, Suite B (in the Uptown Depot at the traffic light), offers two 55-minute tours—one heading uptown, the other to West Sedona—the help you get the lay of the land. The tours run all day. $12 adults, $6 age 12 and under.

WHEN TO COME Sedona's a busy city every month of the year, except for Aug. and Jan. The best weather happens in the spring and fall, along with the biggest influx of tourists. Summer sees near-daily thunderstorms, which locals consider an attraction not to miss. December, like the shoulder seasons, is crowded; make sure you have a reservation if you plan on staying.

MEDICAL EMERGENCY **Sedona Urgent Care** (928-203-4813), 2530 W. AZ 89A, Bldg. A, for minor emergencies. **Verde Valley Medical Center Sedona Campus** (928-204-3000), 3700 W. AZ 89A.

✷ To See

Chapel of the Holy Cross (928-282-4069), 780 Chapel Rd. Open daily. Built by artist Marguerite Brunswig Staude in 1956 as a nondenominational monument to God. Staude considered art to be the search for the spiritual side of the universe. Besides spiritual, beautiful panoramas make it inspirational. Free.

Sedona Heritage Museum (928-282-7038), 735 Jordan Rd. Open daily 11–3. One of Sedona's founding family's home and apple orchard, now a red-rock Historic Landmark, gives you a look into Sedona lifestyles back in its pioneer and ranching days. Exhibits change in the main room a few times a year. Several other rooms have neatly arranged displays. Take one of the scenic pathways through the fruit orchard and past vintage farm implements to the museum. The 4,000-square-foot Apple Barn houses a 40-foot-long apple-sorting machine from the 1940s. $3, under age 12 free. For an extra $2, you can have an audio tour of the museum.

✷ To Do

AIR RIDES **Red Rock Biplane Tours** (928-204-5939). Located at the Sedona Airport. Fully narrated tours give a fun side of Sedona by air. From the mouth-stretching (g-force-induced) takeoff to the smooth-as-silk glide around the red rocks, with a few tummy-tickling moments between through vortexes (a.k.a. updrafts). $99–129 per person; $489 for a private hour-long tour for two; $575 per person for an hour of "stick time."

ARIZONA HELICOPTER ADVENTURES (928-282-0904), 235 Air Terminal Dr. Located in the Airport Main Terminal Building. For 12 to 35 minutes you can glide around the folds of spectacular red-rock canyons along the Mogollon Rim, enjoying eye-level glances into Indian ruins and dramatic sweeps along curious rock formations that seem only a touch away. Sure, the world tilts when the helicopter banks around canyons, and the bottom falls out when you zoom back down crevices, but who cares about updrafts and tilts with scenery this pretty? $65–155 per person.

If you're looking for a more docile aerial experience, your best choice is the oldest form of aviation—a ride in a hot-air balloon. Drift 1,000 feet above the ground in a basket held up by a balloon eight stories high. **Northern Light Balloon Expeditions** (928-282-2274) travels at dawn nearest the red rocks above the Coconino National Forest. **Sky High Balloon Adventures** (800-551-7597) floats above the Prescott National Forest.

Redrock Skydiving, LLC (928-649-8899), 1003 W. Mingus Ave., Cottonwood. If a biplane, helicopter, or hot-air balloon isn't enough, maybe an exhilarating free fall toward the red rocks will do? $225 per person.

FISHING **Rainbow Trout Farm** (928-282-5799), 3500 N. AZ 89A, No. 88. Open Mon.–Fri. 9–5, Sat. and Sun. 9–6. Even if you don't fish, the scenery here is gorgeous—ruddy Oak Creek Canyon sandstone walls in a riparian forest. The $2 admission fee includes fishing equipment, bait, use of grill and picnic tables; under age 6 free.

GOLF **Oak Creek Country Club** (928-284-1820 or 888-703-9489), 690 Bell Rock Blvd. Sedona's original championship course was designed by Robert Trent Jones. The 145-acre course looks more midwestern than arid southwestern with its three lakes. The player-friendly links features tree-lined doglegs with strategically placed fairway bunkers in the landing areas, and slightly elevated greens surrounded by large, swirling bunkers. $65–99.

Sedona Golf Resort (928-284-2093), 35 Ridge Trail Dr. This is the course that lures golfers from around the world to its emerald greens winding around jaw-dropping red rocks. The 6,646-yard, par-71 course presents one of the most unforgettable golf experiences in the world. Designer Gary Panks worked in a number of challenges that demand your attention, no matter how you rank in the game. Rates include green fee, cart, and range balls. $79–105.

HIKING In this enchanting landscape full of legends and lore, hiking takes on new meaning, if only being bedazzled by the red-rock cliffs and sensual smells of the canyon forest. Check out the **Secret Canyon**, **Bell Rock**, or **Loy Canyon trails**. The **West Fork Trail** is the most popular (and beautiful) in

A HIKER ON THE VERY POPULAR, AND BEAUTIFUL, WEST FORK TRAIL IN OAK CREEK CANYON

Oak Creek Canyon. $5 parking pass required to park on national forest land; $8 parking fee at Call of the Canyon parking area for West Fork Trail.

Sedona Creek Adventures (928-593-9221) provides private hikes and fishing trips. John Meyes will take you on hikes off-the-beaten-path and to secluded spots along Oak Creek to flip a spinner or fly rod. $90 for three hours and $125 for four hours. The four hours includes a picnic lunch.

SEDONA'S PINK JEEP PLAZA

HORSEBACK RIDING See *Jeep Tours.*

INDIAN RUINS/ROCK ART Sinagua Indian signs appear all around the area. You may serendipitously spot a ruin in a tucked-away alcove during a canyon hike, or relics on a road or trail. Look, but don't take. Guided tours are the best way to guarantee sightings. Also, you can see an excellent site at the **Palatki Heritage Area** (928-282-3854) managed by Coconino National Forest Red Rock Ranger District. Open daily 9–3. You must make reservations to visit the site.

JEEP TOURS A number of tour companies will accommodate your every whim when it comes to exploring red-rock country; usually each tours a particular area exclusively. Iconic **Pink Jeep Tours** (800-873-3662), 204 N. AZ 89A, for instance, exclusively visits the Broken Arrow and Diamondback Gulch areas. Only **Sedona Red Rock Western Jeep Tours** (800-848-7728), 270 N. AZ 89A, visits Soldier Pass Trail area. Both offer everything from jeep tours (adrenaline rushes included) to guided horseback rides, as well as spiritual and archaeological tours. Tours start at $37. If you want a personal tour, contact **Southwest Outside** (928-284-1816). NOLS (National Outdoor Leadership School)-certified Mike Krajnak will take you off the beaten tracks in Sedona and points beyond in northern Arizona. He'll also do overnights, supplying all the gear and food. $125/person for three hours; two-person minimum.

MOUNTAIN BIKING Although much of the national forest area is designated wilderness where nothing mechanized (as in motorized vehicles or bicycles) is allowed, there are still a number of trails you can cycle on. Contact **Coconino National Forest** for more information. **Absolute Bikes** (928-284-1242), 6101 AZ 179, Suite C, village of Oak Creek, rents bicycles, and has information on where to ride.

SCENIC DRIVES **Schnebly Hill Road**. From AZ 179 and AZ 89A, drive south to just past the bridge over Oak Creek and turn left onto Schnebly Hill Road (FR153) Drive 6 miles to the Schnebly Hill Vista for an unforgettable view of Sedona and its red-rock landscape. Four-wheel drive recommended.

SPIRITUAL Peace Place Sedona (928-203-7755) 355 Jordan Road. Open daily 10–6. Wondering where to start for a more intimate metaphysical experience amid the layers of psychic wisdom and cosmic debris in this spiritual point on the planet? Peace Place, located a little off the beaten path, provides a peaceful portal among the astral chatter with a "true Sedona experience." Loaded with crystals (including the mother of all crystals, Leilani, a chunk from the famous Cave of the Giants in Mexico), gemstones and plain old good vibes, Peace Place is fascinating just to visit and peruse. But you can experience energy healing sessions, massage, shamanic journeys, crystal healing, and professional-quality spiritual healing classes. Owners Laurelle Shanti Gaia and Michael Arthur Baird have practiced the healing arts for more than 25 years. "The concept of using crystals to transmit energy has actually been mainstream for many years," Gaia said, citing their use to generate, modulate, and transmit energy to computers, satellites, watches, radios, and LCD screens. Why not use them to transmit healing energy? Call for services and prices.

VORTEXES In the mid-1970s, a medium channeled information describing four major electromagnetic energy sources called vortexes. The town has never been the same since. **Boynton Canyon**: Go west on AZ 179 to Dry Creek Rd., turn right and follow the signs to the canyon and trailhead for the 2-mile-long Boyton Canyon Trail just outside the entrance to the Enchantment Resort. **Airport Mesa**: Go west on AZ 179 West and turn left onto Airport Road; drive about a half-mile to reach a trailhead for 3.5-mile-long Airport Mesa Trial; **Bell Rock**: Located in the Village of Oak Creek along AZ 179 just north of Jacks Canyon Rd. **Cathedral Rock**: Take the Red Rock Crossing Trail in Crescent Moon Picnic Area (see *Wilder Places*).

Sedona Heart Center (928-282-2733), 1385 W. Hwy 89A, gives vortex tours in air-conditioned vans twice a day for $75 a tour; $130 for both. The vortexes may inspire you to experience more energy work, and the Heart Center offers individual energy work sessions, as well.

✱ Spas

A Spa for You (928-282-3895), 28 Kayenta Ct., #2. Owner Thea Draaisma got the name for the spa when her significant other said she should "open a spa for you." It took Draaisma, then the leading massage therapist at the Hilton spa, about a year to actually open this spa. When she did, she discovered it's not only a spa for her, but a spa for you. "It's all about my clients. My treatments are created for my clients." The spa "is a very organic, moving thing that evolves with each session." The sessions are unique as the owner. The signature, and most popular, is the gemstone chakra polarity balancing, which blends into a massage incorporating Trager, Swedish, therapeutic, and connective tissue massage therapies, hot rocks or cool marble. She also has Aromi di Lucca, which she describes as "the Swedish massage you possibly have never received" drenched in warm oil aromatherapy. The most unique is the Japanese Facial Massage. You won't find it anywhere else, nor will you feel results like it from anything else. Draaisma describes it as "truly a massage for the face" that improves your physical, spiritual, and emotion balance. Massages $105–145, Japanese facial $75–95.

Sedona's New Day Spa (928-282-7502), 1449 W. AZ 89A, Suite 1. Nurturing and soothing, the luxury starts in the waiting area, when a meltingly warm pillow filled with calming and restorative herbs gets wrapped around your neck. In the treatment rooms, therapists use natural products, from Alpine goat butter to Yon-Ka facial products from Paris to high-quality herbal products made in town by Body Bliss. Several dozen treatments—from simple massage to Ayurvedic and exclusive body therapy—are tailor-made to fit your needs. Aura-Soma therapy uses color for internal insights. Nail care and waxing available. Body treatments $130–185, massages $65–155 (60–90 minutes), facials $105–190 (60–90 minutes).

The Spa at Sedona Rouge (928-203-4111), Sedona Rouge Hotel, 2250 W. AZ 89A. Dedicated to calming the mind, balancing the emotions, and connecting the body to the rhythms of nature. Although the spa offers a menu, albeit short and sweet, the sky is the limit when it comes right down to the treatment, inasmuch as each 60- or 90-minute session is tailored to the needs of the guest and administered with some of the best hands in the Southwest. Therapies include Ayurvedic, deep tissue, craniosacral, energy work, and reflexology; hot stones, essential oils, brown sugar, or fresh fruits (depending on the season); facials, couples, and exclusive treatments. Deepak Chopra presents a five-day program here several times a year. Call for information. The signature olive oil–lemon–mint soap is a hit—even men come to buy it at the spa shop. Men's and women's steam rooms, outdoor whirlpools, and Tranquility Room and Garden. Call for spa retreat packages. Massages $120–225 and couples $235–435 (60–120 minutes), body treatments $130–225 (60–120 minutes) and couples (60–90 minutes) $250–365, facials $120–180 (60–90 minutes); waxes available.

Stillpoint . . . Living in Balance, Inc. (928-301-0830), 415 Juniper. Call for appointment. Most spa therapies cater to relaxing the body. Stillpoint . . . Living in Balance provides a more therapeutic experience for the mind, body, and soul. Therapies take place in a quiet atmosphere dedicated to their clients' personal space. Owners and therapists Joy and Cynthia mix massage with energy and essential oil therapies to produce a powerful experience. Their signature, The Stillpoint, is a blend of therapeutic massage and energetic balancing with the use of essential oils, crystals, and hot basalt stones. The intriguing menu includes more than 30 therapies, including aroma, lymphatic drainage, and craniosacral; reflexology; and integrative massage that includes Swedish, deep tissue and neuromuscular. They carry a comprehensive line (more than 200) of medicinal-grade essential oils you won't find elsewhere else, and you can add oxygen therapy to your treatment, as well. $85–250 (one to three hours).

DESTINATION SPAS **Mii Amo Spa** (928-282-2900), Enchantment Resort, 525 Boynton Canyon Rd. Situated in a red-rock canyon sacred to the Apache, and containing a powerful vortex, this destination spa has that distinctive Sedona atmosphere of peace and contentment. The spa deservedly rates among the top in the world. You can get a number of classic treatments here from top therapists, including facials, massages, and popular body treatments, as well as sessions that incorporate energy; or you can choose from a menu of "journeys" with different emphases (de-stressing, losing weight, antiaging, spiritual, and more). Whatever you decide, it feels somehow more redemptive because of that special Sedona aura. There are a number of classes and activities you can partake in during the day, such as a session in a meditation room with a large amethyst crystal to coax you into a more intuitive state. Mii Amo even makes three squares a day more special: the restaurant serves delicious healthy meals with a gourmet touch from an exhibition kitchen. Call for reservations and prices.

✷ Wilder Places

♥ **Crescent Moon Picnic** Area (contact the Coconino National Forest). Open daily 8 AM–dusk, Memorial Day–Labor Day 8 AM–8 PM. Many visitors come to this pretty space to see one of the most photographed scenes in the Southwest: Cathedral Rock reflected in the waters of Oak Creek at Red Rock Crossing. You can also fish, swim, and wade in Oak Creek, and picnic on its banks. $8 per car, $1 for walk-ins.

Red Rock Secret Mountain Wilderness (contact the Coconino National Forest). One of the state's most charismatic designated wilderness areas has several memorable hiking trails. Some lead to vortexes, others travel distinctive canyons, and some climb up to extraordinary panoramas. All travel through the distinctive red rocks that made Sedona famous. A Red Rock Pass ($5 per day, $15 per week) is required on all National Forest lands.

Slide Rock State Park (928-282-3034). Call for hours. Once a homestead owned by the Pendley family, this streamside park provides a grandiose experience along the slickrock shelves that brace Oak Creek; you can ride the water as it blasts through a chute. For a more mild-mannered experience, peruse the grounds and the apple orchard that Frank Pendley planted in 1912. The trees still supply enough fruit for bears and humans to enjoy—self-service for the bears, while whole fruit and containers of fresh juice are sold at the park's Slide Rock Market to humans. $20 (Fri. before Memorial Day to Labor Day; be prepared for a long wait!) and $10 all other days per car, $3 per bicycle.

✷ Lodging

BED & BREAKFASTS ♥ **Briar Patch Inn** (928-282-2342 or 888-809-3030). The 9-acre creekside grounds drip with natural opulence and serenity. The property has 18 cottages, decorated in a southwestern style with Indian art and crafts. Each cottage has king or queen bed(s), radio, CD player, and private entrance, bath, and patio. Most cottages have full kitchen or kitchenette, some have mini fridge, and three have a TV; all include a hearty and homemade buffet breakfast. In summer a classical duet plays music on the lawn where breakfast is served. Yoga happens during summer weekends. The inn's gentle and kind atmosphere inspires your personal celebrations to bubble up: People fall in love, children dance barefoot, and professional dancers take a few impromptu swirls during breakfast. An on-site aesthetician gives marvelous facials in the creekside gazebo or your cottage. The inn has a long list of loyal guests; plan your stay early to be sure to get a room. Two-night minimum on weekends, three-night on holidays. No pets. $219–385.

♥ **Sedona Cathedral Hideaway** (928-203-4180 or 866-973-3662), 2130 Red Rock Loop Road. This ultraboutique hideaway has up-close views of Cathedral Rock, one of Sedona's vibratory centers. Whether you believe in the power of vortexes or not, the views are magnificent and inspiring. The trail to the formation is only a few minutes' walk away. However, the formation is only one facet of this hidden gem. When you don't want anyone else to know where you are, you want total romance, and/or you just want to bask in some self-indulgent doting, this hideaway can become a destination in itself. Open space, so attractive to the human spirit, plays a big role here. The home's huge rooms have a line of windows that bring the outdoors in. Room amenities like comfort-number king beds, fireplace, double shower, Jacuzzi tub, surround sound, iPod jacks, DVD player, flat-screen TV, mini fridge, microwave, and personal safe match those found in any large resort. But the 4,500-square-foot hideaway has only two rooms (700 and 1,000 sq. ft.). Innkeeper-owners Kathy and Larry attend to your every need and request, from a gourmet breakfast (included with accommodations and served where you like) to facials, massages, and antiaging treatments (extra). "Tell us what you want, and we'll try to accommodate you," Kathy said; "we have a lot of fun trying new things for people." Larry added, "It's all about people feeling like they are at home. When we hear them say that, we know we've done our job." The 1-acre property has a medicine wheel patio, a power-point of a place that's perfect for wedding ceremonies or when you need a surge; a bocce ball court; a labyrinth; and sundecks for you to soak in rays from the sun, energy from Cathedral Rock, or your own glow from all things wonderful. $285–340 double occupancy; $20 per extra person.

HOTELS AND INNS **Baby Quail Inn** (928-282-2835), 50 Willow Way. The neat and tidy rooms make this a pleasant place to lay your head in this quiet, residential inn. All rooms have a mini fridge, microwave, coffeemaker with coffee and tea, cable TV, use of year-round hot tub, free local calls, and free continental breakfast. Pets not allowed. $59–95.

El Portal (800-313-0017), 95 Portal Lane. This one-of-a-kind 12-room inn was built of recycled wood, handmade adobe, vintage art tiles, and 200-year-old wood beams to replicate a 1900 Spanish hacienda while staying true to original style and construction methods. Decorated with Frank Lloyd Wright in mind, the inn is a mecca for architectural aficionados. Gracious innkeeper-owners Steve and Connie Segner and part owner Lynda Bourgeois make the rounds with guests in the inn's great room, which converts into a dining area that serves gourmet breakfasts and exquisite weekend dinners (meals extra) prepared by Eden Messer. The trio elucidates upon the inn's fascinating architecture and its special location—it was built on a piece of land that a water diviner claimed has vortexes—as long as your interest holds. Make sure you know if you want to relax or have energy, because one vortex energizes and the other relaxes you. $199–350 specials July–Sep.

Kings Ransom Sedona Hotel (928-282-7151), 771 AZ 179. One of the best deals in town. The rooms, newly and nicely decorated, have tons of amenities—cable TV, free WiFi, mini fridge, whirlpool tub, private balcony or patio with views, and free continental breakfast. The grounds have a heated pool, heated spa, fitness center, yoga classes, and a trailhead in its "backyard." Kids are welcome; pets are allowed. $99–140.

♥ **L'Auberge Inn** (928-282-1661 or 800-272-6777), 301 L'Auberge Lane. This quiet, wooded Sedona classic offers the height of relaxed Old

Word class and romance. The property mixes rustic opulence with a storybook atmosphere on the banks of Oak Creek, and it's just gotten better. The grounds have new landscaping and new cabins have been added. Its boutique spa, open to guests only, meets the sensuous standards of the inn and has experienced service-minded therapists. You'll also find the four-star L'Auberge Restaurant (see *Dining Out*) and a business center; fresh scones, coffee, and tea are served daily 7–9 AM, and cocktails and wine each evening 6–7 in the lobby. There's astronomy on Friday evenings. Individually decorated lodge rooms have a king bed and private patio or balcony. Garden and creekside cabins look like French country cottages with their wooden details, rustic wood-burning fireplaces, and covered porches that soak in the sweet spicy smell of Arizona sycamore trees along Oak Creek; each has mini fridge. $20 daily service fee covers most tips, and use of business center. Pets get spoiled with a dog bed, mat, feeding bowl, and host of gourmet goodies. $195–650.

♿ ((ı)) ⚭ **Sedona Rouge Hotel & Spa** (928-203-4111), 2250 W. AZ 89A. Quiet and peaceful even though it's situated right along Sedona's main highway, this luxury boutique hotel sidesteps any hint of southwestern influence with a full-spectrum Mediterranean style inspired by Roman, French, and North African cultures prominent in Andalusia—the Venice of Moorish Spain. The highly tactile décor drips with saturated colors on organic appointments of wood, metal, and glass. The owners' vision for a classy, trendy, sexy, and fun hotel works; children are welcome, but adults prevail. You'll find 77 guest rooms, heated lap pool, fitness room with state-of-the-art equipment and personal trainer available, yoga and tai chi classes, 2,500 square feet of meeting space, conference room, complimentary WiFi, and cable TV, along with complimentary bottled water and light snacks. $159–269.

RESORTS ⚭ ♥ **Enchantment Resort and Mii Amo Spa** (928-282-2900), 525 Boynton Canyon Rd. The resort sits in its own private canyon, sacred to the Apache, from which a major vortex emanates. It wears its name well, as guests have repeatedly commented. It's the kind of place where you start to wear a smile for no reason, and find yourself staring at the magnificent cliffs for a long time. Even type A's can't resist the chance to just relax and enjoy the elegance of nature. The property includes two restaurants (Yavapai is four-star), the world-renowned Mii Amo spa, a clubhouse, a gift shop, a game room, meeting rooms, seven championship tennis courts (thanks to former owner and tennis guru John Gardiner), five pools, an outdoor whirlpool spa, a par-3 golf course and putting green, and croquet. Rooms have king or queen beds, sitting area, full bath and dressing area, deck with views; studios have a beehive fireplace, kitchenette and dining area, and gas grill; hacienda studios feature full kitchens. Casita Bedroom $295–425, one-bedroom Casita Suite $640–900, and up.

🐾 ♥ **Forest Houses Resort** (928-282-2999), 9275 N. AZ 89A. If you want to stay in Oak Creek Canyon, you can camp in one of the two campgrounds, stay in a cabin, or have a forest home along Oak Creek all to yourself. Back in the 1930s, Bob Kittredge Sr. drove to the Southwest on a motorcycle from Manhattan. Spurred by the adventure stories penned by Edward White, the sculptor zoomed around the region and settled on 20 acres of land in Oak Creek Canyon.

He built the first of 16 homes, The Cook House, during his first winter. He built the next one in the 1950s to see if it would rent to vacationers, which it did. Bob, Sr. then went to work building more with stones, boulders and logs from the area by hand in the forested canyon. The homes come with one to four bedrooms, fireplaces or woodburning stoves, patios or decks, completely stocked kitchens, and are fully furnished with tub or bath. What they don't have is landline, cell, or Internet service because this is the Canyon, where nature has the final say. Check out the gardens and manicured lawn on the property. $90–145.

✷ Where to Eat

DINING OUT **Elote Cafe** (928-203-0105), 771 Arizona 179. Open Tue.–Sat. for dinner at 5. A sign in the restaurant reads: corn continues in a pattern of infinite regeneration. *Elote*, or corn, is a big thing here because it is with indigenous Mexican communities. You won't find any Tex-Mex items here; this is real Mexican food from recipes Chef Jeff Smedstad collected while studying food in Oaxaca for three years and traveling Mexico for a dozen years—from Elote—fresh shaved corn, mayonnaise, spices, and lime (of which Chef Jeff correctly says, "If you don't have Elote, you've missed the point") to wild Mexican Shrimp to Mole to Pepitas Snapper. Pintos are out, black beans and rice in. It's all sustainable food, and local as it can get. The produce comes from Sedona with the corn from a patch grown against the red rocks across the way and mint for the mojitos, as well as other herbs, grown on the patio. Grass-fed beef appears often on the menu, along with natural pork. The desserts are as *rico* as the rest of the food—such as Lime Crème Brûlée, Chocolate Pie (the all-around favorite), and Pasel de Elote (Veracruz-style sweet corn cake with *dulce de leche* and homemade vanilla bean ice cream. The tequila vuelos ($10) and wines (four from Arizona), which come in jumbo glassfuls, and local beer are a deal. Mexican Altura Coffee is smooth as silk. Plus, you get bamboo to-go containers (which you'll need). It's a small venue, so be prepared to wait, as reservations are only for parties of five or more. Patio diners get gorgeous views of the red rocks. Entrées $9.95–22.95.

Hundred Rox Restaurant (928-340-8900), 100 Amara Lane. Open daily for breakfast 7–10:30, dinner Wed.–Sun. 5:30–9. Executive chef David Schmidt has created a fresh and altogether excellent Cal-Ital menu that leans more toward Ital, just think fresh and soulful—from handcrafted ravioli to tagliatelle pasta with ale-poached Italian sausage to chicken piccata and sides of risotto, grilled fresh vegetables and mozzarella Caprese. If you can save room for dessert, check out the crispy cannoli with mission fig–ricotta filling or Grand Marnier zabaglione. The wait staff knows the menu well and will make suggestions and then dote on you. The wine list is short but strong. Entrées $17.99–25.99.

♥ **L'Auberge de Sedona** (928-282-1667), 301 L'Auberge Lane. Open daily for breakfast 7–10:30, lunch 11:30–2:30, and dinner 5:30–9. One of the state's favorite restaurants for dinner, especially with its creekside patio on which everyone wants to dine, has taken a slight turn toward lighter, brighter cuisine with executive chef David Schmidt at the helm. Oh, there's still foie gras with the Juniper-Scented Duck Breast, and Maine Lobster and Pan-Roasted Diver Scallops remain a favorite at this AAA Four Diamond venue, but you'll find a number of dishes with richness coming from flavor rather than butterfat yet remaining sensuously perfect. The Colorado Roasted Rack of Lamb gets offset by mint-eggplant purée and crumbled feta cheese. Garlic-Glazed Alaskan Halibut (in season) comes with Citrus-Scented Apricots and Cornbread Purée. Chef David will do a personalized tasting menu with 48 hours' notice. The wine list gets the nod from *Wine Spectator*, which has designated it one of the best in the nation. The more casual Terrace Bistro at L'Auberge de Sedona has the same menu, but served outside along the banks of Oak Creek (same hours, too, weather permitting). With the staff aiming for another star, the already excellent food, wine, and service will be impeccable. The breakfast becomes special with omelets, eggs Benedict (also with lobster), and *brioche pain perdu* French Toast; even the Old-Fashioned Steel-cut Oats gets a special touch with Caramelized Apples and Brûléed Muscavado Brown Sugar. Lunch means memorable sandwiches and salads featuring *jambon de Paris* and violet mustard on the Croque Monsieur à la L'Auberge and house-made mozzarella on the Caprese Flatbread and Ahi Tuna Salad Niçoise and Six-Year-Aged Rocca Parmigiano Tuilles in the Classic Caesar Salad. Entrées breakfast $10–22, lunch $14–24, dinner $28–40.

VINTNER BOB PREDMORE (ALCANTARA VINEYARDS IN THE VERDE VALLEY) AND CHEF RON MOLER (REDS RESTAURANT IN SEDONA)

Reds (928-203-4599), 2250 W. Highway 89A. Open daily for breakfast 7:30–10:30 AM, lunch 11:30–2, and dinner 5–9 PM. Chef Ron Moler turns out some above-average comfort food, oftentimes with a healthy twist—especially when Deepak Chopra does his five-day healthy living sessions at the hotel's spa. But all spa cuisine aside, Chef Ron has some excellent dinner entrées, heavy on fish, such as the Seared Scallops with Parmesan Whipped Potatoes, and Seared Ahi Tuna. Beef eaters should not pass up the rib eye. You can order lighter fare, meaning smaller portions for $10 (the locals' favorites), of their signature dish, Scallop Tacos, or Beef or Fish Sliders and interesting salads often made with fare from the farmers' market, such as the Spinach Salad that has goat cheese, wild mushroom strudel, candied pecans, and tomatoes and a light bacon dressing. No one should miss the desserts, all but the cheesecake are house-made (check out the Banana Crepe with lemon Chantilly crème).

Troia's Pizza Pasta Amoré (928-282-0123), 1885 W. AZ 89A. Open Tue.–Sun. at 5 PM. Rosanne and Sam

Troia have created a warm, open dining space serving classic Italian food. Locals are often busy meeting and greeting neighbors and friends as they take their seats (reservations are recommended), as the owners make sure everyone feels welcomed and happy. The magic happens in the exhibition kitchen. Lasagna and shrimp scampi are the most popular entrées, and the olive tapenade appetizer is a favorite. The veal is butter tender, the fettuccine Alfredo rich and sensuous; the minestrone soup is like a garden—thick with beans and pasta and full of veggies. Pizzas are made with fresh dough and house-made sauce. Save room for one of the desserts, many of which are homemade; the spumoni is excellent. Entrées $20–25, pasta and pizza $9–16.

EATING OUT **Black Cow Café** (928-203-9868), 229 N. AZ 89A. Open daily 10 AM–9 PM. At first blush you think this is an ice-cream parlor specializing in gooey sundaes—from classic tin roof to caramel Snicker and the Chocolate Lover's Dream. But it's more. First, it's not just ice cream they sell. It's some of the best ice cream you'll ever taste. The confection, made on the premises, shows up on menus at better local restaurants. Next, the house-made cinnamon rolls and Danishes melt in your mouth. Then the World's Best Hot Dog carries its title well. Pastas and veggie sandwiches are available, too. $3.95–6.25.

Garland's Indian Gardens Trading Post (928-282-7702), 3951 N. AZ 89A. Open daily 8–6. This specialty grocery has all the fixings for a gourmet picnic: great-tasting deli sandwiches and salads, sumptuous sweets, locally grown fruits and vegetables. Take your goodies across the street to eat along the banks of Oak Creek, or have a seat on the outside patio. A lagniappe: The property has a soothing vortex. $6.95–8.95.

Kaiser's West (928-204-2088), 2920 W. AZ 89A. Open Mon.–Fri. 7 AM–8:30 PM, Sat. 8 AM–8:30 PM, Sun. 8–2. Expect to find a packed place during the prime mealtimes here. The staff usually goes the extra mile to serve everyone in a timely manner. And what they serve is good basic favorites with innovative ingredients that make them a little different than the diner experience you expect. The Finest French Toast lives up to its name. At dinner the brisket and barbecue ribs are favorites. Desserts have names like Judi's Famous Pecan Pie and Homemade Ice Cream. Entrées $7–20.

New York Bagels & Deli (928-204-1242), 1350 W. AZ 89A. Open Tue.–Sat. 5 AM–8 PM, Sun. and Mon. 5 AM–3 PM. At first glance, you'd swear this eatery was a franchise. Not so. The owners are New Yorkers—there are enough street-life photos of the Big Apple lined up along the walls to assuage any hint of homesickness a native New Yorker may have—and so is the food, prepared with NYC quality. First to open in a town that likes to lounge with some of the best eye-opening coffee around, you can add bagels (that turn into a satisfying meal with eggs, cheese, bacon, sausage, etc.), Belgian waffles, and omelets. Later, for lunch, filling deli sandwiches and fresh salads are served. From 4 PM until closing, the eatery becomes New York Pizza & Deli. It's more great salads, hot sandwiches, and pizza and calzones. And this is good pizza—by the slice or the pie with house-made dough. The lineup of fresh-baked pastries may whittle down your willpower as you file past the display case to pay for your food. Since the owner—who's there every day at 1 AM to start baking—won third place in a metropolitan

New York City contest for his cheesecake, go on and give in. The place is swarming with locals and few leave without pastry. Breakfast $1.95–7.50, lunch $6.25–6.95, dinner $7.25–10.95, pizza $8–15.75.

Sally's Mesquite Grill (928-282-6533), 250 Jordan Rd. Open daily 11–7. Owner Mike Sally got interested in barbecue when he was the general manager for the Ottawa (Canada) Rough Runners football team and on a recruiting trip in Dallas, Texas. He toyed with recipes, fed friends and neighbors, then opened up Sally's. Everything is smoked fresh (ribs for 3 to 4 hours, beef and pork for 12 hours, and chicken for 3 hours) and melts in your mouth. The (secret) sauce has a homemade taste, the beans carry only a kiss of sweetness and (secret) flavors, and the coleslaw contains other (secret) vegetables and spices. $7.25–19.95.

✷ The Arts

When surrealist painter and sculptor Max Ernst moved to Sedona in 1950, a trail of other artists and writers followed. The Cowboy Artists of America started here in 1965 (at the present Cowboy Club restaurant). Today more than 200 artists in every medium and style, contemporary to Native American, live in Sedona. Galleries cluster in **Tlaquepaque Arts and Crafts Village**, **Hillside Sedona**, and **Hozho Shops and Galleries** (see *Selective Shopping*). The **Sedona Arts Center** (928-282-3809), AZ 89A and Art Barn Rd., holds regular exhibits. You can attend openings, technique demonstrations, and talks at several galleries every **First Friday** of the month from 5 PM–8 PM. The Sedona Trolley will shuttle you for free to participating galleries (928-282-7390).

✷ Selective Shopping

Shops line the main highway here, congregating especially in uptown and a few shopping areas. **Hillside Sedona** (928-282-4500), 671 AZ 179, and **Hozho Distinctive Shops & Galleries** (928-204-2257), 431 AZ 179, have distinctive shops, world-class galleries, and award-winning restaurants in a multilevel marketplace.

Hoel's Indian Shop (928-282-3925), 9589 N. AZ 89A. Open daily 9:30–5; best to call first. You'll find one of the finest selections of quality Indian jewelry, fetishes, pottery, baskets, kachinas, and rugs here, made by Navajo, Hopi, Zuni, and Santo Domingo artists.

Tlaquepaque Arts & Crafts Village (928-282-4838), 336 AZ 179. Open daily 10–5. You'll find more than 45 galleries, shops, and restaurants in this open-air shopping venue of Spanish-style buildings.

✷ Special Events

February: **The Sedona Marathon** (800-775-7671) brings runners from around the nation to fartlek through the red rocks.

Sedona International Film Festival (928-282-1177) presents more than 100 features, documentaries, and shorts from around the world, plus workshops.

May: **Sedona Century Bicycle Tour** (928-284-1242) winds through Sedona and the Verde Valley on two routes, a metric century and one 40 miles long.

June: **Sedona Taste** (928-282-0122). Fine food and drink at Los Abrigados Resort & Spa benefits the Boys & Girls Clubs of Northern Arizona.

Festival of Native American Culture (928-284-4764) features a Native

American Film Festival, a Celebration of Native American Music and Dance, a Native American Invitational Art Show, and a variety of cultural awareness activities, including archaeological opportunities to learn, tour, and maybe even get dirty.

August: **Red Rocks Music Festival** (877-733-7257). This week-long classical music festival features world-class chamber and flamenco music, orchestral performances, master classes, and workshops.

September: **Fiesta Del Tlaquepaque** celebrates Mexican independence with food and music in Tlaquepaque.

October: The **Sedona Arts Festival** (928-204-9456) is rated as one of the top in the nation and features fine arts and crafts, cuisine from Sedona's finer restaurants, and continuous entertainment at Sedona Red Rock High School.

Mid-November–New Year's Day: **Red Rock Fantasy** (928-282-1777 or 800-521-3131). More than a million lights are used in almost 50 displays made by families.

December: **Festival of Lights** (928-282-4838) shows off thousands of luminaries at Tlaquepaque Arts and Crafts Village; entertainment, too.

Central Arizona

2

GREATER PHOENIX
AND THE VALLEY OF THE SUN

SCOTTSDALE

MINING COUNTRY:
GLOBE, MIAMI, AND SUPERIOR

WICKENBURG

THE MOGOLLON RIM—WEST

THE MOGOLLON RIM—EAST

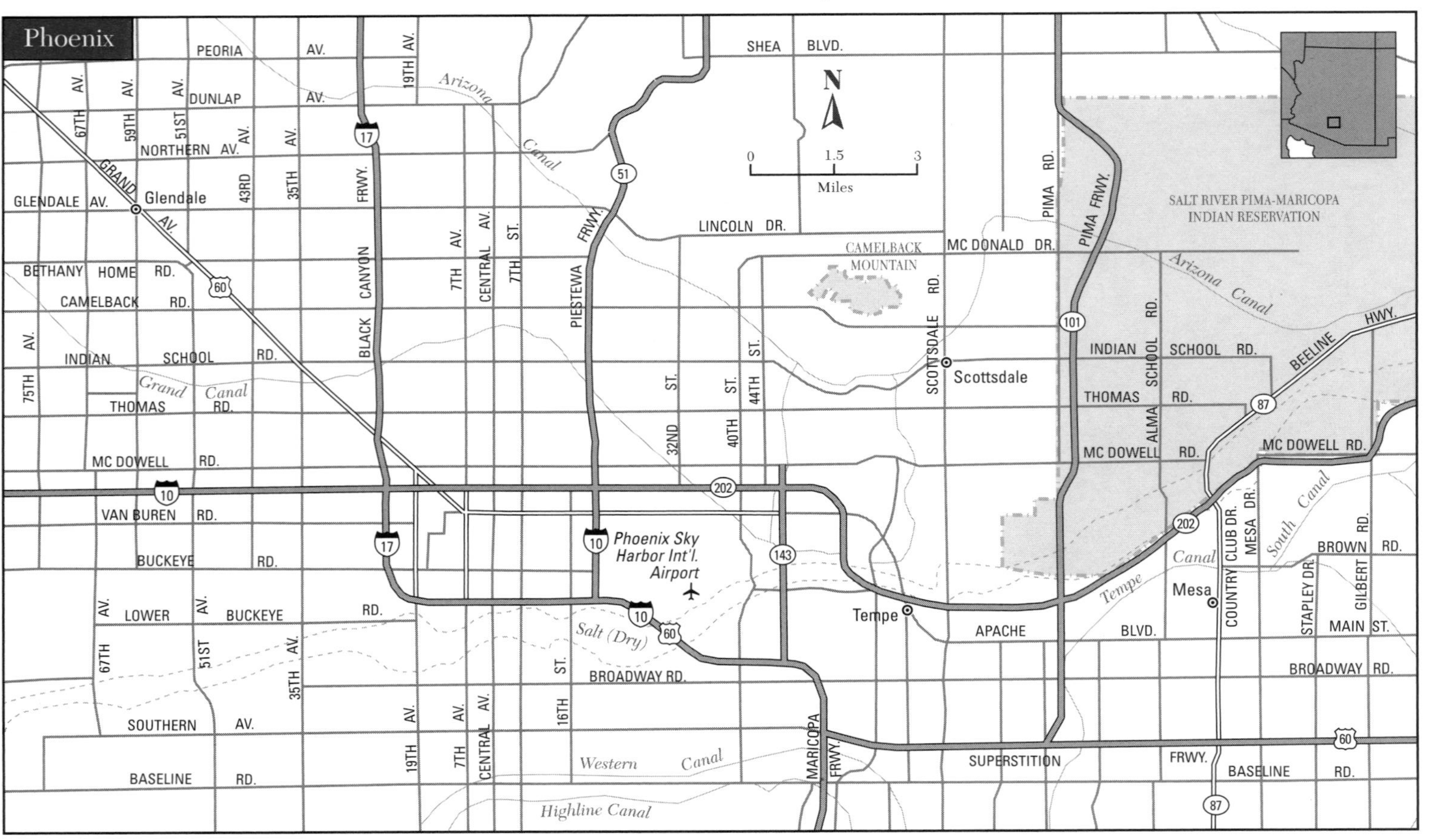

Phoenix
PEORIA AV.
SHEA BLVD.
DUNLAP AV.
NORTHERN AV.
GLENDALE AV.
Glendale
GRAND AV.
LINCOLN DR.
MC DONALD DR.
CAMELBACK MOUNTAIN
BETHANY HOME RD.
CAMELBACK RD.
INDIAN SCHOOL RD.
THOMAS RD.
MC DOWELL RD.
VAN BUREN RD.
BUCKEYE RD.
LOWER BUCKEYE RD.
BROADWAY RD.
SOUTHERN AV.
BASELINE RD.
75TH AV.
67TH AV.
59TH AV.
51ST AV.
43RD AV.
35TH AV.
19TH AV.
7TH AV.
CENTRAL AV.
7TH ST.
16TH ST.
32ND ST.
40TH ST.
44TH ST.
BLACK CANYON FRWY.
PIESTEWA FRWY.
PIMA FRWY.
PIMA RD.
SCOTTSDALE RD.
Scottsdale
Arizona Canal
Grand Canal
Western Canal
Highline Canal
Salt (Dry)
Tempe Canal
South Canal
Phoenix Sky Harbor Int'l. Airport
Tempe
APACHE BLVD.
Mesa
SALT RIVER PIMA-MARICOPA INDIAN RESERVATION
ALMA SCHOOL RD.
BEELINE HWY.
COUNTRY CLUB DR.
MESA DR.
STAPLEY DR.
GILBERT RD.
BROWN RD.
MAIN ST.
MARICOPA FRWY.
SUPERSTITION FRWY.
N
0
1.5
3
Miles
17
51
60
10
202
143
101
87

GREATER PHOENIX AND THE VALLEY OF THE SUN

At first blush you might never guess that the nation's fifth largest city lies in one of the world's principal deserts, averaging only 7 inches of rain a year. Lushly landscaped, bejeweled with swimming pools, and gushing with fountains, Phoenix is an oasis in a sear landscape. With 325-plus sun-soaked days each year, this city's winters are what many folks might call a good summer day. The temperate shoulder seasons feel Edenic. This weather, and the gorgeous natural Sonoran vegetation, has attracted royalty, actors and actresses, politicos, and artists for decades. Greater Phoenix has consistently ranked among the nation's top cities in the number of AAA Four and Five Diamond resorts.

The name Phoenix was bestowed by Darrel Duppa, one of the founding fathers, who prophetically named the Salt River Valley settlement for the mythological bird that rose from its own ashes. The prehistoric Hohokam Indians, whose archaeological sites and intricate canal system are continually unearthed all over the Valley, prospered in the area centuries earlier, then mysteriously vanished in the 14th century. Duppa declared that this prosperity would rise again. Historians claim history has never witnessed a metropolis grow from barren desert to the cosmopolitan status of Phoenix in such a short period of time.

The Valley of the Sun has Phoenix as its centerpiece; the 22 surrounding incorporated cities include Scottsdale, Tempe, Mesa, Chandler, and Glendale. While growth continues each year in the Valley, sprawling closer to the ring of mountains that defines the Valley's borders, burgeoning urban life in central Phoenix, Scottsdale, and Tempe also has people turning their heads (and sometimes spinning them) with its surge of upscale condominiums and lofts, restaurants, hotels, and gathering places. With tourism the second largest industry in the metropolitan area, Greater Phoenix clearly exists for your pleasure.

GUIDANCE **Arizona Office of Tourism** (602-364-3700 or 866-806-8228; www.arizonaguide.com) 1110 W. Washington St., Suite 155 (open 8–5), and **Greater Phoenix Convention and Visitors Bureau** (602-452-6282 or 877-225-5749; www.visitphoenix.com), 50 N. 2nd St. (open 8–5), have a wealth of information. Call **Echo Canyon Recreation Area** (602-256-3220), **Phoenix Mountains Preserve** (602-262-7901), 2701 E. Squaw Peak Dr., and **South Mountain Park** (602-262-7693) 10919 S. Central Ave., for information on trail use. **Arizona Public Lands Information Center** (602-417-9300), 1 N. Central Ave., Suite 800 (open 8–4), is a clearinghouse of information for destinations and activities on public lands.

GETTING THERE *By car:* Downtown Phoenix lies at the intersection of I-17 and I-10. *By bus:* **Greyhound Bus** (602-389-4200), 2115 E. Buckeye Rd. *By air:* **Phoenix Sky Harbor International Airport** (602-273-3300), 3400 Sky Harbor Blvd., is served by more than 20 airlines, including Aeromexico, Air Canada, Alaska Air, America West/U.S. Airways, American, British Airways, Continental, Delta, Frontier, Northwest, and Southwest JetBlue.

GETTING AROUND Metro Light Rail (602-253-5000) The first of several phases of the light rail system debuted in downtown Phoenix just in time to welcome 2009. The 20-mile line links Phoenix to the neighbors, Tempe and Mesa, with stops at attractions such as Phoenix Art Museum, the Heard Museum, Chase Field. and U.S. Airways Center. You can travel the quiet, air-conditioned trains just about 24/7 (except for a few hours' downtime in the wee hours). $1.75 per person.

WHEN TO COME Admittedly, the triple-digit-degree summers seem to get hot enough to make the asphalt soften, sending Phoenicians into the high country (especially in Aug.); of course, that's when you'll find the best deals. One of the perks of living here is the fantastic discount the best resorts give—easily 60 to 75 percent off. The heat starts to ebb by mid-Sep., and the city resuscitates by Oct. when temps drop into the 80s. Outdoor events start in Nov. The high season, with perfect weather (high 60s to mid-70s), runs from Jan. through Mar.; make reservations for all you plan to do then. Whenever you come, plan to dress in layers, even in the heat of summer—indoors are frostily air-conditioned.

PHOENIX'S NEW LIGHT RAIL TRAVERSES FROM DOWNTOWN TO THE AIRPORT, WITH SEVERAL POINTS IN BETWEEN

✷ To See

Arizona Mining and Mineral Museum (602-255-3795), 1502 W. Washington St. Open Mon.–Fri. 8–5, Sat. 11–4, closed Sun. and state holidays. Minerals quickened the hearts of the settlers who came to Arizona, as well as the visitors who come today. Besides information on gold panning to rockhounding, this museum offers fascinating displays of over 3,000 mineral specimens from around the world. Arizona copper takes up a sizable corner of the collection. A section showcases lapidary arts and glamorous fluorescent minerals. $2 adults, under age 17 free.

Arizona Science Center (602-716-2000), 600 E. Washington St. Open 10–5. What started as a hands-on learning center for children in the Valley in 1984 has evolved into a full-blown science center that will interest folks of every age. More than 300 hands-on exhibits, a computerized planetarium, a five-story giant-screen theater, and live demonstrations deliver enough information to please anyone; a gift shop and food service fulfill appetites. $12 adults, $10 ages 3–7 and 62-plus.

Desert Botanical Garden (480-941-1225), 1201 N. Galvin Pkwy. Open daily, Oct.–Apr. 8 AM–8 PM; May–Sep. 7 AM–8 PM; closed July 4, Thanksgiving, and Christmas Day. The garden, actually a one-of-a-kind museum accredited by the American Association of Museums, has several themed trails, indoor and outdoor exhibits, and 139 rare, threatened, and endangered plant species from around the world. Volunteers lead guided trail tours each day from Oct. through mid-May; bird walks occur weekly all year, and sunrise and flashlight tours take place in the summertime. Trailside Discovery Stations give you a chance to use most of your five senses to learn about desert plants from Oct. through Apr. When gardening happens in the Valley (Oct., Nov., Mar., and Apr.), a stop at the Ask a Gardener Station might get the answer to your desert gardening conundrums via knowledgeable volunteers (weekends 10–1). Kids have a blast with Desert Detective games and interactive seasonal exhibits. Garden shop, patio café, and library on grounds. $15 adults, $13.50 seniors, $7.50 students, $5 ages 3–12, under age 3 free.

Heard Museum (602-252-8848), 2301 N. Central Ave. Open Mon.–Sat. 9:30–5, Sun.11–3; closed holidays. World renowned and a local favorite, the Heard Museum grew from a private collection of Dwight B. and Maie Bartlett Heard in 1929 to about 39,000 works of Native American cultural and fine art. The museum especially describes the culture of southwestern Native peoples through exhibits and special events, such as Indian markets and hoop-dancing competitions. Exhibits include jewelry, textiles, basketry, kachina dolls, pottery, cradleboards, paintings, and sculpture. Bibliophiles take note: check out the annual **Heard Museum Guild Library Book Sale** in Jan. for super deals on low-stressed books priced 25 cents to $20. $12 adults, $11 seniors, $5 students with ID, $3 ages 6–12.

Heritage Square (602-262-5029), 115 N. 6th St. Open Wed.–Sat. 10–4, Sun. noon–4; closed mid-Aug. through Labor Day. The compendium of eight historic buildings here date back to the very beginning of Phoenix (the late 1880s) and appear on the National Register of Historic Places. Styles range from utilitarian regional style (The Duplex)—where the porch often doubled as the bedroom on summer nights—to elegant Victorian.

♿ **Mesa Southwest Museum** (480-644-2230), 53 N. Macdonald, Mesa. Open Tue.–Fri. 10–5, Sat. 11–5, Sun. 1–5; closed Mon. and holidays. The museum has an impressive 48,000-piece collection of information on Southwest cultural and natural history. Kids will cry, "*Awesome!*" over Arizona's largest collection of dinosaur fossils. Call for admission fees.

♿ **Musical Instrument Museum** (480-478-6000), 4725 E. Mayo Blvd. Open 9–5 daily (Thu. and Fri. till 9 PM). The newly opened, and already award-winning, museum has more than 12,000 musical instruments and associated items from every country around the world. The instruments in the collection exist for the fine craftsmanship, makers' reputations, and/or a special provenance or connection to famous performers (such as the piano on which John Lennon composed "Imagine"). You can learn about the instruments through hands-on touching and playing and state-of-the art audio and video presentations, along with information about the culture of the country of origin. The building itself is a piece of architectural art—richly grained Indian sandstone, a courtyard designed to evoke an Arizona canyon, Venetian plaster walls, Italian porcelain floor tile, and stainless-steel balcony railings—all allude to the variety and rhythms of musical composition. Special concerts ($25–75) from performers and artists from around the world occur throughout the year. $15 adults, $13 age 65-plus, $10 ages 6–17, under age 6 free.

♿ **Phoenix Zoo** (602-273-1341), 455 N. Galvin Pkwy. Open daily 9–5 (summer 7–2 weekdays, 7–4 weekends); closed Christmas Day. One of the nation's largest privately owned nonprofit zoological parks (and very kid friendly) has about 1,300 animals, including 200 endangered or threatened birds, mammals, and reptiles from the globe. The zoo has several interesting habitats, including the Wallaby Walkabout, Monkey Village, Desert Lives (bighorn sheep), Baboon Kingdom, and African Savanna. The Harmony Farm petting zoo and Enchanted Forest is great fun for kids. Its ZooLights holiday lighting event is wonderful—see the zoo at night during the holiday season amid thousands of miniature lights (early Nov.–early Jan.). $16 ages 13–59, $11 age 60-plus, $7 ages 3–12, under age 2 free.

♿ **Pioneer Arizona Living History Village** (623-465-1052), 3901 W. Pioneer Rd. Open Wed.–Sun. 9–4 (in summer 8–2). Located just off I-17 at exit 225, 1 mile north of the Carefree Hwy. exit. As Arizona started to grow up in the mid-1950s, historic buildings were demolished to make way for the new. In an effort to preserve the history lost to development, the city created this village and moved 27 vintage buildings and structures here. It's the state's largest collection of historic buildings, from log cabins to stores—and they all have a story attached. In living history fashion, Pioneer Village focuses on life and living conditions in Arizona's territorial days (1863–1912, the year Arizona became a state). $7 adults, $6 age 60-plus, $5 ages 5–18, under age 5 free.

♿ **Pueblo Grande Museum** (602-495-0900), 4619 E. Washington St. Open Oct.–Apr., Mon.–Sat. 9–4:45, Sun. 1–4:45; May–Sep., Tue.–Sat. 9–4:45; closed on major holidays. Hard to imagine that you can step centuries back into the ruins of a 1,500-year-old Hohokam village while standing in the heart of a very modern Phoenix. The city has dedicated this park to the study and interpretation of the Hohokam culture through ruins and exhibits, both ongoing and changing. The Hohokam built irrigation canals that inspired the current canal system in the Valley; you can see some of the last remainders of still-intact irrigation canals as well as an excavated ball court and full-scale reproductions of Hohokam-style homes.

A special program called Dig It shows you how archaeologists study clues and piece together information from artifacts and gives you a chance to build your own version of a Hohokam village like Pueblo Grande. The museum collects historic and contemporary Native American art objects featuring Salt River Valley cultures (Akimel O'odham and Maricopa). $6 adults, $5 age 55-plus, $3 ages 6–17, under age 6 free.

♿ **Rawhide Wild West Town** (480-502-5600), Wild Horse Pass, 5700 N. Loop Rd. Open Thu.–Sun. 5:30 AM–9 PM. Sat. farmers' market 8 AM–1 PM. Celebrating all things Wild West, Rawhide will take you back to an authentic Arizona 1880s town, where the streets popped with gunfights and clamored with townsfolk activities. You can watch musicians entertain and Native Americans share their legacies at an informal seating area, or experience fun burro and stagecoach rides that take you around the park. Test your skills with activities like the mechanical bull and climbing wall. You might even get arrested, all (hopefully) in good fun. **Rawhide Steakhouse and Saloon** excels in cooking up mesquite-grilled cowboy steaks. Chef Jon Andersen (who previously cooked in the five-star Kai kitchen across the way and Napa Valley) cooks a rib eye that is one of the best-tasting in the Valley and worth the trip alone. It might be the only place in the Valley to serve deep-fried rattlesnake and mountain oysters (not, the menu warns, a "trendy seafood dish"). The bread pudding and fresh-baked apple pie are dessert favorites. The whole attraction is a special place to experience a bygone era of Phoenix when it didn't even have its name yet. A farmers' market on Saturdays has local produce, food made by local Native Americans, and a cooking demonstration by Chef Jon Andersen. Free admission to farmer's market. Assistance animals only.

✷ To Do

DAIRY TOUR **Shamrock Farms** (602-477-2462), 40034 W. Clayton, Stanfield. Closed in summer. Reservations required. Join the herd as a tractor-pulled wagon shows you the ins (the different components of the farm) and outs (how milk gets delivered around Arizona) of one of the nation's largest working dairy farms. Everyone gets to participate in interactive displays and games. You learn about the nutritional values of dairy products, then see how the ladies (the dairy's 10,000-cow stable) lead a life of luxury as they produce milk. There's a sweet treat at the end of the tour. Call at least 48 hours in advance. $9 adults, $7.50 seniors, $6 ages 3–12.

DOG PARKS **Steele Indian School Park** (602-495-0739), 300 E. Indian School Rd. A gated area on the northeast corner of the park has a drinking fountain and two sections: one for dogs under 20 pounds, the other for larger pooches.

♿ **PETsMART Dog Park at Washington Park** (602-261-8559), 6455 N. 23rd Ave. This 2.65-acre park has a 6-foot-high fence, two double-gated entrances, a water fountain, two doggy watering stations, benches, mutt mitt dispensers, and garbage cans for dog waste. Large trees provide shade. Fenced area for smaller dogs.

Phoenix Sky Harbor International Airport (602-273-3300), 3400 E. Sky Harbor Dr. Bone Yard at Terminal 4 is a shaded, bone-shaped gravel area with mutt mitts plus two water faucets with buckets. Terminal 3 Paw Pad has water spigots and bowls, mutt mitts, and a red fire hydrant.

FISHING Greater Phoenix has some great fishing holes. This is not a fisherman's tale. The Department of Game and Fish stocks lakes and ponds (1 big fish for every 20 little ones) with rainbow trout Nov.–Mar., channel catfish Mar.–July and Sep.–Nov., and sunfish three times a year. Log onto www.azgfd.gov to find urban fishing spots around the Valley. Hot spots are Papago Ponds (Galvin Pkwy. between McDowell Rd. and Van Buren St. in Papago Park in Tempe), Chaparral Lake (off Hayden Rd. between Chaparral and Jackrabbit roads in Scottsdale) and Water Ranch (Greenfield and Guadalupe roads in Gilbert). Bass, crappie, bluegill, white amur, tilapia, and carp roam the waters as well. Most lakes get stocked biweekly from Sep. 20–July 10 on an arbitrary day between Mon. and Sat. This includes Incentive Stocks with 2- to 4-pound lunkers. Contact the Arizona Department of Game and Fish (602-942-3000) for more information. You will need a fishing license if you're age 14 or older. Spend $16 on a Class U urban fishing license that's good for the calendar year, or get a Class D one-day-only license for $8.50.

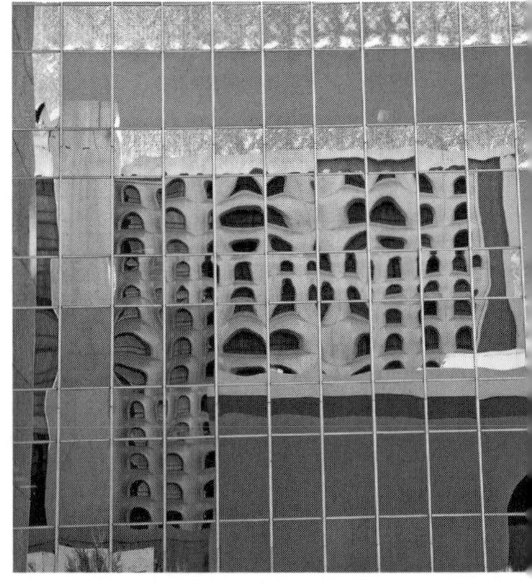

DOWNTOWN PHOENIX

GLIDER RIDES AND PARASAILING **Turf Soaring School** (602-439-3621), 8700 W. Carefree Hwy. (AZ 74), Peoria. Open daily 9–5. You can take flight in the Arizona sky in a glider. The experience is basically your first lesson in piloting a glider plane, and it's entered in your official logbook. You can choose to be released from the tow plane anywhere from 3,000 to 5,000 feet (the higher the altitude, the longer your ride); also select what type of ride you want, from smooth and scenic to a hair-raising loop-de-loop aerobatic deluxe. $109–189.

GOLF Golf may not be the sole reason people come to Phoenix. The mild fall through spring weather and scenery may have something to do with it. But maybe not. From its start as a resort town, Phoenix has always enjoyed golf, and today you'll find some of the world's best courses here. The National Golf Foundation dubbed Greater Phoenix the Golf Capital of the World.

Arizona Biltmore (602-955-9655), 24th St. and Missouri. Few golf courses can match what this time-honored course has in spades: tradition. The stately **Adobe**, second oldest in Phoenix, came on the scene long before modern designs. Its architecture—a triumph of beauty over trickery—forces you to think through your game. The par-71 course provides a relaxing yet challenging round with a couple dozen rugged bunkers with bays and grassy capes and several water traps. Watch that 60-year-old Aleppo pine tree on the 15th hole. The younger **Links** adds some glam to its capricious personality. Pine-lined fairways roll past some of the most stunning homes in Phoenix. Water hazards are big in this course, and well-bunkered greens are reminiscent of the deep and well-set seaside links of the British Isles. No two holes are alike here, so you'll always have a different game that requires thoughtfulness and precise shot selection. No denim allowed; collared shirt and Bermuda shorts required. Championship putting course included in fees. Award-winning golf shop. Private lessons and daily clinics offered. $49–185 for 19 holes.

ASU Karsten Golf Course (480-921-8070), 1125 Rio Salado Pkwy., Tempe. This championship classic Pete Dye Scottish Links produces champions. Arizona State University's 18-hole, par-72 course has rolling hills, railroad ties, and greens partially hidden by bunkers and water. In keeping with scholarly tradition, you will be tested on this college course. The 16th tee is the major challenge. Besides the distraction from the course's beauty, a lake that runs the entire length of the hole guards the hole's right side while mounding the left and backsides. It takes a 217-yard carry over the water to reach the greens. To bogey or birdie, that is the question. Golf cart and locker included in fees. Collared shirts, no denim. $48–105.

Gold Canyon Golf Course (480-982-9449), 6100 S. Kings Ranch Rd., Apache Junction. You have a choice of two 18-hole championship courses here. Both are challenging, both are scenic. The one that gets all the attention and high-profile ratings is the elevated **Dinosaur** (par-71/72). Once you wind your way a few holes up the mountain, the scenery gets phenomenal. Signature hole 4 is the most picturesque; hole 5 comes with a challenge. Sibling course, the **Sidewinder**, also a par-71/72, is flatter and about half the price. Sidewinder winds through canyons and arroyos. Both are impeccably groomed, both carry enough stars from *Golf Digest* to form a constellation, and both give you good golf and plenty of views. Cart included in fees. Dinosaur $75–190, Sidewinder $49–89.

Papago Golf Course (602-275-8428), 5595 E. Moreland St. This hot municipal course will have you arriving in the early hours of the morning to get a tee time. William Bell (think Torrey Pines in San Diego) designed the challenging course with large mature trees and traditional undulating fairways; it has a 132-slope rating from the back tees. This is where golfers qualify for the Phoenix Open. Like most of the Valley's difficult courses, it's beautiful, too: set next to the distinctive Papago Buttes. $59 riding, $44 walking.

The Phoenician Golf Course (480-423-2449; 24-hour reservation line, 480-423-2450). The Phoenician Resort, 6000 E. Camelback Rd. With three championship 9-hole courses named for the type of terrain in which they spread, the game here mixes challenge with diversity. The **Oasis Nine**, designed by Homer Flint, boasts a tropical setting loaded with water features. The **Desert Nine**, designed by Ted Robinson Sr., who calls it one of the prettiest courses in the Southwest, hugs the base of Camelback Mountain. Quintessential desert vegetation decks the greens. The **Canyon Nine**—a combined effort of Flint and Robinson—features lush landscapes overlooking panoramas of the Valley. The dress code is strictly enforced here: collared shirts, slacks, or Bermuda-length shorts for men; for women, sleeveless shirts must have a collar, and slacks or Bermuda-length shorts are required. Denim, tank tops, and T-shirts are never permitted. Green fees include golf carts and practice range balls prior to play. Callaway Rentals clubs with two sleeves of Callaway golf balls and FootJoy rental shoes are available upon request. $60–200.

The Raven Golf Club (602-243-3636), 3636 E. Baseline Rd. If you play this, the highest-rated golf course in Phoenix, you may be rubbing shoulders with some professional baseball players, as it's also the Official Home Golf Course of the Arizona Diamondbacks. Impeccably manicured to be tournament-ready, the course gets overseeded with poa and bent grasses; tees, fairways, and approaches have overseeded winter rye. Impeccable applies to the guest service here, too, which makes your experience just a little sweeter no matter how your game turns out on this par-72 course. If you plan to play during the hotter months to nab a bargain, the course provides mango-scented cooling towels. No denim allowed, but golf mocs are okay. $65–175.

Whirlwind Golf Club (480-940-1500), Sheraton Wild Horse Pass Resort & Spa, 5594 W. Wildhorse Pass Blvd. You won't find houses surrounding this golf course, but you may see wild horses. This Troon-managed facility has two 18-hole courses designed by Gary Panks. **Devil's Claw** has a combination of fairway elevations changes, signature bunkering, and superb course conditioning. Every hole carries the name of a significant legend or landmark of the Pima and Maricopa Indians. **Cattail** has you navigating over and around several water features and deep canyons. Because this club utilizes the G2, a climate-controlled device that changes the air temperature in and around golf carts more than 40 degrees, you can take advantage of the low summer rates and live to talk about the fabulous play you made at Dragonfly Falls. Green fees include golf cart practice balls, bag tag, and yardage guide; $45–145.

The Wigwam Golf Club (623-935-3811), 300 Wigwam Blvd., Litchfield Park. This course, opened in the 1930s, is synonymous with golf in Arizona. The **Gold Course**, nicknamed Arizona's Monster, showcases designer Robert Trent Jones Sr.'s love of heroic shot-making that produces, in his words, "Easy bogies and hard pars." Even though the course will beat you up unless you're an excellent golfer, the waiting list for tee times is often l-o-n-g. Jones went easy on the **Blue Course**. This short but tricky links has an array of deep and perilous bunkers, ponds, and dogleg fairways. Plus, it's full of contradictions—a roller coaster of golf holes presenting different obstacles and challenges. The **Red Course** is a parkland-style course. The Wigwam even has something for pint-sized beginners: **Little Wigwam Golf Link** has three different holes to help little ones learn to hit the ball, get familiar with strategy, and develop a love for the game. A new state-of-the-art practice range is one of the largest in Arizona. The **Village Green**, a 2-acre putting green and garden, is the American version of the famous Himalayas putting green at St. Andrews, Scotland. The golf club also has a full-service golf shop and Jim McLean Golf School. The only resort course with 54 holes on site, the Wigwam is one of the best golf resorts in the state. Call for rates.

HIKING The city parks have some great trails; locals use them all year long, all day long. If you are not acclimated to the desert, drink a quart of water with electrolyte mix every hour in the warmer weather, and every couple of hours in winter; always wear a hat and sunscreen; and hike during the cooler morning hours in warmer weather. The most popular trail is the **Piestawa Peak Summit Trail** in the Phoenix Mountains Preserve, which climbs about 1,200 feet in 1.2 miles. Around 5 PM–6 PM during the week and weekend mornings you may have to hunt for a parking spot. The preserve's **Circumference Trail** takes you about 4.5 miles around the mountain. Another popular route, and more technical, is the **Summit Trail** on Camelback Mountain—but you will have to wait for a parking space in cooler weather. If you want to get away from the masses and experience desert remoteness, hike the **National Trail** in South Mountain Park. Also see *Wilder Places*.

HORSEBACK RIDING You can ride in any of the mountain parks if you saddle your own steed. Rent a horse from **Ponderosa Stables/South Mountain Stables** (602-268-1261), 10215 S. Central Ave., and ride in South Mountain Park for 1–4 hours for $25–75 (open Mon.–Sat. 8–3, Sun. 9–3; they take a siesta during the day when the temps reach 100 degrees).

MOUNTAIN BIKING South Mountain Park has a reputation for its premier mountain bike routes. The **Desert Classic Trail** presents a signed route; it's the best for all levels of experience. The **Mormon** and **National** Trails, full of technical moments, demand experience and will give you a run for your money. **Sonoran Loop Competitive Track** in the White Tank Mountain Regional Park (located at the end of Olive Ave., 15 miles west of Peoria) has beginning, intermediate and advanced routes. **McDowell Competitive Track** in the McDowell Mountain Regional Park (located off of Fountain Hills Blvd., north of Shea and east of Scottsdale roads) has beginning, intermediate and advanced routes. **Dreamy Draw Park** in Phoenix Mountain Preserves and Papago Park in Tempe draw fat tires, too.

PARKS **Papago Park** (602-256-3220), Van Buren St. and Galvin Pkwy. You can't miss the curious ruddy mounds called Papago Buttes, for which the park is named. These geological formations, pocked with openings, have drawn many cultures, starting with the Hohokam Natives. The park has three urban fishing lagoons lined with palm trees that give an oasis-like effect. Also in the park, check out the pyramid tomb of Arizona's first governor, George Hunt. Follow the bike trail along the Hunt Bass Fishery (license required), a cottonwood-willow riparian area with a secluded feel. Arizona Department of Game and Fish stocks this waterway. Watch for giant blue herons here that wade in the shallows looking for aqueous life to munch.

🐾 **Steele Indian School Park** (602-495-0739), 300 E. Indian School Rd. One of the Valley's most aesthetic green spaces honors Arizona's Native peoples and open space. The design was inspired by the late-19th-century City Beautiful movement, which promoted the idea that city dwellers need open green space to develop civic pride and community. This park celebrates the state's Native American history with design elements that feature Indian concepts of life, earth, and the universe. The park has gardens, Native American poems etched into the concrete walkways, water features, a lake for urban fishing (license required), and a dog park.

SUNSET VISTAS Phoenicians know one of the best points to view a sunset sits at the top of **Dobbins Lookout** in South Mountain Park. Although not the tallest peak in the park/preserve, the lookout gives the best views of the Valley. The road up to the lookout—a winding, twisting route with tight hairpin turns—is an interesting drive in itself. Watch for road bikes on the two-lane road.

✷ Spas

Aji Spa (602-385-5759), Sheraton Wild Horse Pass Resort & Spa, 5594 W. Wild Horse Pass Blvd. Open daily 5:30 AM–8 PM. *Aji* means "sanctuary," and the Gila River Indian Community has created one in a way that invokes the spirit of their traditions and faith, as well as their values of serenity, tranquility, simplicity, freedom, and authenticity. These traditions show up tangibly. The flute music you often hear in spas actually fits here culturally. Round corners and curves, along with placement of things in groups of fours, represent the cyclical nature of life. Artwork of tribal legends appear in every room. Treatments showcase the language and philosophies of the spa's owners. For instance, the Wihosha facial includes Tashogith, the Purifying White Clay Facial, which uses the same white clay important to the Gila River Indian Community for centuries; Blue Coyote Wrap, the spa's signature treatment, personifies the Pima legend of the coyote and the bluebird. Each massage takes place on heated tables with warm towels wrapped around your feet and across your back. Treatments $70–270, personal training in fitness center $75 per hour.

Alvadora Spa (602-977-6400 or 800-672-6011), Royal Palms Spa and Resort, 5200 E. Camelback Rd. Open Sun.–Thu. 9–6, Fri. and Sat. 8 AM–8 PM. The Mediterranean cultures believed that each new dawn offered a special opportunity for rejuvenation. The ancients called it Alvadora. Mirroring the romance and beauty of the Old World in style and treatments, this spa features the herbs, flowers, oils, and minerals indigenous to the Mediterranean in a setting akin to it. The signature treatment includes a tailor-made massage with the resort's trademark sensuous scent, neroli, which smells like orange flowers and calms nervous energy and anxiety. Water treatments are big, too. In antechamber fashion, the steam room has a glass door that opens to the outdoor Jacuzzi. Sitting areas with fireplaces and fountains offer quiet interludes between treatments in which to relax and sip a cup of tea, elixir, or lemon water. These small spaces bring an intimacy to the 9,000-square-foot facility. Two spa suites ensure total privacy for multiday destination spa packages (call for more information). $135–200.

Arizona Biltmore Spa & Fitness Center (602-955-6600 or 800-950-0086), 2400 E. Missouri. Open daily 8 AM–8 PM. World class like the resort in which it's located, this spa has seen a lot of beautiful bodies over the years and excels in attention to details. The staff, gifted with "healing hands" and at least a decade, sometimes two, of experience, apply the purest and most natural spa products; you can't help but come away renewed, if only in attitude. The spa features products made from locally harvested ingredients used by Native Americans in many of its treatments (such as Chaparral Clay Wrap) and draws on ancient treatments from different cultures as well: Europe, medieval China, the Pacific Islands, and Native tribes of the Sonoran Desert. Facials using Intraceuticals Infusions therapies and products are available. Several treatments are specifically designed for teens and men. Hydrotherapies take place in two wet rooms. Your visit includes use of three spa pools, steam rooms, saunas, separate men's and women's locker rooms, power shower, and outdoor retreat areas. The fitness center has state-of-the-art cardiovascular and weight-training equipment and an aerobics room. Treatments $135–205, personal training $65 for 30 minutes. The salon has nail, hair, and waxing services.

Suddenly Slimmer Wellness Center & Day Spa (602-952-8446), 3313 E. Indian School Rd., Suite 8. Open Mon. and Sat. 9–5, Tue.–Fri. 9–7, Sun. 10–3. This family-run spa/wellness center got its start when the owner began her acupuncture practice. She always envisioned a complete wellness center as a service to the community, and her dream has come true. What started as a 1,800-square-foot facility has grown into an 8,000-square-foot space loaded with stained-glass windows, plants, healing music, and a friendly staff. One of the treatments the owner has used (the same used by Dr. Phil's wife, Robin McGraw) to help her clients detox turned out to be successful in helping them shed inches of fat as well—hence the name Suddenly Slimmer. The nondehydrating mineral wrap is a signature therapy. The spa menu has a thorough variety of modalities, and if you're looking for something different or unique, you'll probably find it here. For instance, the Body Bliss Massage incorporates the chakras with classic massage. Other treatments range from traditional relaxing massages to powerful healing therapies from all over the world and very cool facial therapies. Call for prices.

✷ Wilder Places

Echo Canyon Recreation Area (602-256-3220), Tatum and McDonald Dr. Open daily 5 am–11 pm. One of the premier hikes in the Valley, the Summit Trail on Camelback Mountain, is not an easy trail, but it will get you to a vantage point that shows you some upscale surrounding neighborhoods and beautiful Valley panoramas. A cluster of easier trails wind around the mountain park, too.

Phoenix Mountains Preserve (602-262-7901), 2701 E. Squaw Peak Dr. Open daily 5 AM–11 PM. This is where Phoenix outdoor mavens meet, from hoi polloi to world-class athletes. The fairer the day, the more folks come out to play. The large park actually has several trailheads in different locations; this one will take you to the Summit Trail on Piestawa Peak, as well as a handful more trails not as extreme. Also check out the 32nd St. (and Lincoln) access. The whole park has classic desert scenery at its best, with wildlife sightings (coyotes, owls, ringtails, and snakes) common occurrences. Drink plenty of water, wear sunscreen, and watch where you put your hands and feet. Free.

South Mountain Park (602-262-7693), 10919 S. Central Ave. Open daily 5 AM–11 PM. One of the largest parks in the nation, this park gets three million visitors a year—second to the Grand Canyon. The South Mountain system comprises three distinct ranges—Ma-Ha-Tauk to the north, Gila Mountain to the south, and Guadalupe Range in the east. In typical Sonora Desert fashion, the ranges run diagonally across the desert floor. Among them a network of multiuse trails travel into canyons, up slopes, and across ridgetops. Free.

AFTER A WET WINTER, THE SONORA DESERT'S MEXICAN GOLDPOPPIES BLOOM IN SOUTH MOUNTAIN PARK

NATIONAL PARKS AND MONUMENTS Agua Fria National Monument (Bureau of Land Management, 623-580-5500), located 40 miles north of Phoenix off I-17,at the Badger Sprints exit 256. This relatively new national monument will appeal to hikers who like an adventure. The park has no maintained trails. If you want to explore, you're on your own. You can canyoneer in the Agua Fria River or in several of its rugged side canyons. Mesa top hikes cross lava-cobbled grasslands where antelope, deer, and javelina hang out. It used to be where Native Peoples hung out—the monument contains the largest complex of archaeological history in central Arizona and parts are listed on the National Register of Historic Places. If you find traces of humanity, look but don't take. The courts in Arizona don't think twice about prosecuting pillagers to the fullest. Free.

Sonoran Desert National Monument (623-580-5500), located southwest of Phoenix. You can explore three wildernesses ensconced by this national monument—**North Maricopa Mountains Wilderness**, **South Maricopa Mountains Wilderness**, and **Table Top Wilderness**—all made up of quintessential Sonora Desert terrain. It's a surrealistic terrain: pristine, untrammeled, and extraordinarily remote for its close proximity to such a large city. Hikers exploring this area might find it's just them and the lizards. The landscape shows boulders the size of small rooms and large saguaro cactus forests. You might spot an Arizona jumping bean bush, kin to the bushes that produce the infamous Mexican jumping beans. Ironwood trees, big enough to produce significant shade, grow in the washes. Contact the Bureau of Land Management 623-580-5500 for information on hiking. Free.

✱ Lodging

HOTELS **The Clarendon Hotel Suites** (602-252-7363), 401 W. Clarendon Ave. This boutique hotel, situated in a neighborhood setting in uptown Phoenix, keeps you close to the city's hot spots. The Phoenix owner has kept the spirit of the 1970s-built hotel alive by creating a retro décor with a modern twist that turns out utterly hip, yet pleasing. Rooms display work from local artists and offer WiFi, free telephone calls (including international), newspaper, fitness room, business center, and covered parking—all complimentary. Rooms also have locally roasted coffee, loose-leaf teas, cable TV, triple 310-thread-count sheets on the same brand of bed you'll find at the Ritz Carlton and Sheraton, down pillows, L'Occitane amenities, and tons of character. Several nearby restaurants provide delivery service. The property has an 80-degree swimming pool surrounded by a cobalt-blue deck, whirlpool, and access to a rooftop fitness center with personal trainer available Mon.–Sat. The Rooftop Deck not only gives some superb views, it's (along with the pool) one of the hottest spots in the city to hang out. Actually the whole hotel has given itself over to the community. So the people who stay here are not necessarily travelers from afar, although you may bump into some interesting folk, such as the Who, Rolling Stones, New York Dolls, and news channel faces. The hotel's restaurant, **Gallo Café**, features local foods and serves breakfast all day. Free upgrades if they're available at check-in! $99–179.

RESORTS **Arizona Biltmore** (602-955-6600), 2400 E. Missouri. When it comes to Arizona's evolution into a world-class tourism destination, this is where it all started. Called Jewel of the Desert when it opened in 1929, the AAA Four Diamond Award winner (it's also garnered a pages-long list of other awards) has hosted royalty, every president from Herbert Hoover through George W., and an array of Hollywood stars and sports figures. With a location to die for, a design by Frank Lloyd Wright, and ever-improving service to meet guests' trendy needs, the Grande Dame of Arizona is still one grand resort and a pleasure to experience at least once. One thing that stays the same is the level of personal service. Any and every request gets fulfilled. After all, this is the Biltmore. The recent addition of Ocatilla separates you from the rest of the resort in a renovated building with rooms that have exquisite details—Old European elegance of pastel colors and rich ivory trim with a ribbon of gold, fine ceramic tilework depicting the signature Biltmore block design and granite in the bathroom, and historic resort photos for art. A ground-floor guest/business center has coffee, tea, and soft drinks all day, chef-selected light evening fare, complimentary beer and wine, an honor bar, dessert, and a continental breakfast in the morning. Ocatilla has a slew of amenities, including head, neck, and shoulder massages; therapeutic bath drawn for you at turndown; shoe shine; daily newspaper delivery; its own concierge; and a swimming pool, to name a few. The whole property has eight swimming pools; two PGA 18-hole championship golf courses; a spa and fitness center; seven night-lighted tennis courts; a lighted basketball court; lawn chess with life-size pieces set out at 9 AM; croquet and bocce ball; a business center; six restaurants, including Wright's; and Kids Korral and Kids Korral Playground. Large guest rooms have king or two queen beds, cable TV, in-room movies, WiFi access, mini bar, safe, spa amenities, and music suites featuring iPods and Bose SoundDock. Preferred Pet Pals provides pets up to 50 pounds with a welcome treat, room service pet menu, walking tours, and room to run. A $100 pet deposit is required, $50 of it refundable on good behavior. Classic room $295–875.

Crowne Plaza San Marcos Golf & Conference Resort (480-812-0900), 1 San Marcos Plaza, Chandler. Back in 1912 when it opened, this facility wasn't just the epitome of class and opulence in the east Valley, but also Arizona's first golf resort. Listed on the National Register of Historic Places and newly remodeled, it remains a beloved and classy hotel. Its 18-hole USGA golf course lures players back again and again; you'll also find a pool, a whirlpool, three restaurants, and a tennis court. Rooms are large, and each has a new comfy bed with eye mask, drape clip, earplugs, lavender spray, and night-lights to promote sleep; a patio; amenities that include weekday delivery of *USA Today* and the *Arizona Republic* on the weekends; an hour of free local calls; incoming faxes (first two pages); bottled water replenished every day; two hours' free time on the tennis court; and an overnight shine of one pair of shoes per night. High season $150–339, low season $71–179.

♥ **Royal Palms Resort and Spa** (602-840-3610 or 800-672-6011), 5200 E. Camelback Rd. This Mediterranean- inspired AAA Four Diamond resort gushes with solar colors and elegant Old World charm. The grounds are so intimately wrapped in mature landscaping, you'll forget you're in the city. In Mar. the heady scent of orange blossoms from property trees and surrounding groves saturates the air. Rooms are far removed from the generic hotel style and full of color and texture. An enclave of 70 rooms surround the intimate Montavista, a romantic Mediterranean-style courtyard with a colorful tiered garden, tranquil reflecting pools, and fireplaces for a taste of ultraluxury. Romance thrives here and is celebrated unabashedly. Romantically challenged guests can rely on the resort's director of romance, who deftly knows just what it takes to make yours an evening to remember. Impromptu weddings at the resort are a specialty. If making the shopping rounds, rather than romance, is your style, check out their director of shopping, Nancy Shina, who will have you whisked away in the chauffer-driven limo to the spots where you can shop till you drop via behind-the-scenes trunk shows, sales, and exclusive merchandise. The property has T. Cook's restaurant (see *Dining Out*), the Alvadora spa, a pool, and a fitness center. Each room and suite includes a private patio or balcony, custom furnishings, a 25-inch TV, and WiFi. $189–3,200. Daily $22 service fee covers general expenses such as gratuities for all but restaurant or room service, valet parking, daily newspaper, and business services.

🐾 ✎ ♿ ((ı)) ꝏ **Sheraton Wild Horse Pass Resort & Spa** (602-225-0100 or 888-218-8989), 5594 W. Wild Horse Pass Blvd., Phoenix. This resort literally lives up to its name: Native American owned and operated, it lies in the Gila River Indian Community, where wild horses still roam. Basically out in the middle of nowhere, but only a few minutes' drive to the Valley, the resort remains pristine. Couple that with the authentic renditions on the property of the Akimel O'odham and Maricopa Indian cultures, and the result is a unique upscale stay in a rugged and beautiful land. Along with typical Sheraton amenities come unusual tribal associations. The domed lobbies of the main resort, golf clubhouse, and the spa represent *olas kih*, the native roundhouse. Native American art (mostly from the Community) decks the walls in a variety of media, and murals color the ceilings. Outside, a convincing 2.5-mile-long replica of the Gila River, replete with wetlands, winds through the resort; a riverside pool has cascading waterfalls and bridges after the ancient (nearby) Casa Grande Ruins. A cultural concierge offers guests a wealth of authentic tribal information and tours of the property. Amenities include high-speed Internet, the Aji Spa, several dining venues including Kai restaurant (see *Dining Out*), Whirlwind Golf Club, Koli Equestrian Center, Love That Dog program for pets up to 40 pounds, two tennis courts, a riverside jogging and hiking trail, three pools with wheelchair access, Wild Horse Pass Casino (adjacent to the resort), and one very real cultural experience. $249–649; $129–349 off-season.

((ı)) **The Tempe Mission Palms Hotel** (480-894-1400), 60 E. Fifth Street, Tempe. The hotel's attractive plaza just off the main street where everything (Arizona State University, shopping, restaurants, and night spots) is happening gives the venue a landmark presence. It's a friendly place with great rooms at a reasonable price. You can't help feeling the elegance of the roof-top heated pool and tennis courts. The venue also has a fully equipped fitness center and business center. Newspaper delivery to your room Mon.–Sat. The hotel's Mission Grille serves a good meal and is known for its buffets. Ask for a remodeled room. $129–219.

🐾 ✎ ((ı)) ꝏ ♥ **Wigwam Golf Resort & Spa** (623-935-3811), 300 Wigwam Blvd., Litchfield Park. While some Arizona inns and resorts are veering away from classic Southwest styling, the Wigwam is relishing it, to the point it has kept the dignified details the bean counters in other resorts have done away with. The resort has even trademarked its slogan, Authentic Arizona, and celebrates its Santa Fe styling, adobe casitas, and cowboy culture. If that weren't enough, the resort's new owners, Jerry Colangelo and his two partners have renovations in mind that will open up the doors and bring guests outside so guests can enjoy the feel of Arizona. Were it not for the boll weevil, this classic resort might not exist. When the weevil decimated cotton crops in South Carolina, Goodyear Tire and Rubber Company looked elsewhere for a perfect spot to raise long-staple cotton. They found it in today's towns of Goodyear and Litchfield. The resort, built in 1918, originally provided a place for Goodyear executives to stay when they came to visit the cotton ranches. Soon family members joined them. On Thanksgiving Day 1929, the resort opened to the public. The town has grown up since then, and the resort resides in a quiet residential neighborhood, which adds peace and quiet to the down-home elegance of the property. Casitas are spread over 463 acres landscaped with gardens and manicured lawns. Rose bushes are big here (8,000 bushes and 800 different varieties), and are pruned and preened under the direction of Ed Fisher, the director of roses, who has worked at the resort for more than 40 years and doubles as the resort historian. Bellman, Michael Kelly, created several of the sculptures inside the resort. The property has three 18-hole championship golf courses, nine outdoor-lighted tennis courts, two swimming pools (one designed for kids with a water slide and the other for adults with a Jacuzzi) with fire pits, Red Door Spa, putting green, croquet, Ping-Pong, billiards, and bike rentals. Oversized rooms have private patio, southwestern décor with ceramic tile, 27-inch remote-control television with cable programming, in-room movies, video games, computer hookups, and enlarged bath with walk-in closet. Annual Signature Events open to the public include Easter on the Front Lawn, Old Fashioned Fourth of July, Patriot Day Breakfast (Sep.11), Oktoberfest, and Holiday Tree Lighting. Check out **Red's Steakhouse** for some excellent dry-aged steaks. GM George Liapas and his staff bring a level of class you don't see too often. Chef Michael Scott creates a number of tasty items to accompany your beef, such as Crab Cakes, Creamed Corn with Gruyère and Parmesan, excellent French Onion Soup, and imaginative desserts. Colangelo has gone on record that he plans to make this AAA Four Diamond venue even better. $159–349.

BED & BREAKFASTS AND INNS

🐾 **Maricopa Manor** (602-274-6302/800-292-6403), 15 W. Pasadena Ave. The first, and currently only, approved B&B establishment in the city of Phoenix continues in the same gracious style it started with when it opened its doors in 1989. This is not your stereotypical B&B that demands the guest's adoration with its uniqueness and history, nor does it demand participation in group breakfasts. The compound's three buildings, located a short light-rail ride to downtown Phoenix, sprawl ranch house style on a large lot full of fountains, pools, and mature landscaping. Each oversize suite has its own entrance, and breakfast (quiche, fruit, juice, and coffee or tea) comes in a picnic basket. Guests can eat in-room or outdoors on the premises. "This is an urban inn," said owner-innkeeper Jeff Vadheim. "Guests that never stay at a B&B stay here because of the privacy. You don't have to eat with strangers or be dressed. And there's no squeaky beds." There's covered parking, some units have fireplaces and/or kitchenettes, and guests may use pool and hot tub. $129–239 double occupancy, $25 per extra person, under age 13 free; small pets on occasion.

✱ Where to Eat

DINING OUT Barrio Café (602-636-0240), 2814 N. 16th St. Open Tue.–Fri. 11–10 (Fri. till 10:30), Sat. 5 PM–10:30 PM, Sun. for brunch 11–3 and dinner 3–9. You'll think you've stepped into the *barrio* at this neighborhood venue featuring southern Mexico cuisine interpreted by Chef Silvana Salcido Esparza. Chef Silvana culled back-road and village experiences during a two-year foray into Mexico and melded them with modern culinary expertise to create one of the hottest (as in *caliente*, not necessarily *picante*) Mexican menus in the Valley. Fresh concoctions include fish tacos, lobster quesadillas, and *chiles rellenos* stuffed with shrimp and scallops. Start your meal with guacamole made tableside and end it with goat's milk caramel–stuffed churros for dessert. Barrio serves about 200 top-shelf brands of nectar of the gods (a.k.a. tequila) and wine made from Baja California vineyards, coined a mini Napa Valley. On Sundays, they feature a special Domingo menu featuring eggs and crepes as well as live acoustic guitar. Entrées $11–24.

Durant's (602-264-5967), 2611 N. Central Ave. Open for lunch Mon.–Fri. 11–4; for dinner Mon.–Thu. 4–10, Fri. 4–11, Sat. 5–11, Sun. 4:30–10. Not much has changed here since founder Jack Durant opened the steakhouse in 1955, including Durant's motto: "Good friends, great steaks, and the best booze are the necessities of life." You still enter through the kitchen, power lunches reign, and the meals still contain some of the best beef around. Nor does the wait staff change often here; many have made a career serving at this bastion. Meals are full of moxie, and as hale and hearty as the motto. Lunch $11.95–29.95, dinner $21.95–49.95.

Fez on Central (602-287-8700), 3815 N. Central Ave. Open Mon.–Fri. 11 AM–midnight, Sat. and Sun. 8:30 AM–midnight. Cool, chic, and ultra-modern, Fez steadies itself with the old axiom that the best way to the heart is through the stomach. Fez's wonderful menu (traditional American favorites with Mediterranean or Moroccan twists created by award-winning chef-partner Tom Jetland) has won the hearts of people of all ages, cultures, and colors. The dining room is a melting pot of humanity. This is not the place for a quiet evening meal. Life happens here, and it's rollicking. But do come hungry, because portions are as generous as the food is good. The *kisras* (like a pizza) are popular items; lamb *kisra* looks beautiful and tastes excellent. The hamburgers, considered the best in town, are big and juicy. Signature dishes (with Fez in the name) include poached pears, nuts, and heady spices. Lunches are a local favorite. Check out the wine fusions: Pomegranate Cabernet and Apricot Chardonnay. Signature drinks make it a meeting place, too. Entrées $10.95–21.95.

Frank & Albert's (602-955-6600), 2400 E. Missouri Ave. (Arizona Biltmore Resort) Open daily 6 AM–10 PM. It's a fresh spot with fresh, organic and local food, taking after its namesake's (architect Frank Lloyd Wright and his student Albert Chase McArthur, both of whom built the Biltmore) way of thinking—"The philosophy is organic: Draw inspiration from the terrain, build on natural elements and engage the senses." And the restaurant does all that, especially engaging the senses, thanks to Chef Conner Favre's thoughtful flavor profiles. Breakfast features some elegant classics to unique breakfast pizzas with creative waffles and pancake dishes in between. Lunch has sumptuous wood fired pizzas and hamburgers on English muffins and a host of soups, salads, sandwiches. and Daily Blue Plate Specials. Dinner has a great grouper and fried chicken that just might be the best you ever tasted along with mac & cheese and cream corn. It's comfort food that's actually good for you. Breakfast $7–15, lunch $10–19, dinner $13–27.

Kai (602-225-0100), Sheraton Wild Horse Pass Resort & Spa, 5594 W. Wild Horse Pass Blvd., Phoenix. Open Tue.–Sat. 5:30–9. Kai serves up an authentic Native American culinary experience that features cuisine from the Pima and Maricopa tribes and locally farmed ingredients from the Gila River Indian Community. Seeds and spices make a strong statement here. It's a one-of-a-kind cuisine that united the past (Native American traditions) with the culinary future. At the time of this writing, Kai is the only AAA Five Diamond and Forbes Five Star venue in the city. Michelin trained executive chef Michael O'Dowd incorporates traditional Native plants such as beans, corn, and squash as well as Sonoran Desert ingredients like saguaro blossom syrup, cholla buds, and agave lacquer in his menu. If you taste influences from James Beard Award–winning chef Janos Wilder, it's because he's the consulting chef. The waiters take the time to explain every dish you order—listing ingredients and traditions attached to them. The staff's low-key, polite approach has incredible appeal—a perfect foil for the strong, attractive menu with iconoclastic ingredients. Chef O'Dowd, who compares the restaurant to Disneyland, has created a magic kingdom of food and art, pairing unusual ingredients (wild boar bacon, smoked eel, white Alba truffles, sandalwood powder) with the familiar seafood, poultry, and meats. Some foods appear in the most unusual ways—seeds, cotton candied, or foamed. Entrées $39–52.

♥ **Quiescence Restaurant** (602-276-6360), 6106 S. 32nd St., Phoenix. Open for dinner Tue.–Sat. at 5 PM. Talk about fresh—this farm-to-the-table venue has a major source right outside its door at Maya's Farm. Inside, the kitchen buzzes with neighborhood farmers who bring their produce to Chef Greg Laprad. Chef Greg not only loves this community purveying, but he's always on the lookout for backyard gardens as a source for his menu's ingredients. He sources most of his food from the state's farmers, herdsmen, and craftsmen. The result is one of the state's only daily-changing locavore menus and it features a handful of artisanal cheeses, house-cured meats, local produce, house-made pastas, and pastured meat or game. Chef Greg has racked up a list of awards for his young (under 30) age, including the recent honor of cooking a meal at the James Beard house; and he has the eye of *Food & Wine* magazine. The daily dessert menu has after-dinner cheeses, pastries, ice creams, and house digestifs and dessert wines. The Brick Oven Table lets you feast on a made-to-order multicourse fresh market dinner next to the outdoor brick oven for $85 per person. Sit indoors for the signature Farmer's Feast for $65 per person, or order off the menu (entrées $19–29).

Monti's La Casa Vieja (480-967-7594), 100 S. Mill Ave., Tempe. Open Sun.–Thu. 11–10, Fri. and Sat. 11 AM–11 PM. The birthplace of Carl Hayden, a prominent historical figure in the Valley, has harbored several restaurants since it was built in 1872.

DIAMONDS (AND STARS) ARE A RESORT'S BEST FRIENDS

Achieving Four or Five Diamond status is no little event. The awards, started by Arizona Automobile Association in 1977, recognizes the country's finest accommodations and restaurants for exceptional quality, outstanding customer service, and first-class amenities. The Five Diamond winners represent a fraction of 1 percent of about 60,000 properties throughout North America.

"Service is what distinguishes Four and Five Diamond facilities," says Jim Prueter, AAA vice president of travel. "Anticipating a guest's need before the guest expresses—or even realizes—that need, greeting the guest by name, quickly answering the phone—all these things make a visit more pleasurable and more memorable."

In 2010, only 21 restaurants in the United States (including Kai in Arizona) received the Forbes Five Star rating and 156 (including Talavera in Arizona), the Four Star rating. Arizona has three (out of 160 in the world) Four Star accommodations.

The house, which still has the original latilla mud ceiling in the oldest section, is listed on the National Register of Historic Places as well as historic registers for the state and the city of Tempe. The family's hacienda had a diner for weary travelers until the Depression. And there was a restaurant/bar during WWII. When Leonard Monti opened his steakhouse in 1956, naming it for the Haydens' homestead (known as La Casa Vieja, or "the old house"), who could have guessed that the place would rate among the favorites a half a century later with half a million people dining here each year? You get a good steak (seafood, chicken, or chops) at a good price at the Old House. This includes their infamous Roman bread circa 1970 (rosemary focaccia). Daily specials hover around $10. Entrées $11–24.

Mucho Gusto Taquería & Mexican Bistro (480-921-1850), 603 W. University Dr., Tempe. Open Mon.–Thu. 11–10, Fri. 11 AM–11 PM, Sat. 4–11. Not just a Mexican eatery, Mucho Gusto has style, and it racks up local awards consistently. The menu presents gourmet authentic Mexican dishes—several vegetarian—with a simple but flavorful wine list that features selections from Spain and South America. Favorites include *picaditas* (thick corn tortillas), gaucho steak, shrimp in a spicy amaretto garlic sauce, and *chiles rellenos* puebla style. The food is prepared with as much local organic products as possible. Lunch $6–8.50, dinner $10–16.

Pizzeria Bianco (602-258-8300), 623 E. Adams. Open Tue.–Sat. 5–10. The only thing better than a good, handmade pizza baked in a brick oven is one made by a James Beard Award recipient—a first for a pizza chef. Chris Bianco makes these wonderful pizzas, one at a time, which turn culinary heads all around the nation. He also uses the best local ingredients, serves house-made bread with the salad and antipasto, and uses handmade mozzarella. Be prepared to wait for a table (no reservations except for six or more). Pizzas $10–14.

♥ **T. Cook's** (602-840-3610), Royal Palms Spa and Resort, 5200 E. Camelback Rd. Open for breakfast daily 6:30 AM–10 AM; lunch Mon.–Sat. 11–2 (Sun. 10–2); dinner daily 5:30 PM–10 PM. Every meal is special and excellent, including breakfast (a favorite for area professionals) and lunch (where the wood fired pizza has house-made pepperoni). At dinnertime the dining room's Spanish colonial–style with rich earth tones and woody aroma from the wood oven becomes a savory scene. The venue is a local favorite for special occasions, thanks to director of romance Robert Vikery. Executive chef Lee Hillson takes Mediterranean traditions to new levels, where every ingredient has a reason and each taste is tantalizing. The charcuteries on the antipasti trays and mozzarella cheese are all made in-house. Produce is often local and always top quality; and the meat and fish some of the world's best, such as the Poulet Rouge chicken, George's Bank scallops, and 21-day dry-aged rib eye. Chef Lee's Carbonara with garlic cream, prosciutto, house-cured pancetta, and egg yolk came by way of his stint on *Iron Chef*. If you have the Chocolate Napoleon for dessert, it will haunt you pleasantly for days afterward. Entrées $24–32.

Wild Thaiger (602-241-8995), 2631 N. Central Ave. Open Mon.–Thu. 11–9, Fri. and Sat. 11–10, Sun. 5 PM–9 PM. Those who crave the perfumed flavors of lemongrass, galangal, ginger, and mint and the piquancy of peppers will feel as if they are sitting in Thailand here. Thai-born chef Olashawn Hasadinratana and sous-chef Mans Lekkla serve traditional dishes made with creative twists. The food is cooked fresh, and they will tailor Thai specialties the way you want them—from mild and delicate to flaming hot. Culinary wags agree that this small-scale venue serves some of the biggest and best flavors in town. Lunch entrées $6.95–9.95, dinner entrées $8.95–19.95.

EATING OUT ✿ **Carolina's** (602-252-1503), 1202 E. Mohave St. (between Buckeye and I-10). Stand in line with the rest of humanity that crowds here for some good old-fashioned Mexican slow food. From neighborhood boys to politicos, you'll find all strata of society here. What the eatery lacks in ambience (zero if you don't count the entertaining flow of personalities arriving and departing with shopping bags full of fresh-made food), it makes up in quality of food. Look at the north wall as you stand in line. It's covered with accolades and awards swooning about the food; especially the handmade tortillas for which Carolina repeatedly wins awards. You can bring your order to a large dining area to eat in or take out. $1.75–5.75.

Chestnut Lane (602-535-5439), 4225 E. Camelback Rd. Open Tue.–Fri. 7 AM–2 PM, Sat. 8–1. This tiny venue, looking as Old English as it gets, serves up some tasty, fresh foods. *Old-fashioned* is the oft-used description here, referring to the good, fresh foods. For breakfast, the granola is house-made, oatmeal is slow baked, eggs are poached, and ham means La Quercia prosciutto. Breads and pastries are homemade. The salad and sandwich ingredients are house-made roasts, fresh, often using local produce, and pedigreed. $5.25–15.

Cornish Pasty Company (480-894-6261), 960 W. University Dr. #103. Mon.–Thu. 11–10, Fri. and Sat. 11 AM–midnight, Sun. noon–10. You may feel like you've just stepped into a

Cornwallian mine tunnel when you enter the black-walled restaurant that's as narrow as a galley kitchen. The bar goes on forever, almost the length of the venue; but this is a college town, after all. Behind the bar and in the kitchen, things look no-frills industrial, just like the subterranean life of the miners who ate pasties fresh baked from home. And just like those miners, you'll get fresh-baked pasties. The menu's list of pasties goes on about as long as the bar with themes from just about every culture. The Oggie is traditional (steak, potato, onion, and rutabaga served with red wine gravy) and Shepherd's Pie (with ground lamb or beef) a favorite. The Strawberry Pavlova dessert may seem more at home at a high tea than at a restaurant emulating a tin mine, but it's consistent with miners' propensity to have the finest dainties at their disposal. Ditto for the impressive number of brews: 6 on draft and 21 in bottles ($2–5), most of which are imported. Pasties $6.50–9, desserts $5.

Fry Bread House (602-351-2345), 4140 N. 7th Ave. Open Mon.–Thu. 10–7, Fri. and Sat. 10–8. If you have heard of, or better yet tasted, a Navajo taco, you will know the deliciousness that awaits at this small eatery. Owner, Cecilia Miller, raised on the Tohono O'odham reservation, serves up frybread the way she learned it back home, with house-made ingredients. You can sample this traditional pillowy, chewy fried treat with a variety of toppings. For a meal, red or green chile is best. If you have room for dessert after finishing off one of these huge meals, try more frybread, topped with honey or chocolate and butter. Entrées $3.50–6.50.

The Gelato Spot (602-957-8040), 3164 E. Camelback Rd. Open Sun.–Thu. noon.–11,Fri.–Sat. noon–midnight). When you were in Rome, you did as the Romans did and imbibed in the sweet frozen confection once made of the snow gathered from the Alps. One taste of the silken substance offered here might put you back at the Spanish Steps. Some of the staff even speak a bit of Italiano. Dozens of gelato flavors made fresh every day line up in display cases. You can also order a cup of exotic tea. Next door is Hava Java, Arizona's most awarded coffeehouse since 1992, that attracts all sorts of interesting folks, from professional cyclists to movie stars to neighborhood java junkies. $2.50–4.50.

Kim's Dim Sum (602-224-5439), 3015 E. Thomas Rd. #7. Open daily 11–9. Takeout and delivery. You can't sit and dine here, but you can get some of the best take-out Chinese food in the Valley here. Owner and Canton-born Kim Yee started cooking his homeland food in Phoenix in 1995. When he helped supply hors d'oeuvres for a local hotel event, "Oooo," Kim described the comments he received about his cooking, "Everybody like it. I thought, *I have to open my own restaurant*." As word spread around, one hotel led to another, and Kim supplied his crème de la crème of the Valley Chinese hors d'oeuvres to some of the best resorts, including the Phoenician. Kim makes every one of his menu items fresh in his simple kitchen. He has a following of regulars that call and say, "You know what I want," and Kim has it ready and waiting. You won't find fried wonton fat with cream cheese and chunks of crabmeat like you do at Kim's. Nor will you taste pot stickers as good as his. The third item in his trinity of appetizers that made him famous, spring rolls, could be a meal in themselves. But don't stop with the appetizers. Everything at Kim's is good. Kim even makes his own sweet-and-sour sauce and customizes his soy sauce with spices. Perhaps the best part about all this wonderful food is Kim offers the meals in small and large portions so you can indulge and try several items. $4.25–$7.95.

La Grande Orange (602-840-7777), 4410 N. 40th St. Open Sun.–Thu. 6:30 AM–9 PM, Fri. and Sat. 6:30 AM–10 PM. From breakfast (think giant muffins, house-made English muffins, fresh fruit, whole-grain cereals, and fresh egg dishes) through lunch (distinctive salads and fresh sandwiches made on artisan bread), and from 4 PM when the pizza starts baking (make that specialty pizzas with toppings like oyster mushrooms, *prosciutto di San Danielle,* avocado, and caramelized fennel) until closing, this neighborhood venue does not stop. Commuters line up for coffee, mothers bring in their young tykes, professionals sip and forge deals, and regulars help themselves to upscale items lining shelves and coolers. This is where you want to come to people-watch; you'll see every culture to match the world music playing in the background. After 9 PM the Original Pizza Happy Hour gets started (cheese pizza $5, toppings $2–3 each). Breakfast $5.25–7.50, lunch $6.75–9.50, pizza $11–14-plus.

Luke's Italian Beef (602-264-4022), 1604 E. Indian School Rd. Open Mon.–Sat. 10–8; closed Sun. Travelers from cities with an Italian neighborhood know how important it is to know where to find the best Italian beef. Luke's shows its Windy City roots with memorabilia from Chicago and Italian beef good enough to hail straight from Taylor Street. Be sure to get peppers and a double dip of natural juice (and extra napkins) for the perfect nepenthe. Entrées $5.95–7.95.

Matt's Big Breakfast (602-254-1074), 801 N. 1st St. Open Tue.–Sun. 6:30–2:30. The orange, cream, and yellow colors of the '50s diner motif have become the darling breakfast joint of the city. You may catch Mayor Gordon on a Saturday morning here. Matt's menu is old-fashioned simple—free-range eggs raised humanely, fresh milk, and real butter are used, as well as organic ingredients whenever possible. You'll get a pitcher of warm real maple syrup to pour over handmade waffles and pancakes. The bacon is meaty grain-fed natural Iowa pork. The beef is all natural. You'll also get a glop of jam in a condiment bowl, rather than a peel-back packet, to put on thick slices of country toast. The meals don't stray from the comfort level when lunch rolls around at 11. Hamburgers (Angus beef) get fried in butter, tomato sauce has cream, and the chili has chunks of cheese melted in it. Breakfast $4–6.50, lunch $6–7.50

Tonto Bar & Grill (480-488-0698) 5736 E. Rancho Mañana Blvd., Cave Creek. Open daily 11 AM–9 PM. One of the mainstays of the Valley's food scene, Tonto has been around since the early 1990s. It recently went local—in the truest sense of the word: Chef Aaron has taken to foraging native foods. This back-to-the-land wildcrafting combined with cultivated native foods (from Native Seeds/SEARCH and area farmers) has turned his menu into an intriguing festival of flavors. Don't miss the Indian Harvest Torta appetizer. Far-from-rote salads have creative ingredients: Compressed Arugula & Spanish Manchego Cheese salad has candied Arizona pecans, sun-dried cherries, tart green apples & pistachio vinaigrette; Fresh Beet Salad with watercress; and Shaved Romaine with Fried Brie. Entrées feature all-natural meats and fish with interesting wild ingredients that Chef Aaron tames extraordinarily well. Entrées $17–32..

INSIDE TWO HIPPIES

Two Hippies Beach House (602-277-0399), 501 E. Camelback Rd. Open Mon.–Wed. 10:30–8 PM, Thu.–Sat. 10:30–10 PM, Sun. 10:30–7 PM. Peace—Love—Understanding—Health—Happiness. The spirit of the '60s is alive and well here, from the walls bedecked with posters, signs, and tchotchkes to all organic food (locally grown whenever possible). All this 1960s counterculture fits perfectly with today's credo. The food is basic Mexican (kind of) burritos and tacos and frozen lemonades—all made fresh. "We don't fry anything here and it's not loaded down with cheese," explained one of the two hippie-owners, Andy Goldstein. The other hippie, 80-plus-year-old Bob Altman, said the 400 sq. ft. joint (no pun intended) has been dubbed "the new Pink's (on La Brea) of Arizona." Goldstein, correctly reported, "People say they feel good after they eat here." This is especially true if they've partaken of a Magic Brownie (don't tell anyone where you got it) for dessert. Whether or not the brownies truly are magic, the two hippies do have the magic formula for a great restaurant—good-size portions of good food at a good price. Entrées $1.50–4.

✷ The Arts

ASU Art Museum (480-965-2787), Herberger College of Fine Arts at Arizona State University, southeast corner of 10th St. and Mill Ave., Tempe. Open Tue.–Sat. 11 AM–5 PM. An impressive and innovative art venue exhibiting more than 10,000 pieces of contemporary art, American ceramics, American and European prints, and southwestern art with a heavy emphasis on Latino artists. Free.

First Fridays Art Walks (602-256-7539). One of the most beloved events in the city teeters between a fine arts soiree and raw-edged social scene. Part of the Walk's success is the iconoclastic venues, which vary from distinguished galleries to homes and businesses that display exhibits; or you can just hang out in street parties to experience the art of living. On the first Friday of every month, thousands converge in the Roosevelt Historic District up to Indian School Road to view every medium and form of artistic expression. Artlink Phoenix provides shuttles through the evening for each First Friday, and many galleries cluster close enough to walk to.

Phoenix Art Museum (602-257-1880), 1625 N. Central Ave. Open, Wed.10–9, Thu.–Sat. 10–5, Sun. 12–5 (First Fri. evenings 6–10); closed

Mon., Tue., and major holidays. With a constant temperature of 72 degrees and 50 percent humidity to protect the art, it doesn't matter what time of the year you come to visit here; it's always cool. And so are the exhibits. The collection of more than 17,000 works of American, Asian, European, and Latin American artists includes modern, contemporary, and western American art. Classics include works by Monet, Picasso, Frida Kahlo, and Georgia O'Keeffe. Some innovative exhibits have you interacting in the ArtWorks Gallery, viewing historic interiors of the Thorne miniature rooms, and learning about great fashion designers and their work in the fashion design gallery; a sculpture garden gives you space to rest and relax. $10 adults, $8 seniors and full-time students with ID, $4 ages 6–17. Free admission Wed. 3–9.

SCULPTURE IN THE PHOENIX ART MUSEUM PLAZA

✷ Spectator Sports

Only 13 other cities in the nation have top professional teams in all four major sports. And Phoenix gets a double dose because of spring training.

Arizona Cardinals (602-379-0102 or 800-999-1402). One of the two charter members of the National Football League plays at their own stadium in Glendale.

Arizona Diamondbacks (602-462-6500), 401 E. Jefferson St. The 2001 World Champion baseball team began playing the majors in 1998.

Phoenix Suns (602-379-7867). Basketball games at U.S. Airways Center in Phoenix often sell out.

Mercury Basketball (602-252-9622). The WNBA team also plays at U.S. Airways Center.

Coyotes Hockey (480-563-7825). The NHL team plays at the Glendale Arena.

SPRING TRAINING Cactus League Spring Training games start in Mar. Fourteen major-league baseball teams make Arizona their home in spring. The 11 teams that play in the Greater Phoenix area are spread throughout the Valley at the following locations. You can purchase tickets direct from the stadium or call Ticketmaster (480-784-4444).

Chicago Cubs, Hohokam Park (480-964-4467), 1235 N. Center St., Mesa. **Cleveland Indians** (623-882-7525), Goodyear Ballpark, 1933 S. Ballpark Way, Goodyear, Kansas City **Royals** and **Texas Rangers**, Surprise Stadium (623-594-5600), 15960 N. Bullard Ave., Surprise. **Los Angeles Angels of Anaheim**, Tempe Diablo Stadium (480-350-5205), 2200 W. Alameda Dr., Tempe. **Los Angeles Dodgers**, Glendale, Camelback Ranch (623-930-2000), 10710 W. Camelback Rd.,

Glendale. **Milwaukee Brewers**, Maryvale Baseball Park (623-245-5500), 3600 N. 51st Ave. **Oakland Athletics**, Phoenix Municipal Stadium (602-392-0074), 5999 E. Van Buren. **San Diego Padres** and **Seattle Mariners**, Peoria Sports Complex (623-878-4337), 16101 N. 83rd Ave., Peoria. **San Francisco Giants**, Scottsdale Stadium (480-990-7972), 7408 E. Osborn Rd., Scottsdale.

✷ Selective Shopping

You'll find a collection of **antiques and collectible shops** on 7th Ave. south of Camelback and north of McDowell. Also head to the city of Glendale's historic district.

🐾 **Biltmore Fashion Park** (602-955-8400), 2502 E. Camelback Rd. Open Mon.–Sat. 10–6, Sun. noon–6. Exclusive, chic, and the place to see and be seen, this open-air pet-friendly mall has some exquisite appointments, from the floral landscaping in its courtyard setting to the hacienda fountains. Shopping leans toward the lap of luxury here; shops like Saks Fifth Avenue, Ralph Lauren, Gucci, Cole-Haan, and Godiva Chocolatier have merchandise you won't find elsewhere. There are also several upscale restaurants.

COFCO Chinese Cultural Center (602-244-8600), 668 N. 44th St. Unless you've studied the Chinese influence in Arizona, you would never know that this culture was once represented in just about every community in the state. Most cities razed their Chinatowns. This cultural center has the most advanced facilities in the Americas featuring Chinese architecture. The property has Chinese gardens, replicas of ancient Chinese pagodas and statues, retail stores featuring Oriental merchandise, restaurants, and the incredibly intriguing **99 Ranch Market**. If you have a hankering for any type of Asian food, you'll find it here, from durian to salted duck eggs; fresh crabs to live eels; lime leaf to bunches of basil. It's a fascinating market to peruse.

Phoenix Public Market (www.phoenixpublicmarket.com), 721 N. Central. Open Wed. 4–8, Sat. 8 AM–1 PM). Often farmers' markets become a happening. This one gives you a look at the best of Arizona produce, products, and talents in a historic neighborhood. Pick up something to eat—from pulled beef to seafood gumbo or a pastry—or a piece of art. Of course, you can always get some fresh produce, too. During the week, check out the store of the same name (Tue.–Fri. 11–8, Sat. 8 AM–8 PM). The community still gathers here for local produce and food items and special events, like wine tastings, Edible Film Festivals, and cooking demonstrations.

✷ Special Events

January: P**. F. Chang's Rock 'n' Roll Arizona Marathon and Half Marathon** (800-311-1255). Bands, cheer squads, prizes, and a finish-line party makes this Boston qualifier a big bash. **Tostitos Fiesta Bowl** (480-350-0911) presents the champion of the Big 12 Conference and an at large BCS team.

February: **Hoop Dance Festival** (602-252-8848) at the Heard Museum presents top Native hoop dancers from North America who compete for cash prizes and the international title.

March: **Art Detour** (602-256-7539) is a yearly art happening in which artists open their studios and galleries showcase top local artists. **Heard Museum Guild Indian Fair and Market** (602-252-8848) presents museum-quality arts and crafts made by Native American artists. **Tres Rios Nature Festival** (623-204-2130) is a two-day

THE SUPERSTITION MOUNTAINS RISE OUTSIDE PHOENIX

outdoor event focusing on the rich natural and cultural diversity of the Gila River.

April: **Arizona Asian Festival** (www.aaaa-az.org). Asian cultures are celebrated here in dance, music, and food. Maricopa County Fair (602-252-0717) features food, games, exhibits, livestock, and a carnival.

July: **Fabulous Phoenix Fourth** (602-262-7176), Steele Indian School Park.

October: **Arizona State Fair** (602-252-6771) features food, games, exhibits, livestock, entertainment, and a carnival. **Cowboy Artists of America Sale and Exhibition** (602-307-2007) is a Phoenix Art Museum fundraiser featuring new works by Cowboy Artists of America members.

November: **Arizona Winegrowers Festival at the Farm** (602-276-6360). Arizona's winegrowers gather at the premier foodies spot in the Valley, **The Farm at South Mountain**, to elucidate about and promote Arizona wines. **ZooLights** (602-273-1341) shows you the Phoenix Zoo decked out in miniature lights for night viewing. **Las Noches de las Luminarias** (480-941-1225). Stroll the Desert Botanical Gardens by the light of thousands of hand-lit luminaries with entertainment, food, wine, and hot beverages.

December: **Christmas Mariachi Festival** (480-558-1122) presents the greatest mariachis in the world. **Fiesta Bowl Parade** (480-350-0900). Early comers will get grandstand seating, and thousands line up standing-room-only to see floats, helium balloons, marching bands, and equestrian units. The two-mile route starts on Central Avenue just south of Bethany Home Rd. and travels south to Camelback Road, where it zigzags east to 7th St. and then south on 7th St. to Campbell.

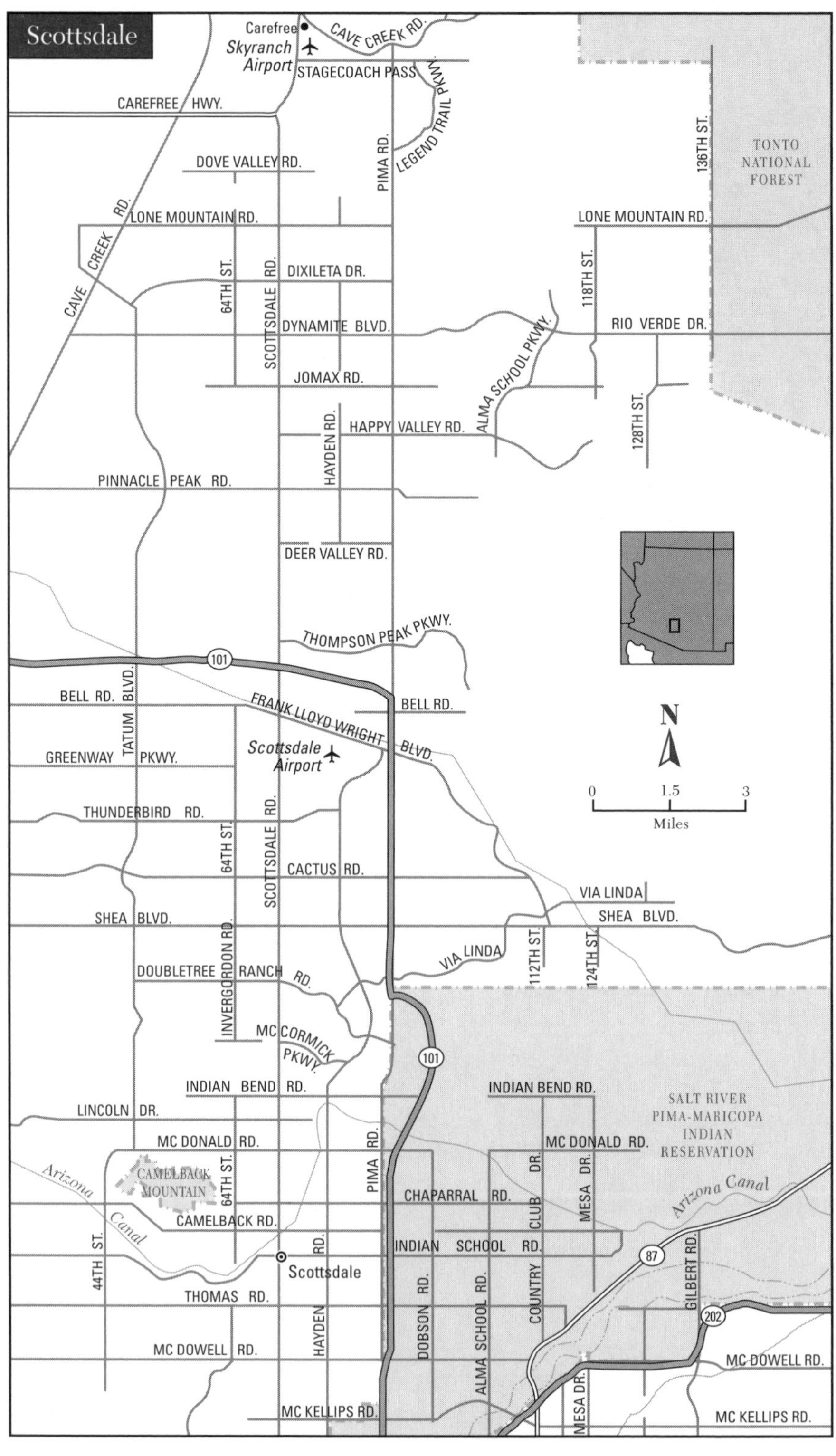
Scottsdale
Carefree
Skyranch Airport
CAVE CREEK RD.
STAGECOACH PASS
LEGEND TRAIL PKWY.
CAREFREE HWY.
DOVE VALLEY RD.
PIMA RD.
TONTO NATIONAL FOREST
136TH ST.
LONE MOUNTAIN RD.
LONE MOUNTAIN RD.
CAVE CREEK RD.
64TH ST.
SCOTTSDALE RD.
DIXILETA DR.
118TH ST.
DYNAMITE BLVD.
RIO VERDE DR.
ALMA SCHOOL PKWY.
JOMAX RD.
128TH ST.
HAYDEN RD.
HAPPY VALLEY RD.
PINNACLE PEAK RD.
DEER VALLEY RD.
THOMPSON PEAK PKWY.
101
BELL RD.
TATUM BLVD.
BELL RD.
FRANK LLOYD WRIGHT BLVD.
N
Scottsdale Airport
GREENWAY PKWY.
0
1.5
3
Miles
THUNDERBIRD RD.
64TH ST.
SCOTTSDALE RD.
CACTUS RD.
VIA LINDA
SHEA BLVD.
SHEA BLVD.
INVERGORDON RD.
VIA LINDA
112TH ST.
124TH ST.
DOUBLETREE RANCH RD.
MC CORMICK PKWY.
101
INDIAN BEND RD.
INDIAN BEND RD.
SALT RIVER PIMA-MARICOPA INDIAN RESERVATION
LINCOLN DR.
MC DONALD RD.
MC DONALD RD.
PIMA RD.
CAMELBACK MOUNTAIN
64TH ST.
Arizona Canal
CHAPARRAL RD.
CLUB DR.
MESA DR.
Arizona Canal
CAMELBACK RD.
44TH ST.
INDIAN SCHOOL RD.
87
GILBERT RD.
Scottsdale
THOMAS RD.
DOBSON RD.
ALMA SCHOOL RD.
COUNTRY CLUB DR.
202
HAYDEN RD.
MC DOWELL RD.
MC DOWELL RD.
MESA DR.
MC KELLIPS RD.
MC KELLIPS RD.

SCOTTSDALE

Some cities know their calling. Scottsdale, founded in the late 1890s by Rhode Island banker Albert Utley—whose goal was to create a Utopian community—has fulfilled it in a world-class way. Scottsdale's resort scene indulges the senses with everything from cutting-edge spas to championship golf courses; sumptuous lodging to fine dining. Its urban élan came with a growth spurt that redefined its downtown. Once a strictly tourist haunt specializing in cowboy art and Native American crafts that rolled up its sidewalks after sunset and flirted with ghost-town status in the depths of summer, Scottsdale's downtown has become an ever-more-active place to live, work, and play. *Play* is the operative word here. You should never have to leave Utopia wanting.

Not one to forget its roots, Scottsdale blends its urban sizzle with the Old West. Amid new trends and latest styles in food, art, and architecture, cowboy hats still pop up, equestrian paths memorialize the town's enduring equine love affair, and western art makes a big statement in the gallery scene. It's still one of the best places to procure museum-quality Native American arts and crafts.

Whether your leanings are contemporary or cowboy, Scottsdale knows you still have to eat. The town has restaurants that rub shoulders with the best in the world, run by chefs who continually appear in the best-new-chef pages of *Food & Wine* magazine, receive James Beard Foundation Awards of Excellence, or earn AAA diamonds.

Finally, for those of you who think the best part of the day begins when the sun sets, the best nightlife in the Valley happens at its world-famous nightclubs, Axis/Radius and E4, which draw A-listers. Kazimierz's World Wine Bar, owned by self-titled "Wino" (and restaurateur) Peter Kasperski, has become an archetype for wine bars in other cities. But remember, what's said and done sub vino does not always remain sub rosa, even in a Utopia like Scottsdale.

GUIDANCE **Scottsdale Convention and Visitors Bureau** (480-421-1004 or 800-782-1117), 4343 N. Scottsdale Rd., Ste. 170, has in-depth information for the types of experiences you want to tailor your visit around: shopping, golf, spas, art, and food. Call **McDowell Mountain Regional Park** (480-471-0173). **Pinnacle Peak Park** (480-312-0990), 26802 N. 102nd Way for information on trail use. The **Arizona State Land Department** (602-364-2753) provides permits for entering state lands.

GETTING THERE *By car:* From Phoenix, take Camelback Rd. east to downtown Scottsdale. From Loop 202, exit at Scottsdale Rd. and go north. The 101 Freeway takes you to the far north and eastern edges of town. *By air:* **Phoenix Sky Harbor International Airport** (602-273-3300), 3400 E. Sky Harbor Blvd., Phoenix, is about 15 minutes from downtown. If you have your own craft, fly in to the **Scottsdale Airport** (480-312-2321), 15000 N. Airport Dr.

GETTING AROUND **Scottsdale Trolley** (480-421-1004) runs every 10 minutes 11 AM–9 PM (free), hitting all the high spots from Scottsdale Fashion Square south to downtown and beyond. For a map, log onto www.scottsdaletrolley.com. Roam the streets on a rented Segway from **ContempoRide**. (www.contemporidesegway.com). The company offers hourly, half and full-day, weekend, weekly and even monthly rentals. $75–100. Check out **Ecocab's** human-powered pedal cabs (602-435-5284) for $75 per spin.

WHEN TO COME Peak season lasts from Jan. to late Apr.; rates are high, rooms fill, and streets buzz with activity. Summertime, from June to late Aug., lures visitors with restaurant specials and the best deals in accommodations. You can get a room at the toniest resorts for budget prices. The locals know this, too, so plan ahead even in summer.

MEDICAL EMERGENCY Dial 911, or **Mayo Clinic Hospital** (480-301-8000), 13400 E. Shea Blvd.

✷ To Do

BIKING **ABC/Desert Biking Adventures** (602-320-4602), 7119 E. Shea Blvd., Suite 109-247, offers mountain and cross-country downhill adventures. They provide support vehicle, equipment, and water. Bike Haus (480-994-4287), located downtown at 7025 E. 5th Ave., rents mountain and road bikes by the half ($25) and full ($35) day, providing helmet, lock, and water bottle.

DOG PARKS 🐾 **Chaparral Park** (480-312-2331), 5401 N. Hayden Rd. Open dawn–9 PM. The largest dog park in the city has drinking fountains and seating areas. It's divided for passive and active dogs.

🐾 **Horizon Park** (480-312-2331), 15444 N. 100th St. Open dawn–dusk. Two-thirds of an acre with a 10- by 20-foot shade ramada and a people/dog drinking fountain. When the canines kick up too much dust, just push a button and the dust-control feature waters the area to settle the dirt.

GAMING The Salt River, Pima, and Maricopa Indian Community has two casinos in Scottsdale. **Casino Arizona** (480-850-7777), 524 N. 92nd St., has around 1,026 slot machines, a poker room, $100,000 live-play keno, and blackjack. Its world-class show lounge presents top acts; there are five restaurants, including fine dining at the **Cholla**, which has exceptionally good food in large portions. **Casino Arizona II** (480-850-7777), 9700 E. Indian Bend Rd., has over 637 slot machines known to pay big, a poker room, and 42 blackjack tables. Locals crowd for specials served at its **Wandering Horse Bar and Café**.

© Scottsdale Convention & Tourist Bureau

GOLF Golf transcends game status here to a way of life. Some of the best courses in the world splay across Scottsdale soil, and the greens mecca attracts all things golf from every corner of the world: pro players, schools, equipment manufacturers, and legendary tournaments. Not all the best courses will set off alarms on your credit card, especially if you follow the good advice of Harry Vardon: "Don't play too much golf. Two rounds a day are plenty."

Camelback Golf Club (480-596-7050/800-242-2631), 7847 N. Mockingbird Lane. Playing one of the two club's courses can turn into an adventure. The **Club Course**, designed by Jack Snyder in 1978, is typical American links-style laid out in a landscaped natural wash. The course's 7,014-yard, par-72 course gives no little challenge to the best of golfers, with its secluded sand traps, gently rolling terrain, and abundance of water holes; not to mention great mountain panoramas bold enough to distract the most disciplined pro. One of the state's best water holes lies at the **Resort Course's** ninth hole. The Arthur Hills course is known for its water holes and strategic layout. Tall trees, subtle topography, and interesting bunkering make an interesting game. More than 20 PGA golf professionals will help you get through all the challenges. If that's not enough, you can sign up for the John Jacobs Practical Golf School (one of the most innovative in the country) located on the grounds. Other services include club and shoe rentals, driving range, putting greens and chipping areas, club cleaning, golf shop, and grill. $79–189.

Grayhawk (480-502-1800), 8620 E. Thompson Peak. Listed as one of the top 100 courses to play in the U.S., Grayhawk stands out among the 200 courses in the Valley. It has two courses—Talon and Raptor. Both are 18 holes desert courses with a par-72. **Talon**, designed by U.S. Open and PGA Champion David Graham and architect Gary Panks, melds with an exciting landscape full of par-3s to give you drama, challenge, and views—the McDowell Mountains the north and City of Phoenix to the south. The 7,001-yard plays well enough to have gotten listed in *Golf Magazine*'s Top 10 You Can Play in U.S. The **Raptor Course**, designed by Tom Fazio, plays with your pluck. Take a risk, get a reward. Maybe. See how close you come to its par-72, 7,108 yards from the back tees. Just remember to double-check your first impressions of shots. Greens fees include golf cart, practice balls, yardage card, pin placement sheet, bag tag. $180–225.

Kierland Golf Club (480-922-9283), 6902 E. Greenway Pkwy. Golf has always been big in the Kierland family, and the club goes out of its way to equip golfers with great greens and the equipment to tackle this course. First, the course (rated one of the most women-friendly in the nation) plays with adventure. Designer Scott Miller put 300 bunkers, lakes, washes, and classic desert vegetation between you and 27 holes on the Audubon-friendly rolling greens. Next, instructors high on the golf-industry-lauded ladder present a fitness training system guaranteed to increase driving distance while improving overall fitness and stamina. Even weekend warriors have no more excuses. Husband and wife teaching team Mike and Sandy LaBauve of LaBauve Golf Academy are available for instruction. The club's exclusive FORE-MAX Training Systems, developed by fitness director Steve Heller melds traditional golf tips, on-course play, fitness, training, nutrition, and custom club fitting. For your ambulatory comfort, you can zoom around the course on a Segway or an air-conditioned golf cart. Finally, you can rest under 83-foot-long Callaway Cool Shade canopies after chasing Callaway Golf Big Bertha Blue range balls driven by the latest Callaway woods and irons. One the more esoteric side, Kierland indulges in a couple Scottish traditions, including their Bagpipes at Sunset Series, which features bagpipes playing at the signature ninth hole, and Scottish Gold Experience (wear a kilt, sip Johnny Walker scotch, and enjoy a hand-rolled cigar). $69–189.

Legend Trail Golf Club (480-488-7434), 9462 Legendary Lane. One of the North Scottsdale beauties (nearby views include Pinnacle Peak and the McDowell Mountains; to the south is Camelback and Mummy mountains, then the City of Phoenix beyond) is listed among the best in the nation. The championship 18-hole course will give you a run for your money, inasmuch as the large undulating greens are a challenge to read. Rees Jones designed the par-72 course to follow the lay of the land, and so it winds through stands of paloverde trees and saguaro cacti. Hole names like Water Chant, Good Medicine, and Stones That Speak might evoke some good juju. The course doesn't really start going until its signature hole no. 7, where a cascade tumbles into a pond hidden from the tee box. From there, the variety continues. Four sets of tees match your skill level. Golf Shop (rated in the top 100 of a Zagat survey), restaurant, and home of Golf Digest Schools. $75–190.

Sanctuary Golf Course (480-502-8200), 10690 E. Sheena Dr. Hard to believe environmentalists and golfers can shake hands, but this one did it. Designer Randy Heckenkemper made golf history by transforming the Bureau of Reclamation's storm water retention area into one hot par-71 golf course with a range of 4,096–6,624 feet. And he did it by following the environmental guidelines established by the staid Audubon International Institute. The Audubon Signature Status Golf Course has to manage its effluent usage, pest control, water quality, and storm-runoff storage to Audubon's standards. Heckenkemper remained true to the lay of the land of the sexy rolling desert foothills of the McDowell Mts.; and vegetation and washes often interlope on your area of play. Wildlife makes a big show here, especially coyotes, roadrunners, jackrabbits, and quail; sometimes mule deer, javelina, or bobcat. The end product is a nature sanctuary that requires intense accuracy from its players. Fees include golf cart. $59–129.

Talking Stick (480-860-2221), 9998 E. Indian Bend Rd. Ben Crenshaw and Bill Coore designed two completely different, but user-friendly, golf courses for the Salt River Pima and Maricopa Indian tribes. Worlds away from target golf so predominant in the area, these courses present traditional style play for golf purists. The 7,133-yard **North Course** has a par-70 rating; chip-and-run is a valuable tool here. Views of Camelback Mountain, the McDowell Mountains, and Pinnacle Peak surround the slightly crowned course that has no trees. The golf course lands in top state and national ratings by various golf venues. The **South Course** is 6,833 yards with a par-71 and more straightforward regarding plays. Parkland-style and full of cottonwoods and water, the course has slight elevation changes, fingered bunkers, and tiered landscaping. Fees include carts; soft spikes only allowed. $60–175.

Tournament Players Club of Scottsdale Stadium Course (480-585-4334 or 888-400-4001), 7575 E. Princess Dr. This over-the-top 18-hole course rests like an emerald in a gold-plated mountain setting. Known for numerous history-making moments by the world's greatest players during the PGA Tour's FBR Open (formerly Phoenix Open), the course is rife with class standards and excellence. This is where Tiger Woods made his famous hole-in-one on no. 16. Tom Weiskopf and Jay Morrish created a course that blends challenge with playability. Additions of an award-winning golf shop, practice facilities, full-service men's and women's locker room facilities, and ESPN Golf School keep this course on the national lists. If you're a guest at the Fairmont Scottsdale, the Golf Concierge program (an extra service which attends to all the details of itineraries, arranging locker facilities, lessons, rental, coordinating transportation for tee times, and supplying aromatherapy iced towels, lip balm, sunscreen, and water) gives golfers more reason to become one with this class course. Fees include greens and cart fees, practice balls, yardage book, bag tag. Dress code: No denim or gym shorts; no T-shirts, halter tops, or bathing suits. $77–287.

Troon North Golf Club (480-585-7700), 10320 E. Dynamite Blvd. Described as "the best course ever built," with a price tag and list of awards to prove it, the immaculate greens winds through natural ravines and hillsides in the Sonora Desert. Course renovations in 2007 by designers Tom Weiskopf created the "ultimate golf experience." You can now play your game exactly as the land dictates. Compelling panoramas, slinky slopes, and desert vegetation are the natural features this club's two championship courses (**The Monument** and **The Pinnacle**) dwell upon. The 18th hole of The Pinnacle gives golfers the illusion of teeing off directly into the area's landmark Pinnacle Peak mountainside. Greens fees include golf car, bag tag, yardage book, and divot tool and practice balls. $140–295 (residents get up to 60% discount).

We-Ko-Pa Golf Club (480-836-9000), 18200 E. Toh Vee Cir., Fountain Hills. It didn't take long for the **Cholla** course, located on land owned by the Fort McDowell Yavapai Nation, to achieve global status. Two days after it opened in 2001 it was named one of the best 10 new courses in the world. Things have not changed here. With no homes, no roads, and plenty of desert vegetation that gives some holes an isolated feeling, this course is about you, nature, and the game of golf. Mountain scenery rubs shoulders with challenges on this pristine course, from bunkers to double-doglegs. Four sets of tees give you a choice of yardages that range from 5,289 to 7,225 with a par-72. Regular back tees play to 6,644 yards. The **Saguaro** course was still in planning at the time of publication. Designers Bill Coore and Ben Crenshaw plan a course that will provoke golfers to play different shots and be open to thinking out new challenges. $75–175.

HIKING Check out the **Scenic Trail** in McDowell Mountain Park and the **Pinnacle Peak Trail** in its namesake park, both in North Scottsdale. Hiking here during spring through fall requires drinking much more water (fortified with electrolyte mix) than you anticipate; plan on a quart every hour or two, depending on the temperature. Make sure your hike ends by 10 on summer mornings, and wear sunscreen and a hat.

HORSE SHOWS Horse events happen all year long in Scottsdale, but the big ones—the **Arizona Sun Circuit Quarter Horse Show** and the **Scottsdale Arabian Horse Show**—take place around Jan. and Feb., featuring a variety of world-championship performance competitions and traditional rodeo events. Glamour still prevails at the Arabian horse show. While more than 2,000 spirited Arabian horses from around the world compete with each other in two big arenas, movie stars, over 400 commercial exhibitors, food vendors, and show-goers garbed in several-thousand-dollar outfits grab attention on the rest of the grounds. Most all of the events take place at WestWorld (480-312-6802), 16601 N. Pima Rd.

HOT-AIR BALLOONING **Hot Air Expeditions** (480-502-6999), 2243 E. Rose Garden Loop. takes off every day at dawn with a champagne breakfast. Dusk flights are available during cooler months. Vincent Guerithault, chef-owner of Vincent Guerithault on Camelback, creates the gourmet menu. $183 adults, $133 ages 5–12.

MUSIC **Sunday A'Fair** (480-994-2787), Scottsdale Civic Center Mall, Jan–Apr. The Sunday afternoon arts festival has music, arts and crafts, and activities for kids. It's a favorite with the locals, who bring blankets and laze on the grass. Free.

RAILROAD **McCormick-Stillman Railroad Park** (480-312-2312), 7301 E. Indian Bend Rd. Open 10 AM (9 AM in summer); call for closing times. This small-scale reproduction of the Century Narrow Gauge Railway equipment caught the eye of Walt Disney, who offered to buy it for one of his theme parks. You can ride the train along its mile-long tracks, peruse the museum, and then stop by the general store for hot dogs and ice cream. Kids (of all ages) can head for the playground or spin on the park's carousel. Rides cost $1 per person; they're free for those under 3 (with a paying adult).

ROCK CLIMBING **Pinnacle Peak** (see *Wilder Places*) has a number of routes for experienced climbers, including the 200-foot granite peak and Cactus Flower and Y-Crack Boulder. **AZ on the Rocks** (480-502-9777), 164447 N. 91st St. Suite 105. Open Mon., Wed., and Fri. 3–10, Tue. and Thu: 3–7 (members till 10), Sat. and Sun. 9–7. Whether you're a competitive climber or a Tyrol, your wall awaits in this air-conditioned warehouse-size climbing gym. Acrophobics can take a yoga class while their Spiderperson climbs. $15 for day pass; membership and family rates available.

✷ Spas

Agave, The Arizona Spa (480-624-1500), Westin Kierland Resort & Spa, 6902 E. Greenway Pkwy. Open daily 6 AM–8 PM. Indigenous plants and oils are big here, especially the namesake agave plant, which is used in spa products, treatments, and even the complimentary energy drink. The signature skin treatment is Agave Enchantment; Tui' Na is the spa's signature massage treatment, which establishes harmonious Qi (energy) and blood flow. Wellness treatments give you an alternative look at harmony based on health rather than getting zoned. The Agave Signature Oil custom-blends agave with hazelnut, lemon, and lime oils for some ultrasmooth skin and shiny tresses. Facials can contain oxygen infusions and enzymes. The spa treatments include some interesting work with basalt (True La-Stone Therapy) gemstones (Rollersage—created at Agave and now featured in all Westin spas) and rainsticks (Rain Massage); Eastern therapies such as *tui' na* and acupuncture, wraps and hypnotherapy; and spa journeys featuring several treatments lasting 2–6 hours. The wet room has a sun ceiling that gets a dousing of light so enticing guests often pull up a chair and relax to the sound of water features. Treatments (Never-Too-Soon Teen Facial and Razzle-Dazzle Manicure/Pedicure) cater to the whole family. Facilities include 20 treatment rooms, a full-service beauty salon, a movement studio, a weight-training/cardio studio, and men's and ladies' locker rooms (each with whirlpool, sauna, and steam room). Body treatments and massages $180–270, facials $140–210 training sessions $100 and up.

Bliss Spa (480-970-2100), 7277 E. Camelback Rd. One of the Valley's newest spas correctly describes itself as a "massage and facial mecca" with "a fun, no-attitude atmosphere." Since this one of eight Bliss spas around the world has opened, Scottsdale's spaland will never be the same. No singing whales or Indian flute music here. It's jazz, blues, and '60s retro. Your therapist might have a tattoo or a diamond stud festooning his/her body. And the Brownie Buffet in the spa lounge—whatever happened to soothing teas and thrice-filtered water? Remember, we're talking bliss here. Anything less, as their slogan goes, is stress. The signature facial is the Triple Oxygen Treatment that has such a following, you'll hear guests gush all over the hotel about how they use the product three to five times a week at home. The "peeling groovy facial" is the most popular antiaging quick-fix facial. But what do these massage therapists know about aging? They're all young, energetic, and attitude-free. Those high-energy hands do such a masterful job at melting stress knots, you may never want to go anywhere else for a deep-tissue treatment, no matter how many times you've been around the block. "Herbies" feature essential oil wraps (the Hangover Herbie is self-descriptive). The spa menu states it has "super effective services" and the service backs the boast whether you get a massage, body treatment, slimming treatment, peel, wax, and so on. If you're looking for a spa experience that only coddles and cuddles the psyche, it's best you head for the call of the whales. Bliss Spa gives results, and a lot of fun on the side. $115–225.

Centre for Well-Being (480-941-8200 or 800-843-2392), The Phoenician Resort, 6000 E. Camelback Rd. Open daily 7 AM–7 PM. One of the world's most innovative spas, and very high on must-experience lists, the Centre for Well-Being presents a whole cadre of treatments from traditional Swedish massage to cutting-edge energy therapies. The treatment menu is pages long (more than 75 treatments). Experienced therapists with a propensity to nurture create an extraordinary spa experience. This was one of the first spas in the country to offer optimal aging and wellness medicine; you can get naturopathic and homeopathic consultations, an exclusive Optimal Aging and Wellness Consultation, and antiaging Facial Rejuvenation Acupuncture from licensed naturopathic physician Dr. Amy Whittington. The spa's Circle of Intuitive Guides (who have given consultations with names known in every household) leads guests into metaphysical realms with remarkably accurate Tarot, astrology, and guided meditation. Treatments $140–250, personal training in the fitness center $100 for 50 minutes.

Joya Spa (480-627-3200), InterContinental Montelucia Resort & Spa, 4949 E. Lincoln Dr., Paradise Valley. Open daily 8:30 AM–6:30 PM. You know a spa has a distinctive sense of place when a guest soaking in the Jacuzzi takes the initiative to say (correctly) to a complete stranger, "This place is really special, don't you think?" The simple statement says it all about Joya Spa. The blend of sensuous elements culled from every corner of the Mediterranean and lighting rarely brighter than twilight continually encourages you to dream. A huge crystal in the antechamber invites you to go ahead and believe. The whisper-silence lounge room, with its double-wide loungers cocooned with gossamer curtains begs for a girlfriend tête-à-tête to whisper secrets to each other. Head into the wet area and sit in the steam room until you break a sweat, and then stand in the cold-bucket shower and brace yourself as you pull the chain to unleash a deluge of 48-degree water, and then dash to the whirlpool to be lulled back to serenity again. This is just the start of your spa experience. Your treatment, which you choose from a distinctive menu of massages, treatments, or rituals, come next. The Joyambrosia Signature Massage uses Morocco's "liquid gold" argan oil, rich in vitamin E and essential fatty acids so healing to the skin, scented with Spanish citrus, Moroccan mint, and spices. Hour-long meditative sessions can take you into the labyrinth, on a Kabbalah experience with sounds and vibrations from the Aramaic language, a Hemi Sync brain synchronization meditation method, or focused meditation with deeksha energy transfer. Facials feature Nature Blisse products from Barcelona, Spain. Massages and body treatments $155–295, facials $155–325, meditation and metaphysical $145, wellness $195–295.

Jurlique Spa (480-424-6072), Fire Sky Resort & Spa, 4925 N. Scottsdale Rd. Open daily 8 AM–8 PM (till 7 PM in summer). Decorated with rustic knotty-pine floors in the treatment room, slate ones in the bathroom, and glass and metal all around, this spa has an earthy feeling balanced by dainty, colorful chandeliers. Therapists use Jurlique's organic products grown in the Adelaide Hills of South Australia (the most mineral-rich spot on earth) in fabulous facials, polishes, wraps, hot stone therapies, and glows. Jurlique makes unique herbal, antioxidant blends that are free of chemicals, animal content, and artificial fragrances and colors. The products have an intense aromatherapy influence. All this becomes important when you consider that what goes on the skin seeps into the body. Each treatment room is a private, self-contained refuge. That means no locker rooms. No sharing dressing space. No stall showers. And your own private bathroom. The rooms are big enough to add breathing space between the treatment table, an elegant curtained-off tub to receive special baths ($50), and the workstation where those wonderful-smelling oils get mixed (often your choice of which ones). This makes any treatment ever so special and luxurious. $120–190. Packages available.

The Lamar Everyday Spa (480-945-7066), 5115 N. Scottsdale Rd. Open daily

9–7. Often (correctly) described as an oasis in the desert, this day spa is one big find. The Caribbean theme prevails in names of treatment rooms and décor and extends into the whole of the spa, whose casual but sensuous demeanor has that subtle element of elegance found on tropical islands. A coed area has sauna, steam room, cooling pool and whirlpool (bring your bathing suit), a private garden with fireplace, water features, ballroom dancing classes, and views of Camelback Mountain from the patio. Your treatments can run from a chair massage or mini mani to a full day of luxury—facials to body treatments. The spa uses Yon-Ka products for facials and offers an oxygenated one that just might keep you from plastic. A variety of body treatments include shiatsu, Swedish massage, body buffs, and hot rock therapy. The best part is that the price is right. The locals once had the spa to themselves, but now the secret is out; make reservations early if you want a weekend or night treatment. Massage and body treatments $60–160, facials $50–185.

Spa Avania (480-483-5558), Hyatt Regency Scottsdale Resort and Spa at Gainey Ranch, 7500 E. Doubletree Ranch Rd. Open daily 8 AM–10 PM. You won't find another spa like this one, with its slate, black granite, and solid cherry hardwood details and a Grecian name that means "an ideal state of being." Every detail of the spa experience is based on the science of time and your body's internal clock. The spa menu is divided into morning (awakening and rejuvenation), midday (restoration and balance), and evening (relaxation and renewal) offerings that work with your body's metabolism and biorhythms. Treatment rooms have natural light, rare exotic teas from Mitea are offered, mineral water from Macedonia is served, men have their own treatment room with flat-screen TV and mini bar, couples can reserve oversized treatment suites, garden treatment suits have private entrances, a French Celtic mineral pool (no chlorine) provides the ultimate soak, hot- and cold-water immersion pools add elements of Kneipp Therapy, a dry inhalation room infuses eucalyptus oils, outdoor storm showers give an alternative to the oversized showers in the men's and women's changing areas, a yoga studio teaches YogaAway to restore and recoup your clarity and balance, and a state-of-the-art fitness center stays open all day. After all this, *avania* is almost a guarantee. Rituals $120, massages $115–180, body wraps $165–180, aromatic Vichy $150, facials $165–200, waxing services $20–75, gentlemen's grooming $30–75.

AT THE HYATT SPA AVANIA

The Spa at Camelback Inn (480-596-7040 or 800-922-2635), 5402 E. Lincoln Dr. Open daily 6:15 AM–7:30 PM. The biggest and the first comprehensive spa in the Southwest is perennially voted among the best spas in the Valley by the locals. People like this spa because it has what they want—great treatments from great therapists (all the movie stars ask for Harrison) at great prices. Plus it's the only one in Scottsdale with a restaurant (Sprouts). The journey starts outside the spa doors in the garden courtyard where aromatherapy scents waft from open doors, music plays, and flowers color the grounds. Once you're through the lobby and separate from the rest of the spa, peace happens. Treatments range from traditional Swedish and shiatsu massage to more meditative therapies that precipitate awareness of self and a sense of inner balance. The signature massage treatment combines elements to detox and relax (hot and cold stones, reflexology, castor oil, a scalp massage and aquamarine stones on the face—very different). The signature body wrap features a head-to-toe vitamin C treatment, Facilities include a heated outdoor lap pool, coed Jacuzzi, men's hot tub and cold plunge pool, women's hot tub, complete men's and women's locker rooms, separate Turkish steam rooms, and Finnish saunas. Salon services tend to hairstyling, cuts, weaving, and coloring and nail services. The fitness gym is hot—the latest equipment, classes, personal training, nutritional counseling, Pilates, water, and lavender towels to cool your brow. Bodywork $1,150–135, facials $135–145, and training sessions $45–80.

The Spa at Four Seasons Resort Scottsdale (480-513-4145), 10600 E. Crescent Moon Dr. Southwestern elements play prominent roles at this spa: adobe-style architecture, southwestern décor, and treatments using mud, herbs, hot stones, and honey. Therapists and aestheticians use 14 treatment rooms, including two spa suites, to work their magic. Facials use the Academie Scientifique skin care line—which means facials are de rigueur here. As a lagniappe, therapists give guests a Tip to Take Home, techniques to assuage dry skin, relieve tension headaches, and exfoliate skin. One of several signature offerings is The Hiker. What's meant for active guests is one of the most exquisite experiences for even couch-potato muscles akin to Thai massage. Plus you get a chocolate-covered strawberry after the 120 minutes of stretching and kneading of muscles. The state-of-the-art fitness center includes every type of machine you think you need, and more. Personal trainers assist with tai chi, yoga, stretching, and Pilates, as well as sport-specific training to improve performance for golfers, tennis players, and joggers. Bodywork $90–310, facials $155–235, and training sessions $110 and up.

VH Spa (480-248-2000), Hotel Valley Ho, 6850 E. Main St. You won't get the dose of tranquility and Om-like peace most spas exude when you make yourself at home in the lounge. Oh, it's quiet—no cells phones are allowed, and whispers are preferred—but the colors remain vibrant light green and turquoise, urging guests in color-therapy language to speak from the heart. Every treatment is meant to transform you in some way, from the facials to quantum biofeedback. This spa caters to the stressed-out businessperson, presenting massages and shiatsu. You can even customize your treatment with guided massage. VH Spa also offers exercise training sessions, guided hikes, and special classes such as Belly Dancing with Veils, Pool Scuba, Yoga, and Yamuna Body Rolling. Massages $95–185, body treatments $185, facials $95–145, and training sessions $65–85.

Willow Stream—The Spa at Fairmont Scottsdale Princess (480-585-2732), 7575 E. Princess Dr. Like the rest of the resort, this spa has a magnificent layout. Patterned after the western Grand Canyon's red-rock-walled Havasu Canyon (stunning waterfalls and all), the spa wraps itself in a natural environment with rock walls, water, and wood. Even products have local traditions and ingredients. The spa interior has natural elements and specially chosen colors to reflect its philosophy of discovering your internal pool of energy. No assembly-line therapies here. Treatments are original, schedules liberal (1–2 hours with 15 minutes in between), and therapists doting. Many of the treatments, such as the signature 2-hour Havasupai Body Oasis Experience, incorporate water. If you can't decide between a massage or facial, get the Tranqwillow Face & Back Experience. A rooftop pool replete with waterfalls is the epitome of elegance. Schedule your session at night when you may end up having the spa to yourself; the after-dark beauty when the water features light up add to the experience. Fitness facility, salon services, meditation gardens, men's and women's spa and lounge areas. Bodywork $175–319, massages $159–269, and facials $169–279.

✷ Wilder Places

McDowell Mountain Regional Park (480-471-0173), 16300 N. McDowell Mountain Rd. Open Sun.–Thu. 6 AM–8 PM, Fri. and Sat. 6 AM–10 PM. Considered one of the most scenic of Maricopa County's mountain parks, this one stretches along the eastern edge of the Valley to offer views of the famous Superstition Mountains. The park has 50 miles of trails crossing mountains rising 3,000 feet for every experience level. $6 per vehicle

McDowell Sonoran Preserve (480-312-7013), end of Alma School Rd. north of Dynamite Rd. Some trails require a $15 State Lands Department permit.

Pinnacle Peak Park (480-312-0990), 26802 N. 102nd Way (a mile south of Dynamite and Alma Schoolroads). Open dawn–dusk; closed Christmas Day. The bouldery, low-lying ridges at the north end of the Valley make a scenic spot to get outdoors and enjoy the desert. You may see rock climbers, loaded with gear, heading for a favorite route via the manicured Pinnacle Peak Trail.

✷ Lodging

🐾 ✐ ♿ ⚭ ♥ **Camelback Inn** (480-948-1700 or 800-242-2631), 5402 E. Lincoln Dr. The Marriotts were so enamored of this desert resort, they finally bought it after repeated vacations there. Bill Marriott Jr.—son of the late hotel chain founder, chairman of the board, and president of Marriott Corporation—says it's where he spent his happiest day. The resort, the first in Scottsdale, has been the lodging of choice for presidents, Hollywood legends, and travelers since original owner Jack Stewart opened it in 1936. For those who demand the threefold braid of privacy without seclusion, posh without pretense, and friendliness without familiarity—kick off your shoes and stay awhile; like Marriott, you may not want to leave. The inn has recently undergone a $50 million remodel and still remains totally Southwest inside and out; Native American, authentic adobe architecture, and nature are big here. Some bellmen don't mind donning a cowboy hat. The blend of cultural tradition and glamour works. The resort shares the distinction of earning AAA's Five Diamond status from 1977 to 2007—the only Arizona property—with only three properties nationwide to do so. The resort has six all-weather tennis courts (five lit for night play, one screened for privacy, and the inn will match unpartnered players with others of equal skill level); the largest spa in the Southwest; championship golf; basketball and volleyball courts; three swimming pools; several restaurants; and a 24-hour fitness center. Rooms have a private patio or balcony, microwave, refrigerator, iHome clock/radio, safes, $199–900.

🐾 ✐ ♿ ⚭ ((Ī)) **Doubletree Resort** (480-947-5400), 5401 N. Scottsdale Rd. Known as "the resort with the horses," this property turns heads as people pass by on Scottsdale Road. The bronze sculpture *My Friends* by Snell Johnson—three Arabian horses at full gait in a fountain—evokes energy. Inside the grounds, life decompresses to match the resort status. You would never know you're *this close* to the best shopping, restaurants, and entertainment venues in the Valley. The Frank Lloyd Wright architecture, manicured lawns, and fountains bring a lush touch to the desert. The gray stone walls of the buildings are textured to look like the bark of the 200 palm trees planted on the property. The 22 acres hold two swimming pools (adult and children's with playground), tennis courts, a nine-hole PGA regulation putting green, a health club, and racquetball courts. Inside each room, all oversized, you have a private balcony with a pool, courtyard, or fountain view, wet bar, WiFi access, cable TV, and movies on command. There's no resort fee, and you get free parking. A Kid's Club takes place in summertime. Pets up to 25 pounds are welcome for a $50 nonrefundable fee. Low season $99–249, high season $189–299.

🐾 ✐ ♿ ⚭ **The Fairmont Scottsdale Princess** (480-585-4848), 7575 E. Princess Dr. The resort's Spanish Colonial–style terra-cotta buildings spread like a southwestern ranch over wide-open spaces. An impressive array of water features spout fountains, cascades, and refreshing streams appear around the grounds, creating an atmosphere reminiscent of a Roman plaza. The outlay marries casual with class, comfort with style. A five-star rating promises over-the-top service. The

THE TRADEMARK HORSE SCULPTURE IN FRONT OF DOUBLETREE RESORT TURNS HEADS

THE FOUR SEASONS RESORT KEEPS AN ELEGANT PROFILE WHILE SHAKING HANDS WITH THE DESERT

resort is ideal for guests who like a little elegance mixed with Southwestern casual. Kids have a blast in the National Geographic Explorers Camp and fishing (catch and release) in the lagoon. The rooms have a spacious design and filled with thoughtful amenities. Seven tennis courts are the site of the ATP/ Franklin Templeton Men's Tennis Tournament; five heated pools and two 200-foot waterslides present great aqueous moments; and a Golf Concierge team hooks you up with the world class courses to play or get lessons. The resort's spa, Willow Stream—The Spa, mirrors the red-rock walls of Havasu Canyon replete with waterfalls. LV Bistro has farm-to-table New American cuisine with a menu that changes seasonally. Meats and cheeses are often local and the fish sustainable. Try one of it organic libations (house-made organic bar and garden infusions and wines made with grapes grown biodynamically. A children's section keeps the young ones occupied with movies and toys while you savor that second cup of (organic) coffee. Call for rates or log on at www.fairmont.com/scottsdale for great specials. Up to two pets under 25 pounds are welcome, $30 each.

🐾 ♿ ♥ **Four Seasons Resort Scottsdale at Troon North** (480-515-5700), 10600 E. Crescent Moon Dr. Situated on the northern reach of Scottsdale, where the edges of the city blur with the desert. Regardless of how close it lies to the backcountry, you still stay spoiled with AAA Five Diamond service. The staff members don't just meet guests' needs; they anticipate them. The resort, one of the few in the state able to hold hands with the desert, presents stunning views of the Valley from its aerie in the boulder-strewn Sonoran Desert foothills. Unpretentious territorial-style buildings and suites keep a low profile to the beautiful desert surroundings. Inside, primary colors create elegant yet lively interiors. This is no longer your grandfather's Four Seasons. All rooms (500 sq. ft.-plus) have a fireplace, down duvet and pillows, soaking tub, L'Occitane bath products, safe, flat-screen TV, MP3 docking station; suites have an outdoor garden shower, private plunge pool, and outdoor kiva fireplace. Besides a 6,000 sq. ft. heated saltwater swimming pool and two night tennis courts the resort's association with Troon North Golf Club just down the road makes it a hit with golfers. Its spa always appears on best lists and maintains a Forbes Four-Star rating. Kids will love it for its Kids for All Seasons program (parents, because it's free), not to mention the potential outdoor adventures waiting all around. Complimentary resort amenities include: morning coffee and tea in the lobby, use of Fitness Center, wine-tasting, salsa and margarita demonstrations, guided morning hikes on local trails, shuttle to local restaurants, poolside cabanas, parking. Pets (dogs and cats under 15 pounds) get special amenities upon arrival. $149–825.

Hotel Indigo (480-941-9400), 4415 N. Civic Center Plaza. One of the best deals in town sits right next to where everything happens in downtown Scottsdale. Taking a cue from the Fibonacci Sequence, the hotel's logo is the nautilus shell, and murals of the sequence found in nature, such as the agave, hang on the outside. Inside, the owners display photography in the hallways taken by up-and-coming local artists using abstract indigenous imagery. The hotel works with Arizona State University students, awarding them scholarships if their art is chosen. The property includes the open-room **Phi Bar/Restaurant**, a heated pool, Phitness room, and parking. Rooms (full of indigo color) have king or two double beds, 32-inch flat-screen TV, complimentary WiFi, MP3 player hookup, spa-inspired shower, Aveda amenities, windows that open, a sitting area and free shuttle service within 3 miles. The hallways have an emerald glow from low green lights. $69–229.

Hotel Valley Ho (480-248-2000), 6850 E. Main St. When it first opened in 1956, celebrities couldn't stay away from this desert property. Over the years it lost its footing in the world of resorts and finally closed. Reopened and remodeled to reflect its 1950s heydays, this once trendy resort has regained its standing in the community as one of the places to see and be seen. It's pure retro made hip. Guest rooms have color schemes of turquoise and goldenrod and black, red, and white; geometrics; and creative baths. Signature guest rooms have baths with frosted glass walls and an azure blue light above large tubs. In studio guest rooms, the tub stands behind a curtain, rather than a wall, and the executive suite has a circular bathtub large enough for two. Rooms have suede platform beds with quality linens, carpet tiles, flat-screen TV, WiFi, and large and wonderful patios (terrace rooms have glassed-in patios). Each month the hotel features the work of a local artist. Low season $159–319.

Hyatt Regency Scottsdale Resort (480-444-1234), 7500 E. Doubletree Ranch Rd. Expansive, active, elegant but playful, this Hyatt has a multiple but appealing personality. Known for its picture-perfect view of the McDowell Mountains, the resort offers a compendium of interesting features many locals don't know about. In all-things-to-all-people fashion, the resort entertains cross-generationally. Its double-H design provides courtyards in which to relax. Nightly entertainment brings crowds to the open-air courtyard. A 2.5-acre water playground provides 10 pools, a three-story waterslide, and sand beaches where adults and kids play. Hard-surfaced tennis courts, three nine-hole golf courses, and jogging and cycling trails keep guests active. The Lost Dutchman Mine has kids digging in a sandpit for semiprecious stones, while Camp Hyatt Kachina teaches them about the flora, fauna, culture, and geography of Arizona. A Native American and Environmental Learning Center feeds the mind, a Native American

PONDS ON THE GROUNDS OF THE HYATT REGENCY

Sculpture and Mineral Garden feeds the soul, while environmentally friendly wetlands and a Native Seed Garden honor the land and its people. Also on the premises are four restaurants (check out SWB for Southwest fare and Alto, which features light Italian food with some classic dishes and a salumi cellar) and Spa Avania. Rooms offer a taste of the Southwest in copper, eggplant, and sand hues, along with cable TV, private balcony, mini service bars, and WiFi access. The casitas along the lagoon give you privacy and your own Jacuzzi. You can upgrade any room with the Regency Club, which provides complimentary amenities (European-style breakfast, light snacks, hors d'oeuvres and cocktails (extra), cordials and desserts, and beverages throughout the day. $190–350.

🐾 ⚭ ♥ **InterContinental Montelucia Resort & Spa** (482-627-3200), 4949 E. Lincoln Dr., Paradise Valley. The mission statement of this resort is, *to fulfill the innermost dreams of our guests and to make them feel as if they are in heaven.* With a backdrop full of designs and architecture styles fresh from the Mediterranean, where legendary mortals become gods and real-life commoners can become royalty, your innermost dreams might bubble up easier than you think here. The resort attends to just about every sensual bone in your body with sights and sounds familiar to Andalusia. The Alhambra walkway is inspired by the Alhambra in Grenada, Spain. The signature restaurant, Prado, takes after Michelangelo's Villa San Michele in Tuscany and the ballroom at Hotel Cipriani in Venice inspired the wedding chapel, Castillo Lucena. The resort has rooms, suites (two presidential), and villas. Amenities include ultra-luxurious Divine Beds with featherbeds, 42-inch flat-screen TV, iPod docking station, dining table, in-room

THE INTERCONTINENTAL MONTELUCIA RESORT HAS A DOGGIE COCKTAIL HOUR, WHEN GUESTS AND LOCAL RESIDENTS CAN BRING THEIR THIRSTY DOGS TO THE CRAVE CAFÉ

THE INTERCONTINENTAL MONTELUCIA RESORT DISPLAYS GREAT EXAMPLES OF MEDITERRANEAN ARCHITECTURE ON ITS PROPERTY

coffee and tea, sunken tubs and dual-head showers. Resort has spa, fitness center, art gallery, Planet Trekkers Kid's Club, golf course, bocce lawn and equipment, Hammond, hidden courtyards, in-room grilling with private chef, five pools and cabanas. Dogs get their own happy hour (Yappy Hour) at Crave Café. Call for rates and specials. Call for rates (which are great in the summer).

🐾 ✐ ♿ ⚭ **The Phoenician** (480-941-8200 or 800-325-3589), 6000 E. Camelback Rd. This 250-acre resort spreads at the feet of the Valley's trademark Camelback Mountain. Created solely for luxury and pleasure, this AAA Five Diamond facility culls comfort from several cultures—warm southwestern colors; haute European accents of marble, gold leaf, and crystal; a $25 million art collection; and island-inspired landscaping. Centre for Well-Being Spa, nine pools, three USGA-approved golf courses (one a championship course designed by Homer Flint and Ted Robinson Sr.), a 12-court Tennis Garden featuring four surfaces, Funician Kid's Club, three restaurants, and private dining in **The Praying Monk** working wine cellar keep guests busy inside the resort. Guided tours to places of interest around the state accommodate those

THE PHOENICIAN

who like an adventure. Even if you don't rent the presidential suite ($3,500–5,000 per night includes a personal butler, limousine transportation, someone to unpack and press your clothes, a choice of cotton or satin linens, and a poolside cabana), the staff goes way beyond the call of duty to make each guest's experience a special one with a your-wish-is-my-command attitude. If you call for a sewing kit, for instance, you'll have a seamstress knocking at your door. Bellmen have been known to personally buy a teddy bear for a distressed child. To appease the discerning palates, guests order cocktails not by the name, but by the name of the liquor that goes into it. Wines are ordered from the largest list comprised by one of only two master sommeliers in the state. No one who stays at The Phoenician goes lacking, anything, at any time. Rates for a Super Room (standard 600 sq. ft.): $375–675. Log onto www.thephoenician.com for special packages.

Sanctuary on Camelback Mountain (480-948-2100), 5700 E. McDonald Dr., Paradise Valley. Tucked away on a spot the Hohokam revered as sacred, this 53-acre resort lives up to its name in the aesthetic sense and in essence. Threaded with Asian hues, the whole resort plays with yin–yang design concepts. The AAA Four Diamond property has a pleasing graceful demeanor, so common to Oriental hospitality, without pretentiousness. Cathy Hayes, of Hayes Architecture Interiors, Inc., balanced mindfulness with beauty during a recent remodel of the property's 98 casitas terraced on a mountainside. The interiors blend Zen architecture with the original clean lines from the 1960s and '70s, colored with hues of the desert. The resort features elements restaurant with its gorgeous views of the Valley, a negative-edge and lap pool, Sanctuary Spa, and a fitness room. Casitas include flat-screen TV, featherbed and down pillows, Mascioni linens, large bath, high-speed Internet, and in-room safe. Call for rates.

Scottsdale Cottonwoods Resort & Suites (480-991-1414) 6160 N. Scottsdale Rd., Scottsdale. This may be the only resort with a popular shopping mall, Borgata Shopping Village, in its front yard. This makes for some interesting sojourns, if only to peruse and listen to Friday-night jazz. The property sits in the center of spas, hiking, golf, and shopping (beyond Borgata). The Scottsdale Trolley will take you in the right directions. Shopping aside, this tucked-away property will give you privacy and romance, if that's what you'd prefer. It's a place where you kick back and relax. The rooms, casita-style suites, have a rustic blend of wood-beamed ceilings, an arched niche wet bar, and a sunken outdoor hot-tub spa on their private patio; cable TV, WiFi access, a newspaper delivered to your room, and shoeshine service are included. Many rooms have real functioning fireplaces. Mature landscaping surrounds the rooms, two pools, four tennis courts, croquet green, putting green, and Ping-Pong tables. A complimentary restaurant, **Courtyard Tapas**, is open Oct.–May. More than 40 tapas are offered on the menu (meat/poultry, seafood, vegetable, and dessert), along with a Spanish cheese cart and Spanish and Californian wines. $75 nonrefundable sanitation fee for pets. Low season $79–309.

W Hotel (480-970-2100), 7277 E. Camelback Rd. One of the Valley's newest, and most sophisticated hotels, has YOUTH stamped all over it. It's Hello Kitty meets James Bond. But it works. Zany (they use their own words to describe features and services), colorful (color is fabulously splashed all over the property), classy (collector's item prints and books and art books by Taschen in the Living Room) and the most comfortable bed in the Valley. The rooms will appeal to any gender with rich purple faux suede furniture, mint velvet curtains, 37-inch LCD TV, iPod docking station, a flagstone wall in the bathroom and a thick epoxy shower floor finished to look and feel like the surface of water. Actually, everything has a "feel" to it, tactile and attractive. But you won't necessarily want to stay sequestered in your room. While W will appeal to wallflowers, it's custom made for the scene, located in the part of Scottsdale where the It-crowd goes. Its logo—*whatever /whenever*—means your wish is the talents' (a.k.a. staff's) demand, as long as it's legal and moral. Just remember one thing—if it doesn't say "complimentary," it isn't. Call for rates and specials.

🐾 ✐ ♿ ⚭ **The Westin Kierland Resort & Spa** (480-624-1000), 6902 E. Greenway Pkwy. With a mind to make Arizona's history come to life, Westin titled this property with the theme "Treasuring the Essence of Arizona." And it works, thanks to Arizona state historian Marshall Trimble, who wrote narratives to explain the names for rooms and areas in the hotel, as well as assisting with historic artwork displayed throughout the property. The property sits right next door to Kierland Commons shopping area. But you don't have to go off-grounds to keep yourself occupied. The library gives you a place to cocoon indoors. Two large pools (the main pool—8,000 square feet—is heated and 4 feet deep, with a zero-entry sandy beach) give you all the sun-drenched space for outdoor lounging. Kids may actually say thank you when they see the water park that gushes 575,000 gallons of water for two large pools two hot tubs, 900-foot-long flowing "river" for "tubing," and a 110-foot-long waterslide. The Family FUN Program gives families the fun of their lives with special programs like Kids in the Kitchen, Adventure Water Park, Poolside Movies, Lazy River, Kids Club, Digital Kids Zone, Arizona S'mores, and the Phoenix Zoo. At sunset, Scottish piper Michael McClanathan plays songs with his bagpipes every day for the Scottish Pipes at Sunset Series. Later, you can sit by the piñon wood firepit in the Dreamweaver's Canyon courtyard next to the seasonal flower garden patterned after a Navajo blanket. The resort also features eight dining venues (check out the paintings of Cuban artist Nelson Garcia-Miranda at deseo restaurant downstairs); Agave—The Arizona Spa; the Kierland Golf Club; and, of course, that Heavenly Bed and Shower. $129–549.

✷ Where to Eat

DINING OUT BLT Steak (480-905-7979), (Camelback Inn) 5402 E. Lincoln. Open for dinner Sun–Thu. 6–10, Fri. and Sat. 6–11; call for summer hours. Bistro Laurent Tourondel (for whom the initials BLT stand) has a number of these restaurants in the great cities of the world. The standard menu, designed by Laurent, has real Japanese Kobe Strip (at $26/oz.) and American Wagyu steaks (a cross between Angus and Kobe, for substantially less) and classics like Dover Sole and Maine Lobster, and à la carte appetizers, vegetables, potatoes, and desserts. The daily Blackboard Menu, created by chef de cuisine Marc Hennessy, is the cream of the crop. Chef Marc has the alchemeic ability to bring unusual ingredients together with flavors that work seamlessly. The board's seasonal menu that changes daily might have Cedar River Farms Rib Eye, a splash of 100-year-old balsamic vinegar to garnish a dessert plate (Chef Marc likes to think about what was going on in history about that time), rhubarb with seared lobster tails (tart with sweet), or dishes featuring local fruits and veggies. The meal starts out with a giant popover (eggily delicious, and comes with the recipe) for each diner. You can end it with a perfectly made soufflé (Chef Marc correctly states, "It's hard to get a real soufflé these days"). Everything is real and it's all real good. Entrées $26–92.

Bourbon Steak (480-513-6002), 7575 E. Princess Dr. Open Tue.–Sat. 5:30–10:30. Dark wood, low lights, funky music, and leather tabletops create a sensuous scene for a menu created to satiate appetites with comfort on the mind. The menu features the finest cuts of beef slow-poached in butter then seared over wood flames. This is definitely a beef-eater's delight that leans on the decadent side. Oh, there's fish (like Maine Lobster Pot Pie) and poultry (Fried Chicken with Truffled Mac & Cheese) on the menu, too. But steak is what's happening here, from all-natural USDA beef to American Kobe to Japanese A5 Waguy. If you want less formal, order one of the wood-grilled Bar Burgers with Chef Mina's duck-fat fries and a milkshake designed for adult tastes. On Thursday's Bourbon and Blues night, eat Chicken and Waffles to the tune of live blues. Pastry chef David Blom's desserts make a grand finale to a luxurious meal. Entrées $22–150.

Café ZuZu (480-421-7711), 6850 E. Main St. Open daily for breakfast 6–11:15, lunch 11:30–2:30, dinner 5:30–10. One of the hot meeting places of the Valley, where the edges of the sophisticated Hotel Valley Ho lounge spill into the café on a busy night. This makes for fascinating people-watching. Inside the restaurant's line of demarcation, Chef Charles Wiley, who has racked up kudos from *Food & Wine* and televisionland (and who also designed the restaurant and lounge area) presents an eclectic menu leaning toward local ingredients. Chef Charles has a knack of taking classic flavor profiles and turning them into delightful dishes. From Warm Maytag Blue Cheese Fondue and Butternut Squash Ravioli with Pumpkin-seed Cream to Beef Rib Eye with Shallot Marmalade and Mashed Potatoes and Beef Stroganoff. Noshers can order from the small plate side of the menu and cull from 20 different dishes. The wait staff here are young and, refreshingly, come with few or no airs. Entrées $10.25–26.

Cowboy Ciao (480-946-3111), 7133 E. Stetson Dr. When Peter Kasperski opened this venue more than a dozen years ago, he continued with the irreverence-meets-quality concept introduced in the Lettuce Entertain You venues of which he was a part in his hometown, Chicago. You might describe the menu as Traditional food run through a kaleidoscope of (often Mediterranean, as in "Ciao") flavors that produce culinary twists as bold as the big guy, Duke (as in "Cowboy"). The signature dish, Exotic Mushroom Pan Fry, is a bona fide mushroom festival with cremini, button, oyster, cepe, lobster, black trumpet, shiitake, morel, and yellow foot mushrooms in ancho cream over double-cooked polenta, topped with grilled portabellos, avocado, tomato and cotija cheese. The Stetson Chopped, a favorite, takes the concept of salad into a different dimension. Buffalo Carpaccio (rolled in a cumin-espresso dry rub, seared, and served with red onion/honey marmalade and chêvre) could cause a diner to say, "I have to tell you, I can't find the words . . . I feel like I just had a massage" (actual guest quote). Peter Kasperski has created a legendary list of wines that has gotten the *Wine Spectator* Awards of Excellence every year since 1997. Advice: avoid the flights; go with a glass or bottle. Entrées $20–36.

♥ **deseo** (480-624-1000, 6902 E. Greenway Pkwy. Open for dinner Wed.–Sun. 6 PM–10 PM. The concept here is Latino, inspired by Chef Douglas Rodriguez, who introduced Nuevo Latino cuisine to America. Chef de cuisine Roberto Madrid carries the torch beautifully, mixing wisdom with wit as he serves up the creative menu. deseo specializes in ceviche, the South American/Mexican version of sashimi that has citrus juices to flavor and "cook" the fish (depending on how long the ingredients marry). Chef Madrid uses fresh fish flown in from California to make the dozen or so ceviches on the menu, the favorite being Millionaire Tacos made with hamachi, ahi tuna, lobster, and mangoes. The exhibition kitchen gives you a chance to watch the food being made. Entrées include the favorite, beef tenderloin *churrasco* style; seafood, steaks, and chops; and vegetarian dishes, The foods' flavors are succinct and thought-provoking. You will probably keep seeing flashes and hearing cell phone cameras going off to take pictures of the ultracreative presentations. You'll be impressed with the unique libations, too. Muddled cocktails feature fresh fruits and herbs. Sommelier Gerardo Mendoze has some esoteric beers and wines you may not find elsewhere. Entrées $26–32.

♥ **Estate House** (480-970-4099), 7134 E. Stetson Dr. Dinner only, 5—10. Designed to evoke the feel of the home of a worldly estate owner, the restaurant makes an intriguing setting for a special dinner. The extensive art collection of drawings, photographs, and paintings have a sophisticated appeal, silk drapes over French doors add elegance, wooden floors akin to the decks of a New England sailboat add rustic warmth. World music wraps it all together into a seductive/wistful float that lasts throughout the evening. The food, contemporary American, is ingenious and prepared well—salads with ice-wine vinaigrette or almond-crusted Manchego cheese; Berkshire Pork Belly Achiote Rub, Pickled Red Onion, Lime, Cilantro; Grilled Colorado Lamb with Tuscan Chestnut Torte, Thyme-roasted Fig, Pinot Noir Toasted Hazelnut Reduction and Handmade Fettuccine with Wild Mushrooms, Herb Crema, and White Truffle Oil drizzle. The staff works harmoniously to produce a special experience by fawning ever so professionally over every dinner guests—from making meal suggestions to pairing courses with the right wines to making sure you have a black napkin to match your black dress. The Estate House is distinctly different from other venues in the area. Entrées $22–42.

FnB (480-425-9463), 7133 E. Stetson Dr. Open daily for dinner at 5. If there's truth in the saying, "Good things come in small packages," you're in for a real good thing at this downtown Scottsdale restaurant. The 14-seat counter and about as many seats at tables may cause a wait, but it's worth it. The small place has some BIG elements. First, the owners, Pavle and Emily Milic, who work the tables, have star-quality personalities. Executive chef Charleen Badmen learned at the side of Donna Norton (Café Terra Cotta in Tucson, now closed), worked with Chrysa Robertson (foodies' favorite Rancho Pinto down the street) racked up kudos in NYC with her restaurant, Insight, and picked up (what she didn't learn from Chrysa) a purist food ethic on the West Coast's Chez Panisse. FnB has a short menu with huge flavors that keeps your taste buds at rapt attention. And speaking of huge flavors, the venue (the only one in town) serves only Arizona wines, which have (correctly) bowled over diners. Tony interiors, reminiscent of East Coast big city, speak elegantly to the venue's casual desert city. And big band music spiced with seductive jazz notes of Miles Davis, Nina Simone, and Sarah Vaughan has diners murmuring about how the atmosphere makes them feel so good. It's a bundle of big stuff, but it's all good. Entrées $18–25.

The Grill at TPC (480-585-4848), 17020 N. Hayden. Open daily for lunch 11–2 and dinner Thu.–Mon. 6–9. Boston or Scottsdale? You decide. The fish is fresh enough to be Boston (right down to the Friday night clambake), but the scenery looking out those big-view windows is pure Sonora Desert golf. You'll find some of the best sustainable fish in the Valley here—Salt Spring Island mussels, Laughing Bird Shrimp, Loch Duart salmon, Florida spiny lobster, Higha Island Scottish halibut—and a daily market whole fish special. Chef Erik Forest prepares the dishes with simple yet sensational techniques and flavors. Because all the fish is sustainable (Cleanfish Alliance), you feel good in body (farm-raised catches are clean and excellent quality) and soul. There's rib eye steak, pork osso buco, and Parmesan tagliatelle for the landlubbers. Lunch features an informal menu of sandwiches, soups, fried fish, and steaks. Lunch $12–23, dinner $18–38.

La Hacienda (480-585-4848), Fairmont Scottsdale Princess, 7575 E. Princess Dr. Open for dinner Thu.–Tue. 5:30–10. Back after two long (too long) years, the Valley's favorite modern Mexican food venue is better than ever. Chef Forest Hamrick is at the helm and has created, with executive chef Richard Sandoval (called the Father of Modern Mexican Cuisine), a menu with an "Old Hand, New Ways" twist—classic Mexican cuisine with European cooking techniques. Try the Sopa de Elote (roasted corn, cream, and *huitlacoche*) or Atun pistachio chile ancho–crusted tuna, sweet potato, green apple salad, and *mole verde*); or the or the Pipián de Puerco (pork shoulder with roasted corn purée, pumpkin seeds, and *pipián* sauce, and you'll understand what the axiom perfectly. Chef Hamrick's travels to Mexico, to research the foods and stoke his imagination, lends a purist's touch to each dish. For instance, the *mole* is one of the most harmonious you'll taste, the *masa* moist and tasty, and the ceviche well balanced. At meal's end, try the Flaming Coffee. More than 100 different tequilas (38 different labels) are available. You can get artisan tastings at the Tequila Bar. Entrées $19–31.

The Mission (480-636-5005), 3815 N. Brown Ave. Open daily for lunch 11–3; dinner Sun.–Thu. 5–10, Fri. and Sat. 5 AM–11 PM. Grabbing foods and flavors from Mexico, Spain, and Central and South America, Chef Matt Carter comes up with some savory dishes you won't soon forget. He mixes French techniques with a *plancha*-style grill, a style that originated in Spain, stoked with pecan and mesquite wood. The glow from the kitchen on the other side of the wall of Himalayan block salt, which looks like quartz, sheds the only utilitarian light in the restaurant. The dining room remains Old World dark, lit moodily by chandeliers. At least a dozen, each, specialty margaritas and martinis are available. Chef Matt has become an expert in cooking pork, so it comes with no surprise the specialty is Pork Shoulder Tacos (with handmade corn tortillas). The Uruguayan Rib Eye and Swordfish Veracruz are pretty tasty, too. If you don't order black bean or white bean purée, get an order of Mission Fries (sweet potato and potato fries with lemon, chile, and cumin) and/or Grilled Street Corn. For dessert, the Expresso Churros (with an Ibarra chocolate milkshake) is addictive enough; the Pumpkin Bread Pudding (with scotch, butter, pepitas, and pomegranate) may not be legal. Be sure to try the coffee—a blend of Free Trade and herbs (which are legal). Entrées $19–36.

Olive & Ivy (480-751-2200), 7135 E. Camelback Rd. Market open daily 7–3:30; restaurant Mon.–Fri. 11 AM–11 PM, Sat. and Sun. 10 AM–10 PM. Arizona restaurateur Sam Fox combines Old World Mediterranean with new at this ongoing hot spot. This is where the ladies love to congregate for their white wine lunches and after-work fun. The huge venue has several different areas, from its community dining bar to patio nooks to private dining rooms. The fare has Mediterranean names and ingredients, and the wine list is large. The small plates and flat breads shine. Grab some house-made gelato in the market for dessert. The market also makes a quick stop for baked goods, specialty quiches, rustic loaves, and gourmet espresso and coffee. Entrées $13–36.

Prado (480-627-3200), InterContinental Montelucia Resort, 4949 E. Lincoln Dr., Paradise Valley. Open for breakfast Mon.–Fri. 7–11, Sat. and Sun. 8–12; lunch Mon.–Fri. 11–3, Sat. and Sun. 12–3; dinner 5:30–10 nightly. Italian-born Chef Claudio Urciuoli (from the southern Italian region of Campania, which means "happy") is well known in the Valley and highly respected. Continuing his commitment to Slow Food (as he did in celebrated venues such as Osteria del Circo/Le Cirque at Bellagio in Las Vegas and Il Fornaio in San Francisco) Chef Claudio uses the freshest ingredients (local whenever possible) in his creations. High-quality food is what he lays his claim to fame to; "the rest is talent." The six-foot brick-lined open wood-fired oven adds the outstanding tastes and aromas to his rustic yet elegant creations. Signature dishes include Yellow and Red Gazpacho, New Caledonian Prawns with Rosemary and Controne Beans, and Prado Paella, which changes daily (as any portion of the menu is apt to for freshness). The best part is the food is priced for the locals to indulge regularly. And they do. The restaurant also has the state's most comprehensive collections of Spanish wine. Entrées $15–38.

♥ **Talavera** (480-515-5700), Four Seasons Resort Scottsdale at Troon North, 10600 E. Crescent Moon Dr. Open nightly 6–10. The restaurant matches the colorful Mexican pottery for which it is named with brightly upholstered furniture and wall hangings. Get a sofa table situated at one end of the room to get a full-room view or right next to the plate glass wall that shows off the gorgeous view of the Valley. When the weather cools, a 12-foot firepit blazes right outside the window. These natural elements create a relaxed atmosphere–a little different for a Four Seasons. But it works. Chef Evan Goldstein shows shades of his California cuisine background from the Four Seasons Hotel San Francisco. Things are fresh and innovative. The bread is artisanal from a master baker, the fish is always excellent, and steaks and chops prime and done well. The sea bass with oxtail reduction, alone, is worth the drive to the edge of the

Valley. Desserts have a little verve with pastry chef Lance Whipple's penchant to create something different. Expect little extras, such as sugar cubes for your French-press coffee and chocolate cream–hazelnut lollipop lagniappes. Entrées $28-44.

EATING OUT **The Breakfast Club** (480-222-2582), 4400 N. Scottsdale Rd. Open Mon.–Fri. 6–3, Sat. and Sun. 8–3. Come breakfast time—the traditional time for breakfast, that is—this is one of the hottest spots in town. Breakfast is served all day here, so if you don't want to stand in line, you can merely check out the menu and return when things quiet down a bit . . . though that might not necessarily happen on the weekends. With several TVs, music, and newspapers scattered here and there, you can catch up on the latest buzz, too. Choices run from distinctive Bar Harbor flapjacks (the king of blueberry pancakes) to delicious Belgian waffles (with a variety of toppings), Southwest-style eggs to Benedict-style eggs (both featuring a number of versions), and steak and eggs to omelets—as in build your own with a couple dozen different choices of ingredients. Portions come big. $5.95–12.95.

Frank and Lupe's Old Mexico (480-990-9844), 4121 N. Marshall. Open Mon.–Sat. 11–10. One of the locals' favorites, especially when the weather suggests that sitting on a patio is the best place to dine. The New Mexico cuisine, all house-made, has endured the test of time since 1980. The favorite is Lupe's Enchilada Plate, made with homemade corn tortillas. The chicken mole enchiladas and open-faced chile poblano (stuffed with chicken) rates right up there, too. If you want, you can substitute regular corn for blue corn tortillas. Entrées $6.75–10.75.

Sugar Bowl (480-946-0051), 4005 N. Scottsdale Rd. Open Mon.–Thu. 11 AM–11 PM (Fri. and Sat. till midnight, Sun. till 10). One of the Valley's favorite places for ice-cream yummies was immortalized in Bil Keane's comic strip *The Family Circus*. Keane was a neighbor of the Huntress family owners. Truly a sugar plum daydream, the retro ice-cream parlor, dressed in pink vinyl booths and a wooden soda fountain–style counter lined with chrome stools, has not changed much since the day it opened—Christmas Eve 1958. This includes some of the staff, who see kids of the kids coming back to satiate their sweet tooth The Sugar Bowl serves Dreyer's Grand ice cream, has the best hot fudge in town, and serves up sodas of all kinds and Top Hats (a cream puff filled with ice cream and topped with a sauce) like they were going out of style. There are also meals—things besides peanut butter and jelly sandwiches—on the menu, along with daily specials. Entrées (ice cream) $3.75–6.95, meals $3.95–8.50.

✷ The Arts

Ranked as a top art destination in the country, Scottsdale has visual arts scene full of variety and talent. Some of the best displays appear in the five-star resorts, with the Phoenician at the top of the list. Although art pops up all over the city, it's concentrated in the downtown area, especially Main Street and Marshall Way. Here, the predominance of western and Native American art has made way for a strong contemporary scene that even lets some photography in now and again. Join the locals at the **Scottsdale ArtWalk**, every Thu. 7–9 PM, where galleries offer special receptions, demonstrations, and exhibits. Several themed ArtWalks happen during the year.

Scottsdale Museum of Contemporary Art (480-874-4666), 7374 E. Second St. Open Tue., Wed., Fri., and Sat. 10–5; Thu. 10–8 (free); Sun. noon–5; closed Mon. (and Tue. in summer). The museum has a collection of contemporary art from around the globe presented in a variety of venues—interactive, changing exhibits, art nights—and goes a step further by hosting programs with a social twist, such as discussion panels, yoga nights, and artist talks and performances. $7 adults, $5 students, under age 15 free; free to members.

Taliesin West (480-860-2700), 12621 N. Frank Lloyd Wright Blvd. The great FLW built homes in beautiful places all over the country. The Valley has several such domiciles. Taliesin West is the queen—the repository of Wright's lifetime efforts. You can take a 1- to 3-hour tour to see how the master blended genius with nature. The property also headquarters the Frank Lloyd Wright Foundation and is home to the Frank Lloyd Wright School of Architecture. Tours $27–60.

✷ Selective Shopping

Kierland Commons (480-348-1577), 15210 N. Scottsdale Rd. Open daily; shop hours vary. Open air and perfect for just strolling, this shopping area is one of the hottest in the Valley, full of uncommon shops and dining. You can have an enjoyable time whether you take out your wallet or just take in the sights.

Old Town Scottsdale, 7201 E. Indian School Rd. Open daily; shop hours vary. The 2-mile-long strip of Scottsdale Road blends Scottsdale's roots with where the city's at today. Hitching posts and wood-front shops remind you of the days when sheep were herded down the main drag (Scottsdale Road) and open space prevailed. It still exudes an Old West flavor through a variety of shops that offer traditional, southwestern, and trendy merchandise. You'll also find a number of dining, entertainment, and spa venues, as well as historical districts.

Scottsdale Fashion Square (480-945-5495), 7014 E. Camelback Rd. Open Mon.–Sat. 10–9, Sun. 11–6. The end of the rainbow when it comes to shopping, this mall brings you all kinds of shopping adventures, from exclusive boutique designer shops such as H&M, Barneys New York, David Yurman, Louis Vuitton, and Tiffany & Co. to such department stores as Macy's, Neiman-Marcus, and Nordstrom, with just about all of the popular franchises in between. The largest mall in Arizona (and growing) has a food court, seven restaurants, two theaters, a full-service concierge desk, valet parking, and taxi and limousine services.

✷ Special Events

January: **P. F. Chang's Rock 'n' Roll Arizona Marathon** (800-311-1255) is an annual 26.2-mile race through Scottsdale, Phoenix, and Tempe with live music at every mile. Celebration **of Fine Art** (480-443-7695) features more than 100 artists selling gallery-quality work. The event runs from mid-January through March. **Barrett-Jackson Classic Car Auction** (480-421-6694) draws more than 1,000 collector automobiles from around the world as well as 200,000 admirers who can buy (or salivate over) them. **Arizona Sun Circuit Quarter Horse Show** (623-869-8037) presents about 1,500 of the country's best quarter horse athletes, who compete for $200,000 in prizes. The show starts the end of the month and runs for eight days. **FBR Open** (602-870-0163) has gained near-legendary status over the past 72 years as one of the five oldest events on the PGA Tour.

ARABIAN HORSES—DARLINGS OF THE HORSE WORLD

The Arabian carried prestige in ancient Arabian communities as a symbol of wealth. This tradition trickled down through the centuries, and came to prominence during the 1970s when the Arabian's image had a brush with glamour; especially in Scottsdale, which had the biggest market in the world where some of the very best horses in the whole world resided.

At that time, horses, in general, were an investment. Arabians, in particular, were promoted heavily; and some of the best horses sold for $1 million or more. Because a change in tax laws in 1986 de-escalated the market, the same horses would sell for a fraction today. Since the tax revisions, all horses took on a more affordable value. This included the darling Arabian, who went back to its roots and became a family-oriented horse.

Although people get involved with Arabians now for their love of the breed rather than an investment, an element of glamour still prevails at the Scottsdale Arabian Horse Show. While over 2,000 spirited Arabian horses from around the world compete with each other in two big arenas; movie stars, over 400 commercial exhibitors, food vendors, and show goers frocked in several-thousand-dollar outfits grab attention on the rest of the grounds.

February: **Prada del Sol** Parade (602-996-8289) is the world's largest horse-drawn parade. **Scottsdale Arabian Horse Show** (480-515-1500) at West-World features more than 2,000 Arabian horses showing off their beauty and talent with plenty of booths selling gifts and products, food and art. **Scottsdale Indian Market** (480-948-923) has Native American artists from around the country, entertainment and food.

March: **Celebration of Fine Art** (See January.) **Giants Spring Training** (480-312-2586). The San Francisco Giants practice all month at Indian School Park. **Scottsdale's Ultimate Block** Party (info@scottsdalesultimate blockparty.com). What started as a big block party bash has evolved into a party-hearty St. Patrick's Day event. The night offers food, drinks, and entertainment, including a midnight fireworks display.

April: **Scottsdale Culinary Festival** (480-945-7193) in Scottsdale Civic Center Mall draws more than 40,000 people looking to enjoy great food.

October: **Scottsdale International Film Festival** (602-410-1074). The best in current international films are shown at Harkins Camelview Luxury Cinemas.

November: **Artfest of Scottsdale** (888-278-3378) is the highest-rated fall art festival in Arizona, featuring more than 220 fine artists from around the country.

December: **Holiday Lights** (480-312-2312). McCormick-Stillman Railroad Park lights up with more than 100,000 holiday lights.

MINING COUNTRY: GLOBE, MIAMI, AND SUPERIOR

Like three pearls strung together by US 60, Globe, Miami, and Superior are gems that all have much more to offer than first meets the eye. Minerals have always played a big part in their history, but life goes on: Superior leans toward art and movies, Miami antiques, and Globe exquisite architecture with European craftsman influences.

With gold strikes foremost on their minds, prospectors were swooning in this mineral-rich mining country by the 1860s. Fueled by reports of "silver-streaked rocks, silver nuggets, and ledges of precious metals" by a New Mexico doctor who traveled to Arizona to treat the Apache peoples for an epidemic eye infection, activity centered on Sombrero Butte in the Sierra Ancha Mountains north of Globe. A strange mix of drifters, cowboys, preachers, unlucky prospectors, merchants, and investors gathered.

The Sombrero Butte lead was suddenly dropped when a soldier named Sullivan found a chunk of silver near Camp Pinal (Superior). All eyes turned toward finding Sullivan's silver lode. And what a lode it was: enough to call the area Arizona's silver belt and the mine, the Silver King. But before that happened, silver claims had been filed in the present-day Globe area two years earlier; one, the Globe Ledge, by the group that discovered the Silver King Mine. The Apaches' resistance delayed any further development of the Globe Ledge, so the group groped for that elusive Sullivan find and found it.

The Silver King Mine drew hundreds of miners to the Superior area in 1875. Among the brood came famous opportunists Wyatt Earp and Doc Holiday. It was a boom situation. As the ore ebbed by 1888, so did the people. However, the town didn't actually appear on the map until the turn of the 20th century, and then as a tent city for several years. Copper brought the miners back in 1910 when it was discovered beneath the silver cap.

Meanwhile, back in Globe, claims multiplied, the Apache relented, and the Globe Mining District formed by 1875. A year later, Globe got its start as Globe City and eventually became the county seat, with the state's first school district. In the downtown, Mesquite Street marked the boundary of respectability. Fair ladies never ventured south, where brothels abounded. The town was so raucous, the original 16-cell jail wasn't big enough to house the clientele. The sheriff's office

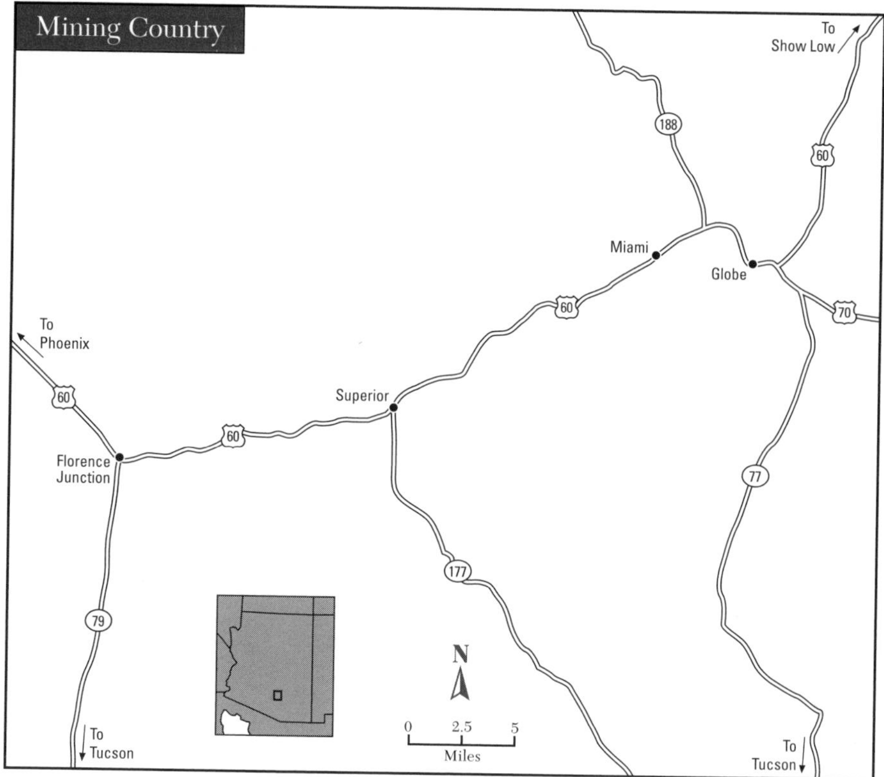

looked more like a revolving door—men never lived long in the position, and unmarried men need only apply.

During this silver boom, claims spread out to present-day Miami. The commute to work from Globe became drudgery, as all modern-day commuters can understand. After no little resistance, Miami developed into a separate city continually promoted by sly businessman Cleve Van Dyke. Years down the road, the minerals in Miami kept Globe alive.

Today Superior's sensational setting along the perpendicular ridge, Apache Leap, and old historic buildings makes it a natural for Hollywood. Almost a dozen movies and several commercials have been filmed there, including *How the West Was Won*. You can take walking tours in Globe to view the exquisite architecture built by Italian masons who worked on the Roosevelt Dam, walk the red-light district, and tour the jail where things were always hopping. In Miami, ever the merchant like its founding father, antiques shops give you a chance to peruse past generations' treasures.

The Apache built a casino on their land, providing an outlet for modern-day gold diggers to test their luck. Perhaps the surer treasure is the backcountry they own—pristine, beautiful, and full of watchable wildlife. All the land around Mining Country is that way—a rich, untrammeled landscape of mountains and desert canyons. Metaphorically, it's the Mining Country's gold that the old prospectors never found.

GUIDANCE **Globe-Miami Regional Chamber of Commerce and Economic Development Corporation** (928-425-4495 or 800-804-5623), 1360 N. Broad St., Globe. **Superior Chamber of Commerce** (520-689-0200), 300 Main St., Superior. Contact the **Globe Ranger District** (928-402-6200), 7680 S. Six Shooter Canyon Rd., or the Tonto Basin Ranger District (928-467-3200), Roosevelt, for information on national forest backcountry, and the **Bureau of Land Management Tucson Field Office** (520-258-7200), 2661 E. Broadway, Tucson, for information on public lands south of US 60 not in the national forest.

EXQUISITE STONEMASONRY CAN BE FOUND THROUGHOUT THE TOWN OF GLOBE

GETTING THERE US 60, AZ 88, AZ 77, and US 70 meet in Globe. Miami lies only a few miles west on US 60, and Superior 24 miles west on US 60 at AZ 77.

WHEN TO COME Cooler than the lower deserts, Mining Country gives a reasonable reprieve from the summer heat. Spring and fall offer the best weather and the most activity. Winter days hover around the 60s, and the nights flirt with the freezing mark.

MEDICAL EMERGENCY **Cobre Valley Community Hospital** (928-425-3261), 5880 S. Hospital Dr., Globe.

✷ To See

🐾 ✐ ♿ **Boyce Thompson Arboretum** (520-689-2723), US 60, 13 miles east of Florence Junction. Open daily Sep.–Apr. 8–4, May–Aug. 6–3; closed Christmas Day. Mining magnate and philanthropist William Boyce Thompson opened Arizona's oldest and largest arboretum in 1923 as a center for research. The arboretum has about 3,200 different species of plants from arid climates around the world, including a mature eucalyptus forest; boojum trees; and rose, wildflower, butterfly, hummingbird, and cactus gardens. Dozens of species of wildflowers bloom, unattended, after a wet winter. Queen Creek's sliver of a stream that runs through the arboretum beneath a dramatic backdrop of volcanic tuff cliffs attracts more than 230 bird species throughout the year, and staff- and volunteer-led bird walks take place each weekend, along with wildflower and plant hikes. Several trails wind around the grounds from which you can peruse the botanicals Check out the 1.5-mile Main Trail meanders among the gardens and the half-mile High

Trail climbs onto the rim of the Queen Creek Canyon into a more rugged landscape. $7.50 adults, $3 ages 5–12, under age 5 free.

Historic Gila County Jail and Sheriff's Office (928-425-9340), 149 E. Oak St. Open Mon.–Fri. noon–4. The town built four jails, each one bigger than the previous, and somehow still couldn't keep up with the rowdy clientele (one look at the graffiti and you'll understand how rowdy the clientele was). Historian Kip Culver tells you all about the people and history related to the jail and Globe. $2 per person, $3 per couple.

INDIAN RUINS ✐ **Besh-Ba-Gowah Archaeological Park** (928-425-0320 or 800-804-5623), Jesse Hayes Rd., Globe. Open daily 9–5. One of the Southwest's largest single archaeological sites sits at the confluence of Pinal Creek and Ice House Canyon Wash. The 600-year-old Salado ruin (a ceremonial, food storage, and redistribution complex) is one of the most significant finds of the century. The Salado culture lived from 1150 to 1450 on the Tonto Basin. $4 adults and age 12-plus, $3 age 65-plus, under age 12 free.

🐾 ✐ **Tonto National Monument** (928-467-2241), 3 miles southeast of Roosevelt Dam on AZ 88. The Lower Cliff Dwelling is open daily 8–5; closed Christmas Day. Guided tours of the Upper Cliff Dwellings are by reservation only, Nov.–Apr. Two sets of cliff dwellings constructed in natural alcoves were occupied by the Salado Indians AD 1300–1500. Farmers of the Salt River Valley, the Indians also produced some of the most exquisite polychrome pottery and meticulously woven textiles in the Southwest. You can see their handiwork displayed in the visitor center museum. To get to the ruins, you walk a 0.5-mile-long paved trail to the Lower Cliff Dwelling. Leashed pets are permitted on this trail. You can only view the Upper Cliff Dwelling via a guided tour (reservations required; pets not allowed). The 3-mile round trip takes 3–4 hours. $3 adults, under age 16 free

SCENIC DRIVES The **Apache Trail**, one of the state's classic scenic drives, winds between Roosevelt Lake and Apache Junction. Always keeping its eye on the string of azure-colored lakes pooled along the Salt River, the road actually follows an old Apache footpath. During construction of Roosevelt Dam, the road provided transportation of equipment and supplies. The narrow, hairpinned, unpaved (but graded) track has no guardrails, which tends to give novices white knuckles. They are advised to drive it from west to east, with the reassuring cliffs right next to the vehicle; an east–west crossing puts your wheels inches from a precipitous drop. There's plenty of scenery; some excellent hiking trails; and Tortilla Flats, with a single-digit population, has a restaurant to refresh you.

✷ To Do

BOATING The largest of the reservoirs, **Roosevelt Lake**, pooled from the Salt River, gives you a chance to partake in a rather anomalous desert activity—boating. You can rent craft ranging from a 14-foot fishing boat to a 56-foot-long houseboat from **Roosevelt Lake Marina** (602-977-7171), AZ 88, open daily 7:30–5.

FISHING **Roosevelt Lake**, located about 30 miles northwest of Phoenix off AZ 88, has 88 miles of shoreline and a variety of fish just itching to put up a fight—largemouth and smallmouth bass, crappie, sunfish, catfish, bluegill, and carp.

Contact the Tonto National Forest or Arizona Department of Game and Fish (602-942-3000) for information.

GAMING Apache Gold Casino (800-272-2438), about 17 miles east of Globe on US 70 in San Carlos. Named for a lost treasure of gold known only by the Apache. The casino has 500 video and progressive slot machines, live bingo, $50,000 keno, blackjack, and "one of the West's most liberal Poker Rooms."

GOLF Apache Stronghold (800-272-2438), about 17 miles east of Globe on US 70 in San Carlos. Legend says a deity named Usen created a mystical area in the midst of the Chiricahua, Aravaipa, Superstition, and White mountains that the Apache call the Stronghold. Here tribe members could walk invisibly among their enemies. The San Carlos placed an award-winning golf course in this area. Now, that doesn't necessarily mean you can pick up those sand-trapped balls without anyone seeing you, but it does mean you will play golf in a landscape like no other. Cliffs, rather than swanky homes, surround you, and archaeological sites, not hotel rooms, appear among the desert vegetation. $20–35.

HIKING See also *Wilder Places*. You can take your pick of what kind of environment you like to hike in, and how close, or far, from civilization you want to get. Globe's in-town **Round the Mountain Park** (from US 60, turn north on South St.) has a small network of trails that can give you a good workout and take you away from the city's sights and sounds. If you want to get into the backcountry and the higher elevations, the **Pinal Mountain Recreation Area** (contact the Globe Ranger District) has several trails. The **Six Shooter Trail** travels through several biomes, from high desert to aspen-fir. The **Ice House Trail** has the best fall color in the area (mid-Oct.). **Picketpost Mountain** (contact the Globe Ranger District) calls for experience if you want to hike its unmaintained route, which climbs almost 2 miles (sometimes requiring hand-over-foot work) to a 4,375-foot peak. The 360-degree view makes the climb worth it.

ARIZONA TRAIL There are several segments of trail you can hike in this general area that take you through cloistered canyons, up desert mountains covered with saguaro cactus forests and wildflowers in spring, and across desert flats. Contact the Globe and Tonto Basin Ranger Districts or log onto www.aztrail.org.

ROAD BIKING Located among some of the most thrilling mountain ranges as far as road biking goes, Superior understands those road bicyclists who live for rollers and challenging slopes. There are several annual road biking events. In Mar. the **Mining Country Challenge**—and it is a challenge—tests your cycling mettle on a 66- or 96-mile route through the surrounding mountains. In early Apr. the 62-mile **OMYA/Superior Road Race** begins in Superior and travels to Winkelman and back, paying a cash purse of $2,000; the next day the **OMYA/ Superior Criterium**, a 0.7-mile loop, earns a cash purse of more than $1,200. For information on these events, call 520-689-0200.

ROCK CLIMBING Devil's Canyon, located along US 60 about 4 miles west of Superior near Oak Flat Campground, is a premier climbing spot that draws climbers from around the world. Contact the Globe Ranger District.

✷ Spas

Adobe Ranch Wellness Spa (928-425-3632), 138 S. Broad St., Suite 2. Open Mon.–Fri. 10–6. While spas naturally lean toward luxury, not all have luxury prices. You can get a nice spa package here and feel just as pampered as you would in an upscale resort spa for half the price. Packages here cost about as much as a single spa treatment elsewhere, and a 90-minute session costs half what you'd pay for a 60-minute treatment elsewhere. The reason? You're in the best-kept secret of the state's historic Mining Country. Enjoy. Massages $50–85, facials $55–150, special treatments and packages $110–225, nail services $25–45.

✷ Wilder Places

Pinal Mountain Recreation Area (contact the Globe Ranger District). The sky island Pinal Mountains vary in vegetation from scrubby chaparral mix along mountain slopes to quaking aspen trees on the peaks. In between, the landscape ranges from high-country pines to New England–style hardwood forests and classic high-desert vegetation. Trails travel several miles and climb several thousand feet. The most scenic are **Six Shooter** and **Ice House Trails** (see *Hiking*).

San Carlos Apache Reservation (928-475-2344 or 888-475-2343), located about 17 miles east of Globe on US 70. World-class for big-game hunting, the Apache reservation also has some great backcountry routes perfect for exploring. Even if you don't hunt, those trophy animals make good wildlife-watching. You can fish, camp, hike, and bike on the land for $10 a day. Get the required (and strictly enforced) permits at the Recreation and Wildlife Department, located at US 70 and Geronimo Road.

✷ Lodging

Apache Gold Casino Resort (928-475-7800 or 800-272-2438), US 70, San Carlos. The San Carlos Apache give this Best Western a cultural spin. The property includes a heated outdoor pool, meeting facilities, a bar/lounge, a restaurant, golf, a hot tub, a sauna, a fitness center, a game room, an arcade, and a guest laundry. Rooms include free local calls, cable TV with in-room movies, high-speed Internet, and coffeemaker. The **Apache Grill** features authentic Apache and southwestern cuisine, and the gift shop offers Apache basketry and beadwork. $79–89.

♿ **Noftsger Hill Inn Bed and Breakfast** (928-425-2260 or 877-780-2479), 425 North St., Globe. Built in 1907 as the North Globe Schoolhouse, the school immediately underwent expansion. It was the place for education until 1981, when its last class graduated. Ten years later owner-innkeepers Dom and Rosalie Ayala started renovation on the building to convert it to a

THE NOFTSGER HILL INN BED AND BREAKFAST

B&B. The classrooms-turned-guestrooms have become huge studios furnished with antiques; double, king, or queen beds, sitting area; TV; and private bath, formerly a cloakroom. Chalkboards have messages from former guests, many of them students with fond memories of the school. Each room has a view from windows you won't see crafted quite so beautifully these days. In the morning Rosalie makes sure you won't go hungry with a hearty (but not fat-laden) delicious southwestern-style breakfast. Birding specials in May include a "lesson" given by a birding expert on Friday nights with a complimentary bird walk on Sunday morning. Breakfast is included with all accommodations. $90–125.

✷ Where to Eat

DINING OUT Back 9 Bistro (928-473-4442), Cobre Valley Country Club, 2 Pinal Canyon Dr., Globe. Open for lunch Mon.–Fri. 11–2, dinner Wed.–Fri. 5–8. In a town that excels in Mexican food served from family-run kitchens, this bistro makes a find if you're looking to go non-Mexican. They are known for their various half-pound burgers, including chipotle blue cheese and green chile cheeseburgers, as well as pastas; the blackened halibut is a nonmeat-eater's favorite. Meals are simple and fresh, with a special every day. Friday nights (prime rib night) get crowded; best to make a reservation. Entrées $9.95–17.95.

Café Piedra Roja (520-689-0194), 507 W. Main St., Superior. Open Mon.–Sat.11–3. Colorful and serving consistently good Mexican food, this café upholds the town's propensity to support the arts. Its bold-colored walls have local artwork that you can purchase. The food is cooked with canola oil; no animal fat. Refried beans are homemade. And the salsa is *pico de gallo* (tomato, onion, cilantro, and chiles). Along with a daily special, the menu has salads (the chicken salad with mango has grilled chicken strips and mango on lettuce with chips and salsa, tomatoes, and lime); Mexican dishes (burritos, tostada, and nachos); and sandwiches (hamburgers, grilled chicken, and ham or turkey tortas). There's always a special, and the enchiladas are exceptional. So are the prices. Entrées $4.95–6.95. BYOB for a $1 setup fee.

Guayo's on the Trail (928-425-9969), 1938 Hwy. 188, Globe. Open Wed.–Mon. 10:30–9; closed Tue. An enduring Globe favorite that's been around since 1938. Eddie y Karen Esparza cook up classic Mexican delights, including *albondigas* and *menudo*, every day. The traditional bowl of chips (the first one's free) come hot and homemade, like everything else. Beer is served in frozen mugs. Seniors get a 10 percent discount. Entrées $6.50–13.50.

EATING OUT Burger House (928-473-9918), 812 Live Oak St., Miami. Open Mon.–Sat. 5:30 AM–8 PM. Mexican at its fast-food finest. The made-to-order food is dependably good, and you can get it on the fly or sit down for a quick, simple meal. $2.50–5.95.

El Ranchito (928-402-1348), 686 Broad St., Globe. Open Tue.–Fri. 11–9, Sat. and Sun. 8–9; closed Mon. As the name says, it's a tiny restaurant, but the food has big flavor. All of it's made on the premises, and the green chili is the town favorite. On weekends a breakfast of *pozole*, *menudo*, *huevos con jamos*, and *machaca* is served in addition to the regular menu. Entrées $5.95–7.95.

Los Robertos (928-425-3030), 340 S. Broad St., Globe. Open Mon.–Sat. 7 AM–9 PM, Sun. 8–3. The dine-in or

LOS ROBERTO'S—SOME OF THE BEST MEXICAN FOOD AROUND

drive-through eatery has some great fresh food. You can order the usual Mexican food dishes, plus some unusual ones, such as *lengua* (tongue) *burro*, *menudo*, and *adobada* (pork with chiles), plus a vegetarian burro that has everything but the meat and more. The salsas are made fresh daily. $2.39–6.99.

✷ The Arts

Blue Mule (928-425-4920), 656 N. Broad St., Globe. Open Tue.–Sat. 10–5. Artist-owners John and Laurie have created a space for themselves and local artists to show their creativity. The floor is a work of art in itself—pieces of wood John glued down, sanded, and varnished; a tedious process with gorgeous results. Besides painting, Laurie specializes in cat adoptions. If you love cats, take your armor with you if you don't want to walk out with one of the cute, forlorn, homeless critters.

✷ Selective Shopping

The biggest finds in the Mining Country are antiques and art. Globe still has a working, operating downtown with all the basics you need in life from clothes to auto repairs and a saddle shop. **Broad Street** (named for the number of broads working in the whorehouses) in the downtown historic section has a number of collectible and antiques shops. Also check out antique shops on **Mesquite St.** (where the tallest three-story building in the world is located) south of Broad St. and north of the railroad tracks. Miami has a national reputation for its antiques business on **Sullivan St.**, just northwest of US 60. Plan your shopping for the weekend, however; stores tend to be closed during the week or open by appointment only.

Copper Mine Picture Café (928-473-4367), 418 Sullivan St., Miami. Open Thu.–Sun. 11–5. For a small town, an honest-to-goodness gallery is a rare find. This one, located in an attractive old building among a line of antiques stores, gives you a chance to view some quality art from local artists. Owner Jim Coates, a native Arizonan

GLOBE'S BROAD STREET

who has lived in several places around the country, has new shows monthly. You can get a cup of coffee and shoot the breeze with Coates, too.

Pickle Barrel Trading Post (928-425-9282), 404 S. Broad St. Open daily 10–6. The first thing you notice as you walk into this authentic trading post that has the feel of an old-time western curio shop is the 8- by 10-foot pencil-on-canvas of Geronimo on horseback titled *One Last Ride*. Next, you might notice glass cases of authentic Native American jewelry, buckskins, and Apache basketry. But you probably won't notice the architect's floor stamp at the doorstep dated 1902, Globe, AT (*AT* stands for "Arizona Territory"). Once you get to exploring Jim and Kelly Moss's 2,000-object warehouse of authentic art, collectibles, antiques, and sundry items, you might feel like you're in a museum. A kids' corner has minerals and fun things to keep active minds fascinated. The outside is loaded with metal yard art from Mexico.

✷ Special Events

Unless otherwise noted, call 800-804-5623 for more information.

January: **Gila County Gem and Mineral Show**. The three-day show at the Gila County Fairgrounds features loose gemstones, minerals, finished jewelry, lapidary equipment, books, and artisans demonstrating the many facets of working with gems and minerals.

February: **Historic Home and Building Tour** and **Antique and Quilt Show** in Globe features architecture and antiques via tours around town (admission) and exhibits at the Cobre Valley Center for the Arts (free).

March: **Annual Pow Wow** presents Native American performances from around the United States at the Apache Gold Pavilion.

April: **Gila County Championship Rodeo** at the Gila County Fair Grounds, where cowboys and cowgirls compete in professional rodeo events. **Annual Miami Boomtown Spree** features the Arizona State Mining Championships (hand and machine drilling, spike driving, and mucking) along with a parade, pancake breakfast, food, arts, crafts, and music.

May: **Annual Gold-N-Oldies Car Show and Blues Fest** blend 29 classes of historic and unusual cars with music, arts and crafts, and food in Miami.

September: **Bye-Bye Buzzards** (520-689-2811) at Boyce Thompson Arboretum promises a whimsical time to say farewell to the buzzards that glide on the area's updrafts and thermals with cake, a bird walk and animal exhibits. **Annual Gila County Fair** at the Gila County Fairgrounds features a beef cook-off, rodeo, arts and crafts, music, games, carnival, and livestock judging. **Annual Apache Jil (Day) Celebration** in downtown Globe celebrates Native American arts, crafts, and performances. **Indian National Finals Rodeo** has the best Native American riders, ropers, and cowboys and cowgirls competing at Apache Gold Pavilion.

October: **Fall Festival and Ghosts of Globe Tour** takes place on Halloween night, beginning at the Old Gila County Jail and heading to other historic, and haunted, buildings.

November: **Fall Color Festival** (520-689-2811) at Boyce Thompson Arboretum celebrates the last autumn color in the state with fall color, music, and spiced cider.

December: **Festival of Lights** Luminaria and Native American performers at Besh-Ba-Gowah Archaeological Park.

WICKENBURG

Casual history pegs the genesis of Wickenburg on Henry Wickenburg's discovery of gold in 1863. But Hispanic pioneers Ramon and Juan Macias had already established their 6M Ranch above the Hassayampa River six years earlier. These brothers, and other families from Sonora that followed, had mining and ranching in their blood—a perfect match for the land in which they settled.

After Wickenburg started the Vulture Mine, which turned out to be Arizona's most productive gold mine, prospectors flooded into the desert. Gold made it a place on the map, the Hispanic pioneers made it a town. Señor Ygnacio Garcia donated land for the school at Vulture City (located near the Vulture Mine) to be moved into town (now the Little Red School House in the old Hispanic neighborhood across from Basha's Market). He also donated land for a cemetery (now the historic Garcia Cemetery about a mile north of the Chamber on AZ 93, where the town's Hispanic pioneers rest). Hispanic families helped build the current structure for St. Anthony de Padua Catholic Church (232 N. Tegner St.), started in 1892.

VAQUERO ANGEL MORALEZ STILL RUNS ANGEL'S RANCH PIONEERED BY HIS SPANISH PARENTS NEAR THE HASSAYAMPA RIVER

With its appealing meld of classic Sonoran scenery, mining history, and dude ranches, Wickenburg correctly calls itself "Arizona's Most Western Town." Cowboys, the steeds they ride, and the open spaces where they roam are key to what Wickenburg is all about.

Take a walk along a trail in its backcountry, just a short few minutes from town, and experience the magnificence of the Sonoran Desert in bloom. Or visit an old mining site strewn with relics on a hardscrabble hillside and pause to wonder how strong the drive for riches must have been to keep prospectors working under a broiling summer sun. Or watch a 60-year-old

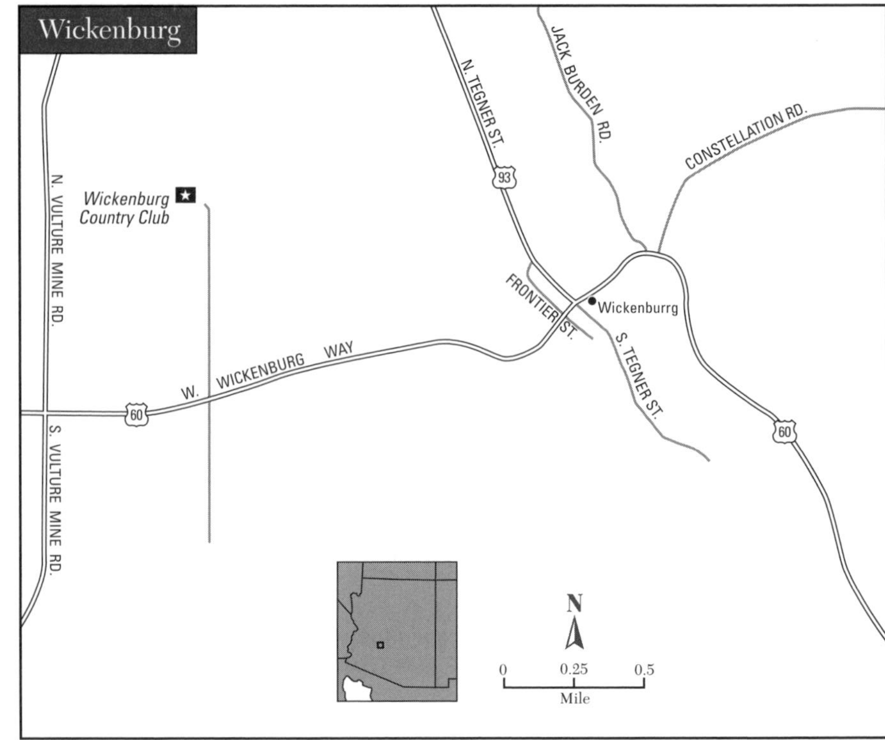

cowboy in a rodeo beat the buzzer in a bull-riding event, then limp out of the arena with a smile on his face.

Unless you value the views of an unhindered horizon or can identify with Baxter Black's poetry, you may not quite understand Wickenburg. No problem. Just stick with the high points of enjoying an untrammeled backcountry trail, enjoying scenic drives as close and easy as they used to be in Arizona's more populated desert cities three or four decades ago, and getting a look at a cowboy at work without going too far off the highway.

If you just plan to stay in town, don't forget the legend of the Hassayampa is alive and well here. This decades-old miners' lore declares that one drink from the Hassayampa River will compel imbibers never to tell the truth again. Visitors will be hard pressed to get a drink from the Hassayampa, which flows mostly underground, unless they head to the chamber offices and pick up a bottle of "genuine" Hassayampa River water—probably a by-product of that silly miner's legend. But don't trust them; they drink the water. Go see for yourself.

GUIDANCE Wickenburg Chamber of Commerce (928-684-5479), 216 N. Frontier St. Open Mon.–Fri. 9–5, Sat. and Sun. 10–2 (call for summer weekend hours). Get information on backcountry use on public lands in the area from **Bureau of Land Management—Phoenix Field Office** (623-580-5500), 21605 N. 7th Ave., Phoenix, open 8–4; or **State Trust Land Department** (602-364-2753), 1616 W. Adams, Phoenix.

GETTING THERE *By car:* It's an hour's drive from Phoenix on US 60, and some 60 winding miles south of Prescott via AZ 89. The Valley Metro has a commuter bus along US 60 that travels between Wickenburg's West Plaza and Glendale's Arrowhead Towne Center in the West Valley. *By air:* **Wickenburg Municipal Airport** (928-684-0754) services private planes. *By shuttle:* **Wickenburg Airport Express** (928-684-2888 or 866-245-5351) is available 24/7.

WHEN TO COME Wickenburg's high season runs from Nov. through Apr., when the mild winter weather appeals to everyone.

MEDICAL EMERGENCY **Wickenburg Community Hospital** (928-684-5421), 520 Rose Ln.

✷ To See

Desert Caballeros Western Museum (928-684-2272), 21 N. Frontier St. Open Mon.–Sat. 10–5, Sun. noon–4; closed Mon. in July and Aug. Former governor Napolitano named this western art and history museum one of Arizona's treasures. A collection of more than 400 pieces of western art includes works from Remington and Russell. Western life comes alive in the outstanding cowboy and Native American exhibits, street scenes, and dioramas. $7.50 adults, $6 seniors, $1 ages 6–16, under age 5 free.

The Jail Tree, Tegner and Wickenburg Way. With the huge placer and lode gold discoveries going on around town, seems no one thought about building a jail. The powers that be merely chained scofflaws to the trunk of a mesquite tree. Now around 200 years old, the old mesquite could probably write a book on its times with some of the town's saltier characters who sat in its shade. Free.

SCENIC DRIVES **Skull Valley**. This drive, about 50 miles one way, takes you through the mining town of Yarnell, then up to the green grasslands of Skull Valley along the historic Peavine Railroad. From downtown, head northwest on US 93 about 6 miles, then turn right onto US 89; go up the Yarnell Hill and through the town of Yarnell (stop at the Cornerstone Bakery for the richest pastries, good sandwiches, and homemade soups) to Kirkland Junction (about 31 miles). Turn left onto Thompson Valley Rd., continue 4 miles to Kirkland, and turn right onto Iron Springs Rd. Go 7 miles to the town of Skull Valley. Just north of the railroad tracks, make a hard left onto 3-mile-long Old Skull Valley Rd. (unpaved after 0.5 mile, but graded) for a look at the countrified side of Arizona. This makes for a refreshing walk along a country road.

BACKCOUNTRY ROADS TAKE YOU INTO GORGEOUS PARTS OF THE SONORAN DESERT AROUND WICKENBURG

✱ To Do

GOLF **Rancho de los Caballeros Golf Club** (928-684-2704), 1551 S. Vulture Mine Rd. This is not your traditional desert course with lots of forced carries. It's solid grass from tee to green, and the greens are some of the fastest in the state. This makes for a pace of play that hovers around 4 hours. Lady-friendly, only an hour's drive from Phoenix, and challenging to all abilities, the front nine present a classic layout of wide landing areas and ample greens. The hilly back nine will make you use just about every club in your bag. Hole 13 is consistently ranked as one of the most challenging par-5 holes in the state. What makes this par-72 course special, first, is the natural surroundings—Vulture Peak, the Bradshaw Mountains, and wildlife. Second, it's a deal. Such a wonderful deal, in fact, that it ranks among the world's best courses in popular magazine surveys. Driving range, putting greens, short game practice, and golf shop. $80–150.

Wickenburg Country Club (928-684-2011), 1420 Country Club Dr. The 50-plus-year-old course is called Wickenburg's best-kept secret. The newly rebuilt 18-hole championship green has a total yardage of 6,400. Par-71. $59 for 18 holes.

HIKING Some of the best desert hiking in the state is located in the wilderness areas surrounding Wickenburg. The popular **Vulture Peak Trail**, short and steep, is just outside town. Pick up a copy of *Wickenburg Adventures* at the chamber of commerce for other trails in the area

HISTORICAL WALKING TOUR Get a map from the chamber of commerce for the self-guided tour to more than 30 historical buildings and other points of interest around Wickenburg.

JEEP TOURS **BC Jeep Tours** (928-684-7901) takes you out into the backcountry around Wickenburg for a short trip to see the local scenery or a day trip to historical mines and/or scenery. Call for reservations and prices.

ORCHARDS **Date Creek Ranch** (928-231-0704). Go 22 miles on US 93, and turn right (north) at milepost 177.5 and go 4 miles to the ranch. Fruit trees in the desert? In the high desert, yes. You can pick your own pesticide-free peaches and summer apples from mid-July through August; Red and Golden Delicious apples in September and October. Check out their Apple Harvesting Fest in September. You can also order grass-fed beef (by the quarter to whole cow) and pork. The ranch uses no pesticides in the orchard and no antibiotics, steroids or hormones on the animals.

DOZENS OF DISTINCTIVE HIKING ROUTES ARE LOCATED RIGHT AROUND WICKENBURG

✷ Wilder Places

Hassayampa River Preserve (928-684-2772), 49614 US 60 (near mile marker 114 on the west side of the highway). Open mid-Sep.–mid-May, Wed.–Sun. 8–5; in summer, Fri.–Sun. 7 AM–11 PM. Trails close at 4:30; closed Thanksgiving and the day after, Christmas Eve and Christmas, and New Year's Eve and New Year's Day. Known as a bird watchers' paradise, this is a spot where you can, and should, bring your binoculars, comfortable shoes, and a bird book—but not your pet. The area is a protected streamside habitat that attracts all kinds of wildlife. A marsh draws waterbirds and the endangered southwestern willow flycatcher. The preserve has some interesting cultural history as well. The headquarters building, built in the 1860s, is listed on the State Register of Historic Places. The property evolved from a working cattle ranch in 1871, to a guest ranch called the Garden of Allah in 1913, and then the Lazy RC Ranch. The Nature Conservancy finally bought and preserved the land and allowed nature to have its way once again. $5 per person.

✷ Lodging

Best Western Rancho Grande Motel (928-684-5445 or 800-854-7235), 293 E. Wickenburg Way. This family-owned property is a guest-friendly favorite that gets repeat business. Includes a pool and spa, horseshoes, volleyball, and a children's playground. Rooms have cable TV, complimentary high-speed Internet, free local calls under 30 minutes, coffeemaker, and refrigerator; many have kitchenette and microwave. Pets $8 per night. $80–94.

Super 8 Motel (928-684-0808), 975 N. Tegner. The unique feature about this chain is it has corral space to board your stock. Laundry facilities on the premises. Rooms have cable TV, Internet access, and free local calls. Free continental breakfast. Fee for pets. $91.

Los Viajeros Inn (928-684-7099 or 800-915-9795), 1000 N. Tegner Rd. Rooms here are large, with Southwest appointments. King or queen beds, satellite TV, complimentary WiFi, mini fridge, and private balcony or patio. Pool and heated spa. Continental breakfast is included. No pets. $90–100

GUEST RANCHES Wickenburg's history as the Guest Ranch Capital of the World for more than 40 years makes it one of the best destinations for dude moments. The handful of ranches, though each different in style, offer an out-West experience as genteel or rugged as you want to go.

Flying E Ranch (928-684-2690 or 888-684-2650), 2801 W. Wickenburg Way. Open Nov.–May. Known as the Riding Ranch with its 20,000 acres of riding countryside, the Flying E is a small, informal operation. The property has a solar pool and hot spa, sauna, tennis, and horseback riding. Rooms have king or twin beds, hand-painted Monterrey furniture, heat and air-conditioning, wet bars, and private baths. You get your meals served family style in a laid-back, homey atmosphere that's for guests only, and BYOL. Minimum stay; $295–378 for a double.

Kay El Bar Guest Ranch (928-684-7593 or 800-684-7583). Open Oct.–May. Eight guest rooms—located in an authentic adobe building listed on the National Historic Register—have king, queen, or twin beds; no TV or phone. The property includes a pool and horseback riding. All meals are home-cooked from scratch and served in private dining room. Minimum stay; $375–485 per double.

Rancho de los Caballeros (928-684-5484), 1551 S. Vulture Mine Rd. Open from the second week of October through Mother's Day. With a name that translates to "gentlemen on horseback," the resort exudes class and over-the-top hospitality, from making notes of what pleases clients to ensure they experience the same on their next visit (guests from four generations are not uncommon) to the dinner dress code. This family-owned historic guest ranch thinks of itself as "high touch" rather than "high tech" by awakening the senses with basic pleasures. Like riding a horse. Although life doesn't always center on the corral around the resort today, the cowboy spirit reigns, and it certainly is in the blood of the owners and wranglers who work there. Love of the outdoors is celebrated here, with horseback riding, nature hikes, skeet shooting, cookouts, jeep tours, four tennis courts, swimming (in the hand-dug pool), golf (rated as some of the best in the country), and a spa (to massage out those sore muscles). Traditionally, guests congregated in the main lodge to unwind via card games, billiards, and gossip. Handcrafted Santa Fe–style furniture and Mexican tilework make each of the guest rooms and suites a different home on this 20,000-acre range. TVs and phones were begrudgingly added to rooms in the last two decades. Complimentary WiFi is available in the main lodge, but not allowed at the bar. Guests can no longer land on the private airstrip (they have to land in Wickenburg Municipal Airport), but they can pay with a credit card, circa 2004. One thing that hasn't changed is the running of the 100 or so horses in the morning and at dusk; that's enough to ignite the spirit of the cowboy in anybody. Call for rates.

Williams Family Ranch (928-308-0589). Open Sep.–May. Located about 20 miles north of Wickenburg at the end of a twisting mountain road on the edge of the wild and practically uncharted Hassayampa River Canyon Wilderness, this ranch will give you a valid taste of life on a working cow ranch. Nothing fancy here, just wild open spaces and real ranching. Minimum stay; $155 per person; no credit cards accepted. Rates include three meals per day and several-hour rides each day.

✱ Where to Eat

DINING OUT Rancho de los Caballeros (928-684-5484), 1551 S. Vulture Mine Rd. Open daily for buffet lunch and dinner Oct.–May; call for hours. Reservations for nonguests required. Although it's part of an all-inclusive guest ranch where ranch life is celebrated, the restaurant truly leans toward the "Caballeros" part of its name, rather than the "Rancho." The menu, which changes daily, features fresh and/or organic ingredients. Often the ingredients are not only local but indigenous. You might see desert quail dusted with seasoned flour and pan-fried, and aged beef so fresh, it travels directly from the ranch to the table. The menu also has variety, such as Lobster Romanoff or Chef Lupe's special featuring her native Sonoran cuisine. The southwestern fare has a spiciness that keeps a low profile while making its presence pleasantly known. The breakfast buffet includes fresh foods, cereals, eggs, and more. The lunch buffet offers a couple of entrées, a large variety of salads, and breads, always the best quality. Keep a spot in your tummy open for dessert. There's a whole tableful of rich yummies—so big, a staff member stands by to answer questions regarding what's what in the sugary spread. Breakfast buffet $13; lunch buffet $16 weekdays, $18 Sunday; dinner $41 (sports coat or western vest required for men) for starter, entrée, dessert, and coffee or tea.

EATING OUT **Anita's Cocina Family Restaurant** (928-684-5777), 57 N. Valentine. Open daily for lunch and dinner 11–9. The local gathering spot serves warm chips, salsa with a mild kick, and dependably good food. Make that big portions of dependably good food. Arrive late for lunch or early for dinner to avoid a wait. $5.95–12.95.

Cowboy Café (928-684-2807), 686 N. Tegner. Open daily for breakfast 6–11, lunch 11–2; call for dinner hours. This is where the real cowboys eat breakfast. The owners are rodeo riders, and meals are named for rodeo greats—such as the Bodacious Bacon Burger named for a famous bull. If you can't make breakfast, make sure you can come by for dinner and taste their famous chicken-fried steak. Entrées $7.95–8.95.

Rancho Bar 7 (928-684-2492), 111 E. Wickenburg Way. Open Mon.–Sat. 11–9. Having been open for business since 1937, the local favorite has truly captured the flavor of the town, serving Mexican, steakhouse, and homestyle cooking as American as the cowboys that hang out there. Most anything you order will be made in-house and tasty. $5.95–9.95.

Screamers Drive In (928-684-9056), 1151 W. Wickenburg Way. Open Mon.–Sat. 6 AM–8 PM (breakfast 6–10 AM) Sun. 10:30–8. You don't want to be on a diet when you come to this classic drive-in. You do want to prime yourself for some good old-fashioned cooked-to-order fare: hand-packed burgers, delightful fresh fries, hot dogs, onion rings, malts, shakes, and cones. Sandwiches $3–6.50.

PRISTINE SONORON DESERT BACKCOUNTRY NEAR WICKENBURG

✷ The Arts

PERFORMING ARTS Del E. Webb Center for the Performing **Arts** (928-684-6624), 1090 S. Vulture Mine Rd. Often the preferred venue for artists performing in Arizona. People come from around the nation to see the talent in the 600-seat auditorium. Plus, the center provides free art camps for children from cities around the state. Call for schedule.

✷ Special Events

Call the Chamber of Commerce for more information on all events.

February: **Gold Rush Days,** a 60-year-old tradition that celebrates Wickenburg's heritage of cowboys and mining with a shoot-out, parade, rodeo, gold panning, mucking and drilling contest, vendors, art, and food. The Library of Congress in Washington DC recognized the celebration as one of the 100 Living Legacies in the United States.

April: The week-long **Desert Caballeros Ride** brings cowboys from around the world to take part in a horseback adventure.

September: **Fiesta Septiembre** celebrates Wickenburg's Hispanic heritage with folklorico dancers, mariachi music, food, arts, and crafts.

October: **Wickenburg Fly-In and Classic Car Show** at the Wickenburg Airport features airplanes and classic cars.

November: The **Bluegrass Festival** draws thousands from the Southwest to a three-day event that features the Four Corners states' championship contests for fiddle, flat-pick guitar, banjo, and mandolin.

December: Hear poems, songs, and stories about western heritage at the **Cowboy Christmas Poetry Gathering**. The **Christmas Light Parade** has lighted floats, Santa Claus, hot chocolate, carolers, and popcorn balls.

THE MOGOLLON RIM—WEST

When Zane Grey first experienced the Mogollon (pronounced muggy-yown) Rim, his poetic prose met its match as he "saw a scene that defied words . . . For wild rugged beauty; I had not seen its equal." Enthralled with his newfound piece of wilderness, Grey settled down in a cabin there to write novels with heroes and heroines that traipsed the rim's enchanting countryside.

Called the backbone of Arizona, this 300-mile-long escarpment along the state's midsection—it extends into New Mexico—still casts a spell too mesmerizing for some people to untangle themselves. You have only to see its forested rampart where fluted limestone stacks upon blushing sandstone outcroppings, fill your lungs with pine redolence dripping in some of the cleanest air on the planet, or find yourself sealed in an envelope of silence in a remote section of the largest stand of ponderosa pines in the world to understand the rim's lure.

The Mogollon Rim draws those looking to escape the cities. Talk to the shop-keepers when you're there. Many will tell you about their former big-city-corporate-rat-race life. Like a mother comforting a child, the rim's tranquility and simplicity wrap you in security and peace. The sights, sounds, and smells of this backcountry saturate the senses.

In summer lush colonies of wild roses, ferns, and wildflowers cover the forest floor; wild grapevines drape the trees. Autumn ignites bursts of red, orange, and gold from bigtooth maples laced with aspens; russet from the Gambel oaks. Take a slow cruise down Colcord Road at twilight to view herds of elk, or watch a bald eagle splash into Willow Springs Lake in winter for a fish dinner to know how sweet a pine forest can get.

Do be warned, however, that Mogollon Rim weather is often at its worst in summertime. Daily thunderstorms rake across the escarpment, bringing afternoon wind, rain, and hail. Still, by day's end the swollen skies give way to an inky firmament sparkling with stars, and pine trees rock like ships lulled by a gentle wind as they toss their sweet aroma into the crisp night air. The campfire embers flare and pop, relinquishing their flame to ashes. And thoughts like Zane Grey's "For wild rugged beauty; I had not seen its equal" creep into the mind.

GUIDANCE **Rim Country Regional Chamber of Commerce** (928-474-4515 or 800-672-9766) is open daily and provides brochures, maps, directions, and area information. **Payson Ranger District** (928-474-7900) manages much of the

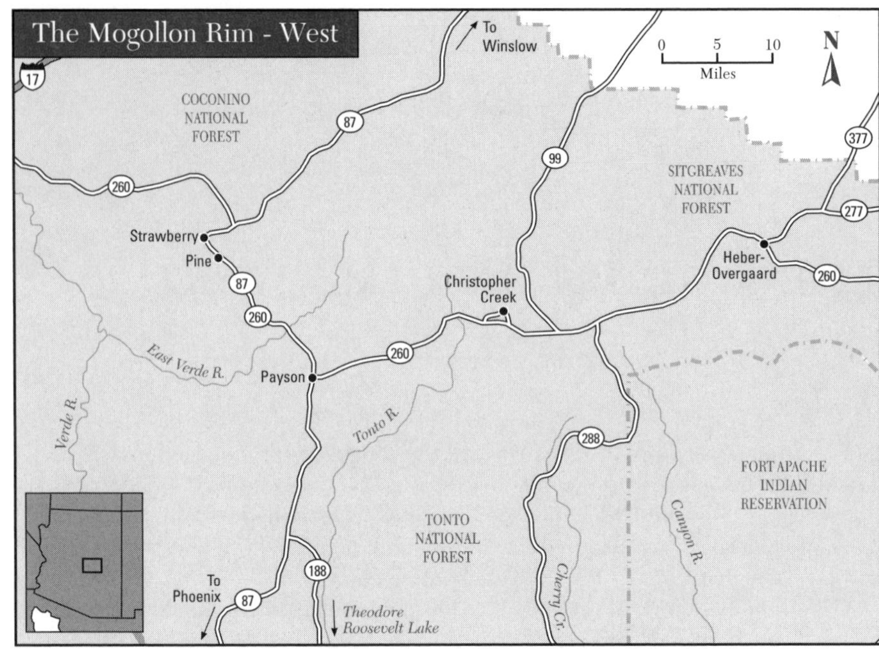

beautiful spread of ponderosa pines on the rim along and south of AZ 260. For backcountry information for points north of the rim, contact **Mogollon Rim Ranger District** (928-477-2255).

GETTING THERE From I-17, Camp Verde exit no, 287, take AZ 260 east; from east Phoenix, take AZ 87 north. I-17 and AZ 87 see heavy backups on the last day of long holiday weekends in the summer.

WHEN TO COME Summertime is high season on the rim. It's only about 90 minutes away from Phoenix and a major destination during summer. Be sure to plan ahead if you travel on weekends and holidays.

MEDICAL EMERGENCY **Payson Regional Medical Center** (928-474-3222), 807 S. Ponderosa.

✱ To See

Rim Country Museum 928-474-3222 (928-474-3483), 700 Green Valley Pkwy. Open Wed.–Mon. 10–4; winter 1–4. Peruse the large collection of artifacts and memorabilia gathered from the early days of the rim and displayed in Payson's 1906 Forest Service ranger station. The museum has a bookstore and gift shop; you can also do guided archive searches. Free.

Shoofly Village Ruins. Contact Payson Ranger Station for more information. Located north of Payson off AZ 87, then east on Houston Mesa Rd. You can take a self-guided tour of the 3.75-acre site where a Native American village stood. The occupants have similarities to the peoples who lived in the Flagstaff area, as well as the Hohokam desert dwellers. Inhabited between AD 1000 and 1250, the village had 79 structures; only rock outlines remain from some. One of the larger structures had 26 rooms and was two stories high. Archaeologists from Arizona State University excavated the site, which is now on the National Register of Historic Places.

Strawberry Schoolhouse. Located 1.5 miles from AZ 260 on Fossil Creek Rd., Strawberry. Open mid-May–mid-Oct. on weekends and holidays, Sat. 10–4, Sun. noon–4. In 1884 county school superintendent Bucky O'Neill answered petitions from the territorial town of Strawberry and established School District 33 in the Strawberry Valley. When the Strawberry folks argued where this seat of higher education should reside, local cowboys employed some common sense to settle the matter: They used a calf rope to measure the lengths between the Hicks-Duncan cabin on the Valley's west end and the Peach cabin to the east, then established the midpoint by splitting the total down the middle. There the school was built with upscale materials and interiors, thanks to the political hobnobbing between a resident and Bucky. It still looks pretty good after all these years (and a series of renovations). Free concerts and free demonstrations on summer weekends given by craftsmen such as a fiddle maker, basket maker, blacksmith, and saddle maker. Free admission.

Tonto Creek Hatchery (928-476-4202). From Payson, drive about 21 miles east on AZ 260, then turn left (north) at the signed turnoff near Kohls Ranch Resort; drive 4 miles to this facility at the end of the unpaved road. Open daily 7:30–3:30; closed Thanksgiving and Christmas days. Call first because of frequent closures. With a high-tech propensity and upscale equipment, Tonto Hatchery has practically perfected the art of raising fish, turning out more than a half-million different trout a year. Stainless-steel raceways, a four-step water purification process, specially designed baskets for fry, and Tonto Creek's cold spring water add up to a survival rate as high as 92 percent. Tonto Hatchery's main products, rainbow trout, end up all along the Mogollon Rim and points northward, including Lees Ferry. The hatchery may have the best computer program in the western United States. You can tour the facility on your own, or call for a guided tour.

SCENIC DRIVE Forest Road 300. The unpaved Rim Road (segments may require high clearance) travels about 43 miles through rich pine forests, to historic sites, and past exquisite views at the edge of the Rim. The side roads on the eastern, and higher, end provide scenic diversions into mixed conifers and aspen forests. This is a great drive during Oct. for autumn color.

✷ To Do

DOG PARK 🐾 **Payson Off-Leash Park**, McLane Rd. next to the library. Open 24 hours. Trees, water, poop bags, and picnic area. Fenced area for small dogs.

FISHING Anglers claim that some of the best fishing anywhere takes place in the streams and lakes on the Mogollon Rim. Easy to reach, and often crowded, the **East Verde River** is only 4 miles north of Payson on AZ 87, just beyond Flowing Springs Rd. Turn left at East Verde Estates Rd., then turn right into the parking and camping area. **Christopher Creek** and **Tonto Creek** (above Kohl's Ranch, 22 miles east of Payson on AZ 260) are regularly stocked. To reach **Woods Canyon L**ake—an easy access on paved roads—drive 30 miles east of Payson on AZ 260, then left (north) onto Forest Road 300 and continue approximately 5 miles. It's the only rim lake with boat rentals and bait shop. **Willow Springs Lake** also enjoys easy access on paved roads and is located 31 miles east of Payson on AZ 260; head 1 mile past the Woods Canyon Lake turnoff, then go left (north). **Chevelon Canyon Lake**, the largest of the rim lakes, is also the most secluded and the most difficult to access. Drive 3 miles east of Payson on AZ 260 to Forest Road 300 and turn left (north); continue 10 miles to Forest Road 159, turn right, drive about 10 miles, then hike about a mile to the lake.

HIKING Rim Country has some of the best canyon hikes in the state. Some follow a maintained trail along a creek (such as the **Christopher Creek** and **Horton Creek** trails); others, like **West Clear Creek**, are full-blown canyoneer adventures. Check out the **Woods Canyon Lake Trail** for scenery and watchable wildlife. Contact Payson Ranger Station or Mogollon Rim Ranger Station.

HORSEBACK RIDING **Kohl's Ranch Stables** (928-478-0030), behind Kohl's Ranch Lodge, 15 miles east of Payson on AZ 260 on Christopher Creek. Open daily 9–4; closed Christmas Day. Trail rides can last from 1 hour to half a day. Guides give fun facts about plants and animals in the area. Kids under age 6 ride in the stable area only. $25 per hour or $100 for half-day per person.

LLAMAS ✐ **Fossil Creek Llama Ranch** (928-476-5178), located on Fossil Creek Rd., about 3.5 miles from AZ 87. Open daily mid-Apr.–Oct. 31 9–5, Nov. and Dec. weekends only. Hum with the llamas on a hike in the ponderosa pine forest or just visit with them at this off-the-beaten-path ranch near Strawberry. Owners Joyce and John Bittner elucidate on these gentle creatures and their unique characteristics. They also have goats and turn their milk into goat cheese (used by several chefs serving local foods) and fudge—both of which you get to taste if you take a tour of their certified creamery (tours every Saturday at 4 or by appointment May 1–Oct. 31; $5 per person). You can stay for the night in a yurt (Apr.–Nov.), too, and get hands-on experience in morning activities including barnyard detail and feeding and milking of the animals; something kids find fascinating, if not fun. Half-day hikes include lunch: $65 adults, $40 under age 12.

✷ Lodging

INNS **Majestic Mountain Inn** (928-474-0185 or 800-408-2442), 602 E. AZ 260, Payson. High-country ambience at a decent price. You'll find an outdoor pool in the pines, a meeting room, athletic club privileges, and complimentary coffee, tea, cookies, and fruit all day. Rooms have queen or king bed, TV-VCR, coffeemaker, and refrigerator; deluxe rooms have cathedral ceilings and gas fireplace; luxury rooms have spas. $60–145.

LODGES AND CABINS **Strawberry Lodge** (928-476-3333), Strawberry. Homespun with a mountain-town atmosphere, this lodge has been a favorite for decades. Former owners Jean and Dick Turner—who bought the lodge after spotting a two-line ad in the *Los Angeles Times* and making one visit—used to say, "We didn't buy this place to get rich, but to make a place where people want to come." And they did. Current owners Jan and Adrian Marnell have kept this friendly personality alive. The property includes a restaurant that sells some tasty pies. The rooms, basic mountain-retro. have an old-time cabin identity.

Most have double and queen beds with fireplace; some have a balcony. $65–75.

Christopher Creek Lodge (928-478-4300), 21 miles east of Payson. Christopher Creek, an off-the-highway niche along the rim, has been a mountain getaway of choice for Arizonans since the 1950s, and this lodge has the longest history of family-owned status. This makes for a more personal and personable experience. Rustic log and stone cabins with modern features, shaded by ponderosa pines, bigtooth maples, and Arizona walnut trees, cozy right next to or near spring-fed Christopher Creek. It's the only place to stay right along Christopher Creek. You can rent a motel room or cabin here. All rooms have cable TV and heat; cabins have cable TV, fully equipped kitchen with oven, gas furnace, wood-burning fireplace, cookware, and utensils. $49–199.

Elk Haven Cabins (928-478-4582), 2 miles south of AZ 260 on Colcord Rd. (1 mile east of Christopher Creek). Located off the highway, deep in the pine country that edges along colonies of aspen trees, this cluster of cabins rests in a peaceful environment where wildlife feels comfortable, especially elk and deer. Cabins include linens; fully equipped kitchen with microwave, stovetop, and refrigerator; gas log fireplace; love seat; air-conditioning; BBQ; and satellite TV/VCR with free movies. $100–125.

BED & BREAKFASTS Up the Creek Bed and Breakfast (928-476-6571), 10491 Fossil Creek Rd., Strawberry. Two words come to mind when you first spot this property, a contemporary farmhouse home on 5 acres next to the national forest: fresh and simple. The descriptive becomes even more appropriate when you get inside. The three guest rooms, though ultra-comfortable with private bath, pillow-top mattress, down pillows and comforters, CD player, robes for two, and environmentally friendly amenities, have a clean and uncluttered look. You can lounge around on the wrap-around porch to soak up the sun, head for the Loft to take in views, or the Gathering Room where a fireplace radiates heat in the cooler weather. Breakfast (included) is served in the cherry red dining room. The rooms have no television, telephone, fax machine, or computer hookup, and the owners advise, "Your cell phone probably won't work, either." Kids over age 12 are okay, but no pets allowed. $125–170.

♥ **Verde River Rock House** (928-472-4304). You'll need directions to get to this tucked-away gem located along the East Verde River just a few miles north of Payson. Owners Maggie and Steve found the 40+-year-old home while looking for a newer one. The logic of no maintenance went, you might say, the way of the river when they saw this home's unique character. The riverine vegetation of sweet-smelling Arizona sycamores, cottonwoods, and willows create a special enough atmosphere. Once inside the rock house, life takes a storybook twist. The great room looks like a museum and its adjacent porch gives stunning views of the canyon. Guests (only one person/couple/family scheduled at a time) have run of the downstairs, which has two bedrooms (one has granite boulders built into one wall), a sitting room, massage room, porch with a standard refrigerator stocked with complimentary water, juice, sodas, beer and wine. The bed might be the most comfortable you've slept in, and the bathroom's stocked with soaps, sponges, tons of towels, and Gilchrist & Soames amenities. Breakfast, hors

THE GREAT ROOM IN THE VERDE RIVER ROCK HOUSE

d'oeuvres, and snacks are included with your stay. Maggie will also cook up a great dinner (extra) of grilled steak, grilled yellowfin tuna or chicken. $199 single, $235 double occupancy.

✷ Where to Eat

DINING OUT **Beeline Café** (928-474-9960), 815 S. AZ 87, Payson. Open daily for breakfast 5–11, lunch and dinner 11–9. This local favorite goes back almost 50 years. About five years after husband and wife Millard and Millie Sexton opened the restaurant, a paralyzing snowstorm made them famous. When everything else in town closed, the Beeline stayed open to feed utility workers—round the clock for 12 days. The townspeople never forgot that. Word got around you could get a good meal at a fair price there. Although Millie's since passed and the Sexton's sons have taken over, nothing's changed. All the food is "homemade," and goes beyond diner food (such as the Santa Fe–Style Macaroni and Cheese special). The hand-formed patties make good burgers, and the old-fashioned milkshakes are, as one local described, "out of this world." Another local said, "It's all good." The food and prices keep people coming "back, and back and back from all over the place," reported Karen, a waitress; "you can't beat the prices." $3.50–7.

Creekside Steakhouse and Tavern (928-478-4389), 1520 E. Christopher Creek Loop, Christopher Creek. Open daily from rooster crowin' (6 AM) for breakfast and 11 AM for dinner until the cows come home. You have to veer off the beaten path several miles (take the Christopher Creek Loop from AZ 260) to eat here. The venue has been around for 40 years, and has grown itself a good reputation. It's a favorite with the locals and the visitors just passin' through. Breakfast is simple—steak and eggs, omelets, homemade muffins, and biscuits and gravy. For lunch, Cindy serves house-made soups and interesting sandwiches (like slow-roasted chuck roast . . . or bologna, because she likes it). The cowboy/American food—steaks, ribs, shrimp—are known far and wide. The house-made cobblers are famous, and the bourbon pecan and coconut cream pies make the list of favorites.

Mama Joe's Italian Grill (928-476-3910), 5076 N. AZ 87, Pine. Open Thu. and Fri. 4:30 PM, Sat. and Sun 12:30 PM. They close if they're not busy, so call before you come. Owner

Dawn Napier serves up house-made foods from family recipes in a smartly styled dining room—red tablecloths on the table and cane chairs with azure cushions. Specials, like Lobster Ravioli with Alfredo Sauce or Charbroiled Shrimp give menu favorites like Eggplant Parmesan healthy competition. The pizzas have fresh-made dough. The desserts range from the classic tiramisu to specials like Raspberry Swirl Brownies or Lime Cake. Wine specials are $3 a glass.

The Randall House (928-476-4077), AZ 87, Pine. Open Wed.–Sat. 8–3, Sun. 8–2. One of the area's favorite, and best, restaurants serves freshly prepared breakfast and lunch, homemade pastries, gourmet coffees, and teas in the old Randall House, circa 1880. The food is fresh and healthy. The attention to aesthetic details, taste, and service has not changed over the years. Entrées $4–8.

Red Elephant Bakery Café (928-468-6202), 1101 S. AZ 87, Payson. Open Mon.–Sat. 7–5. Owner Leonie Dobbins has created an engaging atmosphere at her two-room bakery with live plants, pictures of scenery and animals from her home, South Africa, and good food. For breakfast, try a Huffy-Puffy (cross between a pancake and omelet with blueberries, cheddar cheese, and parsley). Quiches are popular for lunch. Everything's made from scratch in-house from the freshest ingredients, sometimes local and/or organic. Leonie's breads (sweet or yeast) don't hang around long. Customers usually leave with a loaf. You can also purchase scones, pastries, pies, cakes, and cookies. Leonie especially likes to bake bread from scratch (the tomato, onion and oregano is her favorite) because, "I love the feel of it. It feels alive." Beverages include coffee from Passport Teas & Coffee (which keeps beans green and roasts them when she puts in an order), espresso, and rooibus tea. Bakery items $1.52–4.50, lunch $7.25

Rimside Grill (928-476-3349), 3270 N. AZ 87, Pine. Open Wed.–Sat. 7 AM–8 PM, Sun. 7 AM–7 PM; summer hours, Wed.–Thu. 7 AM–8 PM, Fri. and Sat.7 AM–9 PM; closed Mon. and Tue. year-round. Best known for hearty and tasty breakfasts where everything is house-made, dinner specials, and a Friday fish fry where you can have the cod fried or baked. The dinner menu features steaks, chicken, and homemade sausages. Entrées $7.95–14.25.

✷ Selective Shopping

The rim has an abundance of antique and collectible shops. In Pine, you just park your car and stroll the few blocks of shops. In Payson, go to the northern edge of town on AZ 87.

✷ Special Events

March: **Optimist Fishing Festival** (928-474-5242 ext. 7) gives kids a chance to land the Big One at Green Valley Park through fish clinics given by Arizona Game and Fish Department.

April: **Beeline Cruise-In Car Show** has oldies music, 50-50 drawing, judging of the vehicles, and vendor and food booths.

May: **Aero Fair** (928-978-4748) at the Payson Municipal Airport features aircraft rides and classic, older 4x4 vehicle displays along with food and merchandise. **Mountain High Days** (928-474-4515) celebrates arts and crafts in the Payson courthouse parking lot. **Payson Wildlife Fair** (928-474-5242 ext. 7) has wildlife-based activities at Green Valley Park, including fishing and close-up looks at wildlife.

June: **Strawberry Festival** (800-672-9766), a weekend event in the Pine Cultural Center, serves treats from strawberry shortcake to strawberry salsa.

August: **Longest Continuous Rodeo** in Payson presents a classic rodeo weekend.

September: **Payson Heritage Festival** (928-474-5242 x7) celebrates Payson's Western, Native American, and Pioneer heritage with music, art, and cultural activities.

October: **Zane Grey Days** (928-474-4515) The arts and crafts bazaar and Fall festival celebrates the town's pioneer heritage and takes place at the Gila County Courthouse.

THE MOGOLLON RIM—EAST

When you enter the town of Show Low, you know you're getting deep into the heart of Rim Country: not quite in the White Mountains, but certainly high enough to lift you into the pines where life is at its best here in Arizona in summer. Show Low might be one of the best examples around of Old West pioneer spirit. The town got its name back when arguments were settled via fistfight, gunfight, or card game. As the story goes, soured partners Croyden Cooley and Marion Clark played an all-night card game to determine the ownership of some 100,000 acres of ranchland they shared. When Cooley needed just one point to win the marathon game of Seven Up, Clark blurted out: "You show low, and you win." Cooley cut the deck with the deuce of clubs showing. Show Low and its main street, Deuce of Clubs, memorialize this infamous 1870 moment.

Show Low has the essentials necessary for everyday life, while only a few miles down the road Pinetop-Lakeside exists for your recreational pleasure. In fact, Lakeside got its name when a handful of founding fathers spent an afternoon here lazing in the sun—a style of life you will find highly regarded in these parts. Must be the 40 lakes in as many miles surrounded by the world's largest ponderosa pine forest. Not surprisingly, Lakeside was recently named one of the most popular rim resort towns. Next-door Pinetop incorporated with Lakeside in 1984.

GUIDANCE **Show Low Chamber of Commerce** (888-SHOWLOW), 81 E. Deuce of Clubs. **Pinetop-Lakeside Chamber of Commerce** (928-367-4290 or 800-573-4031), 102-C W. White Mountain Blvd., Pinetop. **Lakeside** (928-368-2100), and **Black Mesa Ranger District** (928-535-7300) can give you information on backcountry hiking, fishing, mountain biking, and hunting.

GETTING THERE *By car:* You can reach both Show Low and Pinetop-Lakeside via AZ 260; the former sits at the intersection of US 60 and AZ 77. By shuttle: **White Mountain Passenger Line**s (928-537-4539) commutes from Phoenix. *By air:* **Show Low Regional Airport** (928-532-4190), 3150 Airport Loop Rd., No. 100. Show Low has two runways (7,200 feet lighted and 4,000 feet unlighted), full taxiways, and commuter service to Phoenix via Great Lakes Airlines.

WHEN TO COME Show Low and Pinetop-Lakeside open their arms all four seasons, but summer is the most popular here given the towns' elevations: 6,331 and 7,200 feet, respectively.

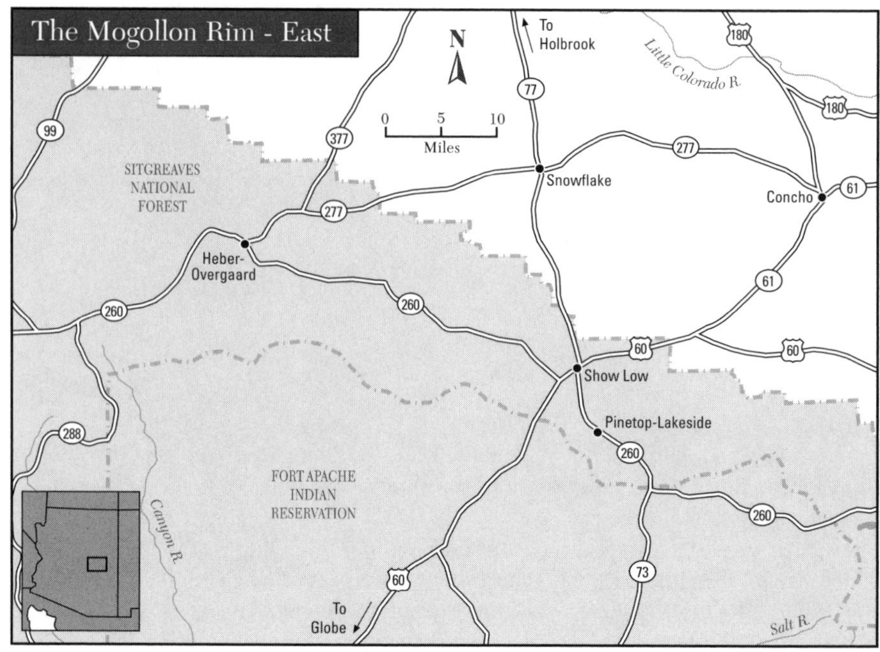

MEDICAL EMERGENCY Navapache Regional Medical Center (928-537-4375), 2200 E. Show Low Lake Rd., Show Low.

✷ To Do

FISHING Silver Creek Fish Hatchery (928-537-7513). From Show Low, go east on AZ 60 about 5 miles, turn left (north) onto Bourdon Ranch Rd., continue 5 miles to Hatchery Way Rd., and turn east to the facility. Open daily dawn to dusk; closed Thanksgiving and Christmas days. The state's smallest fish hatchery raises a fish teetering on the edge of endangered species status, Arizona's native Apache trout. The hatchery sits right at the headwaters of Silver Creek, where 60-degree water flows without fanfare out of the ground. The fish raceways line up, end-to-end, at the spring's mouth, providing a habitat where Apache trout can grow quickly. It's a fascinating object lesson in fish management. Plus, Silver Creek has some good fishing down the creek (away from the hatchery, of course). See Lakes for more fishing hot spots.

GOLF Show Low Country Club (928-537-4564), 860 N. 36th Dr., Show Low. Located 2 miles west of Show Low on AZ 260 off Linden Rd., this 18-hole, par-70 course plays 5,702 yards and features grass fairways and bent grass greens. One end plays in a pine forest, the other in open space. The semiprivate includes snack bar, lounge, driving range, and practice greens. $12–32.

Silver Creek Golf Club (928-537-2744), 2051 Silver Lake Blvd., Show Low. Gary Panks designed this 18-hole championship course that plays 6,813 yards at a par-71. You can play challenging black tees or regular. Semiprivate, the course has a restaurant, lounge, driving range, practice green, and airstrip. $40–60.

HIKING ♿ The **White Mountain Trail System** comprises 11 loop trails ranging from easy to difficult in a variety of terrains. Several of the loop trails, designed for nonmotorized travel, connect. Contact the Lakeside Ranger Station for more information. **Woodland Lake Park** has short trails that work well for a family. The paved, barrier-free **Mogollon Rim Interpretive Trail** (contact the Lakeside Ranger District) runs along the edge of the rim for some great panoramas.

LAKES The **Rim Lakes Recreation Area** (see *Fishing* in "Mogollon Rim—West") includes Bear Canyon, Woods Canyon, and Willow Springs Lakes, where you can fish, swim, boat, and hike. Each pools in a highly scenic area and attracts lots of watchable wildlife, from elk in summer to bald eagles in winter. Contact the Black Mesa Ranger District.

MOUNTAIN BIKING The off-highway roads around here are perfect for exploring on a mountain bike. Get an Apache-Sitgreaves National Forest map and plan your route. The longer trails on the **White Mountain Trail System** are specially designed for mountain biking.

PARK Woodland Lake Park (928-368-6700), Woodland Lake Rd. off AZ 260. More than 100 acres of open space with tennis courts, softball fields, hiking trails, equestrian trails, mountain biking, fishing, and ramadas with charcoal grills.

✷ Wilder Places

Big Springs Environmental Study Area (928-368-8696), Woodland Ave., 0.5 mile south of AZ 260. This outdoor study and recreation area features 40 acres of wetlands, wildlife, and short hiking trails. This is an excellent area for sighting watchable wildlife, with more than 30 different bird species and almost two dozen mammals and reptiles and amphibians.

✷ Lodging

INNS AND RESORTS 🐾 ✐ ♿ **Lake of the Woods** (928-368-5353), 2244 W. White Mountain Blvd., Pinetop. This private resort has its own lake in the pines to give you and the family a night in the forest with a cushion of comfort. Like the owners, Skip and Peggy and her sister, Jan, who came here each year before they finally bought it, many guests make repeat appearances. Cabins come homespun rustic to plush and modern. All have a fireplace and kitchenette or full kitchen, porch, and grill. Many have great lake views. The property includes a playground; a recreation hall with billiards, Ping-Pong, a video arcade, shuffleboard, badminton, and horseshoes; plus a Jacuzzi and dry sauna for adults. Fishing is good—one Tucsonan comes twice a year when the fish are biting (Apr. and Oct.) and he'll catch 100 or more in a week. The best part of this fishing story, is it's free here, and you don't need a license. $99–379.

🐾 ♿ **Lazy Oaks Resort** (928-368-6203), 1075 Larson Road, Lakeside. Private, laid back and quiet, the property along Rainbow Lake fits the name. Oaks, aspen, pines, and weeping willows lend a bit of shade for lounging on summer days, but not so much that's it's too cool when the weather turns. A collection of 15 cabins paneled with knotty pine line along a common area where guests, who start out strangers, end up gathering together for potlucks and s'mores around the fire pit. All the cabins (one and two bedroom) have a full kitchen, fireplace and porch. The two bedroom cabins have two bathrooms. Rainbow Lake is stocked, but fishermen need a fishing license. $79–299.

Mountain Haven Inn (928-367-2101 or 888-854-9815), 1120 E. AZ 260, Pinetop. The rooms, all decorated nicely with their own theme from Victorian to Tree House, are clean and comfortable. Some have kitchens; one has a covered porch. All have coffeemakers, phone, cable TV, private bath, and private entrance. No pets. $64–139.

FISHING IS GOOD (AND FREE) AT THE LAKE OF THE WOODS

Northwoods Resort (928-367-2966 or 800-813-2966), 165 E. AZ 260. These Bavarian-style cottages have all the comforts of home, including queen or king beds, color TV, fully equipped kitchen, fireplace, and deck. The property has a playground, spa, and barbecue area. The resort has a loyal following—it's best to make reservations in summer. Low season $99–249, high season $139–339.

✷ Where to Eat

DINING OUT Charlie Clark's Steak House (928-367-4900), 1701 E. White Mountain Blvd. Open daily for lunch 11–3, dinner from 4:45. They say this rustic spot has accommodated the longest continuously operating restaurant in the state. That's if you count its start as a covert bar dispensing moonshine during Prohibition. When booze became legal, it evolved into Jake Renfro's Famous Log Cabin Café in 1933. Five years later Charlie Clark took over and made steak dinners for patrons—as long as they would tend bar while he cooked. You can get a decent mesquite-broiled steak here, as well as chicken, prime rib, seafood, and classic house-made desserts. Afterward, keep up the ol' Charlie Clark tradition with drinks and dancing in the orchard (seasonal). Lunch $6.95–17.95, dinner $13.95–30.95.

La Casita Café (928-537-5179), 5000 S. White Mountain Rd., Show Low. Open Sun.–Thu. 11–8, Fri. and Sat. 11–9. A few of these restaurants are scattered around Arizona and New Mexico, and Arizona's have dependably good food. The interiors are colorful, and the atmosphere casual and family-friendly. Summer months are crowded at dinnertime. Entrées $6–13.

EATING OUT ⓣ **America's Pie Co.** (928-205-9162), 1001 E. Huning St., Show Low. Open 7–5. Chef Diane Lara opened up this off-the-main-drag shop as a pie shop and bakery. Now she serves breakfast (multigrain pancakes, oatmeal, cinnamon rolls, scones, muffins, and sticky buns) and lunch (quiche, Angus burgers on homemade buns, meatless Farmer's Market sandwiches, and sourdough bread bowls filled with list of different items and salads). People say Chef Diane makes the best pies on the mountain. But they sell out fast. Breakfast and lunch $4.95–8.95, pies $15.

Eddie's Country Café (928-367-2161), 1753 E. White Mountain Blvd., inside Eddie's Country Store. Open Mon.–Thu. 7–5, Fri.–Sun. 7–7. This great little find serves up good food for breakfast and lunch. Owned by Eddie Basha, Arizona's native son and food purveyor extraordinaire. The 40-seat dining room gets filled fast. Weekends (Fri.–Sun.) become a special event when the deli manager, Roland, fires up the combination grill-oven-smoker in the parking lot and cooks some tasty barbecue (baby back ribs, chicken, and tri-tip). Every two weeks they feature a different item on the breakfast or lunch menu. Breakfast $3–9.50, lunch $3.99–8.50.

The Munich Haus Restaurant (928-367-4287), 1443 E. Fir, Pinetop. Open for dinner Thu.–Mon. 4–9; closed Nov.–Apr. With the way Arizona's Western culture and forested high country attracts Germans, it's not surprising to find German restaurant serving some great food, even in the forest. Chef Sebastine Drouillet serves up some classic German cuisine—sauerbraten, rouladen, Wiener schnitzel, pork schnitzel, and sausages. The Saturday special is *jagerbraten* (prime rib). These dishes are accompanied by the also-classic German potato salad, dumplings, spatzle, and red cabbage. Chef Sebastione deviates from the classic German fare when you hit the dessert menu, where decadent chocolate numbers and crème brûlée mix with homemade apple strudel and homemade Black Forest cake. They even carry Henry Weinhard's sodas and a kid's menu. Entrées $10.95–17.95.

Sal & Teresa's Mexican Restaurant (928-537-0230), 1191 E. Hall, Show Low. Open daily 7 AM–7 PM (till 8 PM in summer). Before he and Teresa opened this venue, Sal used to cook at another popular local Mexican food restaurant on the Rim "for years." But, Sal said, "A long time ago, they changed recipes. I have the old ones. Larry Chavez Sr. taught me how to cook food." So Sal brought these recipes, practically historic, to his own place and diners feast at his casual diner. Sal's specialty is the Especial Mixed Burro (with Red Chile Sauce); Teresa's is the Especial Chile Relleno Dinner. They also feature Stuffed Sopapilla (stuffed with beans, and choice of meat, and covered with red or green chile and cheese) and Navajo taco. The Green Chile Cheese Crisp is a must. Kids have a menu with a half-dozen items. Go on Friday for an all-you-can-eat fish fry and live music (4–8). $6–9.25.

✷ Special Events

May: White **Mountain Bike Rodeo** (www.wmrc.org) is a great kid's event with free food, activities, and equipment.

June: **Annual "Best of the West" Fine Art Show and Sale** (928-368-8696) at Hon-Dah Conference Center brings the best of the western artists' works to the rim.

July: **White Mountain Native American Art Festival** (928-368-8696) presents Native American art and crafts.

August: **White Mountain** Bluegrass **Music Festival** (928-368-8696) brings top bluegrass musicians to Hon-Dah Resort/Casino.

September: **Pinetop-Lakeside Fall** Artisan's **Festival** (928-368-8696) has arts and crafts, a talent show, an antiques show and sale, a used-book sale, and entertainment.

October: **Woodland Wildlife Festival** (928-368-8696) at the White Mountain Nature Center presents wildlife during the day and stargazing at night.

December: **Show Low Main Street** (928-537-2326) features a Christmas tree lighting and electric parade.

Eastern Arizona

3

ROUTE 66 EAST:
WINSLOW AND HOLBROOK

GREER

SPRINGERVILLE, EAGAR,
AND THE CORONADO TRAIL

SAFFORD

ROUTE 66 EAST: WINSLOW AND HOLBROOK

Two different towns with two different personalities—one traditional, the other whimsical. Both fill the pages of Arizona history—one with color, the other with class. But these high desert cities, only 33 miles apart, have some strong commonalities. For one, they both make a good base for visiting Petrified Forest and Painted Desert national parks. Both have smidgeons of Old Route 66 running through them. Both have interesting architecture. And they both love history. They just have different stories to tell.

By the 1930s Winslow had evolved into a renowned destination for a west-of-the-Mississippi adventure via railroad. The town, with its beautiful brick storefronts, exquisitely designed La Posada Hotel, vaudeville theater, and trading post, became the home base of choice for visitors who wanted to explore the surrounding reservations and natural wonders. When automobiles prevailed over railroad travel and I-40 bypassed Winslow, the world all but forgot about the town that brought a taste of culture to this rowdy land. The only attraction the town had to offer focused on a street corner where Jackson Browne might have seen a girl, my Lord, in a flatbed Ford.

Toward the end of the 20th century, the grand dame of Fred Harvey hotels where all the beautiful people stayed, the La Posada, caught the eyes of a handful of Californians who not only saved it from demolition but also lovingly restored the building to its former glory. Since then more of Winslow's beautiful historic buildings have gone through the restoration process. The resuscitation has pointed Winslow in the right direction, back to its more refined days.

Holbrook, on the other hand, was one of the reasons the West was called Wild. Before it was a decade old, the town experienced more than 20 deaths by gunfight. A shoot-out at the Blevins household evolved into the famous Pleasant Valley War, a.k.a. Graham-Tewksbury feud, which lasted for years and would eventually be known the world over.

As the countryside around Holbrook filled with ranches, the tiny town surrounded by miles of open space became a modern-day trade route. Far from traditional, organized city life, eccentric personalities flourished. Rotgut whiskey provoked hair-trigger tempers into brawls and gunfights in saloons with graphic names such as the Bucket of Blood—which, by the way, is still in operation. Cowboys, often fugitive outlaws feeling their oats and ready for a little fun, assembly-lined shots of

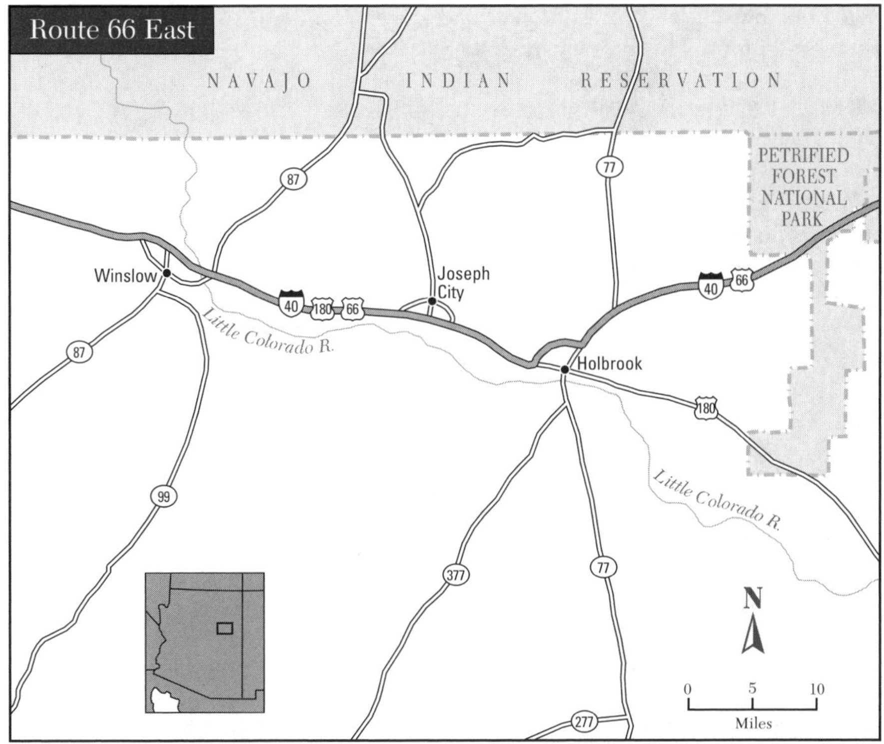

whiskey. It took a lawman named Commodore Perry—a peacock of a man with attractive long locks, who knew how to work a gun—to tame the town. Somewhat.

Cattle ranching grew big in Holbrook; some say there were up to 1.5 million head in the early 1890s. The area's big outfit, Aztec Land and Cattle Company, had the second biggest operation in the nation. The company, which also went by the name Hashknife, declared open season on rustling from inside the company and trolling the outskirts of the humongous herd. This led to the formation of the Arizona Rangers, a hard-bitten group described by state historian Marshall Trimble as "a bunch of rough-ridin' cowboys with a tough-as-nails reputation that made most criminals think twice about messing with them."

If the criminal activity wasn't enough, in 1899 the town carved a notch of notoriety for itself all the way back in Washington DC, when Sheriff Frank Wottron sent out invitations for a public hanging. The invitation poetically stated that the soul of George Smiley, Murderer, "will be swung into eternity on Dec. 8, 1899 at 2 o'clock P.M. sharp. The latest improved methods of scientific strangulation will be employed and everything possible will be done to make the surroundings cheerful and the execution a success." A reprimand was quickly dispatched from President McKinley.

Things quieted down by the time Route 66 made its way through the town, and Holbrook took to its new role as a tourist destination. When I-40 came along, the town coyly kept itself up but never changed its style. Its retro tourist architecture is straight out of the 1950s. Plus, you can still see the buildings and businesses that made the town, hosted cowboy fights, and saw gun battles back in its rowdier days. Just like Winslow, history is big in Holbrook. It's just celebrated differently.

GUIDANCE Winslow **Visitor Center** (928-289-2434), 523 W. 2nd St. The visitor center, located in one of Lorenzo Hubbell's trading posts, features the history of the post and town. Check out the old scales Hubbell used to weigh the wool that Navajos brought into town in their wagons. Hubbell would provide the hay and water for their horses. He often designed those wonderful Navajo rugs once sold at his trading posts. The center has an extensive selection of brochures, maps, and some souvenirs. **Holbrook Chamber of Commerce** (928-524-6558 or 800-524-2459) at the Navajo County Courthouse (100 E. Arizona) has a self-guided tour map of historic buildings gathered within a few blocks' area in the town. **Mogollon Rim Ranger District** (928-477-2255), has information on backcountry use in the national forest.

GETTING THERE **Winslow** is located right along I-40 and intersected by AZ 87. *By train:* **Amtrak** (Los Angeles to Chicago) stops twice daily. *By air:* **Winslow-Lindbergh Regional Airport** (928-289-2422) can handle just about anything from a little Cessna to a 747. If it weren't for the never-ending wind in the Winslow Valley, the airport would have made the short list for space shuttle emergency landings. You might get a special treat and see Bill Reesman's candy-apple-red Russian MiG jet stunt plane sponsored by Red Bull thunder into the ethers.

Holbrook not only straddles I-40 but also lies at the convergence of AZ 77 to the north and south, AZ 377 to the south, and US 180 from the southeast.

WHEN TO COME Most of the year these high-desert towns have a mild climate. Winds cool temperatures down a notch or two in summer.

MEDICAL EMERGENCY **Winslow Memorial Hospital** (928-289-4691), 1501 N. Williamson Ave.

✱ To See

Hopi Mesas. From Holbrook, take AZ 77 north to AZ 264 and turn west; from Winslow, go north on AZ 87 to AZ 264, then turn east or west. The Hopi Mesas jut out like three fingers from Black Mesa. The First Mesa has the views (no picture taking is allowed anywhere on the reservation) and artists' studios producing pottery, basketry, and kachinas. The artistry is generally handed down through generations and has deep spiritual connections. The Second Mesa has the **Hopi Cultural Center** (928-734-6650), open Mon.–Sat. 8–5. You can get a bite to eat, shop, and check into a room if you want to stay overnight. Check out the Hopi Museum to learn about Hopi traditions. Old Orabi, the oldest continually occupied village in North America, is located on the Third Mesa. Free.

La Posada Hotel (928-289-4366), 303 E. 2nd St., Winslow. Open 7 AM–9 PM. Arizona's great railroad hotel—designed by architect Mary Colter (of Grand Canyon fame) and built in the 1930s—was one of the finest in the Southwest and the most elegant Fred Harvey hotel built. Colter was a master at blending light, color, and materials. The world came to La Posada's door, and a who's who of the rich and famous stayed here, from Albert Einstein to Howard Hughes. The hotel briefly fell from grace when it was converted into generic office space and almost destroyed. After a total restoration, the stone and tile floors, glass murals, original furniture, and acres of gardens live once again. It's a remarkable place worth visiting even if you don't plan to spend the night there.

Little Painted Desert Park. Located 13 miles north of I-40 on AZ 87. Smaller, and without the crowds of the national park, the county park has the same "painted" badlands that make a stunning panorama from the scenic rim viewpoint. You can hike down from the rim into the hills for a more up-close and personal experience. Free.

Meteor Crater (928-289-5898), located 20 miles west of Winslow on I-40. Open Memorial Day–Labor Day 7 AM–7 PM, the rest of the year 8–5; closed Christmas Day. The world's first proven meteorite impact site has developed into a fascinating place to learn about the never-ending impacts in our solar system through interactive displays and exhibits in the Learning Center, a 10-minute movie in the big-screen theater, and guided tours and lectures (weather permitting). A collection of meteorites found at the site appears throughout the visitor center, including one that weighs more than 1,400 pounds. $15 adults, $14 age 60-plus, $6 ages 6–16, under age 6 free.

Navajo County Courthouse (928-524-6558 or 800-524-2459), 100 E. Arizona, Holbrook. The rowdiest spot in town when it was first built in 1898, the old courthouse holds plenty of interesting memories, including all-night dances, notorious trials, and an invitation-driven hanging. Today the structure is quieter, describing through displays the historic events and cultures of its earlier days. In June and July, Native Americans hold dances in its plaza. Western and Native American art shows take place there throughout the year.

Old Trails Museum (928-289-5861), 212 Kinsley Ave., Winslow. Open Tue.–Sat. 10–4. Nicknamed Winslow's Attic, this two-room museum located in the historic First National Bank Building built in 1921 building with its original tile floor, marble counters, and a classy vault has a nice compendium of artifacts, vintage clothing, bottles, and historic memorabilia collected from Indian ruins, the Santa Fe Railway, La Posada Hotel, and townsfolk. Check out their little fledgling gift shop full of quality merchandise, including collectible items, at great prices. Free.

Remembrance Garden. Located on 3rd St. and Transcon Lane, Winslow. Two mangled beams from the World Trade Center, 14 and 15 feet tall and the largest pieces given to any community in the country, stand in a brick planter with the words UNITED WE STAND running across. It's an oddly placed memorial with an odd history. The project started when a Phoenix television station called Winslow to see what they planned for the one-year anniversary of the September 11, 2001, terrorist attack. The call spurred residents into action, and they took steps to create a memorial. They got two girders from the World Trade Center by signing a contract agreeing never to use the beams for profit. Next they had to transport them. One of the town's major businesses—Wal-Mart—picked up the beams. The truck entered Winslow on September 6, 2002, immediately starting an impromptu parade through downtown. At the site, everything was ready for placement: Residents had plucked weeds, installed a sprinkler system, and put up a flagpole. The beams were set in place just in time for the memorial's dedication ceremony at 5 PM on September 11, 2002, for all of TV-land to see. Free.

Rock Art Ranch (928-288-3260). From Winslow, go south on AZ 87 to AZ 99 and turn left; go to Territorial Rd., and turn left; go to the signed turnoff and turn right. It's 3 miles to the ranch. Reservations necessary. Open daily except Sundays and holidays. This working cattle ranch has a little bit of everything for the western aficionado. A museum has hundreds of southwestern artifacts, especially Anasazi pots and arrowheads. A centuries-old Hopi rock house and coral, Navajo hogan and sweathouse, and the last remaining bunkhouse of the Hashknife Outfit stand on the grounds. The star of this authentic western roundup is the 0.25-mile panel of rock art in Chevelon Canyon, one of the best such sites in the world. It'll match any national park or monument you may travel to, sans crowds. Call for admission and reservations.

Standin' on the Corner in Winslow, Arizona, Park. Kinsley Ave. and 2nd St. Back around the 1970s, Jackson Browne wrote a song about standin' on the corner in Winslow, Arizona, and seeing a girl (my Lord) in a Ford truck doing a double take. Winslow has memorialized this song—made famous by the rock group the Eagles—with a statue and a mural depicting the story. Winslow has a Standin' on the Corner celebration every year. Whether Jackson Browne did, indeed, get the eye from a girl in a flatbed Ford here, we don't know. Flagstaff claims host to the event, but reliable sources say Browne's car broke down in Winslow. The verdict's out whether or not anyone's willpower did, too.

Painted Desert/Petrified Forest National Monument (928-524-6288). Located 25 miles east of Holbrook off I-40 at exit 311. Open May through Labor Day 7–7, Labor Day to late Oct. and Mar. through early May 7–6, late Oct. through Feb. 7–5; closed Christmas Day. The Painted Desert actually spans from Cameron near the Grand Canyon to just southeast of the Petrified Forest National Park. The short road here takes you through a grand showcase of variety and colors typical of the desert. The various layers of sandstone and mudstone in the Chinle

HOW WOOD GETS PETRIFIED

You have to have volcanic action in the area to get petrified wood. The dry, dusty tableland gives no immediate hint of its ancient status as a fern-stuffed floodplain where dinosaurs roamed, marshes oozed, and volcanoes steamed. But fossils of ancient plants, reptiles, and animals and dinosaur bones give its secret away.

The trees in the Petrified Forest came from a tropical forest atop an ancient chain of mountains once located to the south of the park. Trees died, fell, and washed down to the floodplain and over time, were covered with silt, mud, and volcanic ash. This cover cut off oxygen and slowed the decaying process of the logs and allowed time for silica-laden groundwater to seep through the logs and replace their original wood fibers with silica deposits. Finally, the silica crystallized into quartz. Some pieces spangle with glitters of crystals; most are Technicolor beautiful.

Unless you have a will of steel and a conscience that doesn't quit, you may be tempted to purloin one or more of the pieces as you peruse the park. The park service, in classically bureaucratic fashion, has mounted a number of letters written by repentant wood thieves lamenting their actions by attesting guilty consciences, health problems and broken marriages to their swiping a morsel of petrified wood. With that in mind, it's best to follow Leave No Trace (and honest ethics) by taking only pictures.

Formation took on different colors from various minerals in the sediments and the rate at which the layers formed. Red, orange, and pink hues (predominant at the north end of the park) come from iron oxides and aluminum. When sediments rapidly build up—say, during a flood—oxygen gets depleted from the soil and shades of blue, gray, and lavender form, as you'll see in the south end of the park.

The Painted Desert Inn Museum (928-524-3522), is open 9–5. The museum, built in the 1920s, has wall murals painted by Hopi artist Fred Kabotie. You may hike in the backcountry of the Painted Desert with a permit, which is free and available at the museum. Access the wilderness via the mile-long Wilderness Access Trail located at the northwest side of the Painted Desert Inn. The wilderness area starts when you cross Lithodendron Wash.

Petrified Forest National Monument. The south end of the park contains the state's colorful geological jewels of petrified wood. Actually ancient trees that have agatized into a rainbow of colors, some sprinkled with crystals, the petrified wood lies pell-mell in "forests" along the ground. The park recently went through an expansion doubling its size. However, the paved road that accommodates most travel remains in the central part of the park, far from the extended boundaries. Rainbow Forest Museum provides information on several ways to experience the park: A 20-minute orientation movie runs every half hour; the computer-based Immersive Tour into the Triassic shows the ancient and present environments.

You'll also find exhibits of dinosaurs, reptiles, and petrified wood; a bookstore and gift shop; and access to Giant Logs Trail. $10 per vehicle, good for 7 days

✷ To Do

CANOEING AND KAYAKING **McHood Park** (see *Wilder Places*). If you have your own craft, you can paddle down Clear Creek to secluded Clear Creek Canyon.

HIKING Several hiking trails are located on the national forest within day-trip distance. Contact Coconino National Forest. Petrified Forest National Monument has several short trails; experienced hikers can plan cross-country backpacks.

HISTORIC WALKING TOUR Get a free self-guided map from the **Holbrook Chamber of Commerce** in the Navajo County Courthouse and take a look at some of Holbrook's more historic, and notorious, buildings. From the Bucket of Blood Saloon that withstood gunfights and brawls frequent enough to stain the floor to the Santa Fe Station. In Winslow, walk the six-block pathway along the railroad tracks.

ROCK CLIMBING **Jacks Canyon** is located 30 miles south of Winslow along AZ 87 at milepost 314.7; contact the Mogollon Rim Ranger District. This craggy spot, a climbers' wonderland, has almost 300 vertical to wildly overhanging routes on limestone, and sandstone cliffs have tons of pockets for monos to four-finger sinkers. Vertical walls have bubbly surfaces with edges and blocks. All routes are protected lavishly by cracks. One Winslow rock climber claimed, "Every rock climber in the world knows about Jacks Canyon except Arizonans." Now you know.

✷ Wilder Places

McHood Park and Clear Creek Reservoir (928-289-2434). Located 5 miles from downtown: Go south on AZ 87 to AZ 99, and turn left. The deep rock canyon of Clear Creek makes a magnificent setting with its red-rock shelves bracing deep blue river waters. You can canoe, camp, swim, and fish here.

✷ Lodging

🐾 ⚭ ♥ **La Posada Hotel** (928-289-4366), 303 E. 2nd St., Winslow (see *To See*). You get a gracious dose of history here, at one of the last great railroad hotels along the Santa Fe Railroad line. Each guest room has a full bath and a unique design that incorporates antiques. The 20-inch walls with acoustic insulation are thick enough to soften railroad sounds. The hotel has two tennis courts, a library, and gardens. Well-behaved pets and children are welcome. Pets must be registered at check-in and require an additional $10 fee. $89–175.

🏵 🖉 **Wigwam Village Motel #6** (928-524-3048), 811 W. Hopi Dr., Holbrook. Not many franchise hotels are exclusive enough to warrant a patent like the Wigwam Village. Frank Redford created the first village in Kentucky in the early 1900s to look like tepees he'd seen on the Sioux reservation. The model became a hit with travelers and evolved into a gathering place for the town as well. Redford realized he had

a bankable product, patented it in 1936, and opened six more. Of the seven, only two remain: this one in Holbrook (listed on the National Register of Historical Places) and no. 2 in Cave City, Kentucky. In keeping with the prevailing retro theme of Holbrook, you will feel like you entered a time warp here. Check out the classic cars parked around the property. Tepees—21 feet across at the base and 28 feet high—include bath with shower, cable TV, heat, and air-conditioning. You can check the tepee before you pay. $58–65.

✷ Where to Eat

Holbrook

Butterfield Stage Co. Steak House (928-524-3447), 609 W. Hopi Dr. Open daily 4–10. It's casual here, with a relaxing atmosphere. One of Holbrook's finer restaurants has people consistently commenting about the good food. The name implies steak (with filet mignon the favorite), but they also serve chicken (another favorite) and some good seafood. Salad bar included with the meal. $7.95–22.95.

Romo's Café (928-524-2153), 121 W. Hopi Dr., Holbrook. Open Mon.–Sat. 10–8; closed Sun. As in the rest of the town, the décor here is quintessentially retro—but the food is classic New Mexico. And the place has become a classic. Savory red and green chile sauces, baked (not fried) chimichangas, and sopaipillas with soul. Entrées $7–16.

Winslow

E & O Kitchen (928-289-5352), Winslow-Lindbergh Regional Airport (take AZ 87 south to Airport Rd., then turn right to the parking lot). Open Mon.–Fri. 11–6, Sat.11–5. Named for owners Estella and Oscar, this family restaurant does things a little different. The menu offers a couple dozen entrées with your choice of meat—*asada* (grilled beef), *machaca* (shredded beef), *picadillo* (ground beef), *carnitas* (pork), *adobada* (pork in red chile), and *pollo* (chicken). Entrées $2.95–9.95.

♥ **Turquoise Room** (928-289-2888), La Posada Hotel, 303 E. 2nd St., Winslow. Open daily for breakfast 7–11, lunch 11–2, and dinner 5–9. Chef-owner John Sharpe has resurrected this restaurant—named for the famous Santa Fe Super Chief dining car—to the same level of excellence the original restaurant enjoyed at its finest, and beyond. The interiors are specially designed after the originals—leather-and-wood chairs, emerald brocade booths, Verne Lucero chandeliers, and a stained-glass mural of La Posada patron saints Ysidro, Pascual, and Barbara. As for the food, you won't soon forget a meal you have here. The Wild West still reigns, menu-wise, with entrées such as elk, wild boar, and quail with prickly pear jalapeño glaze or Piki Bread with Hopi Hummus (made with tepary beans). But you'll also see fresh seafood flown from New Orleans, Boston, and Nilinchic, Alaska; and Angus steaks. It just depends what's available and fresh, and often local. Every dish has Chef John's creative twists from his signature yin-yang blend of cream of corn and smooth black bean soup, to the Southwestern Caesar Salad with roasted pumpkin seeds to locally raised heirloom Churro lamb, which people come from all over the world to taste. All these unusual and/or creative dishes are part of a style of food he calls "Regional Contemporary Southwestern with an occasional tribute to the great days of the Fred Harvey Company." Entrées $25–29.

✱ The Arts

Navajo and Hopi Indian Arts & Crafts Center (928-289-4923), 2 miles east of Winslow at Exit 257 off I-40. Open ("usually") 9–4. The Navajo-owned trading post has a large selection of jewelry, pottery, baskets, handwoven rugs and katsinas.

Snowdrift Art Space (928-289-8201), 120 W. 2nd St., Winslow. Open by appointment. Call first. Dan Lutzick, once a partner in the La Posada Hotel, now devotes his time to producing big pieces of art (10-plus feet high) from industrial-grade materials culled from the restoration of La Posada Hotel. More than a dozen pieces stand in an old warehouse with a SNOWDRIFT PERFECT SHORTENING ad on the outside—hence the name. Exhibitions of local artists appear through the year. Call for information and hours.

✱ Special Events

January: The **Annual Pony Express Ride from Holbrook to Scottsdale** leaves the Holbrook Post Office at 8 AM on Jan. 31 and arrives at the Scottsdale Post Office at noon on Feb. 3.

April: **Winslow Railroad Days** draws model train clubs, which set up, and display in locations around town.

July: **Annual Fourth of July Fireworks and Barbecue** in Holbrook.

August: Holbrook's **Annual Old West Days Celebration** (928-524-6558) has gunfight reenactments, **Bucket of Blood** 10K and 2-mile foot races, **Old West Days Car Show**, arts and crafts, and food.

September: **Standin' on the Corner Festival** (928-289-3434) in Winslow celebrates the Eagles' hit, with a two-day rock party that draws thousands of people for food, arts, music, carnival and more. **Navajo County Fair** (928-524-6407), 404 E. Hopi Dr., Holbrook. **Old West Days Celebration** (928-524-6558) in Holbrook includes a Wild West Art Show and Auction, Bucket of Blood Races, Old West reenactors, games, entertainment, a car show, a softball tournament, a chili cook-off, vendors.

October: **Just Cruisin' Car Show** (928-289-3434) brings dozens of classic cars out of the closet to cruise the streets in Standin' on the Corner style. **Piecemakers Quilt Guild Show** has a huge display of handcrafted quilts.

December: **Holiday Tour of Homes** (928-289-8202) in Winslow presents four to six homes, decorated and open to the public. Holbrook's **Parade of Lights Festival** (928-524-6558) has entertainment, art and crafts, food, and Santa during the day, Parade of Lights at 6 PM.

GREER

Located in an 8,500-foot-high valley along the confluence of the Little Colorado River and its West Fork, this hamlet has always been a gathering place for people. Several pioneer families homesteaded here and lived off a very fertile landscape—this area in the White Mountains is where the water is. Farming reports about the hyperproductive land look like something straight out of Genesis, minus the grapes. One pioneer, E. R. Dewitt, recounted how in 1893 he raised "thirty thousand pound of spuds from three acres, 330 bushels of oats, and 26 tons of oat hay on 12 acres." Farmers will understand how Mr. Dewitt must have welcomed the typical 200-plus inches of snow the area gets come winter.

As you peruse the streets around Greer, you might see relics from the old farming days, a truck from a logging business from back when, or historic cabins still standing but unused. But don't get the wrong idea. This is not Jeff Foxworthy territory; rather, well-heeled ranch country. Even though ranching no longer reigns (tourism does), the mind-set lingers, and in Mormon cowboy-land nothing gets thrown away. It's recycled, repaired, or displayed for posterity but never discarded.

Cozying up to the mixed conifers and aspens in the Apache-Sitgreaves National Forest, Greer's population hovers around 120 all year. The big draw today is the forest—for recreation, not logging. Big, beautiful, meadowed, and crossed by trout streams lined with wildflowers, the forest is at its best right here in the White Mountains.

Mixed in among the memories and hidden-in-the-forest-coziness come signs hinting at more cosmopolitan times, such as huge new homes (mostly second) appearing on the mountain slopes and businesses that have become more accommodating to the more distinguished palate. Still, you won't find a gas station here, or a supermarket; only a string of independent businesses that offer food, shelter, and a smattering of gift shopping. Upscale accommodations make life easier in this rugged backcountry than at home. More importantly, there's the fresh air, clean water, and open space. That's enough to attract anyone looking for a great outdoor place these days. It was for the town's founding fathers.

GUIDANCE **Springerville-Eagar Regional Chamber of Commerce** (928-333-2123 or 888-733-2123), 318 E. Main St., Springerville. **Apache-Sitgreaves National Forest** (928-333-4301), 30 S. Chiricahua Dr. (open Mon.–Fri. 8–4:30), has information on backcountry use of the Apache-Sitgreaves National Forest.

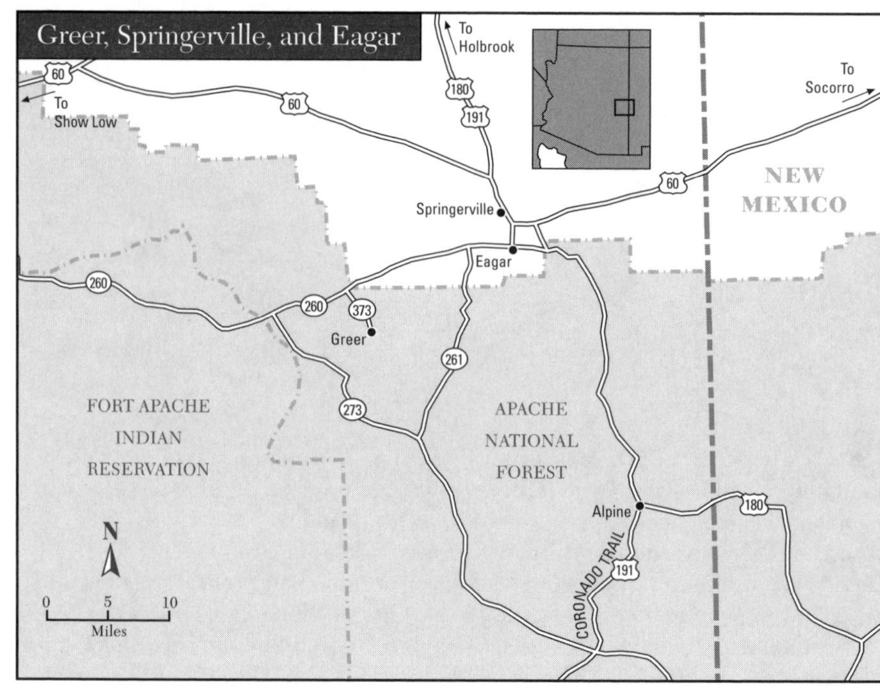

GETTING THERE There's only one road to Greer: AZ 373 about 15 miles west of Springerville off AZ 260.

WHEN TO COME The town's high season runs from Memorial Day through Labor Day, but most of the town stays open all year.

MEDICAL EMERGENCY White Mountains Regional Medical Center (928-333-4368; TDB, 928-333-7156), 118 S. Mountain Ave., Springerville.

✷ To See

Butterfly Lodge Museum (928-735-7414), AZ 373 and County Rd. 1126. Open Memorial Day–Labor Day, Thu.–Sun. 10–5. John Butler (husband of Molly Butler) built this rustic cabin in 1914 for the writer James Willard Schultz who'd take the train to Holl-brook, then travel 116 miles by wagon (later taxi) to the cabin he'd named Apuni Oyis (Blackfoot for "Butterfly Lodge") for all the butterflies flitting about. The town's first tourist cabin is listed on the National Register. Schultz, a hunting guide and trapper from the

WHITE MOUNTAIN WILDFLOWERS DRAW MASSES OF BUTTERFLIES

Glacier Park area and a fighter for Native American rights, wrote dozens of books when he moved to Greer. Schultz's son, Lone Wolf, created the paintings and sculptures exhibited in the cabin. A number of special events and talks are scheduled throughout the season. $2 adults, $1 ages 12–17.

✷ To Do

CROSS-COUNTRY SKIING The national forest has developed a maze of trails in the **Greer Cross Country Ski Area** and nearby **Pole Knoll Recreation Area** just off AZ 260. Some of the routes make great hiking paths. Check out No. 5. It's a pleasant walk in the woods that has potential for sighting a variety of wildlife, especially since Hall Creek cuts through the creases formed by the hilly country. Contact Apache-Sitgreaves National Forest.

DOWNHILL SKIING/SNOWBOARDING **Sunrise Park Resort** (928-735-7669), located in McNary, 11 miles east of Greer on AZ 273, 7 miles south of AZ 260. One of the state's best ski areas has 65 runs for every level of experience. The natural profile of the mountains—more gradual, but long grades and rounded peaks—makes a more manageable terrain for beginner and intermediate skiers. Black diamond skiers should head to Flagstaff. Even when the rest of the state has a dearth of precipitation (including Flagstaff), the White Mountains rarely get skunked. And just in case, the owners (White Mountain Apache Tribe) have snowmaking machines in areas to help nature along. There's a snow half-pipe, implanted wood and metal rails, and a special-event area with jumps ranging from beginner to advanced for snowboarders. Lift tickets $39–49 adults, $34–42 youths, $23–28 under age 12.

FISHING You need only step outside to the Little Colorado River, which runs through town, to do some fly-fishing for rainbow trout (permit required). But why stop there when more than 600 miles of trout streams and more than 20 trout lakes lie within a couple of dozen miles of town? Check out *Fishing* in "Springerville" or contact Apache-Sitgreaves National Forest.

HIKING Greer is located in the national forest, and you have hikes with trailheads right in town: the mile-long **Butler Canyon Loop** and **Greer Cross Country Ski Area** (check out Trail No. 5, see Cross-country Skiing above) at Squirrel Springs Recreation Area, as well as the **West Fork** and **East Fork trails**, both of which follow creeks. The **East Baldy** and **West Baldy trails** travel to almost the top of Mount Baldy (the peak is sacred to the White Mountain Apache, and you need a permit to ascend the last 500 feet) are about 10 miles away. The **South Fork Trail** is just down the road off AZ 260. Contact Apache-Sitgreaves National Forest.

HORSEBACK RIDING **Wiltbank Trail Rides** (928-735-7454), 38735 AZ 373. Open Mon.–Sat. Rides run every 2 hours from 8 AM–4 PM on gentle and experienced horses. Travels trails on the national forest for 30 minutes to 2 hours and you can customize a longer ride with reservations. A Belgian Trots team supplies the horsepower for a wagon ride. In the snowy depths of winter, they pull a sleigh. $30 per rider age 6 and up.

MOUNTAIN BIKING With all the unpaved roads in the national forest, most with little or no traffic, the area offers incredible possibilities for fat tires. This is not gonzo territory with steep, technical grades; rather, it's rolling hills (some with a kick) with awesome scenery in 8,000- to 10,000-foot elevations.

WILDFLOWERS In summer this area has the state's best show of wildflowers. Just head to a river- or creekside and hike. Great finds are long the **Thompson Trail**, the fisherman's trail (beaten path) along the **West Fork of the Black River** from the West Fork Campground, and the first mile of the **West Baldy** and **East Baldy trails**. Contact Apache Sitgreaves National Forest.

✷ Wilder Places

Apache-Sitgreaves National Forest has a variety of biomes, from ponderosa forests to subalpine meadows that take the look of a coastal rain forest in the wet summer months. All this water makes for excellent trout fishing, wildflower viewing in July and Aug., fall color from late Sep. into Oct., and cross-country skiing and snowshoeing in the winter.

✷ Lodging

LODGES 🐾 ♿ ♥ **The Amberian Peaks Lodge** (928-735-9977 or 800-556-9997), located at the south end of Main St. Closed Nov. and Apr. The lodge is like a home away from home in more ways than one. Because owners Don and Ann Poyas live all year in Greer, they're always around to make sure your stay is perfect. Next, the lodge rooms have the most electronics—satellite radio, TV, DVD, VHS player, video games, and WiFi—except a phone. (Ann explains that you don't have a choice about people calling you on a phone, but you do have a choice about turning on the TV.) Rooms have king or two queen beds with triple sheets, private bath,

THE WHITE MOUNTAINS FEATURE FORESTS, MEADOWS, AND LAKES

microwave, refrigerator, and security safe. Some rooms have fireplace and/or whirlpool tub. Occasional murder mysteries take place throughout the year (call for schedule. Pets are welcome in the cabin. $135–235.

Molly Butler Lodge (928-735-7226), 109 Main St. This historic lodge is where everything started in the town. Promoted as Arizona's oldest continuously operating lodge, its Longhouse, originally Molly's Bunk House, was built in the early 1900s. The rooms present a country décor with quilts, antiques, and barn wood furnishings, along with individual heat control and bath. If you want a quiet night's sleep, ask for one of the rooms adjacent to the lodge's porch; the activity from Butler's Bar, where many a tall tale has been told, starting with the owner, John Butler, gets lively. Two pets are allowed at $10 each per night. $65–90 double occupancy; $5 per night per extra person. Three-night minimum stays for holidays; two-night minimum for weekends.

CABINS **Greer Cabin Keepers** (928-735-7617). Take your pick from 40 different cabins located all around the area—from Main Street to meadows to secluded spots in the forest, one-bedroom to veritable lodges, rustic to resort-ish ultraluxury. All cabins are privately owned, furnished and fully equipped with housekeeping services. Most have fireplaces (some more than one) and decks. Some have satellite TV and VCR/DVD; a few even have phones. All you bring is the food. Most cabins have minimum-stay requirements. Pets, when allowed, $15 each per night. $95–550.

Greer Vacation Rentals (928-735-9977), 1 Main Street. You can rent a cozy one-room cabin to a luxury three bedroom cabin with upscale interiors for a day or longer. Most all have kitchens and some form of fireplace (wood or gas fireplace or potbelly firebox) and satellite TV. Pets allowed in Big Ten Cabin. One-time cleaning fee applies. $89–299.

GUEST RANCH **Hidden Meadow Ranch** (928-333-1000 or 866-333-4080). This cluster of cabins located deep in the national forest has been likened to a camp for grown-ups. Kids will love it just as much. All

your meals and most activities are included in the price of your stay (horseback riding, archery, arts and crafts); overnight pack trips or fly-fishing outings incur an additional charge. The 10 log cabins—opulent, quiet, and cozy—provide enough of a lure to this serene setting that decompresses you from the outside world. Each cabin has a living room/dining area, covered porch, woodburning fireplace, oversized soaking tub, Aveda amenities, locally hand-carved wood furniture, and satellite radio. Beds have a pillow-top mattress or featherbed and down pillows. Three gourmet meals at the Ranch House are included with rates (see *Dining Out*). Two pet-friendly cabins provide dog dishes and fleece mat; proof of current vaccinations must be provided prior to arrival. Horse boarding available. $525–600 (includes activities) and $375–450 (without activities) double occupancy.

✱ Where to Eat

DINING OUT ♥ **Amberian Peaks Restaurant** (928-735-9977 or 800-556-9997), located at the south end of Main St. Open Fri.–Mon for dinner at 5; Memorial Day–Labor Day for breakfast 8–9:30, lunch 11–2:30. The beauty of this restaurant is not only the food (it's the only restaurant in town that has professional chefs in the kitchen), but the places where you eat it—in the windowed dining room or out on the deck. The dinner menu, eclectic and fun, presents everything from Wild Salmon Satay to Lamb Lollipops and Mediterranean Sampler for noshing, to Moroccan BBQ Pork Chop, Wild Alaskan Cedar Plank Salmon, and Fire-Grilled Tuscan Steak for entrées. Chef Patrick Boyd has halibut from Alaska and salmon from Oregon flown in when in season. For lunch, check out the Ten Buck Burger or the Peak's Buffalo Chili & Cornbread. Ahi tuna is a favorite, the crème brûlée is a trademark, and the strawberry napoleon "goes out the window" when available. Pizza is a local favorite and popular take-out food. Check out the Gourmet Class every Saturday at 3:30 PM for $15 (guests pay $10). The wine tastings every Sunday during the off seasons (4:30–6) turn into a who's who in the White Mountains. "We get locals from all over the area," said owner Don Poyas. "We call them our Wine Taking Party, but it's educational and entertaining. We pair foods and wines and have music." Lunch $9.95–10.95, entrées $22–32, pizza $9.95–25.95.

❀ ♿ ⚭ **Molly Butler Lodge Restaurant** (928-735-7226), 109 Main St. Open daily for dinner 5–9. Molly Butler cooked for her guests when she and her husband, John, opened the restaurant more than 90 years ago, and her food was not only known as some of the best around but reasonably priced, too. Things haven't changed in these two regards, and the restaurant continues as an area favorite, to the point that reservations are recommended. The prime rib is excellent, and fresh-baked bread a treat. Favorites include Molly's Special Steak, Trout, and Hot Dang Chili. Entrées $15–30.

The Ranch House (928-333-1000 or 866-333-4080). Open daily for lunch 11:30–2 and dinner 5:30–7 for families, then 7–8:30. The restaurant at Hidden Meadow Ranch (see *Guest Ranch*) opens its doors to nonguests for lunch and dinner if there's room available. Meals are special in this open-room log building, with bold touches that marry well. Pan-seared lump crab cake with avocado-corn salad and sweet chile aioli tastes extraordinary and is a favorite. Grilled steaks and fish are generally excellent, and you'll likely have a game selection, such as Achiote-Marinated Elk Tenderloin. The Buffalo Burger and Jack Daniel's Sloppy Joe are not your ordinary sandwiches for lunch. Sides like roasted garlic truffled cream potatoes and campfire Vidalia onions make special accompaniments. Sticky toffee pudding is an unusual treat. Like the menu, the wine list offers quality selections. Entrées $22–30.

EATING OUT **Rendezvous Diner** (928-735-7483), 117 Main St. Open Wed.–Mon. 7–4; closed Tue. This local favorite serves up comforting grub that's done right and tastes good. Hamburgers are juicy, chicken-fried steak a favorite, and pies homemade. The log cabin with a tin roof has loads of old-time memorabilia on the walls. You can eat out on the patio when the weather's right. Entrées $6.95–12.50.

✷ Special Events

Call 928-333-2123 for all events.

June: **Greer Days** has a parade, talent show, vendors, food, and drink.

July: **Chamber Music Concert Series and Art Show**. Residents open their home to chamber musicians from around the world.

SPRINGERVILLE, EAGAR, AND THE CORONADO TRAIL

The two towns of Springerville and Eagar still carry the nickname "Valle Redondo" (Round Valley) given by founder Juan Baca, a Spanish sheepherder. The gorgeous expanse of open space has hills and dales formed by the Springerville Volcanic Field (the third largest of its type in the nation) covered by miles of grasslands that turn emerald in spring and summer after wet weather. Sheep herding, peacefully as it may have begun here in the valley, met with many a bloody battle with cattlemen as settlements developed. History says disputes between the two factions produced more than 50 deaths. Furthermore, bad men who flaunted money freely held a high reputation among the townsfolk, who graciously stayed out of their way. This did not bode well for peace and quiet, to the point that even lawmen wouldn't set foot in the two towns. Perhaps Uncle Pop Pace Wiltbank, who settled in Round Valley in 1879, summed it up the best: "Yah, but the code of living in them days was everybody mind your own business."

Cattle ranching prevailed and ended up having a big influence in the area for several decades. Although it's now on the wane, you may still feel the cowboy spirit in these twin towns—ranching doesn't just get into your blood, it becomes part of your heart and soul.

If you're heading east on AZ 260, Springerville and Eagar are the last towns before you round the bend to head south on US 191 into the White Mountains. Once you pass Alpine, accommodations come sparingly, then not at all south of Hannagan Meadow until Clifton. The land along US 191 once dominated by outlaws and cowboys, now makes a place for outdoor lovers to explore. Wild when the cowboys roamed it, the land remains just the same today—if not more so, thanks to the reintroduction of the Mexican gray wolf.

GUIDANCE **Springerville-Eagar Regional Chamber of Commerce** (928-333-2123 or 888-733-2123), 318 E. Main St. Pick up *The Official Driving Tour of the White Mountain Region* here ($9.95 for tape; $15.95 for CD). The tour includes history and sites of the area and all the creatures and cultures that inhabited the land, from dinosaurs to outlaws. **Apache-Sitgreaves National Forest** (928-333-4301), 30 S. Chiricahua Dr. (open Mon.–Fri. 8–4:30), has information on backcountry use of the national forest.

YOU MAY SEE ANTELOPE GRAZING IN THE GRASSLANDS ALONG CORONADO TRAIL OR IN THE MEADOWS OF THE WHITE MOUNTAINS

GETTING THERE *By car:* You can reach Round Valley from several different directions: Take US 180/191 from the Navajo Nation in the north; US 60 west from New Mexico or east from Show Low; AZ 260 from the towns along the Mogollon Rim; and US 191 (the Coronado Trail) from the south. *By air:* **Springerville Airport** (928-333-5746), 905 W. Airport Rd., has a hard-surfaced, 8,400-foot landing.

WHEN TO COME Located in the foothills of the White Mountains at almost 7,000 feet, the two towns keep comfortable from spring through fall. High season spans from Memorial to Labor Day.

MEDICAL EMERGENCY **White Mountains Regional Medical Center** (928-333-4368; TDB, 928-333-7156), 118 S. Mountain Ave.

✷ To See

Casa Malpais Archaeological Park and Museum (928-333-5375), 318 E. Main St. Open Tue.–Sat. 8–4. Tours at 9, 11, and 2 (0.75-mile hike on a gradual climb that takes1½–2 hours). One of the state's best archaeological sites, and also a National Historic Landmark Site, features an astronomical observatory, great kiva, ancient stairways, and rock art. "Casa Malpais" (House of Badlands) was named for its location on a volcanic rock rim overlooking Round Valley. The Hopi and Zuni have weighed in on excavation at the Ancestral Puebloan site, claiming ancestral affinity. The museum takes a macrobiotic look at the area with not only artifacts from Casa Malpais ruins but also antiques from pioneer days and ancient relics from the days the dinosaurs reigned. The museum is free; admission to the ruins is $7 adults, $5 age 55-plus and students, age 2 and under free.

The Little House Museum (928-333-2286), X Diamond Ranch on South Fork Rd. off AZ 260. Open May 15–Labor Day; tour daily at 11 AM or by appointment. Wink Crigler, granddaughter of the area's founding mother, Molly Butler, created this small museum as a memorial to her late husband, a championship horse trainer. What started with a roomful of awards and memorabilia grew to a community repository, big on cultural history and packed with historical photos, unique musical instruments, antiques, and mementos from the pioneer days. $3 adults, $1 under 12; ranch guests free.

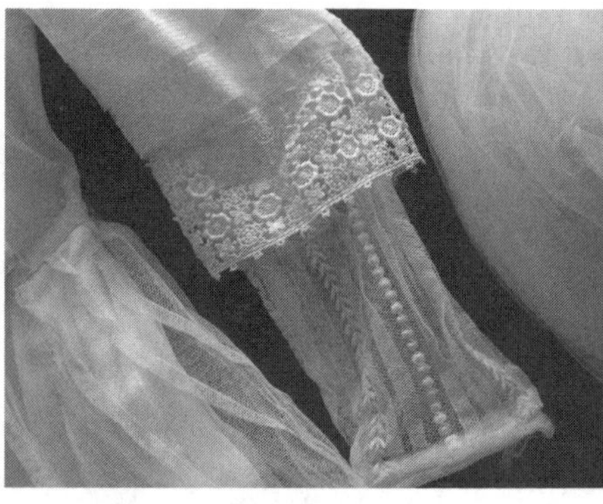

A PIONEER WEDDING DRESS ON DISPLAY AT LITTLE HOUSE MUSEUM

Renee Cushman Art Museum (928-333-2123), Church of the Latter Day Saints, Springerville. By appointment only. The story behind this museum is almost as interesting as its exquisite collection, such as an engraving attributed to Rembrandt, pen drawings by Tiepolo, and other art and furniture dating from the Renaissance to the early 20th century. Although not a member of the church, Cushman, a local rancher, willed the collection to the church as a way of acknowledging her friendship with a bishop who had assisted her in times of need. Free.

SCENIC DRIVES Take any of the unpaved roads south of AZ 260 or west of US 191 to find extraordinarily scenic countryside of huge mountain meadows, aspen-fir forests, lakes, and streams. Many do not require high clearance or four-wheel drive. Purchase a map of the national forest from Apache-Sitgreaves National Forest to help find your way around the forest. For a paved roadtrip, head south on the **Coronado Trail Scenic Byway**. Once called US 666, the forbidding stigma the triple-digit number implied conjured up a movement to save this segment of highway in Arizona (nicknamed the Devil's Highway) with a new numerical designation (US 191). The dramatic drive, which winds between Springerville and Clifton, doesn't exactly follow the historic route its namesake, Francisco Vásquez de Coronado, took during his 16-day pass through the White Mountains. But the road gets close With no services for the second half of the 120 miles, be sure to top off your gas tank and take a lunch or snacks. The scenery is heavenly, but full of devilish hairpin turns (420 by one Forest Service estimate). Take your time and enjoy the scenery.

✷ To Do

FISHING Surrounded by the Apache-Sitgreaves National Forest with the most streams and lakes in the Southwest, you can head in practically any direction and find a stream or lake stocked with trout. Some have native Apache trout. About 10 miles down US 191, **Nelson Reservoir** draws local residents for stocked rainbow trout, waterfowl, and migrating birds. **X Diamond Ranch** (see *Lodging*) allows five anglers at a time onto its segment of the Little Colorado River. Fees run $35–45 per person for half–full day. You can rent the river for $200. **The Speck-**

led Trout (928-333-0852), 222 E. Main St., offers guided trout fishing for $135–225 per day and casting/fishing lessons at $35 per hour (2-hour minimum). If you have your own rig and a sense of adventure, head into the Apache-Sitgreaves National Forest. Hot spots are the **West Fork of the Black River** (Thompson Trail) **Big Lake**, and the **West Fork of the Little Colorado River** (West Baldy Trail). **Pacheta Lake**, located on the White Mountain Apache Reservation (from AZ 260, go south on AZ 273 to Apache Y-20) is known among anglers as *the* spot for lunker trout. Don't be surprised if you nab an 18-pounder in the catch-and-release-only lake.

HIKING Head west to Greer or south on US 191 for the best high-country hiking in the state. Along US 191, check out the first 3 miles of the **KP Trail**, which take you to a waterfall. The **Upper Fish Creek Trail** travels through an aspen-fir forest; the **Bear Wallow Trail** takes you into a remote wilderness where big game roams.

HORSEBACK RIDING **K5 Outdoor Adventures** (see *Reed's Lodge* under *Lodging*). **X Diamond Ranch** (928-333-2286), South Fork Rd. The guest ranch offers rides to nonguests, too. You can spend an hour to all day in the saddle. Prices start at $25 an hour.

MOVIES—**El Rio Theatre** (928-333-4590), W. Main St. One of Arizona's oldest theaters, operating since 1937, might be the perfect spot to hit if the right movie's playing when you're in town.

✷ Wilder Places

Contact **Apache-Sitgreaves National Forest** for information on the following.

Bear Wallow Wilderness Area. The Bear Wallow Trail in this wilderness is where guides take big-game hunters in the fall. With that in mind, don't be surprised to find bear tracks (it got its name from the bears that liked to wallow in the creek), mountain lion sign, prints of elk hooves sunken deeply into the trail, and Mexican gray wolf signs.

Blue Range Primitive Area (located south of Alpine and east of US 191). When mountain man James O. Pattie trapped beaver in the area in 1825, he marveled at its clear running streams, lush canyons, and abundant wildlife. Things haven't changed. The Blue, as locals affectionately call it, remains one of the nation's most unaltered areas of backcountry. Because the Blue never transitioned into a wilderness area, it stays out of books and reference pages.

As remote and lonely as the land remains, it has an extensive trail system that makes it highly accessible. Most of the trails have their roots as Indian paths. Later, ranchers developed the paths to run their cattle between the high country in summer and the Blue River in winter. Hikers can go weeks without seeing another human being in the Blue. If you travel any of these trails, bring a map, compass/GPS, layers of clothing, and a sense of adventure. Don't bring your dog. This is wolf country, where man's best friend is fodder for the territorial Mexican gray wolf.

Escudilla Wilderness. Located about 23 miles south on US 191. This small wilderness holds the state's third-highest peak. Two trails travel the area: the 3-mile-long Escudilla National Recreation Trail, which heads up to the top of

Escudilla Mountain, and the 4-mile-long Government Trail that takes you on a side path firefighters used when a blaze burned the peak in 1951. Because the fire burned the mixed-conifer forests, aspens grew back with a vengeance. The mountaintop has the best autumn golds in the state.

Sipe White Mountain Wildlife Area (928-367-4281), located 10 miles south of Eagar on US 191, then about 5 miles off US 191 on a gravel road. Arizona Department of Game and Fish manages this former streamside ranch. Wildlife watching is big here, and Audubon considers it one of the better birding sites in the area, especially along Rudd Creek.

✷ Lodging

In and near town

Reed's Lodge (928-333-4323 or 800-814-6451), 514 E. Main St., Springerville. Family-owned by local ranchers and one of the favorite accommodations in the area, the lodge offers a rustic exterior with clean, comfortable rooms. They have three different types of rooms, so ask before you sign if you want the best. Rooms have TV, phone, air-conditioning, and heat; some have microwave and refrigerator. Ice is complimentary. Owners Roxanne and Galyn Knight also run K5 Outdoor Adventures and will take you on guided hikes, SUV tours, and off-the-beaten-path places (all extra) privy to locals who have lived on the land for the last five generations because they like their guests to get to know the area a little deeper than just what you can see from the paved highway. $55–75.

Rode Inn (928-333-4365), 242 E. Main St. You can get a decent room at this Main St. inn. The lobby is bona fide western, the rooms clean and comfortable for a night's stay. All have mini fridges. A decent breakfast is included. $60–75.

♥ **X Diamond & MLY Ranch** (928-333-2286). From Eagar, go 5 miles on AZ 260 to the signed South Fork turnoff. Owner Wink Crigler has family roots on this land along the Little Colorado River that go back to 1890, when her grandparents Molly and John Butler homesteaded it. The property, 30,000 acres of grazing land, offers horseback riding, archaeological ruins you can view and even dig when the curator is on site, a museum, private fishing, and hiking. Wink is passionate about the land and gives several-hour tours of it. Kids will be drawn to the animals: horses, cattle, kittens, and glimpses of the wildlife that frequents the property. The grounds are impeccably kept and colored with wildflowers and several gardens. All of the six guest cabins, modern, neat, and clean, run 1,100–2,600 square feet with large, fully equipped kitchen (you just bring your own food), barbecue grill, and views. Most have wood or gas-burning fireplace, all have satellite TV/DVD and Jacuzzi tub; some have a phone or hot tub. $95–175 double occupancy, $20 per extra person. No pets or ATVs.

White Mountains

Blue River Wilderness Retreat (928-339-4426). Located about 20 miles south of Alpine near the confluence of the Blue River and Campbell Blue Creek and 10 miles from a paved road, this is where you go when you want to get away from it all. Three vintage motor homes and a cabin stand on an original 43-acre homestead in the Apache-Sitgreaves National Forest "not on the way to anywhere," as owner and artist Janie Hoffman describes it. Near three roadless areas and a few minutes' drive from trails in the Blue Range Primitive Area, the property is the perfect place for hikers, birders, and couch potatoes. Units are fully furnished, but bring your own towels and linens. Pets okay (bring a leash in case they make chase with owners' cats); use of corral $10 per night. A $25 cleaning fee is returned if your cabin is left clean . $100 deposit required, and applied toward rent. Cell phones don't work here. $190–250 a week; special rates for longer stays.

✱ Where to Eat

DINING OUT ♥ Bistro Escudilla (928-339-1150), 41633 US 180, Nutrioso. Open Wed.–Sun. for lunch 11–4, dinner 5–9. Chef Bill Wise brings affordable gourmet to the high country with his menu featuring "American comfort food with a different spin." For instance, the lunch menu has hamburgers made with American Kobe beef; the Philly Cheese Sandwich and French Dip contains smoked prime rib. A separate dinner menu has fish (ahi tuna and salmon are current customer favorites), steaks and carbonara (which the chef favors). All the food is made in-house, which means Chef Bill roasts his own peppers and create his own condiments. After all is said and done, however, the desserts rule. "People order and then say, 'I'm here for the Bread Pudding, and must leave room for dessert,'" Bill's wife, Leann, said. "They get a doggy bag for what they don't finish so they can have dessert." Lunch $9–12, dinner $13–25.

EATING OUT Buzz's Diner (928-333-2899), 141 E. Fifth St., Springerville. Open Mon.–Fri. 9 AM–9 PM, Sat. 10–9. The local favorite serves up some quintessential diner food. Burgers are big here—especially if you have the Monster Burger). And diners love the shrimp baskets and specials. $2.50–8.

((ɪ)) **Java Blues Coffee Bar & Bistro** (928-333-5282), 341 E. Main St., Springerville. Open Mon.–Fri. 5 AM–7 PM, Sat. 6 AM–7 PM (till 11 if there's entertainment), Sun. 7–3. A meld of local diner, living room, and blues bar, this coffee bar has turned into all things to all people. You'll see everything from flip-flops to cowboy boots here as you sip on some of the best coffee this side of the Little Colorado River. Breakfast, lunch, and dinner served. Beverages include espresso drinks, smoothies, beer, wine, and the plain old cup o' java. Entertainment (most weekends) often includes well-known blues names. Free WiFi and Internet access. Breakfast $3.95–6.95, lunch $4.95–6.75, dinner $6.95–17.95.

Sunny Side Restaurant (928-333-1313), 318 E. Main St., Springerville. Open Tue.–Fri. 4:30 AM–8 PM, Sun.–Mon. 4:30–3. If you're a fan of Joe and Heather's restaurant, rest easy, it's not gone; just has a new name. If you've never eaten at Joe and Heathers, why eat here? "Because the food's good and the price is right." Joe's son and cook, Ryan said with Bostonian pragmatism. The chicken-fried steak is the most popular here, along with the daily specials ($5). Breakfast is served all day "because some people like to eat breakfast for their meal and everyone else in town stops serving it at eleven," Ryan said. It's diner food, but it's decent. And it definitely is the right price.

✱ Special Events

Call 928-333-2123 for all events.

April: **Chrome in the Dome Classic Car Show** features classic cars, vendors, food, and live radio.

May: **Round Valley Roundup** gives you a chance to check out the land and the culture through tours of historical sites, Forest Service tours of the national forest, ATV guided tours on local trails, a fishing derby at Becker Lake, Junior Rodeo, food and dancing.

July: **Fourth of July Celebration** includes a parade, rodeo, barbecue, and fireworks.

August: **Eagar Daze** has a number of fun events that includes an ice cream social, talent show, youth rodeo, and logging activities, as well as vendors and food. **Alpine Chili Cook-Off** serves some of the tastiest chili this side of the Whites, along with entertainment, showmanship, a Bean Jackpot, and Brisket competition to benefit the volunteer Alpine Fire Department and Alpine School.

December: **Electric Light Parade**, **White Mountain Historical Society Home Tour and Tea**, and **Christmas Eve CommunityLuminaria Lighting**.

SAFFORD

In the late 1870s, Mormons from Utah started to head southward into Arizona in what historians call the second generation of Mormon colonization. Apostle Erstus Snow pioneered the movement, and by 1879 a handful of settlers explored the Valley of the Gila to find the best place to dig an irrigation ditch from the Gila River. A few years later, not willing to suffer the impetuous flooding of the Gila River, some farmers headed up the river valley, settled the first Anglo town site, and called it Safford, after a visiting governor. The settlers worked the land and had a ready market for their goods in the mining country of Morenci just up river; life was good. Farmers and merchants pieced together a ragtag route called the Safford-Morenci Trail to pack their goods to the mining country.

Safford and the towns around have always ebbed and flowed with the activity of the mines. When the mines prospered, so did they. When layoffs came, the towns tightened their belts. Lately, Safford has started to promote the wonderful natural and cultural history in its midst. Out in these parts life is down-home and grassroots. The restaurants have old-timer regulars lined up along the counter drinking their cups of Joe, shooting the breeze like they do every morning 'bout this time at El Coronado Restaurant or farmers having their daily lunch kibitz at Bush & Shurtz, just as they did decades ago. You find that special something for your home from a thrift shop instead of a gift shop. The backcountry usually has little or no trace of the managing agencies that supervise the land; exploring comes free in these parts.

Out here, the old-fashioned version of Arizona's independent spirit full of guts and gumption shows through in all its classic glory. They don't call US 70, the road along which Safford lies, the Old West Highway for nothing. The farther out in the country you travel, the more you, correctly, get the feeling things haven't changed all that much. The area oozes so much atmosphere and tradition, it's practically hallowed. Things sure are peaceful here. This calm assurance seems unusual for such a rough-and-tumble spot so full of raucous times and personalities. But a land this rich in culture often exudes such a soothing coziness—especially when the land itself remains unchanged and holds on to its history.

GUIDANCE **Graham County Chamber of Commerce** (928-428-2511 or 888-837-1841), 1111 W.US 70., has information about the town, area activities, and yearly events. **Bureau of Land Management Safford Field Office** (928-348-4400), 711 14th Ave., has information on public lands around the area. **Safford**

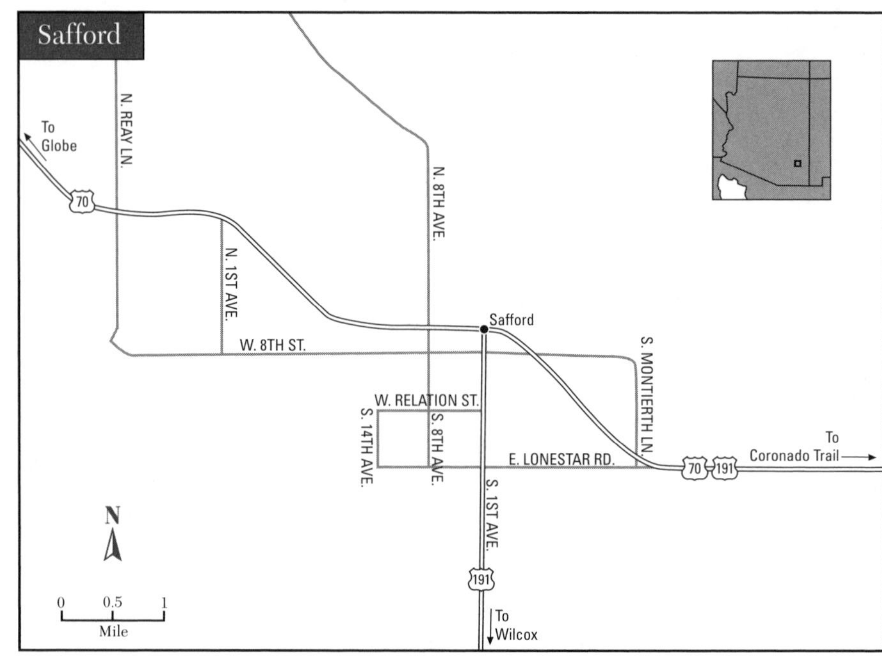

Ranger District (928-428-4150) can tell you about backcountry use on Mount Graham. **Clifton Ranger District** (928-687-8600) has information on the backcountry north of Clifton.

GETTING THERE *By car:* From Phoenix, go east on US 60 and US 70. *By air:* **Safford Municipal Airport** (928-428-2762) 4550 E. Aviation Way, has two well maintained paved runways, tie-downs for transient aircraft, a heliport, and 24/7 fuel service.

WHEN TO COME Safford has a lower Sonoran Desert climate—hot summers and mild winters. With so many outdoor enticements, it's best to plan your trip to match the activity. If you plan your activities on Mount Graham, wait until summer.

MEDICAL EMERGENCY **Mt. Graham Regional Medical Center** (520-348-4000), 1600 20th Ave.

✷ To See

Discovery Park (928-428-6260), 1651 W. Discovery Park Blvd. Open Mon.–Fri. 8–4, Sat. 4 PM–9 PM. Features the Governor Aker Observatory and its 20-inch reflecting telescope and Camera Obscura, as well as an exhibit gallery, gift shop, and educational facilities. A 20-minute simulated ride on the Shuttlecraft Polaris takes a "look" at the planets and their moons. During the day, explore the terrestrial habitats—tree-line paths and a wetlands area. $5 adults, $3 ages 6–11, under age 6 free with ticketed adult, Polaris Space Flight Simulator $6. You can pick up tickets for tours ($20) to the **Mount Graham International Observatory**, which take place Saturdays from early May until mid-Nov., as weather permits. Tours take you up Mount Graham and elucidate geology and natural and cultural history. At the observatory, you can see the Vatican Advanced Technology telescope, the Heinrich Hertz Sumillimeter Telescope, and the Large Binocular Telescope, the world's most powerful, and hear the stories behind it.

Fort Grant Historical Museum. Located at the end of AZ 266 (go about 20 miles south of Safford on US 191, turn west onto AZ 266, and go 21 miles to Fort Grant). Open Mon.–Fri. 8–5. The drive alone is a scenic foray into the high-desert country, with a unique bouldered landscape. The museum, a hidden-away cache of military items and photos and information about its history as a state reformatory and state prison, date back to the late 1800s. Free.

Graham County Historical Society Museum (928-348-0470), 3430 W. US 70, Thatcher. Open Mon., Tue., and Sat. 10–4. The old Thatcher High School building, built in 1917, is a treasure trove of history. Fifteen former classrooms hold a compilation of collectibles and antiques giving insight into the area's cultures—Native peoples, Mormon, and Hispanic. The items—pottery and artifacts, farm machinery, clothes, ranch items, musical instruments, and old electronics—are arranged by room. Free.

SCENIC DRIVES **Black Hills Backcountry Byway**. Contact the Bureau of Land Management. Located off US 70 east of Safford. Scenic and totally undeveloped, this 21-mile route winds through a countryside full of history and geology. If you like to rockhound, check out the Black Hills Rockhound Area. You may find some prized specimens of fire agate. A 1930s Civilian Conservation Camp is located around milepost 16. High-clearance vehicles are recommended on this graded route.

Old West Highway, which starts at Apache Junction and travels on US 60 to Globe, then continues to Safford on US 70, takes you even deeper into the countryside and another 47 miles to Duncan at the New Mexico border. Check out the town of Virden on NM 92, then loop back on US 70.

Swift Highway. Contact the Safford Ranger District. Located off US 191, about 9 miles south of Safford. The 35-mile, mostly paved road takes you up to the top reaches of Mount Graham (see *Wilder Places*). You travel through several different biomes, from desert to subalpine. It's full of hairpin turns and beautiful vistas.

DISCOVERY PARK GIVES VISITORS A MACROCOSMIC SCIENTIFIC LOOK AT THE EARTH AND SKY

Three Way. Take a look at where the Safford merchants sold their products by heading east on US 70, then north on US 191 to Three Way (a place on the map, not a town). Continue north to Clifton and Morenci. On the way back, take AZ 75 to US 70 and stop at Gimee's for a hamburger or classic Mexican food.

✱ To Do

BIRDING There are a number of hidden gems around Safford—ranging from wild and scenic to local ponds and lakes—where you can catch avian activity.

Cluff Ranch (928-485-9430) is located 10 miles west of Safford. Take US 70 northwest to Pima, turn left onto Main St., then left onto Cluff Ranch Rd. Open 24 hours. The ranch, maintained by the Arizona Department of Game and Fish, lies in the foothills of Mount Graham and presents several different habitats that attract a number of different species. The road leads to several ponds with trails that travel riparian woodlands. Free.

Discovery Park. The small pond behind the Graveyard Wash flood-control structure has a stand of cottonwood and willow trees that attract waterfowl, hummingbirds, hawks, falcons, and a number of neotropical migrants. Free.

Gila Box Riparian National Conservation Area. Contact Bureau of Land Management. More than 140 species of birds have been sighted here, including the common black hawk, zone-tailed hawk, and yellow-billed cuckoo. Over 70 species nest right along the creek. Free.

CULTURE Mexican roots go deep around here, and the town celebrates them with **Arizona's Salsa Trail**. Get a map or purchase the book "Arizona's Salsa Trail" at the Graham County Chamber of Commerce and visit a chile pepper market, a handmade tortilla factory (using no preservatives), and a handful of restaurants that serve this state's cultural favorite Mexican food. The book has in-depth information on the restaurants along the trail and more than 30 destinations to visit.

HIKING Check out the 5.1-mile **Arcadia Trail** on Mt. Graham for some great viewpoints. In summer, follow the first few miles of the **Ash Creek Trail** on Mt. Graham. Contact Safford Ranger District for both. Or head up US 191 past Clifton to the **Painted Cliffs** or **Spur Ranch Trails** (contact the Clifton Ranger District).

HOT SPRINGS Located on a lava field, the Safford area has several hot springs—all of different demeanor—where you can go soak yourself. Some require you bring your own towel, so come prepared if you plan to partake of the mineral water therapy. **Essence of Tranquility** (928-428-9312), 6074 S. Lebanon Loop. Open Mon. 2–9, Tue.–Sat. 8–9, Sun. 8–7). The original owners of these hot springs called them "Lebanon" after the biblical Pools of Lebanon, where an angel occasionally agitated the waters and the sick and lame could get healed if they got into the pool when the waters stirred. The premises have six separate pools ranging from 103 to 106 degrees, and they still, many say, hold the healing powers of the Pools of Lebanon. Owner Clarrise Drake attributes healings to faith and the fact that the water has a lot of sodium, which draws out poisons and stress. Her spa's popularity comes from not only the water's health benefits but also its "funkified," homey atmosphere with plastic flowers and kitschy curios, decorative outside lights, and cozy sitting areas scattered around the spa's grounds. $5 per soak; bring your own towels. Camping, tepees, and casitas are available for overnight stays. Body treatments (massage, reflexology, herbal detox wraps, hot mineral baths, herbal sea salt full-body scrub) are available.

Hot Well Dunes Recreation Area. Contact the Bureau of Land Management for hours and availability. Drive 7 miles east on US 70; turn south (right) onto Haekel Rd., and proceed 25 miles to the area. The road is well graded but not paved. Located 25 miles south of Safford, hidden in a gallery of mesquite trees surrounded by desert, the recreation area offers a wilder hot-springs experience. The 106-degree water flows at 250 gallons per minute from a well discovered by accident. Drillers seeking for oil instead hit a pocket of hot water 1,920 feet under the sand. From its two outdoor tubs, soakers can view the rolling sand dunes and the jagged peaks of the Peloncillo Mountains in the distance. One tub sits in the shade of a giant tamarisk; the other basks in the sun. At night bathers soak under a canopy of stars. And because you're surrounded by 2,000 acres of sand dunes, it's almost like a day at the beach. Picnic tables and camping available. Bring your own towels. $5 per vehicle per day.

Kachina Mineral Springs (928-428-7212), 1155 W. Cactus Rd. Open Mon., Thu., Fri., and Sat. 9–4; Sun. 11–2. Located at the base of Mount Graham in an area called Artesia because of its many free-flowing hot springs, Kachina Mineral Springs is fed by a hot thermal pool bubbling with 108-degree water. The spa has a large communal tub and several private mineral baths, which pour into Roman-style tubs cleaned and scrubbed after each use. You can also receive a body massage, sweat wrap, and/or foot reflexology treatment (reservations required) at very reasonable prices. Soak $10 per person, treatments $55–90.

MINE TOUR ✐ **Morenci Copper Mine** (877-646-8687), 4521 US 191 (54 miles east of Safford). Tours are offered Fri. and Sat. at 9 and 1. You get a blend of information and entertainment when you hop on the $2 million haul truck normally used to carry about 270 tons of copper ore to take the 3-hour guided tour in the world's largest open-pit copper mine. The decommissioned truck has 12-foot-high tires and looks every bit like the ones still hauling raw ore for processing. Call for tour times and prices.

✷ Wilder Places

Gila Box Riparian National Conservation Area (NCA). Contact the Bureau of Land Management. Open 24 hours every day. The west end is located 20 miles northeast of Safford: Go east on US 70, then north on Sanchez Rd. near the town of Solomon; follow the road until the pavement ends, then continue on a graded road, following GILA BOX signs. The NCA contains 15 miles of Bonita Creek and 23 miles of the Gila River. Bonita Creek presents a beautiful riparian canopy of cottonwood, sycamore, walnut, ash, and mesquite trees in a narrow high-walled canyon. Beaver ponds pool the creek water, and hikers should be prepared to wade, deeply. The Gila River is more open walled, and its flow is not as hiker-friendly A wildlife-viewing deck overlooks the confluence of the creek and river. If you explore along Bonita Creek, there's a good chance you'll see bear signs. Along the Gila, watch for hawks, eagles, and bighorn sheep. Both the waterways are known for excellent birding opportunities. Free.

Mount Graham. The Pinaleño Mountain range, where 10,720-foot Mt. Graham is located, has a rich cache of wildlife and biological diversity. Scientists call the mountains a biologically unique area because 18 species and subspecies of plants and animals found here exist nowhere else on the planet. The diversity comes from the sky island principle; the range rises almost 8,000 feet above the desert floor. The highest peak in southern Arizona), contains more life zones than any other single mountain in North America. Cacti cover the base of the mountains, and pine-oak forests the midsection. Ponderosa pines blanket the upper realms, and old-growth fir and aspen forests on the mountains' tops. When you plan a visit to the Pinaleño Mountains, stay in their lowlands in winter, and head for the peaks in summer.

Red Knolls. (Contact the Bureau of Land Management.) Located on Red Knolls Rd. off US 70 at milepost 312. Once the accumulated sediment at the bottom of an ancient seabed, the Red Knolls rise Bryce-like from the desert floor in a most majestic manner. The Knolls' elegance comes from several natural amphitheaters etched with flutes, turrets, nooks, and hoodoo columns topped with caps. Native peoples rendezvoused in the formations in centuries past. Cowboys used the natural amphitheaters to round up cattle. Rustlers used to hide out here. Some corralled their clutch of stolen horses in the niches of the Knolls. Some, local legends say, buried their booty and never came back to get it. Tread lightly, as some parts are unstable. Free.

✱ Lodging

BED & BREAKFASTS Olney House Bed & Breakfast (928-428-5118 or 800-814-5118), 1104 Central Ave. The only B&B in the area was built in 1890 and is listed on the National Register of Historic Buildings as one of the finest examples of Western colonial revival architecture in the Southwest. The innkeepers, both retired from the U.S. Air Force, have a veritable museum with all kinds of interesting memorabilia, antiques, and historic anecdotes about the home's first owner, Sheriff Olney. Breakfast included. No pets. $65–85 double occupancy, $10 per extra person.

✱ Where to Eat

DINING OUT Casa Mañana (928-428-3170), 502 S. US 191. When Diane Hoopes purchased this restaurant, she decided to resurrect as many original recipes as she could when it used to be *the* place to go for dinner in the 1950s. "We have several old-Mexico style recipes you can't get anywhere else," Hoopes said. The Rellenos have a red onion sauce; the Sonoran Enchilada is a *masa* patty covered with enchilada sauce, scallions, and green olives. The Shredded Beef, one of the signature dishes then and now, tastes as close as one could get it to the good old days. And, unlike other Mexican restaurants in the area, the menu features some tasty fish tacos. Entrées $4.95–9.95.

La Casita Café (928-428-1882), 3338 W. Main St., Thatcher. Tue.–Thu. 11–8:30, Fri. and Sat. 11–9:30. When owner and chef Ray Villalobos opened his restaurant with his wife, Lorraine, he didn't know much about cooking. But his late grandmother, Salustia, did. Ray took over the kitchen and cooked up dishes using his grandmother's tried–and-true recipes; Lorraine worked the dining room. Salustia, known for her excellent Mexican food, must have put her stamp of approval on her grandson's efforts. The place is usually packed during the dinner hours. The secret ingredient in the mild salsa has everyone guessing and coming back for more. The green chile pork is the local favorite. The *machaca* is juicy. And the sopaipillas are light as air. Entrées $4.99–7.99.

La Paloma (928-428-2094), 5183 E. Clifton St., Solomon. Open daily Mon.–Thu. 10:30–8, Fri. and Sat. 10:30–9. Located a few miles down the highway from Safford, this Mexican restaurant draws a following for a reason—fine food and service at great prices. Some of the same recipes have been used since it opened as Shorty's Café more than 50 years ago. Each time the restaurant sold for the last 25+ years, Fernando and Carmen have come with the deal. This was good business, as Fernando makes killer enchilada sauce that lures diners for miles around and Carmen the perfect *chiles rellenos*. There's always a daily special. $4.99–9.45.

✷ Special Events

September: **SalsaFest** celebrates the chile harvest the last weekend in the month with a balloon glow on Friday night; balloon launch, salsa-making contests, music, food, and fun on Saturday, and another balloon launch Sunday morning.

Southern Arizona

TUCSON

TUBAC

BENSON

WILLCOX

SIERRA VISTA

BISBEE

TOMBSTONE

PATAGONIA, SONOITA, AND ELGIN

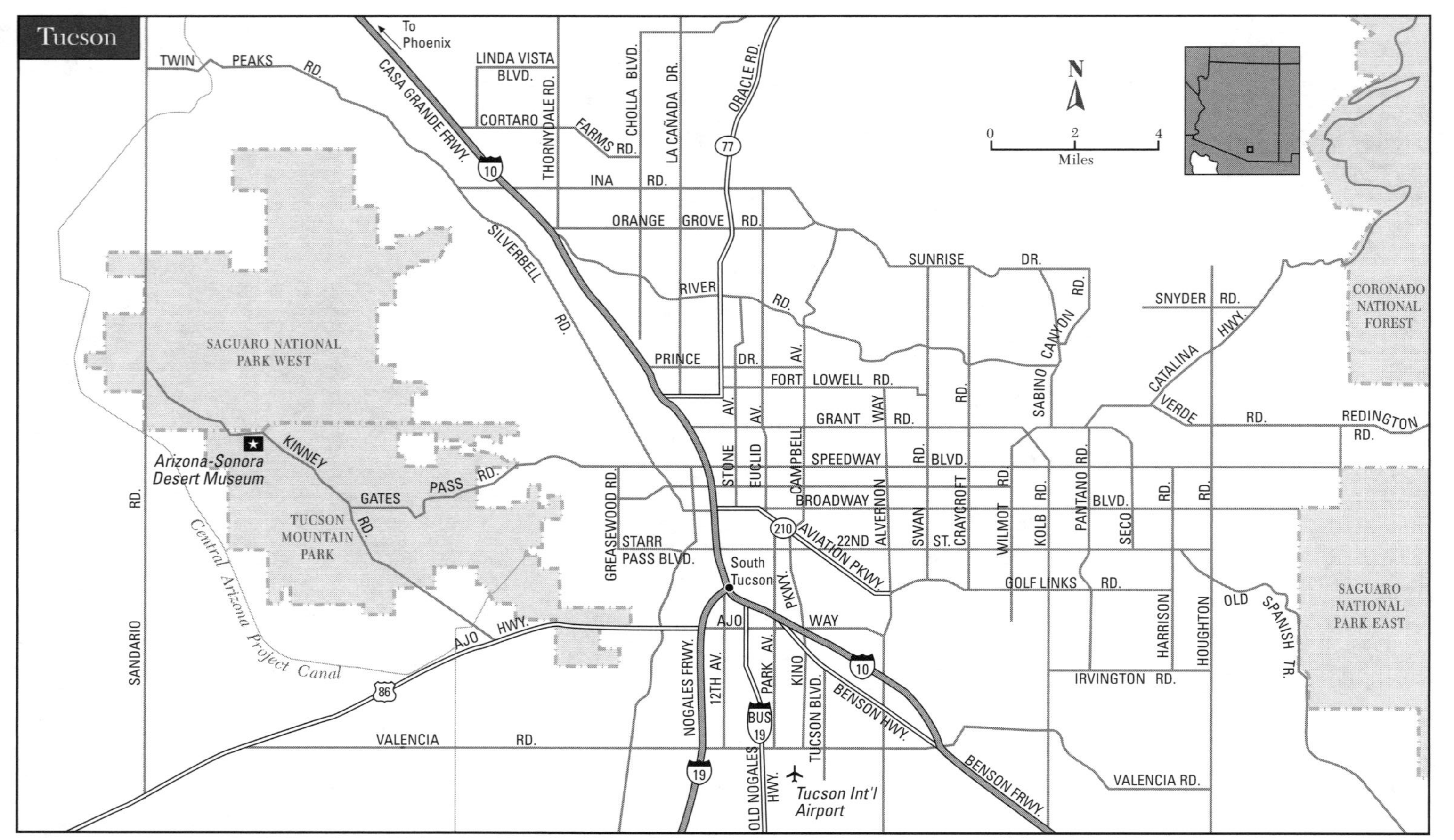

Tucson
To Phoenix
N
0
2
4
Miles
TWIN PEAKS RD.
CASA GRANDE FRWY.
10
LINDA VISTA BLVD.
CORTARO
THORNYDALE RD.
FARMS RD.
CHOLLA BLVD.
LA CAÑADA DR.
ORACLE RD.
77
INA RD.
ORANGE GROVE RD.
SILVERBELL RD.
RIVER RD.
SUNRISE DR.
SNYDER RD.
CANYON RD.
CATALINA HWY.
CORONADO NATIONAL FOREST
SAGUARO NATIONAL PARK WEST
PRINCE DR.
FORT LOWELL RD.
AV.
AV.
AV.
SABINO
GRANT RD.
WAY
RD.
VERDE RD.
REDINGTON RD.
Arizona-Sonora Desert Museum
KINNEY RD.
GATES PASS RD.
SPEEDWAY BLVD.
STONE
EUCLID
CAMPBELL
BROADWAY BLVD.
GREASEWOOD RD.
TUCSON MOUNTAIN PARK
STARR PASS BLVD.
210
AVIATION PKWY.
22ND ST.
ALVERNON
SWAN
CRAYCROFT
WILMOT RD.
KOLB RD.
PANTANO RD.
SECO
RD.
RD.
South Tucson
GOLF LINKS RD.
HARRISON
HOUGHTON
OLD SPANISH TR.
SAGUARO NATIONAL PARK EAST
SANDARIO RD.
Central Arizona Project Canal
AJO HWY.
AJO WAY
PKWY.
10
86
NOGALES FRWY.
12TH AV.
PARK AV.
KINO
TUCSON BLVD.
BENSON HWY.
IRVINGTON RD.
BUS 19
VALENCIA RD.
19
OLD NOGALES HWY.
Tucson Int'l Airport
BENSON FRWY.
VALENCIA RD.

TUCSON

Dressed in Spanish and Mexican architecture, with a Wild West spirit and a Native American soul, Tucson brings visitors back to the state's cultural roots. The desert city, wrapped in mountain panoramas and natural Sonoran Desert scenes, takes visitors as close to the Wild West as they want to comfortably get or as far out into interstellar space as a telescope can take them.

Comfort is the key word here in Tucson, where even the toniest of resorts and restaurants add the word *casual* to *dressy* when defining their dress codes. The town's comfortable with its culture, cares about its surrounding landscape, and knows it has the edge when it comes to independent thinking. Many of its best businesses are homegrown independents that rack up awards and kudos.

As one of the oldest cities in the state, Tucson has blended tolerance with wisdom and comes up with a likable personality akin to that of a doting grandmother who can't do enough to make you comfortable but is able to teach you a new thing or two. The city, like much of southern Arizona, has been around the block a few times. Tucson has seen flags of three different countries and both sides of the Mason-Dixon Line during the Civil War flapping in its breeze.

Long before politics, the first signs of inhabitants roamed the area the same time mammoths did, between 12,500 and 6,000 BC. Next, the Cochise culture built pit houses. By AD 300 the Hohokam farmed the valley. Spanish missionaries came on the scene in 1692 and built the Presidio of St. Augustin a year before the nation's founding fathers signed off on the Declaration of Independence. Tucson changed hands from Spanish adobe village to part of Mexico after the Mexican Revolution of 1821. Looking for railroad land, the United States negotiated the Gadsden Purchase, and Tucson finally flew the U.S. flag when Arizona became a territory in 1854. Of course, not all Washingtonians liked the idea. Some suggested the United States pay Mexico to take Arizona back, at double the original price.

Tucson spent a decade as the territorial capital but never could wrangle the title back after Arizona became a state. This ended up working for them, inasmuch as Tucson has always been able to favor the land and its culture over development. The result is a reputation as one of the state's most livable cities full of personality and a lot of soul.

GUIDANCE **Metropolitan Tucson Convention and Visitors Bureau** (520-624-1817 or 800-638-8350), 100 S. Church Ave. Open Mon.–Fri. 9–5, Sat. and Sun. 9–4. A complete source for information on southern Arizona, from maps to brochures to magazine guides. The Coronado National Forest (520-388-8300), 300 W. Congress St., has recreation opportunity guides and sells maps of each ranger district managing the national forest surrounding the city.

GETTING THERE *By car:* I-10 travels through the city's south and west sides. *By air:* **Tucson International Airport** (520-573-8000), 7250 S. Tucson Blvd., is served by 11 airlines, including Alaska, American, Continental, Delta, Northwest, Southwest, United, and U.S. Airways/Lufthansa. *By bus:* **Greyhound Bus Station** (520-792-3475), 471 W. Congress St. *By train:* **Amtrak's Sunset Limited** (520-623-4442), 400 E. Toole Ave.

GETTING AROUND Tucson's transit system, **Sun Tran** (520-792-9222), will get you around the town's major streets and to or from the airport. The downtown area has the free **Tucson Inner City Express Transit** (TICET). The road bicycle is big here, and drivers honor the bicycle's legal right to the road. Drivers should note most intersections have a delayed left-turn arrow after the red light, several downtown streets are one-way, and many major cameras lurk in several areas to memorialize speeders and red-light runners.

WHEN TO COME The weather is sensational from Oct. through Mar. High season runs Jan. through Apr. In summer, however, you get exceptional deals on resorts, golf, and spas. Surrounding mountains make cool getaways.

MEDICAL EMERGENCY Dial 911.

✷ To See

Arizona-Sonora Desert Museum (520-883-1380), 2021 N. Kinney Rd. Open every day of the year. Oct.–Feb. 8:30–5; Mar.–May and Sep. 7:30–5; Jun.–Aug., Mon.–Sat. 7:30 AM–10 PM, Sun. 7:30–5 PM. The Desert Museum has more than 300 species of native wildlife and 1,300 varieties of desert plants in exhibits designed to replicate natural habitats. Paths wind through Cat Canyon, Riparian Corridor, and a number of botanically correct habitats, from desert to woodland, that include the animals that dwell within. The Raptor Free Flight Program demonstrates the natural inclinations of raptors in the Sonoran Desert. Sep.–May $13, adults, $4.25 ages 6–12; June–Aug. $9.50 adults, $2.25 ages 6–12, age 5 and under free.

THE RAPTOR FREE FLIGHT PROGRAM AT THE ARIZONA-SONORA DESERT MUSEUM

Christine Maxa

WHITE DOVE OF THE DESERT—MISSION SAN XAVIER DEL BAC Christine Maxa

♿ **Arizona Historical Society Museum** (520-770-1473), 140 N. Stone Ave. Open Mon.–Fri. 10–4. The Arizona Historical Society has several museums around the state, and a few in the city. This one has exhibits of life in 1870 Tucson; a history of medicine, including culture and science; the evolution of transportation in Tucson; and a Mining Hall. $3 adults, $2 ages 12–18 and 60-plus, age 11 and under free.

♿ **Arizona State Museum/University of Arizona** (520-621-6302), Park Ave. and University Blvd., University of Arizona campus. Open Mon.–Sat. 10–5. The highly regarded, and oldest, anthropology museum in the nation features Southwest and northern Mexico cultures. The displays come from more than a century of research, and include the Wall of Pottery, the largest whole vessel collection of Southwest Indian pottery in the world. The Smithsonian affiliate museum rotates displays to showcase ancient and contemporary Native American culture. You won't find a better archaeological research center, with the world's top resident scholars and displays. Donations requested.

Mission San Xavier del Bac (520-294-2624), 1950 W. San Xavier Rd. Open daily 7–5. The meld of Moorish, Byzantine, and late Mexico Renaissance styles in the mission is as delightful as it is captivating: angels, peering from the ceiling, wear checkered and striped skirts; statues wear real clothes; and deep, vivid colors—predominantly red, blue, and gold—splash across the ceiling and walls like a richly woven tapestry. The mission, built in 1783, is the oldest original building in the United States. You can learn more about its history in a museum on the grounds (open 8–5 daily). Pilgrimages are common here, and Mass is still celebrated and confessions heard (call for times and days). Donations accepted.

El Tiradito—The Wishing Shrine. Located on Main Ave. just south of Cushing St. in downtown Tucson. There are hundreds of shrines in Arizona, and many around Tucson. This particular one, however, comes with a promise. Legend has it that if, when you make a wish and light a candle, your candle stays lit through the night, you'll get your wish. Be careful what you wish for. Free.

Old Tucson Studios (520-883-0100), 201 S. Kinney Rd. 10–4 daily; open selected Tue. and Wed. for limited hours and tours only; closed Thanksgiving, Christmas Eve, and Christmas. Called "Hollywood in the Desert," this working movie set was originally built in 1939 for the movie Arizona. Since then more than 200 films have been made here, including Lone Ranger films and *Tombstone*. The theme park features a re-creation of an 1880s frontier town with townsfolk dressed in period outfits reenacting life in the lawless Arizona Territory. $16.95 adults, $10.95 ages 4–11.

♿ **Tohono Chul Park** (520-742-6455), 7366 N. Paseo del Norte. Open daily 8–5; Exhibit Hall, museum shops, and greenhouse 9–5; tearoom 8–5. The park weaves a mix of nature, art, and culture with botanical gardens, an Exhibit Hall in a renovated historic home, and excellent breakfast, lunch, or afternoon tea done by Albert Hall of Acacia in the tearoom. You can shop in the greenhouse and museum shops. $7 adults, $5 age 62-plus and active military, $3 students, $2 ages 5–12, under age 5 free; free for members.

Tucson Botanical Gardens (520-326-9686), 2150 N. Alvernon Way. Open daily 8:30–4:30, closed major holidays. As you tour its specialty gardens, you can see that this garden is big on education, with interactive touch carts allowing you to handle props about the desert. Horticulturists and gardeners interface with the public, a feature that makes you feel like you're talking to your next-door neighbor who happens to be an expert. Don't let the summer heat keep you from visiting this garden. During those hot days and warm nights the plants go nuts, especially during monsoon season. The garden gets a huge increase in butterflies during that time. $7 adults, $3 ages 4–12, under age 4 free.

MEXICO Tucson is located only 60 miles north of the Mexican border on I-19, where mileposts are measured in kilometers rather than miles. For day visits, you can simply drive down to Nogales (Arizona), park, and walk across the border to shops and restaurants. You must have enchanced drivers license or passport to enter Mexico and passport or passport card to reenter the United States.

SCENIC DRIVES The preeminent road to scenery (and high-country cool) is the **General Hitchcock Highway**, locally known as the road to Mount Lemmon. Next, check out the saguaros taking Speedway all the way west up **Gates Pass** (the quintessential sunset vista) and then through the Saguaro National Forest—West. Watch for road bicycles.

THE ROAD TO MOUNT LEMMON

✷ To Do

CAVE TOUR 🖍 **Colossal Cave Mountain Park** (520-647-7275), located off I-10 at exit 279. Open daily 8–4 (mid-Mar.–mid-Sept. till 5) The cave has long wooed geology lovers, especially since the discovery of a chamber called La Tetera, which one researcher described as much more colorful than Karchner with "colors that are almost Disneyesque." The cave also drew robbers and other characters in decades past as a perfect

LIST OF TIPS WHEN VISITING MEXICO

To enter Mexico, you must have a passport or enhanced drivers license.

To reenter the United States, you must have a passport or passport card.

Drink bottled water, especially outside major tourist areas. Avoid eating fruits and vegetables from street vendors. However, these foods are generally safe at larger restaurants.

The Mexican peso conversion runs approximately 13 pesos per U.S. dollar. However, merchants usually accept U.S. dollars, and many establishments accept major credit cards.

Bartering is still a major part of the fun of shopping in Mexico. Compare prices before you start bargaining, and be ready to walk away if you want the best price.

Always carry your passport with you.

If you plan to drive in Mexico, buy Mexican insurance and carry proof of ownership of your car. If you rent a vehicle, make certain the rental car company allows it to go into Mexico.

If you are driving in Mexico, note that *alto* means "stop"; *peligro* means "danger." Also, Mexico has a few driving customs that are different than in the States. For instance, a left-turn hand signal doesn't necessarily mean the driver will turn left; it could also signal the driver behind that it's safe to pass.

Safety decreases exponentially when you drive after dark

Pets are usually allowed into Mexico with verification of rabies vaccination within last six months.

Guns are not allowed.

Household effects (such furniture, carpets, paintings, tableware, stereos, linens, professional tools of the trade) are duty-free. Merchandise up to $800 per person is duty-free.

You cannot bring back birds, natural wildlife and plants, unpacked food, fireworks and firearms, whalebones, or coral.

hideout. A 45-minute tour that travels about 0.5 mile and includes 363 steps will give you information on the cave's natural, nefarious, and curious history. The after-hours Candle Tour experiences the cave by candlelight. Reservations are necessary. The Wild Cave Tour (for the physically fit) travels in the dark through rarely seen passageways that extend 0.25 mile deeper into the earth. The park also features a butterfly garden, a desert tortoise exhibit, a mining sluice that bags you gemstones and fossils, and an analemmatic (horizontal) sundial. You can camp in the park's picnic area. Trail rides are available. $5 per car, $2 per motorcycle, $1 per bicycle. Tours $11 adults, $6 ages 5–12, under age 5 free.

GAMING Casino del Sol (800-344-9435), 5655 W. Valencia. The Pascua Yaqui tribe's casinos features Mediterranean architecture, a fresh-air atmosphere, a 4,400-seat outdoor amphitheater, and restaurants. The casino has 1,300 state-of-the-art slot machines with the highest payout in the state and a 12-table poker room with tournaments.

Casino of the Sun (520-883-1700 or 800-344-9435), 7406 S. Camino del Oeste. Another Pascua Yaqui tribe casino. This one has 400 slot machines, a live poker room, a 900-seat bingo hall, and big promotions for members, from cars to cash. An all-you-can-eat buffet attracts out-the-door lines.

Desert Diamond Casino (520-342-2935), I-19 and Pima Mine Rd. A Tohono O'odham Nation casino with slot machines, live keno and poker, a 2,000-seat entertainment center, and gourmet dining at Agave restaurant and lounge.

DOG PARKS 🐾 Christopher Columbus Park (520-791-4873), 4600 N. Silverbell. Open daily dawn–two or three hours after dusk. Enclosed area with Fido Fountain, scrambling area, shaded area with ramada, and pooper scooper dispenser.

🐾 **Palo Verde Park** (520-791-5930), 300 S. Mann Ave. Open daily 6 AM–10:30 PM. Enclosed area (5-foot chain-link fence) for dogs with picnic tables, trash cans, doggy drinking fountain, and pooper scooper dispenser.

GOLF Arizona National Golf Club (520-749-3636), 9777 E. Sabino Greens Dr. Listed among top courses regionally and nationally, the former Raven Golf Club at Sabino Springs gives you a run for your money with challenges and decisions, as well as beautiful scenery in the Santa Catalina Mountain foothills. Robert Trent Jones Jr. designed the course to meld with the natural ruggedness of the land across arroyos and around craggy cliffs. Tee boxes show off views into Mexico. This is where the University of Arizona men's and women's collegiate golf teams play. $135–165.

La Paloma Country Club (520-299-1500), 3666 E. Sunrise Dr. The premier luxury greens operated by Troon Golf touts an armload of awards, including one for being woman-friendly. The 27-hole Jack Nicklaus Signature golf course (designed by The Man, himself) comprising the **Ridge**, **Canyon**, and **Hill courses** spreads amid undulating foothills sheltering century-old saguaro cacti and showing off spectacular panoramic mountain vistas. You share these courses only with club members and other hotel guests. PGA and LPGA golf staff professionals are available for private lessons; complete full-swing and short-game schools are available upon request. La Paloma Dining Room eyes the 19th hole. $50–75.

The Ritz-Carlton Golf Club Dove Mountain (520-572-3500), 15000 N. Secret Springs Dr., Marana. The personally designed Jack Nicklaus courses (Saguaro, Tortolita, Wild Burro) himself (the first in 25 years), makes an exciting place to test your golf mettle. The tournament course, which hosts the World Golf Championships–Accenture Match Play Championship, is located in a saguaro cactus forest where wildlife makes frequent appearances on, or within eyesight of, the open fairways, undulating greens and well-placed bunkers. You'll have to use your three-wood on Saguaro's fifth hole. All of Tortila's 18 holes are extremely difficult, but no. 2, placed in a wash, is the most troublesome. Even the lowest of handicappers will have a run for the money at Dove Mountain. Once you have experienced this

Golfweek Best New Course, where the best players in the country play, your game will never be the same, only better. $189.

Starr Pass Country Club & Spa (520-670-0400), 3645 W. Starr Pass Blvd. This course goes back a couple of decades and has hosted some of the world's best golfers on its meticulous greens, including Arnold Palmer, Phil Mickelson, Payne Stewart, and Nancy Lopez. The course became an Audubon Cooperative Sanctuary Program member, and is currently finishing the requirements to become a certified member of the Audubon Sanctuary Program. Because the course is located next to the wild spaces of the Tucson Mts., this designation encourages the protection of wildlife habitats and the surrounding natural resource. The course, part of a 27-hole Arnold Palmer Signature Golf Facility, has some features meant to challenge PGA Tour's great players. Back in the course's PGA days, hole 3 was ranked the most difficult hole on the PGA Tour in 1996, and hole 5 was ranked in the Top 5 Most Difficult. Bunkers and undulating greens remind you that the bogeyman is alive and well at this historic course. The three nines are named for the wildlife that has shown up at each one: **Rattler**, **Roadrunner**, and **Coyote**. $89–181.50.

Tucson Omni (520-297-2271), 2727 W. Club Dr. Host to the PGA Tour's Tucson Open since 1976, this 36-hole desert course offers plenty of challenge. The pros rank the 18th hole (no. 9 on the Gold Course) as one of the most challenging finishing holes on the tour. The complicated shot—465 yards with water on both sides of the tee shot—has been the deciding factor of several tours. If you want a good score here, plan well on this par-4 trickster. Golf professionals and instructors provide playing tips and individual lessons. Long- and short-game practice areas, golf shop, restaurant, and equipment rental available. Call for rates.

Vistoso Golf Club (520-797-9900), 955 W. Vistoso Highlands Dr. This par-72 Tom Weiskopf course is carved right out of the mountains and is described as desert golf at its finest. Known for its outstanding course conditions and attention to detail, it always ends up on best-of lists, such as *Golf Digest*'s Best Public Course in Tucson as well as the Top 100 Places to Play. The Tucson Open Pro-Am, USGA Mid-Amateur Championship, and PGA Section Championship are played here. Dress code requires men to wear shirts with sleeves and collar; sleeveless is allowed for woman, as are midthigh shorts for men and women; no denim; non-metal spikes only. Putting and chipping greens. $55–145.

HIKING Surrounded by four mountain ranges with several designated wilderness areas, this town is one great place to make a base camp if you like to hike. See *Wilder Places* for information.

HORSEBACK RIDING **Spanish Trail Outfitters** (520-825-1664), 8500 E. Ocotillo Dr. Rides are led by entertaining wranglers who impart fun and interesting facts about the Sonoran Desert. You travel a private trail system that winds through a particularly lush and pristine area of the Sonoran Desert, including streams, mesquite bosques, and stands of saguaro cactus. Watchable wildlife is big, especially during early-morning and evening rides. Of special interest are stops at ancient Hohokam village sites. $35–50 per person for 1–1½ hours. Must be over 7 years old.

Walking Winds Stables at **Hilton Tucson El Conquistador Golf & Tennis Resort** (520-742-4422), 10000 N. Oracle Rd. One of the top stables in the basin takes you into the Coronado National Forest to secluded desert trails. You'll ride through saguaro cactus forests and past interesting rock formations while learning all about the fascinating Sonoran Desert. Call for reservations and prices.

MOUNTAIN BIKING Among all those mountains ranges ringing the city travel perfect single- and doubletrack trails. The unpaved roads in **Saguaro National Park—West** (520-733-5158) are a favorite. It'll cost you $10 to ride them, but admission is good for a week. The trails in the Santa Catalina Mountains are long and steep, taking you more than 4,000 feet from the desert floor to the pine country. There are several designated wilderness areas that will keep you off trails within wilderness boundaries, however. Purchase a national forest map from **Coronado National Forest** (520-670-4552) or an *Arizona Gazetteer*, both of which shows land status If you want to stay in town, **Fantasy Island** (Irvington and Houghton rds.) has a network of hand-built trails that twist and turn across the desert landscape on a tract of state trust land. Be sure to purchase a permit at the Arizona State Land office (520-628-5480), 233 N. Main, open daily 8–4:30. It costs $15 for an annual permit to carry and a hangtag for your car. Check out the **24 Hours in the Old Pueblo** in February. The 3,000+-participant event celebrates mountain biking to the max with fat tire legend Todd Sadow at the helm.

OBSERVATORIES With a strict ordinance against light pollution, Tucson's night skies facilitate stellar sky-watching, weather permitting. **Flandrau Science Center** (520-621-7827), 1601 E. University Blvd. Observatory open Wed.–Sat. evenings 7–10, mineral museum open Tue.–Fri. mornings 9:30–11:30. This center was recently renovated to become a living and working laboratory with hands-on exhibits and programs. It has its eyes on the skies with a planetarium sky show (weather permitting) and its feet planted on terra firma in its Mineral Museum—one of the country's finest. Observatory is free; mineral museum $4 adults, $2 kids.

Kitt Peak National Observatory (520-318-8726), AZ 86 (Ajo Way). Open daily 9–3:45. Closed holidays. This observatory, part of the National Optical Astronomy Observatory, houses the world's largest collection of optical telescopes. Two radio and 22 optical telescopes accommodate dozens of astronomical research projects at the observatory. You can take a docent-led or self-guided tour. At the National Solar Observatory exhibit gallery, you can see how scientists operate the world's largest solar telescope. Hour-long tours occur daily at 10, 11:30, and 1:30, and cost $4 adults, $2.50 ages 6–12. The **Night Observatory Program** (reservation required) is open daily, weather permitting, except during monsoon season (July 15–Aug. 31). Up to 20 people can observe the night sky through three of the observatory's telescopes. $46 adults, $41 seniors and kids age 8 and up; $20 deposit.

ROAD BIKING In a town where professional road cyclists winter and Lance Armstrong trained for one of the earlier Tour de France races he won, you can understand how serious Tucsonans take road bicycles. The city rates as one of the most cycle-friendly in the West. Contact **Pima Association of Governments** (520-792-1093) for a map of the city and surroundings. Check out the country's largest road biking event, the Tour de Tucson (courses run from 30 to 100-plus miles long), which takes place the Saturday before Thanksgiving.

ROCK CLIMBING Granite rock walls, so absolutely perfect for scaling, await you here no matter what your experience. The **Santa Catalina Mountains** (Santa Catalina Ranger District, 520-749-8700) have some sensational routes that fill a couple of books. If you like hanging out with the peregrine falcons (when the area isn't closed for raptor nesting), the **Dragoon Mountains** (see "Benson") and their labyrinthine rise of balanced rocks will give you some sweet climbing time. Contact Coronado National Forest or the outdoor outfitter Summit Hut (520-325-1554) for information.

✷ Spas

Tucson gets special notice as one of the world's harbors for healthful revitalization. The town has some of the most treasured health resorts/spas on the planet. Client names are shrouded in confidence.

Canyon Ranch (see *All-Inclusive Resorts*) offers limited day-use packages based on availability. $200–350.

Elizabeth Arden Red Door Spa (520-742-7866, ext. 7890), 3666 E. Sunrise Dr. Open Sun.–Wed. 9–7, Thu.–Sat. 8 AM–8 PM. The staff dotes on you here even before you enter the decompression chamber—that would be the spa treatment area. The over-the-top service continues in the form of roomy changing areas with spacious vanities displaying quality amenities, and skilled therapists. The service and setting befit the high-profile clients you are apt to see, and may recognize behind dark sunglasses, from politicos to movie stars. Treatments run the gamut from classic massages to energy therapies; water therapies to body wraps; facials to foot treatments. The salon has hair services, waxing, makeup artistry, and a variety of manicures and pedicures. Body treatments and massages $120–235, facials $120–250.

NOVEMBER'S TOUR DE TUCSON DRAWS ROAD BIKERS FROM AROUND THE WORLD

Hashani Spa (520-791-6117), 3800 W. Starr Pass Blvd. They say this spa is located on sacred ground, and a Tohono O'odham Native blessed the premises. That may explain the peaceful, kind, and comfortable atmosphere that permeates the facilities. Of course, the fact that every spa treatment starts with a signature Hashani foot ritual that includes a rejuvenating foot reflexology massage might have something to do with all that good feeling. It's a pretty spa, too, with wonderful tilework and rich colors. The treatments blend ancient healing techniques with the latest in technology. The Petals and

Leaves Body Ritual is the signature treatment that combines a scrub, essential oils, and a full-body mask of rose, lavender, or green tea to balance and rehydrate. When the therapist asks if you want the scalp massage while the body mask works its magic, take it. The spa has a salon and fitness center ($25 a day); personal training runs $65 for 50 minutes. Massage and rituals $125–240, facials $130–200.

Lakeside Spa (520-299-2020), 7000 N. Resort Dr. Open daily 6 AM–8 PM. Part of the Loews Ventana Canyon Resort, where the desert terrain rubs shoulders with the Santa Catalina Mountains. The intimate spa interiors are noticeably different with walls the color of lapis with warm wood trim. Experience the restorative signature treatment, Sedona Sacred Clay Energy Restorer with earthy juniper and cedarwood fragrance or the Hot and Cold Stone Facial. Besides a relaxing massage or invigorating treatment, the spa has an aerobics studio with daily classes, cardio workout equipment, five lighted tennis courts, adult lap pool, saunas, steam rooms, and Jacuzzi. Massages and body treatments $110–165, facials $115–155.

Miraval Arizona Resort & Spa (800-363-0819), 5000 E. Via Estancia, Tucson. Open daily 9–3. Known around the world to have an atmosphere so soothing, it calms even the highest-strung type-A personality, this spa goes delightfully beyond the call of duty in providing a soul-stirring experience. Cutting edge in its therapies (this is where the hot stone massage was invented), staffed with master practitioners who explain the history and effects of your treatment, and permeated with an accommodating atmosphere, Miraval can be described as magnificent. The menu reads more like a book, with everything from the Blue Mint Foot Repair Treatment for tired feet to Trager Psychophysical Integration to help relieve you of chronic tension, exotic Ayurvedic and Oriental body treatments to familiar Swedish and deep tissue massages, and facials from a gentle peel to deep hydration. Plan your spa experience early, because time slots get filled fast. The spa recommends making reservations at least three weeks in advance, and guests get first dibs. Call for prices.

The Sonoran Spa (520-917-2467), Westward Look Resort, 245 E. Ina Rd. Open daily 8–7:15. This boutique spa's whole property has a peaceful and gentle ambience, like a restful garden. Maybe it's the outdoor pre- and post-treatment patio in which spa goers get to relax and gaze at pretty views of the Sonoran Desert. Or the fresh fragrances that waft around the treatment rooms. A labyrinth inspired by a Tohono O'odham symbol titled "the Man in the Maze" adds a spiritual dimension, especially because an elder of the tribe blessed it., The treatment menu grabs from every corner of the spa world—classic aromatherapy massages with oils for soothing tight muscles or relieving virus-riddled sinuses, popular hot stone massages, rituals such as the classic Shirodhara or lesser known Abyhanga, energy-oriented ones like Reiki, healing wraps, and facials for every season and skin type. Ingredients lean toward the natural, like aloe and blue corn, volcanic clay, and a blend of muds and clays. The salon has nail and waxing services. Massages, body treatments, and rituals $109–159, facials $109–149.

✱ Wilder Places

Coronado National Forest (520-388-8300), 300 W. Congress St. This national forest—unique for its collection of mountain ranges that rise abruptly from the desert floor like a group of islands in a sea, called sky islands—spreads across southeast Arizona. The whole cluster is called the Madrean Archipelago. Each sky island has its own characteristics, but they all have incredible diversity and trails that often take you from the desert floor into the pines. The **Santa Catalina Mountains** have long, steep trails. **Marshall Gulch** is a favorite. The **Rincon Mountains** are more wild and remote, especially **Rincon Peak Trail**. The **Santa Rita Mountains** hold the highest peak around the Tucson Basin, Old Baldy. Take the **Super Trail** to its top. Bring rain gear during monsoon season (July to mid-Sep.).

♂ ♿ **Sabino Canyon Recreation Area** (520-749-8700), 5900 N. Sabino Canyon Rd. Open 24 hours. One of the favorite backcountry destinations in the area. The canyon, cut deep into the Santa Catalina Mountains with a crystal stream embellished with granite boulders, is the quintessential natural desert oasis. The water and riparian area along the streambed attract wildlife and people. Up to 1978 you could drive up the 3.8-mile road, full of hairpin turns and nine stone bridges sometimes well underwater. Today you must walk, ride your bicycle, or take a tram up the road as it rises from 2,800 to 3,300 feet. You can duck onto one of several trails accessed along the road and get into a quiet corner of the backcountry in this altogether lovely canyon. Bicycles are permitted daily, except Wed. and Sat., before 9 AM, or after 5 PM. $5 per vehicle.

NATIONAL PARKS AND MONUMENTS **Ironwood Forest National Monument** (Bureau of Land Management, 520-258-7200), about 20 miles northwest of Tucson off I-10. Located in and around the Silverbell Mountains northwest of Tucson, the monument has the highest density of ironwood trees recorded in the Sonora Desert. It's quintessential Sonora Desert with all the trimmings—a nonstop giant saguaro forest, a grid of washes that double as wildlife thoroughfares, a curiously shaped ridge called Ragged Top that holds geological wonders and cultural secrets, and a host of trees that play a role in the development of the desert with the ironwood tree the star of the show. There are no maintained trails, so getting around on foot requires excellent route-finding skills. If you have a high-clearance vehicle, take the partially paved horseshoe scenic drive around the monument (access from exit 242 or 226) for a user-friendly adventure.

SOME SAGUAROS HAVE PERSONALITIES

Organ Pipe Cactus National Monument (520-387-6849), located 22 miles south of Why (which is about 120 miles from Tucson on AZ 86). The 330,688-acre monument gives you a remote look at life in the Sonoran Desert. The desert's distinctive characteristic of two rainy seasons attracts an extraordinary amount of vegetation. The monument showcases wildlife in a desert ecosystem at its unhampered best. So special is the land, the United Nations designated it an International

Biosphere Reserve. You can explore the monument by car or bicycle on the 21-mile Ajo Mountain Drive. Several hiking trails give you an up-close look at some distinctive vegetation you won't find anywhere else north of the Mexican border—such as organ pipe cactus. $8 per vehicle.

Saguaro National Park East (520-733-5153), 3693 S. Old Spanish Trail. Open daily 7 AM–sunset; visitor center open 7–5. Saguaro forests fill the slopes of the Rincon Mountains here and mix with more than 600 species of plants. In springtime, after a wet winter, dozens of species of wildflowers color the desert floor. In May, cacti and trees bloom. Explore the park via the 8-mile **Cactus Forest** loop drive or several trails. Visitor center has maps and information. No pets. $10 per vehicle or motorcycle, $5 per person on foot or bicycle.

Saguaro National Park—West (520-733-5158), 2700 N. Kinney Rd. Open daily 6 AM to sunset. Visitor center open 9–5. You can drive, ride a bicycle, or walk on trails, unpaved roads, and paved highway through the densest saguaro forest you'll find anywhere in the world. The **Wasson Peak Trail** travels through a gorgeous saguaro forest. If you don't want to climb, take the **King's Canyon Trail** and stay in the wash. The park fills with spring wildflowers after a wet winter; especially the King's Canyon Trail. The visitor center has maps and information. No pets. $10 per vehicle or motorcycles, $5 for persons on foot or bicycle.

✷ Lodging

INNS AND RESORTS

♥ **Arizona Inn** (520-325-1541), 2200 E. Elm St. Congresswoman Isabella Greenway, who built the property, did so to "give its guests privacy, quiet and sunshine," But that was half the story. She actually built it to keep the disabled WWI vets working in her furniture factory (The Arizona Hut) in a job making furniture for the inn. Her family carries on a spirit of community service by preserving the sumptuous era of Tucson's past when the inn was built. Formal but not stuffy, elegant but laid back, the inn attracts an often-celebrated clientele from around the world. The pink stucco walls aren't the only original feature you'll find on the property, listed on the National Register of Historic Places. Each room has exquisitely crafted furniture made at The Arizona Hut for the inn, antiques, and unique pictures. An on-site cabinet-making shop restores and replicates these pieces. The property includes the Main Dining Room, Har-Tru clay tennis courts, a 60-foot heated outdoor pool, an exercise facility, saunas, Ping-Pong, croquet, bicycle rentals, a gift shop, a DVD library, a laundry and dry-cleaning service, and business services. Each room has a flat-screen TV, DVD player, iHome clock radio, complimentary high-speed Internet access, refrigerator, coffeemaker, *New York Times* delivered daily, complimentary bottled water, and turndown service. Check out the complimentary bicycles, afternoon tea, and poolside ice cream (in season). $279–579; log onto www.arizonainn.com for special promotions.

♥ **Hacienda del Sol Guest Ranch Resort** (520-299-1501 or 800-728-6514), 5601 N. Hacienda del Sol Rd. One of the more unusual inns in the state and a favorite on world-traveler lists, this Spanish Colonial compound built in the late 1920s has been around the block as it changed hands over the years. What started as a ranch turned into a college preparatory academy for young girls sporting such surnames as Pillsbury, Vanderbilt, and Westinghouse. Next the property became a guest ranch for folks like Clark Gable, Spencer Tracy, and John Wayne. Finally Tucson investors bought and restored the property in the late 1990s. The 30 historic guest rooms have thick adobe walls, original fireplaces, hand-painted tiles, exquisite views, and a down-to-earth comfort level. Each one, however, is decorated differently in classic hacienda-style colors, textures, and style. The property includes the Grill restaurant, a local favorite that consistently makes best-of lists; a boutique spa offering specialty and therapeutic treatments such as craniosacral and shiatsu; and (by appointment only) the Wine Shop, where sommelier Dan McCoog personally selects 30 to 40 exceptional or hard-to-find wines each month that you can purchase in 6- or 12-packs at amazing prices (usually below wholesale . . . yes, Dan has connections). $99–495.

Hilton Tucson El Conquistador Golf & Tennis Resort (520-544-5000), 10000 N. Oracle Rd. Set right up against the Santa Catalina Mountains with the peaks between you and the city—you can't get a better backdrop or setting. Especially if you like outdoor sports. You'll find 45 holes of golf, 31 lighted tennis courts, regulation racquetball, basketball, and volleyball courts, four outdoor swimming pools (including an NCAA six-lane lap pool and a 143-foot water slide), six hot tubs and a cold dip plunge, miles of trails for hiking, jogging, biking, and horseback riding, two major fitness centers, the Camp Quail for Kids, and a spa. This AAA Four Diamond resort has kept its rating just about forever; so expect consistency. Rooms are spacious and have gorgeous views (half have fireplace). In-room movies and Nintendo games come with all rooms, and WiFi is available. If it makes you tired just reading about all these opportunities for activities, keep in mind that the setting and panoramas are so nice, just lolling around to enjoy them is high on the activity list, too. $89–299. Optional sport and fitness facility fee $10 per day.

♥ **Loews Ventana Canyon Resort** (520-299-2020), 7000 N. Resort Dr. You can't get much closer to spending the night in the desert mountains' wild space without pitching a tent in the backcountry. Nuzzled in Ventana Canyon where it starts its rugged 4,000-foot climb into the Santa Catalina Mountains, the resort lures nature lovers of all ranks. Yes, the rooms are over the top with slate tile, earth tones, and a AAA Four Diamond rating, but the resort lies this-close to a popular 6.4-mile (one-way) trail that will take you to a "window" in the upper reaches of Tucson's tallest ridgelines. Even if you've come for some unabashed R&R, the mountain views and smells of Arizona sycamore trees in the riparian forest and mature jasmine vines climbing the resort walls will lull you into lazy submission. Whatever you plan to achieve, you'll have the best the city has to offer here, whether you watch native birds flit among the cottonwood-willow habitat; go celestial on stargazing nights; walk the half-mile nature trail with its 66 different types of plants, 105 different mammals and reptiles, and 80-foot natural waterfall; play a round of golf at its Tom Fazio courses (with new greens); or explore the surrounding mountains and canyons. Even dogs can have their day at the resort, including place mats, bowls, and their own room service. $129–329.

The Ritz-Carlton Dove Mountain (520-572-3000),

15000 N. Secret Springs Dr., Marana. Located a little more out-there than any of the other accommodations in the city, you won't get a more intimate experience with the desert. The property incorporated items from Arizona's history, culture, and natural resources every chance it could get—the lobby floor is made of flagstone and quartzite; the library (with shelves lined with books on the Southwest and filled with native peoples artifacts from Arizona State Museum) has mesquite wood floors; copper elements appear in just about every area; geodes and quartz crystals sparkle from shelves and tables; paintings and photography from local artists deck the walls; a blessing ceremony performed by an Indian flutist takes place every evening; and authentic petroglyphs from Hohokam, Apache, and Conquistador cultures line the pool area in the spa (which has unusual treatments). You wouldn't necessarily think of hiking when you consider the Ritz, but they have created several hiking trails (open to the public) in the Tortolita Mts. on which you can explore the desert on your own or with guides. Each room has a view of the mountains outside; inside, rooms have dark mesquite wood accents, light stones, and leather chairs. Besides a big-screen TV (to which you can connect your laptop), there are tons of amenities. The Jack Nicklaus golf course is a Certified Audubon Cooperative Sanctuary; Fitness and Wellness Center has PRECOR equipment and Pilate, yoga, and stretching classes. The property has three swimming pools (one with a 235-foot water slide), Ritz Kids program, and an Executive Business Center. There are four restaurants: **CORE Kitchen & Wine Bar**'s chef Joel Harrington raises the culinary bar for Tucson; **Cayton**'s great comfort food menu and Frank Lloyd Wright interiors draws the neighborhood; **Ignite** has a menu of 120 different whiskeys and scotches; **Turquesa**'s Latin foods have executives sneaking a Sonoran hot dog or Cubano sandwich. Luxury has its price, but it's relatively low thanks to the ongoing gaggle of specials created for these dollars-are-dear times. Pets welcome. Call for prices.

🐾 ✐ ♿ (ᵢ) ⚭ **The Westin La Paloma Resort & Spa** (520-742-6000), 3800 E. Sunrise Dr. Hard to believe a warehouse once stood where this Westin classic now spreads. The Mehl brothers negotiated hotly for the land, and once they got it, they built this hotel in 1986 to match the Biltmore in Phoenix. Standing in the foothills of the Santa Catalina Mountains, the resort has some of the most seductive views in the city. The mature landscaping with footpaths makes it a most pleasant place to amble around in. And you never know who you might see in the way of famous personalities at this resort, which has held the AAA Four Diamond award since less than a year after it opened in 1986. The best in the business has been gathered onto these premises: local award-winning Janos restaurant (see *Dining Out*), the Red Door Spa, a 27-hole Jack Nicklaus Signature golf course, a tennis and health center (10 courts, 4 clay and 10 lighted), indoor racquetball, five pools, sand volleyball, a 177-foot waterslide, Westin Kids Club, and Children's Lounge. Rooms have WiFi, Starbucks coffee, and the famous Heavenly Beds and Heavenly Baths. Pets of 40 pounds or less are welcome when you sign a damage waiver. The Heavenly Dog Program provides an oversized pillow and a "doggy bag" filled with a plastic bag, glove, and food and water dish. $129–429.

🐾 ♿ ⚭ ♥ **Westward Look Resort** (520-917-2476), 245 E. Ina Rd. The city's oldest resorts loaded with history, originality, and down-home comfort. What started as a homestead in 1912, the year Arizona became a state, evolved into a dude ranch and now a resort. For its AAA Four Diamond and Forbes Four-Star awards, it's incredibly unpretentious and always leans toward the side of nature. The city favorite has beautiful nature trails lush with quintessential Sonoran Desert vegetation, open to the public, which wind through several gardens spread among the property's 80 acres. Check out the Chef's Garden, tended by Raymundo Ocampo. All organic and incredibly lush, the gardens provide herbs, spices, fruit, and vegetables for Chef James Wallace's kitchen. You'll also find tennis courts, a swimming pool, Gold restaurant (see *Dining Out*), and the Sonoran Spa (see *Spas*). Southwestern-style guest rooms each have balcony or patio, king or queen beds with pillow-top mattress, stocked mini bar, oversized bath, cable TV, and movies. Pets okay with a $75 non-refundable cleaning fee. $89–180.

ALL-INCLUSIVE RESORTS 🐾 ♿
Canyon Ranch (800-742-9000), 8600 E. Rockcliff Rd. The nation's first, and the crème de la crème of, health and wellness resorts lives up to every good thing you might have heard about it. It racks up awards continuously and consistently, even wowing *Gourmet* and *Bon Appétit* with its too-good-to-be-true spa cuisine à la Chef Scott Uehlein. Basically, the whole idea behind the resort is to have a great vacation while receiving cutting-edge health therapies and/or medical treatments. The all-inclusive resort gives you spa time, three tasty squares, and a couple dozen (mostly free) classes/seminars to fill your day. It's one of the few places on the planet where you can get an 80-minute physical and talk with the physician the whole time. The adobe-style cottages, roomy, quiet, and pleasantly appointed; have spa amenities, television and phone. The grounds have lush landscape with streamlike water features. Art appears everywhere, inside and out. It's probably the 80,000 sq. ft. spa (with a virtual catalog of treatments that might take a bit of counseling on which is perfect for you) that might lure you to the resort. Some people come to repair and recover after major operations because of the professional medical staff. Many come to kick a habit or enhance health and performance, though there's never a peep from the staff about who's who on the guest roster. There's even a program for teens (14 years and older with some treatment restrictions). Whether you come for quality time with yourself; to heal, repair, or recover; or just to laugh and let loose your endorphins, you'll leave knowing Canyon Ranch is every good thing you've heard about it. Up to two dogs under 35 lbs. allowed

SCULPTURES ON THE GROUNDS OF THE CANYON RANCH SPA

with current registration and vaccination records. They will pick up dog food, pet treats, and toys with 48-hour notice. Doggy massages are available. Four nights $4,600–5,500, seven nights $7,470–9,020, 10 nights $10,050–12,200; all rates per person, based on double occupancy.

♿ ♥ **Miraval Arizona Resort & Spa** (800-232-3969), 5000 E. Via Estancia Miraval, Catalina. A favorite with savvy travelers who know the world, Miraval is one resort that can somehow be all things to all people. With its mantra of living in the moment, the resort aspires to heighten your senses and bring you into balance. And that it does, whether you're a spa-goer looking for that unusual but enlightening treatment, a gourmand wondering how the meals can taste so good yet be so healthy, or closet Outward Bound type who needs a challenge to stay sane. Miraval Arizona embraces all with the warm arm of a friend. Laid out like a lush canyon with a stream traveling through it, the resort grounds look like a garden sanctuary. Rooms are warm Southwest. Amenities over the top. Service engaging yet professional. And what a variety of programs: bodymindfulness; challenge activities; cooking demonstrations; equine activities; golf; hiking; and, of course, the spa. Packages from $399 per person/per night based on rate seasons and/or room type and availability. Log onto www.miravalresort.com for details.

MIRAVAL LIFE IN BALANCE

BED & BREAKFASTS "1" **Adobe Rose Inn** (520-318-4644 or 800-328-4122), 940 N. Olsen. The neighborhood myth holds that builders took the dirt from 2nd Street to make the adobe bricks for this property back in the 1930s. Located in the Sam Hughes District, the home has old Tucson character and style. The property earned the AAA Three Diamond award, highest for this category of lodging. Premise include a hot tub; pool; refrigerator stocked with soft drinks, juice, and water; and tons of sitting areas. Rooms have private bath, coffee, tea, hot chocolate, writing space, complimentary WiFi; cable TV, DVD, and functional fireplaces in two rooms. Breakfast, included with your room, means gourmet coffees, fresh fruit, and meals such as pecan French toast or Brie and apple omelets with fresh baked goods and coffee cake—and sometimes a tableful of astronomers taking advantage of the area's world-class astronomical environment. $95–140.

♥ **Across the Creek at Aravaipa Farms Bed and Breakfast Country Inn** (520-357-6901), located about 40 miles north of Tucson off AZ 77. When Carol Steele decided to open an all-inclusive bed & breakfast on this 300-acre plot of land along Aravaipa Creek in the middle of nowhere, her mother thought she was crazy. Her guests think she's the greatest. Each of the five guest casitas was designed by Carol—all an aesthetic meld of hacienda, Provincial and primitive art. If it has texture, color and soothes (or stirs) the soul, you'll probably find it here. The B&B's location right across Aravaipa Creek gives it a cache, since the Aravaipa Canyon Wilderness just upstream is one of the favorite wilderness areas in the state. Each casita has a queen bed and down comforter; oversize shower; covered patio with fireplace; breakfast bar with coffee pot, toaster, and refrigerator; and fireplace. Phoenicians knew Carol as C. Steele, the woman who introduced Brie cheese and other epicurean wonders to the Phoenix Valley. This inductee to the Scottsdale Culinary Hall of Fame has worked with the best chefs in the world, such as Julia Child, Jacques Pépin, and Barbara Fenzl, so you can imagine how luscious the meals are here. Much of the produce is grown on the property. The price includes three meals (European-style continental breakfast, picnic lunch, and dinner when everyone gathers in the red barn dining room for food and conversation, of which there is no lack because Carol loves to discuss world events). $345 for up to two people per room (June–Sep. $250); minimum two-night stay for weekends; closed Sun. and Mon.

((ı)) **Catalina Park Inn Bed and Breakfast** (520-792-4541 or 800-792-4885), 309 E. 1st St. Closed mid-July to mid-Aug. This classy 1927 home features the quality craftsmanship characteristic of past eras. The inn's layout will have a familiar ring to Bostonians. Each of the six rooms is thoughtfully and impeccably decorated. At the same time, the home has a comfortable feel to it. It's the kind of place where the guests feel pampered, but can have a life—a trickle-down from the proprietors' casual yet professional attitudes. Gardens are big here, for secluded moments and outdoor relaxing. Breakfast (included in the rates) starts with European-roasted coffees and continues with specialties like papaya and lime scones and lemon ricotta pancakes. Rooms have color cable TV, DVD player, iPod dock, iron w/board, and beds with down comforters and pillows (fiberfill for allergic guests). Complimentary WiFi; generally no pets. $99–169.

♿ ((ı)) **El Rancho Merlita Ranch House Bed & Breakfast** (520-495-0071), 1924 N. Corte El Rancho Merlita. Back in the early 1950s, makeup maven Merle Norman built this desert getaway a few miles from Sabino Canyon with partying in mind. Her brother, an architect, designed the sprawling ranch house. His creativity shows up all over the home, in the form of aesthetic brickwork, wooden beams, a fireplace made from rhyolite rocks from the Tucson Mountains with a grill for searing steaks, and flagstone floors. Two of the four rooms have original bathroom tile and fixtures. Now restored and remodeled, the house feels as gracious as ever. Three guest rooms (two with showers and one with soaking tub and walk-in closet) and one suite (with a steam shower, whirlpool tub, fireplace, and walk-in closet) have a big-screen TV, artisanal amenities made locally, engaging bed, and mini fridge. The property, enclosed by an ocatillo fence and a fortress of nightblooming cerus cactuses, has plenty of patio space to sit and take in the mountain views; a saltwater swimming pool; 1950s barbecue; labyrinth; stargazing pad;, massage room; yoga room; and rec room with table tennis, darts, and stationary bike. Guests wake up to daily ground house-blend coffee and Harney & Sons tea. Then innkeeper Pattie Bell (an encyclopedic resource on what's where and who's who in the state) makes a healthy breakfast (included) with as many local ingredients she can purvey.$75–275.

Natural Bed and Breakfast (520-881-4582), 3150 E. Presidio Rd. You may not find a bed & breakfast quite like this anywhere else in the Southwest. The property caters to clients with environmental sensitivities. No chemicals are used for housecleaning, air purifiers and humidifiers are running, and no smoking or pets are allowed. Shoes come off as soon as you pass through the front door. Innkeeper Marc Haberman goes a step beyond the physical and has arranged the home to meet feng shui standards; he cleanses it with sage and offers plenty of interesting book and periodicals; a holistic health practitioner and muscular therapist, Haberman also offers massages. Breakfast consists of all-natural organic (when possible) whole-grain cereals, toasts, jams, and juice. $85–95 two or more nights; $20 extra if only one night.

⁽ᴵ⁾ ♥ **Peppertrees Bed & Breakfast Inn** (520-622-7167 or 800-348-5763), 724 E. University. Located in the cultural heart of where it's happening in Tucson, you can walk in several directions to some great places—University of Arizona, restaurants, theater, and shopping. But you'd never know how close humanity lies for the soothing atmosphere of the four-house (a few 90 to 107 years old) compound cloistered in mature landscaping. The compound has six different units decorated in different styles—Mexican, Persian/French, and eclectic. They all have a separate entrance and private bathroom; a refrigerator stocked with house-made specialties; a microwave, stove, and oven; bathrobes; and cable TV. Because Peppertrees is located so near the university, some of the guests are researchers and can provide some interesting academia chatter in the AM over breakfast—or dinner. Owner-innkeeper Jill McCormick creates both (dinner is extra). The former award-winning chef (who opened the Four Seasons/New York and was pastry chef at Janos) also ran a crazy-cake bakery in Washington, D.C. Now she provides a healthy breakfast to start your day. The breakfast is organic and different (such as breaded poached egg with shredded sweet potato and succotash of corn, asparagus, squash, with bacon along with a fruit plate and sweet bread, such as lemon yogurt muffins). What you get here is a super-personalized form of Four Seasons–type attention to your needs. $155–285 ($99–195 summer).

GUEST RANCHES ♥ **Rancho de la Osa** (520-823-4257 or 800-872-6240), Sasabe. With history going back to the celebrated Fr. Kino's Jesuit priests, the cantina in this old adobe compound is said to be the oldest building in the state. The compound, made of hand-formed adobe (mud) bricks, is one of the last great Spanish haciendas still standing in America. Even though all the buildings, and many of the 18 guest rooms, have experienced centuries of use, the property is neat, clean, and highly aesthetic. Color, art, and memorabilia make each room a point of interest. Each guest room has handcrafted pillows and bedspreads, a private bath, porch, and separate entry. Most guest rooms have a wood-burning fireplace. Original artwork, Mexican antiques, and whimsical designs of these ranch rooms capture the colorful spirit of the desert Southwest. The

THE RANCHO DE LA OSA RESORT IS ONE OF THE OLDEST ADOBE BUILDINGS IN ARIZONA

property has wranglers that manage a corral of horses for guest to ride; a pool, heated to 83 degrees in the winter; and lots of peace and quiet under the shade of a forest of eucalyptus trees more than 100 years old. Three meals described as Southwest fusion included. Double rate is $220–255 per person.

HOTELS AND LODGES 🐾 ♿ **Hotel Congress** (520-622-8848 or 800-722-8848), 311 E. Congress St. The Congress is one of those hotels that seem frozen in time. The period antique furnishings (from iron beds to vintage radios), steam heat and evaporative cooling, and even the original switchboard ringing up your desired numbers are still here. Just to highlight the fact you could get lost in time here at the longest-operating hotel in the state, rooms do not have clocks. Wake-up calls come via live people who call your rotary phone. If you want to watch television, there's one in the lounge. The hotel, built in 1919, catered to the railroad and cattle industry, as well as (unknowingly) such nefarious folks as John Dillinger. A fire at the hotel flushed Dillinger and his gang out of their third-floor rooms, where they'd come to "lay low" after a series of robberies. Today the elegant hotel caters to those who love a sense of place and the original appointments, such as the Old West deco paintings on the walls created by Larry Boyce on a will-paint-for-room-and-board arrangement when he bicycled across the country and stayed for the summer. The Tap Room is the one of the hottest places in the city to go for weeknight entertainment. Their three-day music fest on Labor Day weekend is usually a sellout (www.Hocofest.com). All 40 rooms are located on the second floor and each has a private bath. Some even have ghosts. $79–99; pets $10 extra.

🏵 🐾 ♿ (ı) **La Posada Lodge and Casitas** (520-887-4800 or 800-810-2808), 5900 N. Oracle Rd. Correctly touting itself as Tucson's Best Kept Secret, you will get a sensibly priced room with a themed interior different from what a franchise would offer—Mexican (with tin headboards), southwestern (with tasteful furniture), or

THE OLD SWITCHBOARD AT THE HOTEL CONGRESS IS STILL IN USE

retro (with bold colors). The lobby has a Navajo mural that sets it apart from the norm. Amenities include a pool and workout facility. The on-site Miguels Restaurant features dozens of different tequilas and is a popular after-dinner spot for the locals. Rooms have a king, two doubles, or two queens, along with a microwave, refrigerator, balcony, complimentary high-speed Internet hookup, and satellite TV. A complimentary full continental breakfast is included in rates. Pets are okay with $50 deposit. $89–169.

La Siesta Motel (520-624-1192), 1602 N. Oracle Rd. Back in 1941 when this hotel was built, it was one hot spot. After wobbling with the neighborhood that declined for a couple decades, gentrification is bringing beautification back to this spot on Tucson's Miracle Mile. With, as manager, Kimberly Underwood described it, "some plastic surgery and facelift inside and out," the motel is once again, one hot number. The 13 rooms have pillow-top queen beds, luxury sheets, free WiFi, art from local artists and bathrooms as vintage as possible. Some rooms have vintage kitchenettes. The hosts do special things for their guests, such as parties during special events and spontaneous barbeques and swim parties (in the saltwater pool) because, Kimberly said, "We like people to have fun and do special things." Sometimes even baking a carrot cake to celebrate a guest's birthday. $65–125.

Lodge on the Desert (520-320-2000), 306 N. Alvernon Way. One of Old Pueblo's vintage hotels has evolved through the years from a private residence built in 1936 with seven guest rooms, then hotel upgraded to 35 rooms and finally redesigned to the present version. The recent expansion gives you the best of both worlds—renovated historic rooms or new 140-554 sq. ft. rooms and suites with a hacienda feel. The beds—Simmons Beautyrest Black Beverly Hills—come loaded with pillows and comfortable bedding. Green Natüra bath amenities and coffeemaker with Arbuckle coffee; deluxe rooms have 42-inch flat-screen TV and double sinks. Because the lodge is located in a residential area, the views aren't the draw. Its quiet seclusion is. The grounds—full of grassy stretches and winding sidewalks—are pleasant to meander. The property has a heated pool and Jacuzzi, fine dining restaurant of the same name (see *Dining Out*), and spa (schedule completion in 2010). There are plenty of events going on that draw a mix of people onto the property from the community. Call for rates.

✱ Where to Eat

DINING OUT Acacia (520-232-0101), 4340 N. Campbell. Open Mon.–Sat. for lunch 11–2 and dinner 5–9 (till 10 on Fri. & Sat.); Sun. brunch 11–2 with live jazz. Chef Albert buys local, all-natural, organic, pesticide- and herbicide-free, sustainable ingredients whenever possible. He also recognizes the importance of what goes into ingredients before they're harvested, whether plant or animal, so you'll see Scottish salmon, Wisconsin veal, Arizona Wagyu, Alaskan halibut, and Peruvian chicken on the menu. Chef's cooking style is a mix of Americana with Latin influences wrapped in French techniques. House-made desserts and an award-winning wine list. Order from the Anytime Menu (items available all day) at the bar. Entrées $24–45.

Café Poca Cosa (520-622-6400). Open Tue.–Thu. 11–9, Fri. and Sat. 11–10; dinner served daily beginning at 4. Famous for having one of the most creative Mexican menus in the state, the restaurant itself is a unique meld of cosmopolitan cool filled with Mexican folk art and world music. The familiar menu of innovative Mexican cuisine leans toward Mexico City fare. "No chimichangas here," chef Suzana Dávila advises. The menu changes daily, but one entrée that stays put is the Plato Poca Cosa, "where you give up all control to the chef," Dávila says. This means that the chef chooses three dishes for you, perhaps *pastel de pollo* (shredded chicken layered with tortillas and mole sauce made with Godiva chocolate), *pescado* (slightly breaded cod), and tamale pie. Losing control is not a bad idea here. Entrées $14.95–22.95.

China Phoenix (520-531-0658), 7090 N. Oracle Rd., Suite 172. Open Mon.–Fri. 11–9:30, Sat. and Sun. 10–9:30 (dim sum 10–3). If your friends frequent your restaurant, you either have good food or very good friends. China Phoenix—very popular among the local Chinese community—has both. You'll get classic Chinese meals here, prepared well and without MSG. No tired seafood, and vegetables are fresh. Entrées $8–26.

CORE Kitchen & Wine Bar (520-572-3000), 15000 N. Secret Springs Dr., Marana. Open daily for breakfast 7–11 and Tue.–Sun. for dinner 6–9. Chef Joel Harrington (opening chef from Fearings in Dallas) takes his ingredients seriously. Besides bringing with him a trail of loyal purveyors, he cruised Arizona for a year to source the ingredients for his True American Cuisine featuring America's classic foods à la Arizona. Brilliant with flavor profiles and a personality that tilts on the rad side (you'll see—he visits every table several times during the evening), Chef Joel can talk about anything from art (his major) to mountain bikes (his minor). He also has raised the standards of quality a few notches in the Old Pueblo. Fish dishes are superfresh (he trolls for scallops with his Nantucket purveyor), the beef dry-aged and spiked with peppers and nopales relish and accompanied by signature avocado fries, and the game (quail and rabbit) and produce local. Citrus comes from the mini-grove outside and some produce from Chef's Garden. Dessert creations come from his pastry chef, James Wroblewski, whom he brought from Dallas. Chef James assisted Roland Messner, former White House pastry chef for presidents Carter through Clinton. Entrées $24–35.

AT THE CAFÉ POCA COSA

Feast (520-326-9363), 4122 E. Speedway. Open Tue.–Sun. 11–9. The menu is a brief, two-page, 4- by 11-inch number (three pages in the summer to add customer favorites) and changes the first Tuesday of the month because owner-chef Doug Levy has "a limited attention span." The menu—with an emphasis on fresh, homemade, and different—is full of pedigreed ingredients, and Chef Doug knows how to combine them in surprising ways that marry well. His curious, "What if I did this . . ." produces favorite dishes that get a rise out of your taste buds like the Feast Grilled Cheese Sandwich (seared Halloumi cheese, honey-roasted eggplant, tomato, and shaved red onion on a roll), Lobster, Corn, & Scallion Bread Pudding, or Roasted Strawberry Shortcake. Chef Doug cooks up these feasts to stay or go, so the restaurant can look like Grand Central Station during rush hour. Some dishes can be prepared gluten-free (this does not include the cupcakes, which have a following). Instead of 99 bottles of beer on the wall, Feast has about that many wine bottles displayed on the east wall. This represents one-fifth of an extraordinary, and thoughtful, wine list. Entrées $7.75–18.

Flying V Bar & Grill (520-299-2020), 7000 N. Resort Dr. Open daily 5:30–10. Chef de cuisine Alexis Martinez wanted to be a professional baseball player. Through a few simple twists of fate, he instead became the chef of one of the city's hot eating spots. Totally Lowes Ventana–trained under a five-star chef, Chef Alexis adds Southwest influences to grill favorites and brings food to a whole new level, combining unexpected flavors with local foods from around the state; indigenous flavors from Mexico; and fruits, vegetables, and grains from the Tohono O'odham Nation's nearby farm. The V's baby back ribs rate among the best in town, the guacamole won best in the city (a big thing in a city where there's 150 Mexican food restaurants), and the Sunday brunch tops the list of city bests. Not bad for an aspiring ballplayer. Entrées $20–34.

♥ **GOLD** (520-297-1151), Westward Look Resort, 245 E. Ina Rd. Open daily for breakfast Mon.–Sat. 7–11, Sun. brunch 10–1:30, lunch 11:30–2, dinner 5:30–10. This Tucsonan favorite got a new name (formerly The Gold Room), a new look (mirrored gold tiles, maroon silk upholstery), with the same knock-out views of the Tucson Basin, and a new chef, James Wallace, who defines himself as "the nuts-and-bolts person that just happens to produce some elegantly simple foods." Elegant, yes, but the simple refers to simply delicious. Try the most popular Short Stack, Pan-Roasted Petit Filet Mignon, Seared Rare Yellowfin Tuna, and Grilled Day Boat Scallop in Mission Fig Sauce and Watercress Cream hugged by a swirl of turnip mashed potatoes. The stunning dish got Chef James the job as executive chef (for which 350 chefs applied in 24 hours' time). The "Dry Aged" Beef Striploin is butter tender. Volcano Lamb Shank with Sun-dried Bing Cherry Jus and Porcini Mushroom Risotto presents the "contradictory flavors" that appeal to Chef James. And each dish has "stage presence"—full of colors, textures, and personality. All of the herbs and many fruits and vegetables are plucked from Chef's Garden, which is really Raymundo's (Ocampo) Garden. Oaxacan-born and savvy with the Earth, Raymundo has coaxed impossible fruits (such as avocado, banana, and grapes) in a thriving organic garden. The only thing that tops Chef James's cuisine is the extravagant views of the Rincon Mountains and Tucson Valley twinkling with lights below. Entrées $24–29.

♥ **The Grill at Hacienda del Sol** (520-529-3500), 5601 N. Hacienda del Sol Rd. Open daily 5:30–10. Repeatedly on the list of community favorites as one of the most romantic restaurants. Chef Romero Scavo, two-time Iron Chef winner, is at the helm so you know the menu will always be fresh and novel. The courtyard leading up to the restaurant (part of the Hacienda del Sol Resort) colors with herbs, fruits, and vegetables used in the Grill's kitchen. The food is described as novel American at its best, and it lives up to its reputation.

Freshwater and ocean fish appear liberally. as well as other classics, but they come with a creative yet elegant twist. Some, like the Braised Rabbit Leg with Sous Vide Loin, evolved from a family tradition. The owners are oenophiles, and the wine list leans toward lavish. The Grill has a consistent run of earning Wine Spectator's Award of Excellence since 1997; it has one of the top six wine menus in the country. Entrées $22–42.

♿ ♥ **Janos** (520-615-6100), 3770 E. Sunrise Dr. Open for dinner Mon.–Thu. 5:30–9, Fri. and Sat. 5:30–10; closed Sun. and Thanksgiving, Christmas, and New Year's days. Owner-chef Janos Wilder has played an integral role, nationally, in the use of organic produce and local, indigenous ingredients in restaurants. Janos, awarded Best Chef in the Southwest by the James Beard Foundation, marries the sensible French Nouvelle style with the spicy American Southwest. What you get is a party—colorful, lively, and full of tastes and textures that titillate your palate. From appetizers like Wild Licensed Mexican Shrimp de Ajo to such entrées as Lobster with Papaya and Champagne Sauce, your palate will enjoy one savory evening. The restaurant interiors are as sensually intense as the food: the main dining room is red with a gold-leaf ceiling and beaded Moroccan fabric; art, mostly by local artists, decks the walls, along with a line of Forbes Four-Star, AAA Four Diamond, and DiRona Awards. The wait staff is in constant motion, tending to your needs and desires. Internationally known local musicians play on the patio during summer months. Entrées $28–50.

J-Bar (520-615-6100), 3770 E. Sunrise Dr. Open for dinner Mon.–Sat. 5–9:30; happy hour 5–6:30; closed Sun. and Thanksgiving, Christmas, and New Year's days. Owned by Chef Janos, and an extension of his namesake restaurant, the informal and lively J-Bar is the place to enjoy food, libations, and people. Janos patterned it after the *parillas* in Nogales. The food, with southern Arizonan, Mexican, Latin American, and Caribbean leanings, is created in an open kitchen and served family style. The highly original menu might have dishes such as Oaxacan Lamb Barbacoa and Green Corn Tamale Pie with tangerine *crema*, spicy orange zest, and chipotle–black bean broth. On the other hand, steaks are simply grilled simply with salt and pepper. The bar serves some fun *bebidas*, such as a variety of mojitos and martinis, sangria, and Liquado del Dia (a nonalcoholic blend of fresh fruit and juices). Entrées $13–19.

Jonathan's Cork (520-296-1631), 6320 E. Tanque Verde. Open nightly at 5 PM. Originally a Cork 'N Cleaver way back in the 1970s; Chef Jonathan Landeen bought the venue in 1994 and resurrected the "Cork" part of the name. The restaurant is located in back of a (currently) Chuy's, and not easy to spot from the road, "which might be good," Chef Jonathan reasoned, "because it gets busy." The venue has "a few of the old Cork items that were popular," But it's not necessarily a steak place; though you will get a great steak (the New York strip is the chef's favorite). You will notice a number of hearty items on the menu, including blackened meats and a liberal use of spices. This comes from Chef Jonathan's training at the Commander's Palace in New Orleans under Chef Paul Prudhomme, when the "'N Cleaver" was still part of the venue's name. Now his distinctively bold, Southwest cuisine (and booming voice and laughter) has a following. Some regulars come in once a week to have the chef cook whatever he wants for them. Try the ostrich or grilled romaine for something different. Fish is fabulous (remember his New Orleans training) and steaks great. Desserts are house made by Peggy Forest, who has worked with Chef Jonathan "forever." Entrées $15–28.

♥ **Lodge on the Desert** (520-320-2000), 306 N. Alvernon Way. Open 7–10:30 for breakfast, 11–2 for lunch, and 5–9 for dinner. The glass-walled dining room (which slide open with the right temperatures) has an intimate number of white linen tables that look onto the patio. One of the city's best chefs is also one of the youngest. Like the green-leaning lodge for which it was named, the restaurant uses natural and local ingredients. Couple that with chef's mantra—make it when you can—you get an idea of how fresh your meal will be. Check out the Grilled Beef Fillet with House-cured Bacon. The Cornmeal-Dusted Calamari is the most popular appetizer. The menu changes often to accommodate fresh produce available from the local farmers. The wine list, presented in tame-to-bold order, has great names at great prices. Dinner $18–32.

♥ **Maynard's Market & Kitchen** (520-545-0577), 400 N. Toole Ave. Open Sun.–Wed. 11–10, Thu.–Sat. 11 AM–midnight. The historic train station location gives plenty of inspiration for the venue, starting with the name—Maynard was a conductor who escorted high-profile people on the train. The name also honors local artist Maynard Dixon. Train station memorabilia makes authentic touches, but not as romantic as the Doppler whistle of freight trains passing by. Speaking of romance, this is where you come for a tête-à-tête dinner (flashlights provided if the low light proves too low). Bright and creative chef Addam Buzzalini has put together a tasty eclectic menu. The fare, mostly contemporary, includes classics like Caesar salad, paella, NY strip, oysters on the half shell, and a variety of stone-baked pizzas. The Francophile even puts Cassoulet on the menu now and again. This is slow-foods-ville where everything is house made from local ingredients, when possible, within a 25-mile radius. After your meal, you can go to Maynard's Market next door and pick up some locally produced foods to take home. Entrées $12–30.

Pastiche Modern Eatery (520-325-3333), 3025 N. Campbell Ave. Open Tue.–Fri. 11:30 AM–midnight, Sat. and Sun. 4:30–midnight. Upscale yet casual, eclectic yet dependable, this locally owned bistro has a distinctive menu—American with global influences—that begs experimentation and racks up local awards To accommodate

PASTICHE'S MARKET HAS HUNDREDS OF BOTTLES OF WINE AND PLEASANT DAINTIES

the process of ordering, they provide half and bistro portions (lighter versions of originals) that are perfect for sharing and sampling. For instance, you could get a bistro portion of the thyme-crusted sea bass and a half portion of the Pastiche baby greens and not miss out on either of these signature dishes. Comfort food appears in the form of baked mac and cheese (smoked Gouda, Parmesan, and white cheddar with mesquite-smoked bacon) and San Francisco–style cioppino with mussels, scallops, shrimp, calamari, and sea bass in a spicy tomato broth, served with grilled garlic sourdough bread. These, intelligently, do not come in smaller sizes. Their next-door market has "bottles and bottles" of wine (about 600 labels) and an astounding selection of gourmet cheeses to go with that wine. Entrées $14–23.

Sur Real (520-529-2644), 3001 Skyline Dr. Open daily for lunch 11–4, dinner 4–10; call for summer hours). One step into the restaurant's neon color–saturated world gives you a clue about the lively Latin food Chef Emeliano Sotelo cooks up, a meld of classic flavors with an innovative twist here and there. The cuisine and interiors draw all strata of the social mix, from business suits to hair color that competes with the interiors. The food ranges from tortas to Street Tacos ($10–19), Enchiladas with Dominican rice and Cuban black beans ($18–22); entrées like Sea Bass (*pasilla*-dusted, grilled, and served over *papas rostizadas* and garlic spinach with a carrot-coconut broth), Lamb Mendoza with a Malbec reduction, and platters from the Churrasqueria (seasoned and grilled meat) ($25–28). The Sur Real Paella is a house specialty. At dessert time, the Churro Sundae is a hit.

Zinburger (520-299-7799), 1865 E. River Rd. $10 for a burger might seem steep, but it will be one of the freshest and tastiest you've ever eaten. The onions and mushrooms are Zin(fandel) braised. And you can go vegetarian with Clint's "Almost Famous" Vegetable Burger ($9). With more than a dozen toppings to choose from (American cheese to a fried egg to smoked mozzarella to wild mushrooms) you can come up with quite a burger, The Angus beef gets ground every few hours, and all the sides are made in-house. The cut-above quality of potato makes the French fries and sweet potato fries practically melt in your mouth. You can order a designer milk shake (Crème Brûlée or Bars of Zin, for instance) to go with your burger, or get a glass of wine from the not-so-typical wine list, or order from a dozen different bottles or on-taps of beer. The banana cream pie is worth saving space for.

EATING OUT **Frost—A Gelato Shoppe** (520-797-0188), 7131 N. Oracle Rd., Suite 101. Located in the Casas Adobes Shopping Center. This wonderful gelato shop raised the state's gelato standard to near perfection. Production chef Nazari Melchionda, from Bologna, Italy, has perfected his gelato recipes with trade secrets from master gelato chef Alberto Scagliarini. With dozens of flavors to choose from—all made fresh daily, entirely from ingredients imported from Italy—your experience will not be easy until you get the product in hand and devour. $3.08–4.49.

Ghini's French Caffé (520-326-9095), 1803 E. Prince Rd. Open Tue.–Sat. 6:30–3, Sun. 8–2; closed Mon. Good food at good prices always draws a crowd. This popular albeit tucked-away gathering place serves French Provençal food in a most delicious way. Using locally grown ingredients when possible and La Baguette Bakery bread, the food is fresh, good, and downright comforting. Entrées $5.95–8.95.

Mi Nidito (520-622-5081), 1813 S. 4th Ave. Open Wed.–Sun. 11 AM; closed Mon. and Tue. Tortilla factory or restaurant? That was the question for the couple from Sonora, Mexico. They decided to open Mi Nidito (which means "my little nest"), and generations have been thanking them ever since. They serve a number of Mexican specialties, such as *casuela*, tortillas, *pan birote*, *caldo de queso*, *birria*, old-fashioned flat enchiladas, and *nopalitos*. You'll see mangoes appear often in the menu, from appetizers to dessert. Their *chiles rellenos* are the best in town. You never know who you'll see in this small restaurant that serves up authentic Mexican fare so savory, it packs in clients from every rung of the social ladder, from students on a budget to U.S. presidents. $8.25–12.50.

✷ The Arts

Murals are rife around the Old Pueblo. About 34 mural projects cluster around the downtown area alone. The best public artwork appears at the downtown library on Church and Pennington.

Center for Creative Photography (520-621-7968), Speedway Blvd. and Olive St., University of Arizona campus. Open Mon.–Fri. 9–5, Sat. and Sun.1–4. The world-class collection of photography represents nearly every 20th-century photographer of note and features the nation's foremost collections of Ansel Adams and Alfred Stieglitz. Free.

♿ **Tucson Museum of Art and Historic Block** (520-624-2333), 140 N. Main Ave. Open Tue.–Sat. 10–5, Sun. noon–5; closed Mon. This museum exhibits more than 7,000 pieces ranging from western to European, modern to contemporary. Exhibits change almost monthly. The Historic Block represents five restored homes of the El Presidio Historic District built between 1850 and 1907 that surround the museum. $8 adults, $6 seniors, $3 students, under age 13 free.

University of Arizona Museum of Art (520-621-7567), located near Park and Speedway. Open Tue.–Fri. 9–5, Sat. and Sun. noon–4. This exquisite permanent collection was donated and purchased through the years. Pieces from the 15th-century Spanish Retablo of Ciudad Rodrigo to works by Georgia O'Keeffe, Picasso, Rembrandt, and Zuniga make a trip worthwhile. $5 adults.

✷ Selective Shopping

American Antique Mall (520-326-3070), 3130 E. Grant Rd. Open Tue.–Sat. 10–5 and sometimes Sun. (call). The best thing about this huge mall is that it's located in the heart of Tucson's Antique District (between Speedway Blvd. and Grant Rd.). So if the mall's 100 consigners don't have something to capture your fancy, you can continue the hunt to the surrounding antiques shops.

4th Avenue (520-624-5004), between University Blvd. and 9th St. It's exceedingly retro around 4th Avenue. The area has around 100 venues of shopping, dining and nightlife. You can find antiques, imported gifts, vintage clothing, jewelry, and custom-made furniture. Cultural restaurants and popular bars dot the street as well. Street fairs in spring and winter bring thousands of shoppers.

The Lost Barrio, Park Ave. south of Broadway. They didn't give this shopping area its name out of whimsy. The out-of-the-way spot in the city might be likened to a type of Bermuda Triangle where people end up when they're lost. The locals dubbed it the Lost Barrio, and the nickname stuck. If you land here because you're lost, it may end up serendipitous. To make sure you arrive on purpose, the best way to get to the Lost Barrio from downtown is to go east on Broadway under the Rattlesnake Bridge (which rattles when you cross it), then turn south onto Park Ave. Looking more like a warehouse district than cool shopping haunt, the red-brick warehouses belies the cache of goodies—more global than border-town fare—inside them, antiques from China, lights from Italy, stonework from Morocco, and doors from everywhere else.

Old Town Artisans (520-623-6024 or 800-782-8072), 201 N. Court Ave. Open Mon.–Sat. 10–4, Sun. 11–5; summer hours Mon.–Sat. 10–4, Sun. 11–4. A large collection of local and regional art, fine crafts, trendy clothes and jewelry, and Native American art is presented in a historic 1860s adobe in the El Presidio District.

✷ Entertainment

Fox Tucson Theatre (520-624-1515), 17 W. Congress. The 1929 art deco theater is listed on the National Register of Historic Places as a historically significant building. It was a grande dame in its heyday but almost had a date with the wrecking ball in the 1970s. Now newly restored, the theater shows classic films and hosts concerts.

✷ Special Events

End of January–mid-February: **Tucson Gem, Mineral, and Fossil Showcase** (800-638-8350). The world's largest marketplace, comprising more than 30 locations throughout town (at fine hotels and resorts, in shops and attractions, and under tents) featuring everything minerals and gems.

February: **Southwest Indian Art Fair** (520-626-8381). A high-quality Indian art fair hosted by Arizona State Museum, University of Arizona, featuring artists from around the Southwest, with musical entertainment. **La Fiesta de los Vaqueros: Tucson Rodeo** (520-741-2233). The Celebration of the Cowboys is an 8-day extravaganza centered on the Tucson Rodeo, one of the top 20 professional rodeos in the United States.

March: **Tucson Winter Chamber Music Festival** (520-577-3769). Nationally and internationally known groups perform at the Tucson Convention Center.

April: **Arizona International Film Festival** (520-882-0204). Independent films show in theaters around town, with opportunities to meet the filmmakers at workshops, seminars, and presentations at various venues. **Spring Fling** (520-621-5610) is the nation's largest student-run carnival, with fun rides, midway games, food, and amateur and professional entertainment, all at Rillito Raceway Park. **Pima County Fair** (520-762-9100) is an old-fashioned fair with exhibits, food, stage concerts, and live entertainment, carnival rides, educational exhibits at Pima County Fair Grounds. The award-winning **Tucson International Mariachi Conference** (520-838-3908) features mariachi music, folklorico dancing, student workshops, a concert at Tucson Convention Center, and a community fiesta at Reid Park.

August: Tucson's month-long **Birthday Celebration**. (800-638-8350)

Late September–early October: At the **Oktoberfest on Mount Lemmon** (520-885-1181) you can bring a blanket to relax on the pine- and aspen-forested slopes with German food and beer, music, dancing, and costumes atop Mount Lemmon.

October: **Tucson Culinary Festival** (www.tucsonculinaryfestival.com). Wine dinners and seminars, with more than more than 70 wineries pouring wines and over 30 Tucson chefs presenting culinary specialties.

November:. Thousands of road cyclists from around the world compete in the annual **El Tour de Tucson** (520-745-2033), featuring a prestigious 109-mile perimeter race and 30- and 60-miles rides.

December: Tucson's **Downtown Parade of Lights** (520-837-6504) holiday parade begins at 6 PM. Stroll down luminaria-adorned garden paths amid seasonal music after dark (5:30–11 PM) at the **Luminaria Nights at Tucson Botanical Gardens** (520-326-9686).

TUBAC

Describing itself as the town "Where Art and History Meet," Tubac has evolved over the last two and a half centuries from Spanish presidio to true art town. Red tile roofs, ocotillo wand fences, latilla ceilings, and religious shrines—a meld of Old West and romantic Latino—gives the tucked-away town its inspiring charisma.

As the northern frontier of New Spain and first European settlement, this area of the New World was already happening when the American Revolution got under way. Tubac started in 1691 with the Tumacácori Mission (now a national park) and its Presidio defense post (now an Arizona state park) under the Spanish flag. Juan Bautista de Anza II carved a niche in history by establishing a trail in 1775 that traveled all the way from Tubac to San Francisco. Decades before the gold rush, a third of the City by the Bay's residents named Tubac as their birthplace.

For the next 100 years Tubac roiled with Indian wars, served a stint as a Mexican colony, and wobbled with the rest of the state as a Confederate army pawn until Lincoln declared the Arizona Territory in 1863. With Tubac's war-torn history at a lull and its national status securely in U.S. hands by 1866 (after Geronimo's surrender), the town settled down into some serious peace and quiet. In 1948 artist Dale Nichols established the Artists School here. This eventually transformed the town into an artist community. By the 1960s Tubac became a respite for the East and West coast crowds who doted on its arty élan. And thanks to Bing Crosby and his Hollywood cronies, Tubac even got itself a tony golf resort that's still in operation and better than ever.

Tubac has quietly developed its aesthetic propensities since its art colony days, expanding to a national art destination. Classic western art made room for modern southwestern artists. For a while abstracts and world art have even showed up.

Where artists gather, shopping prevails; and galleries and specialty shops have multiplied. Over the years Tubac favored its free-spirited side and kept a laid-back ambience that visitors still find irresistible, never knowing what to expect. Shops rarely held to a schedule, while shopkeepers displayed their eccentricities. Recently, however, its businesses have actually adopted hours of operation. Tubac may dally with a mañana attitude now and again, but it's definitely open for business.

GUIDANCE The **Tubac Chamber of Commerce** (520-398-2704), 2 Tubac Road, is open Sept.–mid-May 10–4, mid-May–Aug. 10–1. **Nogales Ranger**

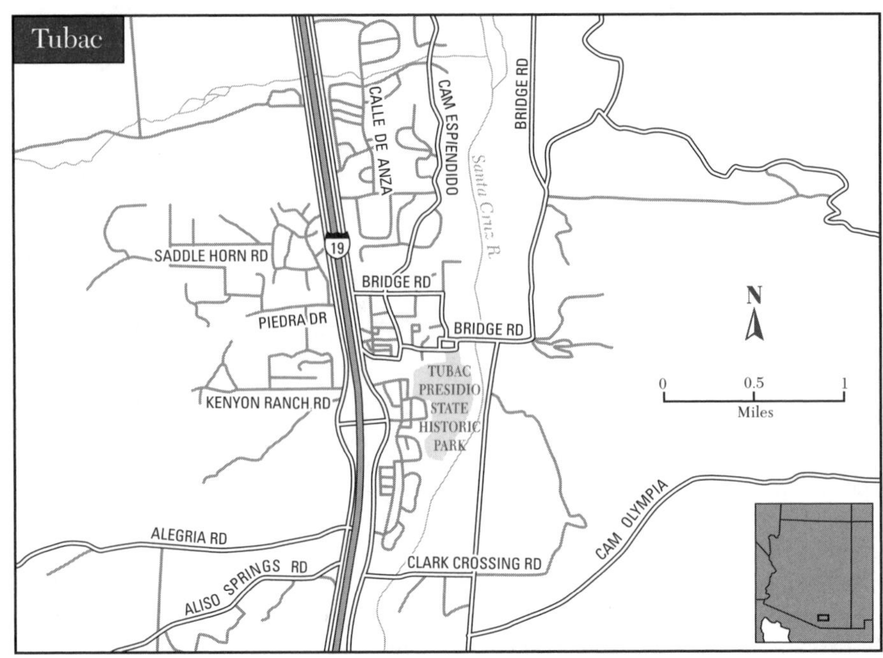

District (520-281-2296), 303 Old Tucson Rd., Nogales, has information about the Coronado National Forest; open 8–4:30.

GETTING THERE Tubac is located about 40 miles south of Tucson on I-19 (this highway is measured and marked in kilometers rather than miles) at exit 34.

WHEN TO COME Tubac's high season starts in Dec. and ends in Apr. During the off-season, May through Nov., the art galleries and shops that open daily during the high season turn laissez-faire as the crowds thin out, making this a restorative time to visit. Summer temperatures hover around 100 degrees during the day, but the nights drop into the 60s.

MEDICAL EMERGENCY **Holy Cross Hospital** (520-285-3000), 1171 W. Target Range Rd., Nogales.

✷ To See

Santa Cruz Chili & Spice Co. (520-398-2591), 1868 E. Frontage, Tumacacori. Open Mon.–Fri. 8–5, Sat. 10–3; closed Sun. and holidays. The Santa Cruz Valley produces some of the best chile peppers around, and this company has grown special and distinctive chiles here since 1943. You can purchase their products, plus peruse memorabilia in their mini-museum for free.

Tumacacori Mesquite (520-398-9356) 2007 E. Frontage Rd., Tumacacori. Open Mon.–Sat. 9–5. Twisted, gnarled, and weathered to gray tones when a living tree, mesquite is the unsung hero of the wood world. When its outer wood is cut away, the wood's beauty comes through with hues that range from lemon, honey, and caramel to burgundy, and the grain from straight as a board (sorry) to highly ornate. The American Hardwood Association classifies this hardwood as rare and exotic. Oak, mahogany, and mesquite have equal status as the most stable hardwoods in the world. This mesquite mill specializes in all things mesquite, from milled wood to furniture, even utilizing the tough burls. Free.

Tumacácori National Historical Park (520-398-2341), located just south of Tubac at 1891 E. Frontage Rd., Tumacácori. Open daily 9–5; closed Thanksgiving and Christmas days. Tumacácori is where everything started in Arizona. Father Eusebio Kino, a frequent face in Arizona history, established the mission here, indoctrinating the Pima Indians in the way of Roman Catholicism via ristras and rosaries. The mission led to the presidio in Tubac. You can tour the mission church, cemetery, and outlying structures. Check out the mission courtyard and garden just off the visitor center. $3 per person age 16 and older.

✷ To Do

BIRDING **The Anza Trail** (see *Hiking*) follows the Santa Cruz River, a major birding thoroughfare. The riparian forest is a welcome habitat for passerines and an interesting variety of mammals, including an occasional jaguar.

Arivaca Lake and Buenos Aires Wildlife Refuge (see *Wilder Places*) present some of the best birding in the state. The refuge has Arivaca Creek (located about 2 miles west of Arivaca on Arivaca Rd.) and Arivaca Cienega (0.25 mile east of town on Arivaca Rd.) to attract avian guests. A free, guided bird walk takes place Nov.–Apr. every Saturday at 8 AM at Arivaca Cienega.

Madera Canyon. Contact the Nogales Ranger District. One of the birding hot spots in the world accommodates one of the darlings of the avian world—the elegant trogan. About 240 species of birds live in the canyon.

GOLF The Tubac area has courses that rate among the state's best. With temperatures running warmer than Phoenix and Tucson, they make an excellent play in winter.

HISTORY IS VISIBLE ALL OVER TUBAC

Palo Duro Creek Golf Course (877-752-9732), 2690 N. Country Club Dr., Nogales. Located along the border, this par-72 foothill course has views of Arizona's Santa Rita Mountains and the San Cayatano Mountains in Mexico. The course has a number of obstacles, from canyons and streams to doglegs all over the place. The eighth hole (par-5) has a 90-degree turn in the middle of the fairway with an optical illusion. From there, the entire back nine will test your mettle. Let's hope it's as tough as the wood of the tree for which the course is named. Restaurant and pro shop. $30–69.

Rio Rico Golf and Country Club (520-281-8567), 1069 Camino Caralampi. This Robert Trent Jones Sr. golf layout hosts qualifying rounds for the U.S. Open and the Senior Open. Rye grass fairways and bent grass greens look gorgeous with the surrounding ridgelines rising all around. The front nine rates among the state's most challenging, and you'll find yourself in trouble if you don't have the skills right from the start with long yardages and sand traps. Private lessons, clubhouse, restaurant, and shop. $29–79.

Tubac Golf Club (520-398-2211 or 800-848-7893), 1 Avenue de Otero. History is a big thing in these parts, and this golf course has some interesting brushes with it. The historic Anza Trail passes through the 17th and 18th holes. More recent history was generated at the 15th hole, where Kevin Costner, a.k.a. the character Roy McAvoy in *Tin Cup*, sank his ball in the pond that fronts it. He then threw the golf ball onto Avenue de Otero. This scene, to Hollywood's credit, is accurate. In 2006, nine more holes were added, and the last four are long and high-par. The bent grass greens are described as slick and tricky, and that pond is a troublemaker. As a counter to the Hollywood glitz, it's the only golf course in the state where you'll see cows on the fairways. The pastoral grounds include a line of giant eucalyptuses, lily ponds, and a couple of meanders of the Santa Cruz River. Players must wear proper golf attire: golf slacks or shorts; soft spikes only. Excellent practice facilities and a shop. $29–79 (cart included).

HIKING **Anza Trail** (4 miles one way; easy). Trailheads located at Tubac Presidio State Park and Tumacácori National Historic Park. Juan Bautista de Anza blazed this trail along the Santa Cruz River on his expedition from Culican, Mexico, to San Francisco. A segment of this historic trail has been reconstructed into a maintained trail that follows the Santa Cruz River from Tubac down to Tumacácori. Free.

THE TUBAC GOLF CLUB OFFERS A PASTORAL COURSE COMPLETE WITH COWS

Atascosa Peak can be conquered via the **Atascosa Lookout Trail** in the Coronado National Forest. The 2.5-mile-long trail takes you to an enchanting panorama that looks into Mexico. Take I-19 to the Ruby Rd. exit, and go about 27 miles west to the trailhead.

Brown Canyon (520-823-4251, ext. 116). One of the state's best-kept secrets has a trail that takes you into land where wildlife prevails. Reservations are necessary. Guided hikes, led by an escort from Buenos Aires Wildlife Refuge, take place Nov.–Apr. on the second Saturday each month and cost $5 per person. Private tours cost $40 for up to 12 people, and it's worth the rare opportunity to see unspoiled grasslands and mountain slopes where subtropical species (including jaguars) roam. Call for reservations and directions.

MOUNTAIN BIKING Singletrack trails are not the Tubac area specialty; rather, it's the network of remote back roads traversing some beautiful backcountry. Get yourself a copy of the *DeLorme Arizona Atlas & Gazetteer* and/or a map of the Coronado National Forest Nogales Ranger District, pick a route, and have some fun. Remember that designated wilderness areas (such as the Mount Wrightson Wilderness Area) do not permit mechanized vehicles, including bicycles.

SCENIC DRIVES You can pick just about any back road in the area and have yourself a scenic drive. However, the Road to Ruby (about 44 miles long) is one of the more memorable. The sedan-friendly route (time and weather may change road conditions; the first 9 miles are paved) starts in Arivaca (take exit 48 on I-10 and go about 24 miles west) and twists and turns through some of the most scenic countryside this side of the border on its way to I-19. Volcano-formed peaks contain stunning colors and shapes. Just beyond Montana Mountain at about mile 15 are the ruins of Ruby. The town's present owners charge $12 to peruse the ruins.

✷ Wilder Places

Buenos Aires National Wildlife Refuge (520-423-4251, ext. 116). From Arivaca (take exit 48 off I-10 and go about 24 miles west), go west about 2 miles on Arivaca Rd. to reach the refuge boundary and another 10 miles to AZ 286 to reach the western boundary. To reach the headquarters, drive north about 8 miles on AZ 286. Once a ranch named Buenos Ayrees, Spanish for "good air," this refuge in southeast Arizona's Altar Valley has recaptured the native characteristic that inspired its name—a sea of rolling grasses that wavers in gentle high-desert breezes. The rich grassland attracts a variety of watchable wildlife, including an occasional jaguar and the masked bobwhite quail. A walk along the Arivaca Cienega or Arivaca Creek gives glimpses of some of the 340 species of birds sighted in the refuge. Free.

Sonoita Creek State Natural Area (520-287-2791). From I-19, take exit 17 (Rio Rico), turn east (left) onto Rio Rico Dr., and continue to Pendleton Dr.; turn south (left) and go to Coatimundi; turn east (right) and drive to the parking area. The state's first natural area recently opened to the public, allowing visitors to see parts of the Sonoita Creek drainage as densely occupied by avian life as its cousin, the San Pedro River—one of the world's most biologically diverse areas. Seven distinct vegetative communities are present in the just-over-5,000-acre space. In addition, the natural area lies in a transitional zone between the Chihuahuan and Sonoran deserts. Species from each zone interlope. Obtain permits from Apr. 16–Oct. 14 from Patagonia Lake State Park Visitor Center (see page 311) or reserve them by calling 520-287-6965.

✷ Lodging

BED & BREAKFASTS AND INNS

♿ ⚭ **Amado Territory Inn** (520-398-8684 or 888-398-8684), 3001 E. Frontage Rd., I-19 exit 48, Amado. Located on the 17-acre Amado Territory Ranch, where gardens and water features are interwoven in the natural desert landscape. Rustic yet elegant, each of the nine rooms has historic southwestern décor kept to impeccable standards. Although the interiors edge toward rugged Victorian, and a traditional high tea is served in the guest ranch, amenities are modern. The four suites have a flat-screen TV, coffeemaker, and mini fridge; two have a Jacuzzi. Check out the two labyrinths on the property. Home-cooked breakfast included. Kids over age 12 welcome. $105–165.

♿ ((!)) ♥ **Tubac Country Inn** (520-398-3178), 13 Burruel St. Located right in town next to the Old Town shopping district in a peaceful garden setting. Owner-innkeeper April has thought of everything: queen bed, microwave, mini fridge, coffee, tea, hot chocolate, tableware, glasses, coffee grinder, WiFi, and TV. The rooms have a casual but polished southwestern elegance reflective of the town. The largest of the five rooms and suites available includes a workroom. A breakfast basket appears outside your door each morning with an assortment of cheese, fresh-cut fruit, juice, baked goods made that morning, and yogurt. The property features garden benches, a *chiminea* niche, and a barbecue; each room has separate access and porch space. $90–175 double occupancy, $25 per extra person. Kids over age 12 okay, but no pets.

RESORT 🐾 ♿ ⚭ ♥ **Tubac Golf Resort & Spa** (520-398-2211 or 800-848-7893), 1 Otero Rd. More caballero than cowboy, the resort stands on part of the former Otero cattle ranch located on the first Spanish Land Grant in the Southwest. Bing Crosby and partners bought the cattle ranch in 1959 and started the golf resort. Many of the original buildings still stand. It's one of the few resorts around that has a distinct gentlemen's appeal and estate feeling with tons of laid-back class. The talents of area artisans show up around the property, down to the details: delicate handmade-paper wall sconces, entry doors fashioned from solid mesquite, latticed saguaro rib ceilings, hand-forged iron door handles, chairs upholstered with strips of serape, and cobblestone floors. The 70 guest rooms include high-speed Internet, triple sheeting on beds, robes, refrigerator, safe, and coffee; 27 casitas feature separate living room and dressing area, fireplace, and private patio; and 24 haciendas have s state-of-the-art sound system, flat-screen TV, jet tub, walk-in shower, sunken living room, fireplace, and patio. The Otero Suite in the historic Otero Hacienda has a bedroom, living room, den with kitchenette, fireplace, and private patio with golf course and mountain views. Casitas have richly crafted interiors that include leather furniture and Native American rugs. The 600-acre property has two restaurants, a swimming pool, chapel, golf course, spa, bicycles, croquet, volleyball, hiking on the Anza Trail, and meeting space. Call for rates. Additional charges apply for additional guests; two-pet limit at $25 each.

✱ Where to Eat

DINING OUT The Artist's Palate (520-398-3333), 40 Avenida Goya. Open Wed.–Sat. 11–9, Sun. 11–3. This themed restaurant, with a menu as creative as the food. Carrying names pertaining to the arts, you can order Masterpieces (main courses) such as Renoir Filet Mignon and Chicken Cordon Louvre. Landscapes (salads) might be anything from Cézannes Caesar to Francis Bacon Baby Spinach Salad. Paints (soups) come in A Different Color Every Day. Multi-Media (pastas) could be as traditional as De Anza Lasagna or as avant-garde as Spaghetti and Warhol Meatballs made with saffron spaghetti. Mona Lisa's Pizzas are self-explanatory. Finishing Touches, like Death by Chocolate Cake and

Windsor's Castle (A Royal Treat), make dessert an extravagant adventure. Water Colors (libations) are drinks from the full bar, with a menu of trendy cocktails. The lovely wine list ranges from Louis Jadot Pouilly Fuissé to St. Francis Old Vine Zinfandel by the glass or bottle; there are several very nice bottles ranging from Pezzi King (Dry Creek Valley, $35) to Roederer "Cristal" Champagne ($350). Entrées $18–26.

Dos Silos (520-398-2211]), 1 Otero Rd. Open daily 4:30 PM–9 PM. Named for the two silos on the patio dating back to the original historic Otero cattle ranch. Inside, the décor is richly Southwest: copper-top tables with cobalt blue glasses and plates. A mural on the wall depicts an agave farm (the plant from which tequila is made). The food is fresh with just the right touch of spices. Everything here is made in-house and often local, which gives classic Mexican dishes a fresh taste. Chef John Wooters's thoughtful choices, such as Anasazi beans rather than the usual pintos and traditional ingredients, make attractive flavor profiles. Entrées $11–30.

Melio's Trattoria Ristorante Italiano (520-398-8494), 2261 E. Frontage Rd. Open Wed.–Sun. 11:30–9; closed Mon. and Tue. Owners Elio and Melinda Trovarelli met in Rome and ran a trattoria there for a decade before moving to Arizona. *Melio* means "the best" in Italian, and it happens to be the combination of their two names. The restaurant lives up to its romantic genesis with its huge views of the Santa Rita Mountains by day and candlelight at night and usually its name. The menu has classic dishes that taste much lighter than Sicilian—15 pastas; 10 meat, fish, and poultry dishes; and almost a dozen antipasti. Plus, they serve authentic Roman-style pizza, with a thin handmade and hand-rolled crust and an assortment of toppings. Popular dishes are the homemade meat lasagna, filet mignon, and veal dishes. Desserts include tiramisu, pies, and fruit mimosa cake. Entrées $8.95–19.95.

Shelby's Bistro (520-398-8075), 19 Tubac Rd. Open daily for lunch 11–4, Wed.–Sat. for dinner 5–9. On a typical day in the high season, owner-chef Anthony can serve more than 200 people for lunch. His restaurant rates high among the locals, which means it's consistently good. Chef Anthony draws from his Mediterranean roots (southern France and southern Spain) for recipes. He makes nine different pastas and 10 different meat dishes. When he describes them as unique, he does so correctly, as he uses lavender, tarragon, fennel, and cilantro in these dishes and goes easy on the cream. Chef Anthony's creativity shows up in appetizers like baked Brie with fresh herb bread and pecans and oven-baked salmon artichoke spread; dinners such as Sonoran rubbed grilled pork chop and lobster with fresh spinach leaves. His pizza—European style with a thin crust and light sauce and cheese—is a favorite. Chef Anthony serves wines from California, Washington, Chile, and Argentina. Entrées $12.95–14.95.

Stables Ranch Grille (520-398-2678) Tubac Golf Resort. Open daily 7 AM–10 PM. Chef John Wooters's menu, refreshingly different from your typical resort fare, draws together the important elements of the people and cultures that makes up the area, using All Natural meats and fresh, often local, produce. The several fish dishes have thoughtful ingredients (such as the grouper, Swiss chard and mashed potato stack) and the steaks and onion hash brown potatoes are topped with a bordelaise sauce. The resort's history (built by the Otero family who traveled from Spain to the area in 1789) inspired the touches of Español (tapas and Spanish wines). The Oteros laid the cobbled floor, now the restaurant's main dining room, as the foundation for their stables. The back dining room has floor-to-ceiling windows that show off the pastoral golf course and Santa Rita Mts. in the background. You may wonder about the German entrées (Pork Schnitzel and warm potato salad or Veal medallions with spätzel) until you find out one of the restaurant's partners, Ernest Andreas, is from Frankfurt. Andreas, formerly a chef, cooked in cities in Europe, Asia and Africa, so you'll see European influences such as risotto, morel sauce, veal liver and mâche on the menu. The Southwest elements in the breakfast menu celebrate the Mexican influence. Chef Wooters wraps everything together with an elegant alchemy that works deliciously. Breakfast $7–17, lunch/dinner $9–30.

EATING OUT Las Trankas De Rio Rico (520-377-7153), 1136 W. Frontage Rd., Rio Rico. Open Mon.–Sat. 7 AM–9 PM, Sun. 7 AM–7 PM. This restaurant feels right at home located this close to the Mexican border. It's real Mexican fare here, including the *queso*, chorizo, *machaca*, and *menudo*. On Sunday mornings mariachis serenade while you decide among breakfast dishes such as huevos rancheros, *huevos Mexicanos*, and *chilaquiles verdes y huevo motulenos*. Lunch entrées, available until closing, are classic Mexicana. Steaks are served 4:30–8. Entrées $6.50–14.95.

Tubac Deli & Coffee Co. (520-398-3330), 6 Plaza Rd. Open daily 6:30–5:30. There are a lot of special things about this deli. Pastries are fresh baked every day. The pecan pinwheels can be hazardous if you're not known for moderation. The coffee is the local Gadsden brand (organic, shade grown, fresh roasted in Arivaca). Sandwiches include deli favorites like Reubens, tuna or turkey melts, and roast beef dip. And it's the only WiFi access in the area. If you're a customer, you need only to open up your laptop and "plug in." Cash or checks only; no credit cards accepted. ATM machine available. Sandwiches $3.50–6.25.

✷ The Arts

The perennial art community has strong southwestern leanings. Several artists in town have galleries in their homes and open them by appointment. You can contact the chamber of commerce or Tubac Center of the Arts for information. Arizona's native son (born when the state was just a territory and now passed on), Hal Empie has a gallery in town: **Hal Empie Studio & Gallery** (520-398-2811), 33 Tubac Rd. **Karin Newby Gallery & Sculpture Garden** (520-398-9662), 19 Tubac Rd., has a penchant for eclectic southwestern art. The gallery just opened up a sculpture garden, one of the largest in the Southwest.

♿ **Tubac Center of the Arts** (520-398-2371), 9 Plaza Rd. Open Mon.–Fri. 10–4:30, Sat. and Sun. 1–4:30; closed major holidays. The Santa Cruz Valley's major art organization exists to provide a venue for artistic activity. The center has three galleries with more than 3,500 square feet of exhibit space, a members' gallery, a performance stage, an art library, and a gallery shop. A number of exhibits run during the high season, as well as a performing arts series, art and cultural workshops for adults and children, an adult choral group, the Tubac Singers, and several benefit events. A month-long arts program takes place in summer and culminates

LA PALOMA DE TUBAC

in July with a reception, exhibit, and performances. Donations accepted.

✷ Selective Shopping

A number of galleries and shops line the village's Old Town area; it can easily take you a full day to peruse them all.

La Paloma de Tubac (520-398-9231), 1 Presidio Dr. Open daily 10–5. Like an open-air Latin American marketplace, this corner market has a collection of about 10,000 pieces of folk art handmade by more than 1,000 different artisans. The owners have dealt with the same families of Peruvian, Ecuadorian, Guatemalan, and Mexican artists for years, and you'll find an interesting collection of quality traditional crafts at good prices. If you don't plan to dip into Old Mexico, head here.

Lee Blackwell Studio (520-398-2268), 18 Plaza Rd. Call for hours. Lee has sculpted metal in Tubac since 1982, and his metal fountains and sculptures of desert plants and animals appear all over the world. He'll custom-design anything made of metal, from gates to countertops to homes.

Old Presidio Traders (520-398-9333), 27 Tubac Rd. Open daily 9–5; closed major holidays. Garry and Lisa Hembree have been here for more than 25 years, offering Native American crafts and jewelry. The Hembrees have traveled the reservations of northern Arizona and New Mexico for more than 30 years and are known for their authentic selection of Indian pawn at very reasonable prices, plus a large selection of fetishes.

✷ Special Events

For more information, call 520-398-2704.

February: **Tubac Festival of the Arts**, Tubac's big event, showcases the work of hundreds of visiting artists, craftspersons, and musicians from around the country and Canada.

March: **Art Walk** gives visitors a chance to take a look at artists' studios.

October: **Anza Days** presents a Living History of the Indian, Mexican and Spanish Colonial Periods with military demonstrations, folkloric dancers, ethnic music, and food.

December: During the annual holiday celebration of **Luminaria Nights/ Fiesta Navidad**, luminaries line the streets and stores stay open until 9.

BENSON

A classic example of the saying, "Good things come in little packages," this small town has a number of niche-type museums and points of interest on subjects you might find in a Trivial Pursuit game. It's a doorway for several points of interest in Cochise County and always has been.

The town started as a stage stop for the Butterfield Overland Stage mail delivery route. When prospectors struck it rich in Cochise County mines, the Union Pacific Railroad laid tracks through the stage stop to cozy up to the silver boomtown of Tombstone. Thanks to the railroad, Benson was born.

Benson became a railroad hub with a global population of Mexicans, Chinese, and Anglo cowboys, miners, and railroad workers, mostly men. As the town grew, so did the saloons, gambling houses, and cache of ladies of ill repute. Oftentimes the town would try its hand at respectability, ridding itself of undesirables, but it took churches and schools to bring stability. By 1913 the railroads expanded to other cities, and by 1920 mine production slowed. Ranching and farming followed, and the wild bachelors of the cosmopolitan hub of the mining towns and camps either moved on to seek their fortunes elsewhere or finally settled down into connubial bliss. Benson's had a few brushes with ghost-town status but has always endured.

GUIDANCE **Benson Visitor Center** (520-586-4293), 249 E. 4th St. For information on the Coronado National Forest, contact the **Douglas Ranger District** (520-364-3468), 3081 N. Leslie Canyon Rd., Douglas. **Bureau of Land Management** (520-439-6400) has information on the San Pedro Riparian National Conservation Area.

GETTING THERE *By car:* With I-10 running through the town, you need only head east from Tucson or west from Willcox to get there. AZ 90 drops to the south from Benson, as does AZ 80, only a few miles east. *By air:* **Benson Municipal Airport** (520-843-5444) is located 2 miles north of the AZ 90/I-10 interchange for private craft. *By bus:* The **Greyhound Bus** stop is located at McDonald's, 618 S. VLG Loop AZ 90. You cannot acquire tickets from this stop, but you may call the Greyhound Telephone Information Center (800-231-2222). *By train:* **Amtrak** (800-872-7245).

GETTING AROUND **Southwestern Aviation** (520-586-3262) offers rental cars starting at $25 per day.

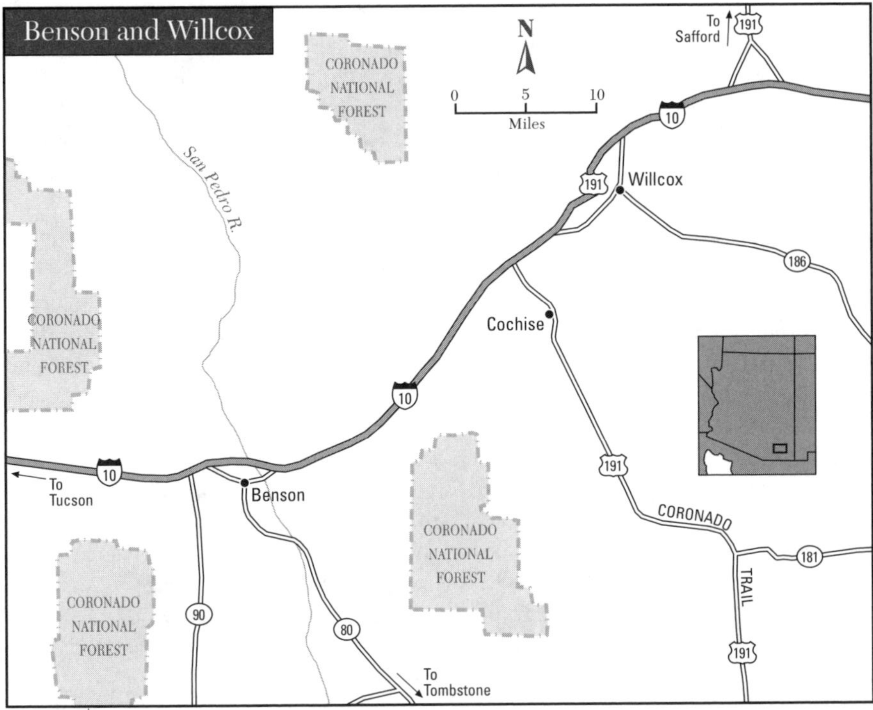

WHEN TO COME Even with its 3,585-foot elevation, Benson sizzles in the high 90s in summer. Fall and winter calm down to agreeable levels, and winter, comfortable to many, averages about 62 daytime degrees.

MEDICAL EMERGENCY **Benson Hospital** (520-586-2261), 450 S. Ocotillo.

✷ To See

The Amerind Foundation (520-586-3666), 2100 N. Amerind Rd., Dragoon. Open Tue.–Sun. 10–4; closed Mon. and major holidays. One of Arizona's more unusual museums gets its name from a contraction of American Indian, to which the foundation devotes itself through art, artifacts, and research. New Englander William Fulton started the foundation, a result of his love of archaeology. The museum, a compound of Spanish colonial revival–style buildings built in 1930–1959, houses Fulton's private collection of ethnographic and archaeological materials, one of the best private collections in the world. $5 adults, $4 age 60-plus, $3 ages 12–18, under age 12 free.

Holy Trinity Monastery (520-720-4642). Located off AZ 80 south of St. David between mileposts 302 and 303. This Olivetan Benedictine monastery, founded by Blessed Bernard Tolomei (canonized at St. Peter's, Rome, on April 26, 2009), glows with a halo of peace, harmony, and beauty. This is where people living in an Andy Warhol painting retreat when they want to experience a Monet world; where the curious come to find out just what goes on in a monastery (usually prayer or meditation, so you won't see many people milling about here). Nevertheless, you can explore the bird sanctuary, Prayer and Meditation Garden, museum; attend Mass every weekday at noon and Sunday at 10:30 AM; and even join the padres for breakfast, lunch, or dinner. Just don't expect engaging conversation, as most of the meals follow the monastic tradition of silence. You can even spend the night in spiritual retreat in the simple visitor quarters. This means following the way of the monks, and exercising silence, solitude, simple living, community, and personal prayer. $50–80. Call for information on the cost of meals.

♂ ♿ **Kartchner Caverns** (520-586-4100) 2980 AZ 90. From I-10, take exit 302 (Benson) and drive 9 miles south on AZ 90 to the signed entrance. Open daily 7:30–6; closed state holidays. One of the world's premier caverns gives you the chance to walk through a live cave still in the process of evolving and growing. The air hangs thick, like a sultry night in a Louisiana swamp; water drips arbitrarily all around. Kartchner is among the top 10 caves in the world for unusual minerals. It contains colorful and diverse formations such as fragile crystalline rods, flowstone walls, and quartz needles. The park includes a discovery center that features a makeshift underground journey plus a video explaining the history of the cave; you'll also find a gift shop, picnic areas, ramadas, campground, restrooms, hummingbird garden, and the 4-mile (aboveground) Guindoni Loop trail. There's a park entrance fee of $5 per car (up to two adults), $2 additional charge per person age 14-plus, or get in free with a tour reservation. Rotunda/Throne Room Tour $18.95 adults, $9.95 ages 7–13, age 6 and under free; Big Room Tour $22.95 adults, $12.95 ages 7–13; no kids under age 7.

San Pedro Valley Art & Historical Society (520-586-3070), 180 S. San Pedro. Open Tue.–Fri. 10–4, Sat. and in summer 10–2); closed Aug. When the old mercantile store, built in the early 1920s, changed hands more than 20 years ago to become a museum, some of its inventory went with it and remains on display here. The museum houses a variety of historic items, from a 1900 horse-drawn school bus to a steam engine, maps, and historic memorabilia of Benson. It showcases changing displays and exhibits highlighting local cultures. Donations accepted.

Singing Wind Bookshop (520-586-2425), 700 W. Singing Wind Rd. Open daily 9–5. If you have any bibliophile blood flowing in you, this bookshop will captivate you. Located off the beaten path a mile north of town on a working cattle ranch, it's known the world over. Books about the West and Southwest and those written by local authors prevail, but don't be surprised to find a few anomalous niche subjects. The shop, more a social happening than a bookstore, has scheduled events throughout the year. The main event, Thanksgiving Fiesta, which happens in late November, is when local authors do readings of their latest books

✷ To Do

BIRDING **San Pedro Riparian National Conservation Area** (520-439-6400), Fairbanks BLM Headquarters. One of the premier birding sites in the world stretches from St. David to Naco, Mexico, along the upper San Pedro River. At the Fairbanks area, located about 26 miles south of Benson, you'll find flycatchers, red-tailed hawks, Gambel's quail, and buntings.

HIKING The **Dragoon Mountains** (see *Wilder Places*) present a unique landscape to explore. If you want to know what the basic lay of the land looks like, hike the popular 5-mile **Cochise Stronghold Trail**. For a more intimate look, take the tucked-away 3.5-mile **Slavin Gulch Trail**. Contact the Douglas Ranger District.

ROCK CLIMBING The **Dragoon Mountains**, one of the best climbing spots in the state, have more than 100 routes in their labyrinthine maze of granite formations. Contact the Douglas Ranger District.

✷ Wilder Places

Dragoon Mountains. Located about 25 miles south of Benson. Contact the Douglas Ranger District. Lying like a lazy dragon stretched across the high-desert grasslands floor, the Dragoons evoke an aura of fantasy with their strangely sculpted peaks and outcroppings. Their curious granite landscape of towering pinnacles, boulders precariously balanced atop one another, and spiny peaks that look like fingers pointing every which way makes a perfect hideaway. The confusing jumble of rocks became the last stronghold of Cochise and his loyal band of Apache. Cochise always retreated to these mountains after bloody battles over his coveted land. Like an impenetrable rocky cocoon, the Dragoons never failed to protect him as he turned southeast Arizona on end. The Dragoons still keep watch over Cochise, never telling where his fellow Apache buried his body in the labyrinthine formations.

✷ Lodging

BED & BREAKFASTS ✐ ♥ ⟴ **Cochise Stronghold Bed and Breakfast** (520-826-4141). Located in a canyon amid the mountains to which legendary Apache leader Cochise retreated, this nature retreat has a special atmosphere steeped in the legends and lore of its colorful past. Tranquil yet wild, the land around the canyon still defers to nature and wildlife. Owner-innkeepers John and Nancy Yates note that any stress guests bring with them dissolves overnight. The Yates built an environmentally savvy casita full of amenities to make your stay as comfortable as the landscape will make it memorable. The straw-bale casita has a fully equipped kitchenette, king bed, private bath, and patio with barbecue grill. For a wilderness experience kids will love, you can stay in the B&B's 700 sq. ft. yurt. It has a double and two single beds, outside running water, fire pit, and hot shower station. You can rent the whole ranch for a totally intimate stay. A full breakfast, made from healthy whole foods and served in your casita or yurt, is included; and you can order provisions (steaks or salmon) to make your own dinner or have John and Nancy get groceries for your stay (extra). Double occupancy for casita $179; yurt $129; add $25 for each person.

Down by the River Bed and Breakfast (520-720-9441), 2255 Efken Place, St. David. This newly built Santa Fe–style B&B has views from all angles. Four rooms have king or queen beds; two have whirlpool and beehive fireplace. The great room, open to all guests, has 12-foot ceilings with ponderosa logs and latilla. Oversized pool table and barbecue open for guest use. No kids under age 8, and no pets. June–Oct. $85–95, Nov.–May $85–135.

RANCHES ✐ **Grapevine Ranch** (520-826-3185), Dragoon Mountains. When you sign in at the Grapevine

Ranch, you get a cup, which you use in the mess hall during your stay. Come back a couple times, and you get to keep the cup, which gets set on a special shelf running along each wall. The shelves are full of cups belonging to people from all over the world, who just can't stay away from Grapevine. It's definitely cowboy here, and no fluff, from the beds to the food to the untamed countryside with clean air filled with the calls of nature and wild demeanor practically unchanged since Cochise and his band of Apache braves lived in them. You can hike the trails in the mountains. But if you believe the owner, Eve, who insists, "If God meant for man to walk, he wouldn't have created horses," you'll ride. Just remember, the horse is going to do what he wants to do; you've got to tell him what to do, and 95 percent of riding is in the sitting, the other 5 percent is balance. Meals are included. De-stressing within 24 hours is practically guaranteed. Call for rates.

✷ Where to Eat

DINING OUT ♥ **Ironwood Grill** (520-586-2525), 926 N. Madison St. Open Tue.–Thu. 10–5, Fri. 10–8, Sat.–Sun. 7–5. Located in the San Pedro Golf Course, the venue has 270-degrees of floor-to-ceiling windows that show you just about the whole golf course. You can watch golfers at the 18th hole try to swing the club hard enough to get the ball over two ponds. One of the town's popular venues serves the perfect hamburger cooked to your temperature specs and a tasty Caesar salad for lunch. They serve beer-batter French fries with the warning that they are addictive. Dinner happens on Fridays, and the entrée of choice is the prime rib (8 oz. is still under $10). Cheesecake desserts (with banana, coconut, and rum sauce or turtle divine) are the diet wreckers here. Lunch $5.25–8.95, dinner $6.25–14.95.

EATING OUT Horseshoe Café (520-586-3303), 154 E. 4th St. Open Sun.–Thu. 6 AM–8 PM, Fri.–Sat. 6 AM–9 PM). The two-story building has one of the area's most enduring and endearing western restaurants. The western art, relics from the past from former workers, and old jukebox have a "sit-down-and-make-yourself-at-home" ambience reiterated by the home cooking served by the new owners, Karla and Bryan. Everything (except onion rings and chicken fingers) is made in-house, and the St. David Farmers' Market provides produce in season. They hand-cut the meats (and Alaskan pollock for Friday's fish fry special), make biscuits in the morning and bake the pies for dessert. Entrées $6.49–17.49.

Magaly's Mexican Restaurant (520-586-2027), 675 W. 4th St. Open Mon.–Sat. 11–9. The local favorite not only has dependably good food, but also goes out of its way to make sure you're happy. They serve the standard Mexican fare, freshly made, and are known for their *chiles rellenos*, red chile, and tortilla soup. $2.95–9.95.

✷ Special Events

Contact 520-586-2842 unless noted elsewise.

February: **Territorial Days**. Entertainment, food, vendors, and a carnival.

May: **Bluegrass in the Park** is a two-day festival featuring the top bluegrass bands in the nation with food and craft vendors and music workshops taught by bluegrass masters. **Fiesta de la Primavera**, Holy Trinity Monastery (St. David) (www.holytrinitymission.com) brings art, entertainment, food, and crafts to raise money.

July: **Fourth of July Celebration** has a parade, entertainment, and fireworks.

October: **Butterfield Overland Stage Days** spans two days that start with a parade; also entertainment, food, art and crafts, rodeo, and fireworks.

November: **Fall Festival of the Arts**, Holy Trinity Monastery (St. David) (www.holytrinitymission.com) brings back all the good stuff, only autumn-themed, of May's Fiesta de la Primavera.

December: **Christmas on Main Street**. Shopping, Santa, and a lighted parade.

WILLCOX

There are a few towns in Arizona that don't seem to budge much when it comes to change. Willcox is one of them. The old cattle capital still celebrates cowboy history. The late cowboy movie star Rex Allen has a monument and festival dedicated to him. The mercantile store still sells western wear and equipment. And the railroad station is still a focal point in the town. Willcox, like many of the cities in southeastern Arizona, has recently become an ecotourism destination. Birds are big here, specifically the sandhill crane. Even better, a number of one-of-a-kind wilderness areas are located just a short drive away. When you get hungry, Willcox and its environs hold around a dozen U-pick orchards, and just down the road in don't-blink-your-eyes-or-you'll-miss-it Kansas Settlement are salt-of-the-earth farms run by Mennonites. It's an interesting mix of Old West meets ecotourism surrounded by orchards and farms run by people that still believe the best things in life are natural and simple. That alone makes it a truly special place.

GUIDANCE **Cochise Visitor Center** (520-384-2272), 1500 N. Circle I Rd. Located on the eastern side of Willcox. You can watch a video on Willcox's history and the building the center is housed in, a historic railroad station. Pick up a free map and details of a self-guided tour in Willcox, as well as brochures on farm produce and birding spots. A small gift shop has books and maps. **Douglas Ranger District** (520-364-3468), 1192 W. Saddleview Rd., Douglas, has information on backcountry use of the Coronado National Forest. Open Mon.–Fri. 7:30–4:30.

GETTING THERE Willcox straddles I-10, and you can reach it by driving 81 miles east of Tucson or 40 miles west from the New Mexico border. The city also lies at the top of the Cochise Circle Route (AZ 186, AZ 181, US 191, and I-10) that takes you past some great history and scenery.

WHEN TO COME The prime tourist season runs from fall through spring. Fruit and nut orchards ripen late July through September.

MEDICAL EMERGENCY **Northern Cochise Community Hospital** (520-384-3541), 901 Rex Allen Dr.

✷ To See

Willcox Commercial Store (520-384-2448), 180 N. Railroad Ave. Open Mon.–Sat. 9–5:30. Built in the early 1880s, this claims to be the oldest continually operating store in the state. It's seen some interesting characters in its heydays. One, for instance, was the great Apache freedom fighter Geronimo. So distrustful of Anglos was the Apache champion that he would risk coming out of hiding to buy a pound of sugar. Why? As the story goes, he didn't trust the white man's pound. He knew how a pound in the hand felt, and Geronimo would hold the sugar in his hand to feel the weight of it. You can still get a pound of sugar (true weight), as well as hats, cowboy boots, and western wear, just like the good old days when Geronimo did his shopping here.

Chiricahua Regional Museum and Research Center (520-384-3971), 127 E. Maley St. Open Mon.–Sat. 10–4. The museum's repository of photos and artifacts gives fascinating insight into Chiricahua Apache culture as well as frontier life, from memorabilia and a rock collection. You'll learn about the town's founding fathers, the Maley Tent City, and railroad. Donations accepted.

Fort Bowie National Historic Site (520-847-2500). Go 20 miles south on AZ 186 to unpaved Apache Pass Rd. and turn left; continue 8 miles to the trailhead. Open daily 8–4; closed Christmas Day. The 1.5-mile-long trail to the fort and several sites tied to the fort's history—the cemetery, an Apache wikiup, the Chiricahua Apache Indian Agency, and the original fort—gives you a chance to stretch your legs through some isolated countryside full of colorful history. This was the land where the Apache lived their last days in freedom. The fort, built in 1862 on a mail route, played a big part in quelling the tribe. The Fort Bowie Visitor Center displays military photos and memorabilia. For nature lovers, it has a virtual computer program featuring natural history of the area. Free.

Headquarters Saloon on N. Railroad Ave. While Wyatt Earp made his mark all around the state, especially in Tombstone, his lesser-known youngest brother, Warren, ran a stage route in the area. Warren wasn't as sharp a shooter with a gun; he was shot and killed here in July 1900 carrying nothing but a half-opened pocketknife. Poor Warren rests in peace in the Old Willcox Cemetery.

Rex Allen Museum and **Willcox Cowboy Hall of Fame** (520-384-4583), 150 N. Railroad Ave. Open 10–4 daily; closed Thanksgiving, Christmas, and New Year's days. The legendary country-western singer made a big impact on his beloved Willcox. This museum celebrates the legend's career with memorabilia, including some flashy outfits the silver screen star wore. $2 per person, $5 per family, $3 per couple.

SCENIC DRIVES **The Cochise Circle** (about 87 miles of AZ 186, AZ 181, US 191, and I-10) makes an excellent day trip. Clockwise, you pass through the ghost town Dos Cabezas with its adobe ruins; the turnoff for Chiricahua National Monument; the cemetery where the homesteaders who discovered the monument and lived near it rest; scenic ridges around the junction of AZ 181 with US 191; the turnoff for the little ghost town of Pearce; and Willcox Playa.

✱ To Do

ORCHARDS The Sulphur Springs Valley has some of the best land and water supplies in Arizona to grow crops. It has the requisite climate for apple orchards and vineyards: sunny days and cool evenings. Locavores will hit pay dirt with a drive down Fort Grant Road. From late spring through early fall, orchard, farms, ranches and vineyards share their harvests. Below is a sample of what's waiting, and when.

Apple Annie's Orchard (520-384-2084), 2081 W. Hardy Rd. You can start picking apples here at the beginning of July. The harvest includes Gala, Red and Golden Delicious, Fuji, Rome Beauty, and Granny Smith. If you don't want to labor for the fruits, you can get already picked apples, pies, cider, or an apple-smoked hamburger. The family-run orchard has the largest cider mill in the state.

The Berry Farm (520-300-0337), 11515 N. Old Fort Grant Rd. Pesticide- and chemical-free boysenberries late May to early July.

Briggs & Eggers Orchard (520-384-2539), go 17 miles north on Fort Grant Road. Quality certified organic fruit from July–Oct.

Brown's Orchard (520-384-3671; www.youpickapples.com), 5774 N. Atwood Dr. Apples, pears, and grass-fed lamb.

Valley Farms LTD—Desert Sweet Organic (520-384-2861), 17½ miles north. Certified organic cherries (June and July) and apples (July–Oct.).

Vernon Dozier's Produce Stand, 84 Frontage Road, York (near Milepost 395 of US 75)—A variety of fresh produce grown out-back of the home.

Stout's Cider Mill (520-384-3696), 1510 N. Circle I Rd. Open daily 9–5; closed Thanksgiving and Christmas days. From apples to ostrich eggs, you get all unadulterated products here. Known as "that apple place in the desert," the orchard has more than 10,000 apple trees and 18 varieties, including Granny Smith, Gala, Fuji, Jonathan, and Red Delicious. Almost 1,000 apricot, peach, pear, and cherry trees provide fruit for preserves. You can pick apples July–Oct.

BIRDING Willcox labels itself as Arizona's Mecca for Wintering Sandhill Cranes, Raptors, and Sparrows. It's the wide swatches of open-space grasslands that attract many of these species. More than 5,000 sandhill cranes winter at the **Willcox Playa Wildlife Area** (520-628-5376), located southeast of Willcox; go 6 miles east on AZ 186, turn south onto Kansas Settlement Rd., and go 4 miles to the wildlife area. You can hike 1.5 miles to the crane roosting area. **Whitewater Draw Wildlife Area** (520-642-3763) gives you a close-up of the sandhill cranes (around 21,000 each winter) from Oct.–Mar., a variety of other waterfowl, flycatchers, and quail during the year; and free camping. Go south on US 191 to Elfrida, continue south on Central Hwy to Davis Rd. and turn right (west), go to Coffman Rd. and turn left (south) to the wildlife area. **Lake Cochise/Twin Lakes Golf Course** (800-200-2272) draws wading birds and shorebirds during migration and for the winter. Go south on AZ 186 to the signed turnoff for the golf course and follow the birding signs. The **Apache Station Wildlife Area** (520-384-4256) also draws wintering sandhill cranes, and other birds year-round. From I-10 east of Willcox, go south on US 191 for 8.5 miles.

HIKING One of the more fascinating places to hike in the state is **Chiricahua National Monument**. **Chiricahua Wilderness** offers trails less traveled and very beautiful. See *Wilder Places*.

ROAD BICYCLING Most of the highways around here are perfect for road biking—there's little traffic, many have good shoulders, and you'll wheel past tons of open space. Services are limited, however; bring plenty of food, water, and a repair kit. **Kansas Settlement Road** travels flat and scenic farmlands. AZ 186 traverses a wild and wonderful landscape full of history and rollers. **Dragoon Road**, a little-known niche, travels past acres of fruit and nut orchards with a tease of the Dragoon Mountains' curious rock formations.

✷ Wilder Places

Chiricahua National Monument. Contact the National Park Service at 520-824-3560. This national monument has some of the most unusual geology in the state. Formed by a cataclysmic act of volcanism, the lava that makes up the strange formations here was catapulted from its subterranean flow, scientists say, some 25 million years ago as incandescent ash and molten pellets of pumice. As the thick layer of stuff cooled, vertical joints appeared and separated over time, then allowed erosion to have its artistic way, forming the rock spires, totem poles, hoodoos, and bridges in the monument. Head for Massai Point for the best panoramas.

As if this spectacular geological history weren't enough, the flora and fauna is askew as well. The monument is a crossroads for plants and animals. It's a mixed-up area, not only because of the sky island concept, but it has Rocky Mountain, Sierra Madre, Chiricahuan, and Sonoran Desert plants and animals living on the fringe of their natural environment. The **Heart of Rocks Trail**, which so typifies the geological landscape of the monument, lives up to its name. The **Echo Canyon Trail**, spiritually important to the Apache, is the soul.

THE WILLCOX TRAIN STATION

Chiricahua Wilderness. Contact the Douglas Ranger District. This designated wilderness lies on the sky island range of the Chiricahua Mountains. Its 13 trails cross some of the most attractive mountainscapes in the Southwest with precipitous canyon walls, pine forests with deciduous tree stands along mountain streams, and slopes colored with wildflowers. Avian sightings are legendary. Check out **South Fork Trail** for birds from May through Sept. and fall color in Oct. The **Crest Trail** has dozens of wildflowers in summer. **Rucker Canyon Trail** has some of the most distinctive scenery.

✱ Lodging

BED & BREAKFASTS **Dos Cabezas Spirit and Nature Retreat Bed and Breakfast** (520-384-6474), 7101 E. White Pacheco St., Willcox. Because most of the buildings in this old mining town, population 27, are historic adobes feeling the hardships of time, this B&B came after no little blood, sweat, and tears (not many straight lines existed in the buildings). The compound contained the Hostess Room built in the late 1800s where chief swindler and town hedonist, T. N. McCauley, sold stock for his Mascot Mine in the Dos Cabezas Mts. Although McCauley sold tons of $10 certificates, the mine never produced. His high-on-the-hog lifestyle, however, kept the town humming along nicely. Around the 1960s, the compound became the Dos Cabezas Craft Center, where a group of renaissance artists created every kind of handmade craft. The Samuelsons cleaned up the compound's buildings, decorated them in Southwest hues and styles, and created a soothing space in the desert. Nature gives some of its finest displays here—animals, scenery and atmospherics. Jon and Charmayne give some of the finest company. Two rooms and a kitchen casita with a mini fridge, microwave, dishes, tableware, and table for guest use. Breakfast is scrumptious gourmet with fresh local foods. $149 for double occupancy.

GUEST RANCHES ♥ **Sunglow Ranch** (520-824-3334 or 866-786-4569), 14066 S. Sunglow Rd. Open year-round. Located on 400 acres in the Chiricahua Mountains, next to 300,000 acres of open-space national forest land, the property is a microcosm of what Cochise County is all about—big sky, beautiful landscapes, and tons of history. The fact that Geronimo once tread through the property along Turkey Creek on his commutes between Arizona and Mexico makes the place a little special. The property has a truly unexpected scene more European than southwestern: an open meadow ringed by mountains with a pond owned by a gaggle of geese. The property's Boston owners, Chrissy and Mitch, meld some East Coast elements with the land's backcountry mein—salons several times a year, gourmet dinners, astronomy weekends (Mitch is an astronomer), an Olympic-size swimming pool, and Ralph Lauren Americana touches in the low-key Southwest casitas crafted by neighboring Mennonites. One-bedroom casitas have a queen bed; two-room casitas have a bedroom with two queen beds, living room, fireplace, and futon; and casita grandes have same with two bedrooms. All come supplied with Harney & Sons tea and organic coffee. Healthy gourmet foods for breakfast and dinner are included in the rates. The restaurant is open to the public, with reservations (see *Where to Eat*). $200–250 per person, $70 per extra person; casita grande $375 double occupancy, $70 per extra person.

✱ Where to Eat

DINING OUT ♥ **Sunglow Café** (520-824-3334 or 866-786-4569), 14066 S. Sunglow Rd. The Sunglow Ranch's restaurant is open to the public for dinner by reservation only. Chef Colleen Stevens surprises guests with gourmet food out in the middle of nowhere. She loves the fact people expect grilled hamburgers and hotdogs but get meals like wild-caught salmon and crème brûlée. It's the best place around for fine dining, and the food is good. The interiors, a mix of Mexican and Provençal enriched with plants and a water feature, create a harmonious atmosphere. Glass tabletops and candles make the room sparkle. The food is farm-to-the-table fresh and, when possible, local; and the portions are hearty. Call for prices and reservations (one day in advance required).

EATING OUT Burger Barn at Apple Annie's Orchard (520-384-2084), 2081 W. Hardy Rd. Open for lunch mid-July–Oct., Sat. and Sun. 11–3. As you can imagine, apples are big here and appear in everything from pies to apple-smoked burgers. Pancake breakfasts take place about six times through the season. Entrées $5.59–7.59.

Rodney's (520-384 5180), 118 N. Railroad Ave. Open Tue.–Sun. 11–8. Looking like an eatery in Bayou Country, this tiny restaurant is where food happens in Willcox. Owner-chef Rodney cooks up some excellent meals culled from a variety of cultures, from Cajun to Southwestern to South Side Chicago. His grandmother was the cook in the family, and he inherited her talent for cooking without a recipe. "We were the kids with pulled taffy and homemade egg rolls," Rodney explains. "Mom was the recipe person, I just watched and could cook without one. We call it passing the spoon." Chef Rodney will serve you in the shop, on picnic tables outside, or even the saloon next door, because he doesn't have a liquor license. Entrées $5.99–7.99.

Salsa Fiesta (520-384-4233), 1201 W. Rex Allen Drive. Open Sun.–Thu. 11–8:30, Fri. and Sat. 11–9. Gladys Olsen and her daughter, Jennifer Regensberg, opened this Mexican Slow Food venue because they wondered why they couldn't have one in their town. They quickly learned, when one cook left after another, if the restaurant was going to work, they'd have to learn how to cook. Although it looks more truck stop than creative, you'll get a blend of tried-and-true barrio and foodie trendy. They use local foods (Bonita beans from down the road, Eurofresh tomatoes from Ft. Grant Rd., wine from Coronado Vineyards a few miles east, handmade tortillas from Mexico, and chile peppers from Ft. Bowie). Jennifer makes about seven different salsa for the salsa bar. The *pico de gallo* is the favorite but, Gladys advices, "Jennifer makes a mango salsa to die for." Entrées $5.95–9.95.

✷ Special Events

Call 520-384-2272 for more information.

January: **Wings over Willcox** celebrates the winter migration of thousands of sandhill cranes to the area, as well as birding in general, with birding tours, seminars, workshops, photo contest, and banquet.

September: **Magic Circle Bike Challenge**. This road biking event takes place on Labor Day.

October: **Rex Allen Days**. Events include the induction of a new cowboy into the Willcox Cowboy Hall of Fame, softball tournament, turtle race, rodeo, country music concert, western dances, and country fair.

December: **Christmas Apple Festival** includes a judged arts and crafts show, bazaar, and local entertainment.

SIERRA VISTA

Located in a biome-crossed area of the state, Sierra Vista has become one of the destinations of choice for ecotourism in Arizona. It has the best of both worlds—civilized comforts and watchable wildlife. Species from Mexico's Sierra Madre feel just as at home as those dipping down from the Rocky Mountains and in from the Sonoran and Chihuahuan deserts. Plus, the city lies on a major avian migration path along the San Pedro River. Hundreds of species of birds pass through the city during their seasonal shifts. Premier watchable wildlife areas lie within a stone's throw of the city limits—it's that close to the backcountry.

The San Pedro River flows only a few miles from the city, and the remnants of centuries of history remain along the riverbanks. This history is not exactly the kind you find in a textbook. It's full of color and cuss, thanks to the mining camps along the river and the tenacious courage of Native Americans who refused to give up their extraordinary homeland. Which brings us to the reason Sierra Vista exists—Fort Huachuca. The fort was established to protect settlers and travel routes in this corner of the state, then a territory, from attacks by resident Native people. That particular spot was selected because it had fresh water, an abundance of trees, excellent observation in three directions, and high ground. Many of the same reasons the birds like this area so much. And once again, we come full circle back to why you might want to visit Sierra Vista—it's the best of both worlds.

GUIDANCE **Sierra Vista Convention and Visitor's Bureau** (520-417-6960 or 800-288-3861), 3020 E. Tacoma St. You can pick up an official visitor guide, an information brochure about birding and watchable wildlife, and a Cultural Heritage Tour brochure, as well as specific information on things to do in the area. Check out the *How the West Was Fun* CDs, full of information on the famous people—Cochise, Geronimo, Buffalo Soldiers, and pioneers—who made the area their home. The late Rex Allen and local rancher and cowboy poet Bud Strom tell you all about these charismatic personalities. Call 520-417-6960 for information, 800-288-3861 to order. The **Sierra Vista Ranger District** (520-378-0311), 5990 S. AZ 92, Hereford, has information, maps, and descriptions of trails for hiking and mountain biking in the Huachuca Mountains. The **Bureau of Land Management** (520-439-6400) has information on the San Pedro Riparian National Conservation Area.

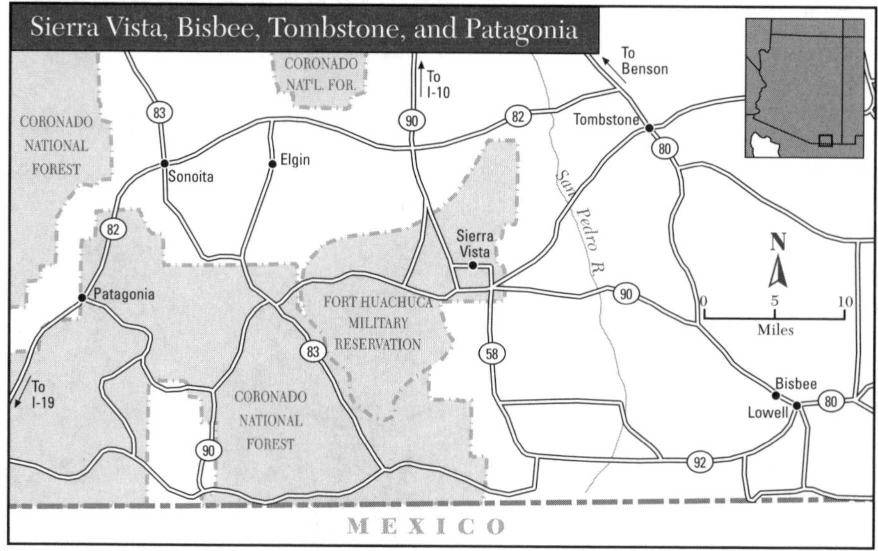

GETTING THERE *By car:* Sierra Vista is located right on the curve of AZ 90, about 24 miles south of I-10. *By air:* **Sierra Vista Municipal Airport** (520-458-5775), 1800 Airport Dr.

WHEN TO COME High season is spring, when the weather is mild and major bird activity starts. The birding doesn't slow until October. Then the secondary birding season begins and lasts through winter.

MEDICAL EMERGENCY **Sierra Vista Regional Health Center** (520-458-4641), 300 El Camino Real.

✷ To See

Arizona Folklore Preserve (520-378-6165). Go 6 miles south on AZ 92, then turn west onto Ramsey Canyon Rd.; go 3.5 miles. State balladeer Dolan Ellis first thought of opening the preserve in the Phoenix area. And then he experienced Ramsey Canyon in the Huachuca Mountains, fell in love with the canyon's beauty, and thought it the perfect place to fulfill his dream of creating a venue where the songs and stories celebrating Arizona and western heritage and culture could be performed and preserved. The preserve is nonprofit, and admission charges are considered a donation. $15 adults, $6 age 17 and under.

Fort Huachuca Historical Museum (520-533-5736), Buildings 41401 and 41305, Fort Huachuca. Open weekdays 9–4, weekends 1–4; closed Thanksgiving, Christmas, and New Year's days. This national landmark and old (established 1877) military complex still operates. You can peruse the grounds and check out two museums. This one tells the story of the U.S. Army on the southwestern frontier. One of the most endearing parts of the history is the segment of the Buffalo Soldiers—African American regiments who patrolled the frontier and its rawboned characters. The Buffalo Soldiers also fought in Mexico and trained infantrymen for World War II combat. Today the fort has evolved into the army's intelligence center. The **U.S. Army Intelligence Museum** (Building 41411) presents the axiom that "Intelligence Is for Commanders," currently the cornerstone of U.S. Army intelligence doctrine. Exhibits discuss how the idea developed over the past 200 years. Both museums are free.

AN ANGEL STATUE AT SIERRA VISTA'S OUR LADY OF THE SIERRAS SHRINE

Murray Springs Clovis Site (520-439-6400). Take AZ 90 about 5 miles east of town, then turn north onto Moson Rd. and follow the signs. When a University of Arizona excavation team found a Clovis Point (a fluted spear point crafted by the Clovis Culture more than 11,000 years ago) here, they had no idea it was only the tip of the iceberg. The site turned out to be an undisturbed cache of a stratigraphic record in time. The team found 15 more Clovis Points dating back some 11,000 years, along with bones of several extinct animals, tools, and a hearth. Free.

Our Lady of the Sierras Shrine (520-378-2950), located in Hereford off AZ 92; turn west onto Stone Ridge (near mile marker 333), and right again onto Prince Placer; turn left onto Twin Oaks Rd. to the parking area. You might notice the shrine's 75-foot-high Celtic cross in the foothills of the Huachuca Mountains from the highway. You can view it up close at its 5,300-foot elevation when you walk the steps up several hundred feet to the shrine inspired by a religious event in Medjugorje, Yugoslavia. The shrine provides an inspiring view and a quiet place to contemplate—even experience a miracle. Some visitors have noted unexplained healings. A stone chapel includes an antique Spanish cross, wooden beams hand hewn in the 1830s over the doors and windows, vigil candles, chairs, and an altar. Free.

✷ To Do

GHOST TOWNS **Fairbank Historic Townsite**. Contact the Bureau of Land Management. Located on AZ 82 at the San Pedro River. Open 24 hours. At this historic railroad stop, you'll learn that the history along the San Pedro is just as prevalent, and colorful, as the birds. Mills that once operated 24 hours a day—as did the brothels and bars—kept the river a lively place. The spot is now quiet, with abandoned adobe buildings and the foundation remains of the post office, a general store, the Montezuma Hotel, a schoolhouse, and a saloon. You can only imagine what life might have been like. Free.

BIRDING

One of the top hot spots in the nation, constantly showing up on the radar of bird watchers around the world, Sierra Vista sees birders flying in at the mere mention of sighting to eye a life-list bird. The spring migration peaks between late April and early May. The best time span to see tropical species such as hummingbirds, trogans, warblers, and flycatchers is from mid-Apr.–Sep. In late summer, monsoon storms coax a wide array of wildflowers that attract hummingbirds and butterflies. Migrating birds pluck seeds, fruits, and insects from the area. Hot spot canyons include **Ash Canyon** and its namesake trail (see Huachuca Mts. in *Wilder Places*). The **Ash Canyon B&B** (see *Lodging*) opens its bird feeding area to the public from dawn to dusk daily for a donation (hummingbirds burn through 7 pounds of sugar a day during peak season). You might catch sight of a plain-capped starthroat or Lucifer's hummingbirds here. Owner-innkeeper Mary Jo Ballator will elucidate about the birds at the feeders and in the area. **Miller Canyon** and its namesake trail has harbored a number of rare birds; and **Beatty's Guest Ranch** (see *Lodging*) holds the record for largest variety of hummingbirds in a day (15 in 2002), where they like to sip from the property's public hummingbird feeders. White-eared hummingbirds are exclusives here. **Carr Canyon** (520-378-0311). Take AZ 90 to Carr Canyon Rd., and turn west; go 8.5 miles to the campgrounds. **Carr House Visitor Center** in Carr Canyon has exhibits, trails and native plantings for hummingbirds and butterflies. The **Southeastern Arizona Bird Observatory (SABO)** conducts regular bird walks in spring and summer in the canyon. Call for dates and times. **San Pedro Riparian Conservation Area** (see *Wilder Places*) Everything they say about birding here is true, especially if you go during migration times, when you'll see a variety of the more than 330 species of birds recorded there. Bring your life list. **Ramsey Canyon Nature Preserve** (520-378-2785) (see *Wilder Places*). Favorite haunt of birders and other naturalists for more than a century. **Sierra Vista Wastewater Wetlands** (520-458-5775). Take AZ 90 3.1 miles east of Fry Blvd. Open Mon–Fri: 7–3:30. Three ponds, part of a pilot project to test natural treatment of secondary sewer effluent, attract thousands of waterfowl, shorebirds, rails, raptors, and songbirds with their lush aquatic vegetation.

Charleston and Millville. Contact the Bureau of Land Management. Located just downriver (north) of the Charleston Road bridge along the San Pedro River. The river's present peaceful demeanor gives no clue of the raucous mining-town life here in the 1880s, the heyday of silver mines in nearby Tombstone. While the West's legendary heroes, bad men, and brazen ladies converged in Tombstone, a rougher breed rumored to be even more ruthless congregated here in the adobe

BIRDWALKS

Casa de San Pedro (see *Lodging*) has tours guided by SABO every Tuesday morning during April and May; reservations required for nonguests. The **San Pedro River Inn** (see *Lodging*) offers guided bird walks every Wednesday and second Sun. each month. Call in advance. **San Pedro Riparian National Conservation Area** (520-439-6400) has guided bird walks Jan–Apr.; call for dates and times. **Ramsey Canyon Nature Preserve** (520-378-2785) (see *Wilder Places*); call for scheduled walks. **Sierra Vista Wastewater Wetlands** (520-458-5775). Take AZ 90 3.1 miles east of Fry Blvd. Guided bird walks on Sundays.

ruins of Charleston. If, as the saying goes, Tombstone was "too tough to die," Charleston was too mean to live. Farther upriver at Brunkow's Cabin, the bloodshed got worse. The tiny shack known as the Bloodiest Cabin in Arizona hosted at least 21 murders.

HIKING **Arizona Trail** (602-252-4794). The 800-mile trail gets its start at Coronado National Memorial on the Crest Trail, located across the parking area at Montezuma Pass. Contact the Sierra Vista Ranger District for trail conditions.

The **Huachuca Mountains**, among the great hiking spots in the state, have a beautiful network of trails that take you through canyons and up mountaintops. Check out the **Hamburg Trail** for one of the most scenic hikes in the area, **Comfort Springs** and **Carr Peak** trails for excellent wildflower activity from mid-July through Aug., and the **Scheelite Canyon** and **Miller Canyon** trails for spectacular autumn color in late Oct. Contact the Sierra Vista Ranger District for more information.

HORSEBACK RIDING **Buffalo Corral Riding Stables** (520-533-5220), located in Fort Huachuca. You can rent a horse by the hour or the month. Guided tours into the Huachuca Mountains are available as well. The stable has a horse for all skill levels. If you're around in Oct. and an experienced rider, you can join the annual ride to Tombstone. Call for more information.

HUMMINGBIRD BANDING (See sidebar next page) Sierra Vista, the Hummingbird Capital of the United States, has a wealth of hummers sipping on the incredible diversity of vegetation in the area. You can watch the fascinating process of banding these little ones at several places July–Oct. Call the Convention and Visitor's Bureau for locations.

MOUNTAIN BIKING The area has a number of dirt roads and singletrack routes to explore, especially in the Huachuca Mountains. Contact Sierra Vista Visitor Center for a map, and the Sierra Vista Ranger Station for information. The **Dawn to Dust Mountain Bike Club** (520-458-0685; www.dawntodustmountainbikeclub.org) leads medium to difficult rides.

HUMMINGBIRD BANDING

"She's a wiggler," declares Sheri Williamson, research director at San Pedro House as she gently maneuvers a squirming runt of a hummer in her hands. "She's a survivor."

Miss Little Bit will have to be. During the routine examination and recording of gender, weight, beak and fat measurements, and overall health, Williamson discovers the top and bottom parts of the bird's bill don't match. This will make sipping from flowers impossible. "She'll need feeders to accommodate her scissor bill, and they're hard to come by in Mexico where she's heading for the winter."

Nevertheless, Miss Little Bit continues to amaze Williamson as much as she fights her. The tiny bird has more fat than most of the others, and weighs 3.9 grams—several grams more than most others banded that day. Her heartbeat, which sounds like static at 1,000 beats per minute, is strong.

The little bird absolutely charms all who watch. The banding process has everyone absorbed and happy.

"Who wants to release her?" Williamson asks as she stations Miss Little Bit at a feeder.

Everyone does. Williamson eyes a little girl and puts Miss Little Bit in her hand for release. The crowd watches as the antsy bird takes off immediately then sends up a cheer in the hopes the handicapped bird will do well on the difficult journey of life ahead.

MULTIUSE PATHS The city has several 10-foot-wide paved trails for walking, running, and biking. Check out the paths along Buffalo Soldier Trail, Martin Luther King, Avenida Cochise, and AZ 92. Contact the visitor center for more information and maps.

NATURE WALKS **Interpretive River Walks** (520-439-6400). Walk 2–3 miles along the San Pedro River and learn about the river, its natural history, and its endangered existence. Call for dates and times; meet at San Pedro House. Donations accepted.

Ramsey Canyon Preserve (520-378-4952) offers walks Mar.–Oct. on Tue., Thu., and Sat. at 9 AM. The preserve opens to the public at 8 AM. Call ahead to confirm walk dates.

STARGAZING University of Arizona South, Patterson Observatory (520-458-8278) is open to the public for special gazing events. Call for information and reservations.

✷ Wilder Places

Huachuca Mountains. The sky island range of the Huachuca Mountains, part of the Madrean Archipelago, has a rich mélange of wildlife activity: birds, insects, butterflies, and animals. These peaks draw rare plants and animals that thrive there while they struggle in other locations.

You can hike all but the mountains' uppermost trails, which get snow in winter, through most of the year. But certain seasons have different attractions—birds migrate in spring and fall, butterflies and hummingbirds proliferate in summer when wildflowers peak, and late autumn brings exquisite color to the canyons and mountaintops. Contact Sierra Vista Ranger District for more information.

Coronado National Memorial (520-366-5515). Visitor center open 9–5. From Sierra Vista, go south on AZ 92 and turn south onto Coronado Memorial Rd. You won't get to walk the path the great explorer Francisco Vásquez de Coronado took when he started out from his Mexican base on a wintry Sunday morning leading a flamboyant entourage of 225 caballeros, 60 infantry, a thousand Native helpers, some women and children, and a handful of servants dressed in garments ranging from chain mail and bull hide to brightly colored festival frocks and body paint. But you will see, from a distance, the San Pedro Valley where the troop was believed to pass. You can explore on several trails. The Crest Trail takes you to the top of Miller Peak where the views are big. The visitor center has a small museum with exhibits explaining the history of the Coronado expedition. The scenic overlook at Montezuma Pass shows great panoramas of the San Pedro and San Rafael Valleys as well as Mexico. Free.

Ramsey Canyon Preserve (520-378-2785). From Sierra Vista, go south on AZ 92 for about 7 miles, past Fry Rd., and turn west onto the signed turnoff. Open Feb.–Oct., daily 8–5; Nov.–Jan., Thu.–Mon. 9–4, Sat. and Sun. 8–5; closed Thanksgiving, Christmas, and New Year's days. Owned by the Nature Conservancy, where land protection reigns. The 300 acres located midmountain present excellent birding opportunities from Apr. through Sept. You can access the **Ramsey Canyon Trail** here. $5 adults, under age 16 free, and the preserve is free to all on the first Sat. of every month. A pass is valid for 1 week from the date of purchase.

San Pedro Riparian National Conservation Area. Contact the Bureau of Land Management. This sanctuary, located on the upper San Pedro River, is the most extensive riparian ecosystem remaining in the desert Southwest. The river still nurtures a lively lineup of wildlife influenced by the Rocky Mountains and Sierra Madre. Almost 400 species of birds, 180 species of butterflies, 87 species of mammals, and 68 species of amphibians and reptiles give the San Pedro the greatest diversity of vertebrate species in the continental United States, and the second greatest diversity of land mammals in the world (the mountains of Costa Rica rank first). You can see an incredible array of these mammals in the 40-mile-long segment of this natural area. Free.

✷ Lodging

SUITES **Sierra Suites** (520-459-4221), 391 E. Fry Blvd. This southwestern-style inn is packed with amenities, including a pool and spa, fitness center, and meeting space. Each room has a refrigerator and microwave, free local calls, free WiFi, pay-per-view TV, and coffee. Continental breakfast included. $79–89.

BED & BREAKFASTS **Ash Canyon Bed and Breakfast** (520-378-0773), 5255 Spring Rd., Hereford. You're pretty much in the center of birding activity at this B&B. Located on an Important Bird Area, it's one of the hot spots where more than 144 species are sighted through the year. It's also located near several hiking trails, and plenty of wildlife congregates around the 6.5 acres the straw-bale casita sits on. The casita has a kitchenette, dining area, queen bed, sofa, and bath. The kitchenette is fully stocked, from coffee grinder to electric frying pan, and includes an assortment of breakfast foods to create your own breakfast whenever you want it. Reverse osmosis provides water for drinking and ice. Well-behaved kids are welcome, but no pets. Call for rates.

Beatty's Miller Canyon Guest Ranch & Orchard (520-378-2728), 2173 E. Miller Canyon Rd., Hereford. Beatty's claim to fame is the variety of hummingbirds that gather at the property's public feeders—the most species (15) ever sighted in the area in 2002. Plus, the property sits right above the trailhead of the Miller Canyon Trail—one of the more beautiful routes in the Huachuca Mountains. Six cabins are available, three turn-of-the-20th-century and three newly built, with breakfast. $80–120.

♥ **Casa de San Pedro** (520-366-1300), 8933 S. Yell Lane, Hereford. Located away from the city along the San Pedro River, this distinctive property is a favorite among bird watchers and guests seeking peaceful and natural accommodations. Xeriscaped gardens contain colorful flowers and fountains to attract hummingbirds and butterflies, so you need not venture far to see them. Each of the 10 guest rooms has hand-carved Mexican furniture, a private bath, a patio, a king or two double beds, telephone (local calls free), and complimentary high-speed Internet access. The property has a ramada with a gas barbecue open to guest use. Out front, you can walk the Four Elements Labyrinth. Breakfast starts with shade-grown coffees and herbal teas, then progresses to a full-blown gourmet meal complete with fresh-baked goods, entrée, fruit, and juices to the sounds of Gershwin (or other classical favorites) in the background. Afternoon goodies include home-baked pies and assorted snacks and beverages. $160–175.

Ramsey Canyon Inn (520-378-3010), Ramsey Canyon Road. Ask any serious birder about Ramsey Canyon, and they'll tell you the chasm has some of the best displays of hummingbirds in the state. "It amazing how many come by the sixteen to twenty feeders," owner/innkeeper, Shirlene said. "They swarm like bees." That's exactly what guests expect when they stay at the world-famous inn. In July, the 15 species of hummers sip through enough sugar water to use up 50 pounds of sugar each week. This avian cloud draws all kinds of people to the inn. You're just as apt to have breakfast with a scientist as a next-door neighbor stopping by for a bite. More than 300 species of birds have been sighted; spotting 95 during a few days' stay is not unusual. But birds aren't the only draw to this forested sanctuary. Guest gush all the time about how magical it is and downright restorative. "Nature heals," Shirlene insisted. Then again, her homemade pies can make you feel pretty good, too. She plucks the fruit from her orchards or buys from local growers to make apple, plum, rhubarb, apricot, peach, and/or pear pies each day. Coffee is fresh roasted from a company in Tucson. The rest of the breakfast is gourmet and fresh and local as she can get it. Six rooms $133–150, two suites $150–225. Kids under age 16 allowed only in suites. No pets.

✷ Where to Eat

DINING OUT The German Café (520-456-1705), 1805 Paseo San Luis. Open for lunch Tue.–Sat. 11–2, dinner Thu.–Sat. 5–8. Owners Peter and Brigitte Volger present a totally German experience in a town where the world meets (because of Fort Huachuca). The menu lists items in German with an English translation: Bratwurst mit Katoffelsalat und Sauerkraut or fried sausage with potato salad and sauerkraut, and Berliner Gulasch mit Spätzle or Berlin goulash with noodles. You can get sides of all the German favorites (noodles, red cabbage, sauerkraut, bread and butter), and desserts (from cheese to rum cake). The Volgers make everything in-house. Entrées $8–13.

Mesquite Tree (520-378-2758), 6398 S. AZ 92. Open for dinner Tue.–Sat. 5–9, Sun. 5–8). When the locals get in the mood for a steak, they head here. Steak, seafood, ribs—it's all here and all pretty descent. Desserts register in the rich category. The building, over 150 years old, was originally a gambling hall called Fletcher's Roundup. The owner, the story goes, was shot in the building and comes back now and again to haunt the place. Entrées $15–25.

The Outside Inn (520-378-4645), 4907 S. AZ 92. Open Mon.–Fri. 11–1:30 and 5–9, Sat. 5–9. Located in a restored home and set back from the highway, it's a favorite fine-dining spot for the locals. The low-lit dining room retains a bit of elegance when the place gets lively, which is often. The food, generally good and thoughtfully prepared, has gourmet touches. Salmon and filet mignon are favorites, as well as chicken champagne and Mediterranean chicken. Entrées $12.95–15.95.

♥ **Peacock Authentic Vietnamese Cuisine** (520-459-0095), 80 S. Carmichael Ave. Open Tue.–Fri. 11–9, Sat. and Sun. 4–8. One of the town's best restaurants (family-owned and -operated) serves a variety of Asian fare. The plain storefront belies the elegant setup inside with white tablecloths and candles. Mom cooks each of the 90 items on the menu from scratch; Dad and the kids serve. The most popular dishes include a variety of curries and sautéed chicken with lemongrass. Entrées $8.95–16.95.

EATING OUT Bobke's Bread Basket (520-458-8580), 355 W. Wilcox Drive. Open Mon.–Fri. 6 AM–5 PM; lunch served 11–2. Not everything at this authentic German bakery is all Bavarian cream and butter. Although Peter Bobke does create some outstanding German treats, which draws people from every walk of life through the bakery's doors, his wife, Michelle, who insists processed foods are the bane of mankind's existence, makes some healthy salads, soups, and sandwiches (even the sausages are very fresh) for lunch. Now, back to the bakery—do not miss the Beehives (a rich Bavarian cream sandwiched between two layers of a coarse, buttery cake) and cheese bars made with quark, or the macaroons, almond horns, Danish, or marzipan kugel dipped in chocolate; after all Peter spent all night (10:30 PM–8 AM) making them for you. Lunch entrées 6.95–8.50, yummies $1.75–2.75.

The Real Taco (520-458-0224), 45 S. Garden Ave. Open Mon.–Fri. 10–5. Everyone says Luiz and Oralia Quijano have the best beans in town. "People come in just to have our burritos," Luiz says. People also say they have the best chips in town. "It's the tortilla"—handmade, which they buy in Cananea Mexico—"and we fry them in vegetable oil." Everything there is pretty special. The chicken is skinless and boneless breast cooked in lemon butter or in its own juice. The steak is real. Sauces are made from scratch. And they make the hard shells for tacos every day. A woman makes special-order green corn tamales in the summer and red chile with beef tamales in the winter. The Quijanos food is world famous—a customer from Germany takes some *chimichangas* with him when he flies home to the Motherland. $1.95–8.95.

✷ Selective Shopping

Fort Huachuca Thrift Store (520-458-4606). Located in Fort Huachuca. Open Tue. and Thu. 9:30–3, and first Sat. of the month 9:30–1:30. One's man's treasure is another one's trash, but at this thrift shop treasures come from military families who have lived all over the world. The store has a loyal following, and some folks spend the whole day seeking their treasures here, which often come at bargain prices. The store is run completely by volunteers and all profits go to local schools, groups, and charities.

✷ Special Events

January: **Sierra Vista Senior Games** (520-458-7922). If you're 50 or older, you're welcome to partake in the competition events.

February: **Cochise Cowboy Poetry and Music Gathering** (www.cowboypoets.com). The Old West comes to life through song, poetry, and stories.

August: **Hummingbird Banding** at the San Pedro House (520-432-1388). This is an ongoing event through September where you watch biologists catch, band, record data about, and release hummingbirds. **Southwest Wings Birding and Nature Festival** (520-432-3554), Arizona's longest-running birding festival, has four days of birding and nature workshops and programs.

October: **Art in the Park** (www.huachuca-art.com). The premier art event of Sierra Vista, this fine art and crafts show features more than 200 booths of original artwork, furniture, jewelry, clothing, and sculptures. **Oktoberfest** (520-458-7922). Come to imbibe massive quantities of beer, eat mountainous amounts of bratwurst and sing "Ein Prozit der Gemutlichkeit."

November: **Festival of Color** (520-417-6960). Around 30 brightly colored balloons participate in this hot-air balloon rally.

December: **Holiday Parade** (520-458-6940). Family-oriented fun to start the mood for the holidays. **Holiday Tour of the Officers' Homes, Fort Huachuca/Sierra Vista** (520-417-6960). View beautifully decorated homes built at the turn of the 20th century at Fort Huachuca. Soldiers dressed in period uniforms greet visitors at each historic home. No kids under age 10.

BISBEE

The first Distinctive Destination Award given by the National Trust for Historic Preservation to an Arizona town went to Bisbee. The terraced community is a bundle of Old World culture and Old West individualism. Counterculture influences play pleasantly with the classic beauty of Greek, Romanesque, Renaissance Revival, Mediterranean, Victorian, and art deco architecture to produce a quirky charisma that actually invites visitors to join in the fun.

Known as the Queen of the Copper Camps, the mineral-rich mining town didn't stop at copper, not its biggest draw even at 8 billion tons. The area produced more gold, silver, and lead than any other mining district. It took little more than a couple of decades for this fast-living mining town to find its place among the nation's cosmopolitan cities. Soon after the turn of the 20th century, Bisbee ranked the largest city between St. Louis and San Francisco. Its Brewery Gulch mining camps won the distinction as the liveliest spots between El Paso and San Francisco, with nearly 50 saloons and who knows how many shady ladies.

By the mid-1970s, though, large-scale mining had hit the skids in Bisbee, and the town's glory started to evanesce—a denouement some liken to Rome in its last days. The counterculture, drawn by affordable housing with beautiful architecture, breathed life back into the city with their art, however homespun it might have seemed at the time. What looks hippie retro to the present-day visitor is actually the town's prevailing personality from the '70s, not a retro movement.

The National Trust for Historic Preservation put Bisbee on its 2005 list of America's Dozen Distinctive Destinations, honoring unique and lovingly preserved communities in the United States. Although Bisbee has reclaimed some of the culture for which it was famous a century ago, it's still quirky after all these years.

GUIDANCE The **Bisbee Visitor Center** (520-432-3554 or 866-224-7233) has information on Bisbee's events, attractions, and accommodations. Stop by for a brochure detailing two self-guided, historic walking tours that feature historic buildings and architectural influences. One tour goes up Brewery Gulch, where the miners' shadows came out to play; the other features the downtown area where they boasted openly about their riches.

GETTING THERE Bisbee is the southern point of AZ 90 and almost at the tail end of AZ 80. Just head south on either road from I-10 to reach the town a few miles north of the Mexican border.

GETTING AROUND **Bisbee Trolley Tours** trace the path of the Warren-Bisbee Railway, which began operating in 1908. As the trolley traverses the steep streets, guides recount anecdotes about historic times in Bisbee and its outskirts. Tours depart Copper Queen Plaza (just south of the historical museum) at 9:30, 11, 1, 2:30, and 4 daily. $10 adults, $7 age 10 and under.

WHEN TO COME Located at 5,300 feet, Bisbee is comfortable just about any time of year. Late fall through spring is high season, but summer is the best-kept secret. Highs may hover around 90, but afternoon thunderstorms cool things down and add some atmospheric drama, then the nights settle into the 60s. Couple that with fewer tourists and lower rates, and you might end up preferring the low season.

MEDICAL EMERGENCY For hospital services, **Copper Queen Community Hospital** (520-432-5383), 7 Bisbee Rd.; for outpatient services, **Chiricahua Community Health Center** (520-432-3309), 108 Arizona St.

* To See

Bisbee Mining and Historical Museum (520-432-7071), 5 Copper Queen Plaza. Open daily 10–4. This museum was the first western affiliate of the Smithsonian Institution. Take a look at how Bisbee got started through changing exhibit displays that showcase numerous artifacts from the mining days explaining the macrocosm of Bisbee: why it happened, who lived here, and what the social issues of the day were. History starts to make sense here. Once you learn about daily life in Bisbee, you'll never again complain about having to walk up a steep hill or an endless set of concrete steps to get around town. $7.50 adults, $6.50 age 60-plus, $3 under age 16.

RESIDENTIAL ART IN BISBEE

Copper Queen Library (520-432-4232), 6 Main St. Open Mon. and Wed. noon–7, Tue., Thu., and Fri. 10–5, Sat. 10–2. Opened when Arizona was still a territory in 1882, not only is this the state's oldest library, but it may have the most interesting inception as well. As the story goes, when mining magnates showed up in town one day and saw a hung corpse swaying in the breeze, they swiftly decided the town needed a strong dose of Christian and cultural distractions. The opening of the Copper Queen Library in a corner grocery store promptly followed. It worked. By 1920 more than 260 people visited the library each day.

Evergreen Cemetery, located just south of Old Bisbee. Listed on the National Register of Historic places, you'll see some interesting gravestones here belonging to Bisbee's influential residents. The graves were moved from their original home in Brewery Gulch when typhoid fever broke out from contaminated well water. Free.

Queen Mine Tour (520-432-2071). Tours available daily at 9, 10:30, noon, 2, and 3:30. A cool 47 degrees year-round, the bonanza copper mine comes alive in this tour, given by retired miners who lend an air of authenticity as they describe working conditions and relate personal anecdotes about working in the mine. A mini train takes you, clothed in yellow rain gear, helmet, and headlamp, into the bowels of the mountain via the Queen Mine Shaft, and you see firsthand how they blasted and stabilized the mine while they excavated ore. They'll tell you how old-timers made a life underground. You'll view the cars, the drilling equipment, and the vertical shaft with its cage, a.k.a. elevator. $12 adults, $5 ages 4–15.

St. Patrick's Church (520-432-5753), 100 Quality Hill Rd. One of the remedies for the bawdy behavior in Bisbee's early years, this Roman Catholic Gothic Revival church (listed on the National Register of Historic Places) copies St. Mary's Catholic Church in Whitehaven, England. Of special interest are the 27 windows designed in 1917 by Emil Frei, the world-class master designer of Victorian-style stained glass. Each, a masterpiece, is created from lead crystal glass. Free.

✷ To Do

BIRDING The **Southeastern Arizona Bird Observatory** (SABO) (520-432-1388), a nonprofit scientific and educational organization, leads tours, workshops, seminars, and trips throughout fall and winter that share the fascination of winged creatures. Feeding areas attract birds for an up-close-and-personal experience. The organization offers half-day and full-day guided walks, tours, and personalized guide services. Take AZ 80 West (north) 2 miles past the Mule Pass Tunnel to the turnoff on the left.

Wezil Walraven Bird Tours (520-432-4697). Wezil Walraven, a professional bird guide, leads you on owl and bird-watching tours in the area throughout the year. Call for information.

COOKING SCHOOL You can create your own homemade masterpieces at the **Bisbee Cooking School** (520-432-3203) under the direction of owner Helen Saul, a professional chef. She teaches four styles of cuisine—French, Italian, Cajun, and Creative Southwest. Only six people participate in each class, which emphasizes the background of recipes, the ingredients that go into them, and having fun. The best part is indulging in the dish you've created at a sit-down meal,

THE STREETS OF OLD BISBEE

including the appropriate wine. Prices include all materials. Call for class schedules. $48 per class.

GOLF Turquoise Valley Golf Course (520-432-3091), 794 W. Newell St., Naco. Open every day but Christmas. This course takes you way back in Arizona golf history; it's the oldest continuously run course in the state. Built in 1937, the course features undulating bent grass greens and rolling Bermuda fairways. Holes 10 through 18, built in 1999, head into the high-desert terrain for some challenge and true desert course action. Watch for the par-6, 727-yard Rattler (said to be the longest golf hole in Arizona) and water hazards on holes 1 and 16. Bar, restaurant, and pro shop on the grounds. $25–50.

GHOSTS 🐾 Old Bisbee Ghost Tour (520-432-3308). Fri.–Sun. 7 PM. The 90-minute walking tour takes you through Old Bisbee's alleys, streets, and stairways to hunt the haunted haunts. $13 adults, $9 under age 12. On the last Saturday of every month at 6 PM, you can join **The Old Bisbee Haunted Pub Crawl**. Choose your spirits at each of the four "spookiest bars" as you learn about their spirits. The tour lasts about 3 hours. $20, over age 21 only!

JEEP TOURS Lavender Jeep Tours (520-432-5369), 1 Copper Queen Plaza. Bisbee's history is fascinating enough inside its city limits, but once you get outside, you experience a whole other form of wild. It doesn't take long to get into the backcountry, and these jeep tours teach you all about the areas they take you to: the Sky Island Adventure takes you through several biological zones as you climb up to 7,400 feet; the Back Roads of Bisbee winds 90 minutes on the narrow, twisting back roads; the Mining Landscape Tour explores the whole Warren Mining District. $35–95 per person.

✷ Spas and Massages

Monsoon Face and Body (520-432-6868), 33 Subway. This spa offers a compendium of therapies: therapeutic massage, shiatsu, Reiki, facials, and 90-minute yoga classes. Hair care includes styled cuts and Goldwell color treatment. Asian-inspired boutique. Massage $85–105, facials $65.

Warm Hands Therapeutics (520-432-5139), 27 Subway St. Licensed massage therapist Nick Night brings the therapy back to the massage. Using skilled techniques to separate and mobilize muscles, vessels and fascia, Nick releases tensions and pains you might not even realize you have. This is because he specializes in relaxation and treatment massage, LaStone Therapy, sacred Lomi Lomi, and craniosacral therapy. All allow release of deeply buried energies. Nick uses a blend of organic jojoba oil and Nature's Gate moisturizing lotion to nourish the skin. $60–120.

✷ Lodging

HOTELS AND SUITES Copper Queen Hotel (520-432-2216), 11 Howell Ave. Built by Copper Queen Consolidated Mining Company to accommodate its East Coast executives, the hotel was the most elegant of its time. Some of its guests from decades past still roam the three floors. Julia Lowell, one of three ghosts who show up occasionally, has a namesake room on the third floor. The hotel management thinks she might be the strange lady in a long black dress and veil who stops clocks, appears half naked on the grand staircase clutching a bottle, whispers to men in the elevator, tinkers with lights, and opens windows. Each room's décor remains historic, and each is different. Some have clawfoot tubs, while all have heat, air-conditioning, telephone, cable TV, and private bath. The property includes a second-floor outdoor swimming pool as well as the **Winchester Restaurant** and **Old West Saloon**. $89–197 double occupancy, $15 per extra person.

Letson Loft Hotel (520-432-3210 or 877-432-3210), 26 Main St. Located in the Letson Block—the oldest brick building and only authentic Victorian structure in Bisbee—this hotel has a well-done blend of Old World interiors with modern amenities. The second-floor hotel has four rooms in front with bay windows to watch the street scenes below, a kitchenette, and a suite. Some have authentic skylight or clawfoot tub; all are spacious. Antique furnishings give a period feel. A lounge gives guests a place to hang out with friends or for business meetings. Rooms have private bath, Lofty Beds with goose-down pillows and blankets, complimentary WiFi, flat-screen TV, air-conditioning and heat controls, authentic wood floors, and 11-foot ceilings. Light breakfast (such as Brie, apricot, and apple phyllo pockets, coffee and tea) is included with your room. Kids age 12 and older welcome. $95–180.

San Ramon Hotel (520-432-1901), 5 Howell Ave. The big and bright rooms at this renovated hotel

THE COPPER QUEEN HOTEL

give you plenty of space, even if you spend some time in them. Each room has several big windows or skylights. Rooms have private bath, complimentary WiFi, complimentary bottled water, and air-conditioning and heat. Snack on fresh-baked cookies in the lobby. Families with kids welcome. Complimentary off-street parking. $79–155 double occupancy, $10 per extra person.

BED & BREAKFASTS AND INNS

Calumet & Arizona Guest House (520-432-4815), 608 Powell St. Most visitors to Bisbee have no idea another side of town exists outside the historic downtown called the Warren District. The mining magnates and families lived in this area while the miners ballyhooed in town. This B&B was built in 1906 for the secretary/treasurer of the Calumet & Arizona Mining Company by regionally noted Henry C. Trost. For those who want to experience the elegant side of the period, this is your place. With its exquisite craftsmanship, well-designed architectural details, and period furnishing, the house takes you back in time to a point in Bisbee's more graceful past. Each room has its own special feature—patio spa, fireplace, and gorgeous antiques. A guest kitchen has full-size appliances. Some rooms have period tubs or patio. Owner-innkeeper Joy Timbers serves a made-to-order breakfast, from scratch, with eggs from her own chickens, homemade jellies and jams, and other fresh ingredients at a table for 16 with a seasonal setting fit for a grand holiday feast. Kids are welcome and she loves pets. $60–90 single occupancy, $20 per extra person.

Mayberry's Place (520-234-1252), 318 Tombstone Canyon. Mayberry's Place, built in 1906, was named for the previous owner of the building and town barber Eskar Mayberry. Eskar lived on the top floor of the building and had his barbershop on the bottom floor. In like manner, current owner Donna Burke runs her Red Shoes Hair Salon on the bottom floor. The two-bedroom cabin has queen beds, washer and dryer, full kitchen, cable TV, VHS library, and a small private rear yard and balcony overlooking Tombstone Canyon. $95 double occupancy, $25 per night per extra person, age 10 and under free; small pets okay. Cash or check.

School House Inn (520-432-2996 or 800-537-4333), 818 Tombstone Canyon. This old brick schoolhouse, built in 1918, is located in a residential neighborhood, yet close enough to Old Bisbee's shops and restaurants. The classrooms-turned-guest-rooms and -suites are big, with 12-foot ceilings and private bath. Rooms have full or king beds, complimentary WiFi, and great views of Tombstone Canyon. Guests can use cable TV in the family room and have plenty of off-street parking. Full breakfast included in the rates. $89–149.

Sleepy Dog Guest House (520-432-3057), 212A Opera Dr. Local artist Tad Cheyenne Miller restored this miner's cabin perched on a hillside. The one-bedroom cabin is simple but elegant, full of art and collectibles and gorgeous views. It sits on an acre of land, which makes it quiet and very private. It also makes it perfect for dogs with its enclosed yard, large Frisbee lot, off-leash trails, and designer doggy bowls. For your comfort, the cabin has a king bed with a down and feather bed, luxury linens, and claw-foot bathtub. Informal breakfast and coffee and tea are included in the rates. $125, cash or check only, two-night minimum on weekends. Weekly and monthly rates are available upon request.

OTHER LODGING **Shady Dell RV Park** (520-432-3567), 1 Old Douglas Rd. The Shady Dell opened in 1927 as a trailer park and campground for travelers on AZ 80, which runs from San Diego, California, to Savannah, Georgia. You can still hook up your own RV here, or you can stay in one of a collection on the property, including a 1949 Airstream, 1950 Spartanette, 1950 Spartan Manor, 1954 Crown, and 1951 Royal Mansion. Trailers have a propane stove, refrigerator, electric percolator, dishes, and linens; cassette tapes of big band, early rhythm and blues, and favorite old radio programs you can play in reproduction vintage radios; and period magazines and books. Some trailers have a bath or vintage black-and-white TV and phonographs with vinyl records. Kids over age 10 allowed. $45–130.

✷ Where to Eat

DINING OUT **Bisbee Grille** (520-432-6788), 2 Copper Queen Plaza. Open daily 11–9. One of the few "late-night" venues serves dependably decent food. The menu leans toward the Southwest with steaks, pasta, seafood, and vegetarian entrées. Fine dining starts at 6 PM. Entrées $8.99–21.99.

Café Roka (520-432-5153), 35 Main St. Open at 5 PM for dinner Thu.–Sat. Jazz on Fridays. This local favorite always gets great write-ups, thanks to consistently good food at reasonable prices. Without reservations you may be able to get a seat at the bar, where you can order dinner, but owner-chef, Rod Kass says, "Reservations prevent disappointment." Chef Rod grabs a bit from Italian, California, and new vegetarian cuisines to create his Modern American menu. This is one of the few restaurants in the nation to serve four-course meals (soup, salad, sorbet, and entrée) without going prix fixe. Tastes teeter-totter—crunchy/soft, tangy/sweet, spicy/muted, or subtle/rousing—to keep your palate's attention. The changing menu has several vegetarian dishes that will capture your attention. Desserts are made in-house. Entrées $16.50–26.50.

Rosa's Little Italy (520-432-1331), 7 Bisbee Rd. Dinner Fri.–Sun. 5–9; reservations required. While the trendy Italian restaurants focus on Mediterranean meals, Rosa keeps to her classic Sicilian cuisine. Everything is house made and it's all good. She's mastered her menu so delectably, just about anything you order will come to the table tasting just as delicious as the last time. If this is your first time, be warned: Rosa's meals come big. Two dinners can easily feed three people. But you want to have leftovers, so order liberally. Rosa, on the other hand, does not believe in leftovers because, she insists, the food is not as good the next day. So, she only makes one pan of her lasagna, which you must place dibs on when you make your reservation (an absolute necessity because her clientele not only have their favorite booth, but their favorite meals; consistency is *big* here). Bring your own wine and beer. Entrées $14.95–20.95.

Santiago's (520-432-1910), 1 Howell Ave. Open daily 11–9. Located at the gateway to Brewery Gulch, where wild and raucous life happened in Bisbee's prime. The brightly colored décor fits the personality of the town. A variety of Mexican provinces inspire the menu, and the food is fresh and good. The signature Rocky Point (fish tacos with corn and rice) is excellent, the Sonoran enchilada has a fried flat *masa* dough, and the fajitas come in pork, chicken, shrimp, or beef. The margaritas have a stellar reputation and may add a bit of old-time Brewery Gulch conviviality to the meal. Entrées $6.95–10.95.

EATING OUT 🏵 **Bisbee Breakfast Club** (520-432-5885), 75A Erie Street, Lowell. Open Thu.–Mon. 7–3. You have to travel just outside Old Town to get to this fabulous breakfast/lunch spot that looks straight off the cover of Super Tramp's Breakfast in America. "This is the kind of building that's disappearing in America," says owner Heather Grimm. She and husband (and chef) Pat put sweat equity into the open and airy diner with distinctive glasswork created by a local artisan. The building, once an old Rexall Pharmacy, may insist diner, but the food says it's a special one. It's a local favorite, and people come from all over the state to eat here. Entrées $3.95–6.95.

Mimosa Market (520-432-3256), 215 Brewery Gulch. Open Mon.–Fri. 7 AM–9 PM, Sat. and Sun. 7 AM–7 PM. This eclectic market has prevailed for the last century as the neighborhood grocery store. Their motto is posted on a sign in the store: NOT EVERYTHING ALWAYS, BUT MOST OF IT A LOT OF THE TIME. It stocks the makings for a perfect picnic featuring the freshest of produce, better beer and wine, and homemade deli items. There are several salads, great cheeses, and wonderful homemade breads. You can also pick up baked chickens, homemade meat loaf, and desserts, or get sandwiches made to order. Come for a hot dinner entrée during the week from 6–9.

THE BISBEE BREAKFAST CLUB

Peddler's Alley (520-432-3733), 17 Main St. Open daily 11–4. Grab a quick bite here in the form of a hot dog, homemade meat loaf, chicken salad sandwich, or chili. If Seth, owner of Bisbee Bean Coffee, is around, you might get a free shot of espresso. $2.75–6.50.

✷ The Arts

You can find art all over the city—from cosmic murals to colorful window covers on the old miners' homes teetering on the steep hillsides to well-polished galleries. Professional and philanthropic **Beeleza Gallery** (520-432-5877), 27 Main St., is owned and operated by the Women's Transition Project, a port in the storm for homeless women and their kids. The gallery features local favorite, established, and emerging artists.

✷ Special Events

March: **Art Auction** (520-432-3554) presents a collection of some of Bisbee's finest artists at the Bisbee Convention Center.

April: **Copper Classic Car Show** (520-432-5421) has food, music, drawings, and lots of dazzle and chrome. **La Vuelta de Bisbee Bicycle Race** (520-432-5795) presents a 3-day staged

A GARGOYLE PEERS FROM HIS PERCH ATOP ONE OF BISBEE'S RESIDENCES

bicycling event that includes time trials, a circuit race, and a road race.

May: **Gem and Mineral Show** (520-432-3554) Find gems from around the world at attractive prices at the Queen Mine Tour.

July: **Fourth of July** (520-432-3554) gives you a chance to take part in mining activities of old, such as mucking and hard rock drilling. Coaster races, parade, and fireworks.

August: **Brewery Gulch Daze** (520-432-3554) you get a taste of the lively atmosphere that once prevailed on Bisbee's liveliest streets—family style, with a pancake breakfast, pet parade, chili cook-off, recycled-art show, kids' carnival games, and skateboard competition.

September: Bisbee's **Blues Festival** (520-432-3554). Warren Field fills with blues bands for the day to raise money for local charities.

October: **Fiber Arts Festival** (520-432-3554) displays more than 30 artists' works made from natural fibers. You can get hands-on fiber experience, too, at workshops. Test your stair-climbing mettle at the **Bisbee 1000 Stair Climb** (520-432-1585), where you get firsthand knowledge of the endurance Bisbee gives its residents via those steep and endless flights of stairs. The **Wine Tasting Festival** (520-432-3554) allows you to taste about 50 different varietals in Brewery Gulch. **Halloween in Bisbee** (520-432-3554) is big; it's one of the city's favorite holidays.

November: The holiday season kicks off at the **Festival of Lights** (520-432-3554). Get an up-close look at some of Bisbee's showcase homes at the **Historic Home Tour** (520-432-3554).

TOMBSTONE

Like many small Arizona towns, Tombstone got its start from precious metal. A relentless, and generally unlucky, prospector named Ed Schieffelin changed his destiny when he poked around the limestone bluffs along the San Pedro River, an area then inflamed with battles among Native Americans, Mexicans, and Anglos. As the story goes, a soldier warned Schieffelin he'd find nothing but his own tombstone. Instead he found a silver lode, big enough for the assayer to say, "You're a lucky cuss." Schieffelin's Lucky Cuss Mine drew a crowd of treasure seekers to Ed's cleverly named town of Tombstone.

The passel of personalities that lived during Tombstone's decades of decadence created a reputation so infamous, the town refuses to die. Many of the main players in Tombstone traveled the whole state following the flow of money to rack in riches from gambling, mines, and business deals. But in Tombstone, where winks, nods, and tolerance allowed outrageous transgressions, the convergence provoked a perfect storm. It's the stuff that creates romance and history today, but at the time could be described as simply raucous and ruthless. Bravado ruled in Tombstone, and its personality grew too big for its own britches. Its aura—a meld of mystique, taboo, and excitement—still wafts from the old buildings and the stories they hold.

GUIDANCE You can pick up a variety of information brochures and purchase tickets for tours at the **Tombstone Visitor Center** (520-457-3929), 4th and Allen Sts.

GETTING THERE From I-10, go south on AZ 80 about 20 miles to the signed turnoff. From Sierra Vista or Bisbee, go east or north, respectively, to AZ 80, turn north, then go 15 miles to the turnoff.

GETTING AROUND The **Tombstone Pharmacy** (520-457-3543), 516 E. Allen St., rents wheelchairs; the **Tombstone General Store** (520-457-3997), 512 E. Allen, rents strollers; and the **American Legion** (520-457-2273), 225 E. Allen, provides free use of wheelchairs to American Legion or VFW members.

WHEN TO COME The season spans Oct.–Mar. With big celebration events going on in October, it's best to make reservations if you plan to stay then.

TOMBSTONE STREETS ARE STILL DUSTY AFFAIRS

MEDICAL EMERGENCY Sierra Vista Regional Health Center (520-458-4641), 300 El Camino Real, Sierra Vista.

✷ To See

Bird Cage Theater Museum (520-457-3421), Allen and 6th. Open daily 8–6. No self-respecting women would be seen anywhere near this dance hall bordello licensed to "Dutch Annie" Smith in 1881 by Cochise County. Anyone with a strong attachment to his or her life stayed away, too. During the bawdy bar's eight-year life, it saw 16 gunfights and 26 deaths; it has 140 bullet holes shot into the walls to prove it. In 1882 the *New York Times* claimed it was "the wildest, wickedest night spot between Basin Street and the Barbary Coast." Randy-minded cowboys, miners, and gamblers gladly paid $25–40 for a bottle of liquor and a gal. The joint was named for the "cages" suspended from the ceiling, where the ladies entertained their customers. You can see part of the bar and get an oration on the history for free. A self-guided tour of the whole building costs $10 adults, $9 seniors and active military, $8 ages 8–18; $28 families with kids up to age 18.

Boothill Graveyard (520-457-3300), AZ 80 just north of Tombstone. Open daily 7:30–6. Some of the town's roughest residents lie here, including the slower draws from the OK Corral shootout. Donations accepted.

OK Corral and Tombstone Historama (520-457-3456 or 800-518-1566), 3rd and 4th Sts. Open daily 9–5. This is where the event took place that made Tombstone immortal: the shootout at the OK Corral between the notorious cowboys and the famous faction of lawmen. You can peruse the museum (the largest in town) and watch a 25-minute multimedia presentation, narrated by Vincent Price, explaining the true history of the town every half hour 9:30–4:30. At 2 PM each day and, additionally, 4 PM on Fri.–Sun. (and for $3.50 extra) you can watch a re-creation of the gunfight that took place near the spot. $5.50.

Rattlesnake Crafts & Rocks (520-642-9207), 10630 N. Doubleuranch Rd., Gleeson (signed turnoff along the road to Gleeson (see *To Do*). Open daily dawn–dusk. When John and Sandy Weber decided to call it quits with the corporate world in 1979, they packed up their belongings, split Rockport, Illinois, and headed west. They ended up in a ghost town, lazing around during the day and hunting rattlesnakes by night. John makes things out of the snakeskins—from wallets to watchbands to cell phone cases; and jewelry from the vertebrae, fangs and rattles. You name it, you'll probably find it in the 150 different items packed in the little trailer that bids the curious and treats everyone as honest (leave your money in the coffee can). True, not everyone is drawn to rattlesnakes or the vipers' hides. But you don't want to miss Memory Lane, an outdoor museum packed with exquisite collections of minerals that will make collectors drool—old bottles, tools, artifacts, cameras, and mass quantities of sundry items of extreme interest.

Rose Tree Museum and Books (520-457-3326), 116 S. 4th St. Open daily 9–5. The 120-plus-year-old Lady Banksia rosebush, which sprawls over 9,000 square feet and has a trunk like a tree, is listed in Guinness World Records as the largest on record. You may catch it full of fragrant blooms in Apr. $5, under age 14 free

Tombstone Epitaph Museum (520-457-2211), 9 S. 5th St. Open daily 9:30–5. Founded in 1880, this notorious and long-running paper published some unique tongue-in-cheek articles (such as about cattle sweating gold dust and nefarious bees taking, instead of making, honey) over the years. It also blared sensational headlines the town generated. The office still has its original presses and equipment, plus archives. Free.

Schieffelin Monument. Located 2.3 miles west of town on Allen St. The man who started all the action lies in repose far away from all the action. The founding father of Tombstone and the Lucky Cuss Mine specifically requested a burial atop the granite hills west of town with "a monument such as prospectors build when locating a mining claim" marking his grave.

Tombstone Western Heritage Museum (520-457-3800), Fremont and 6th St. Mon., Tue., Thu., and Sat. 9–6, Sun. 12:30–6. This private museum has a collection of Wyatt and Virgil Earp personal memorabilia, rare and unique guns, and historic photos. $5 adults, $3 ages 12–18; $13 families.

THE *TOMBSTONE EPITAPH* IS STILL PRINTED

✷ To Do

HISTORIC TOURS In a place as well preserved as Tombstone, you might want to get the facts via a tour. John Rose of **Tombstone & Thunder Valley Tours** (520-378-2539) offers historically accurate tours full of fun and action. The research historian (for 20 years) goes through court records and newspapers to compile his information. He's one of the top collectors of Tombstone and has unusual photographs pertaining to Tombstone (such as a picture of Wyatt Earp as a child). He brings blow-ups of prints on his tours. Call for information.

Old Tombstone Tours (520-457-3018) takes you on tours around town in a stagecoach or covered wagon with a guide announcing the historic high points of the wild times of Tombstone. Tours run 9–5, and you can board them on Allen St. between 4th and 5th sts. $10 adults, $5 ages 5–15, under age 5 free.

HORSEBACK RIDING **Tombstone Livery** Stable (520-457-3559), just past AZ 80 on AZ 82. Trail rides head to spots in the local backcountry, such as Indian rock art and ghost towns. Call for times and prices

SCENIC DRIVE **Ghost Town Trail** (From Tombstone, drive south on AZ 80 to Camino San Rafael (with a sign saying to Gleeson), and turn left; drive across Walnut Gulch to Gleeson Road, and turn right (about 30 miles one-way), Tombstone wasn't the only game in town. The area was littered with mines, and some of them paid handsomely. The ghost town of Gleeson, originally named Turquoise, was a copper town founded around 1890 in the southern tip of the Dragoon Mountains. You can see the old jail, school and a store. The ghost town of Courtland lies a couple miles farther away. The once-thriving copper community has gone the way of the elements almost completely. You'll find only ruins of the 2,000-strong town. Continue farther to the ghost town of Pearce, where John Pearce struck gold in 1894. The Commonwealth Mine produced more than $15 million. Check out the **Old Pearce Mercantile** building. It's open every Thanksgiving weekend for free tours. The **Old Pearce Pottery Shop** is open during the week year-round. The route ends at US 191.

JOE BONO'S STORE ALONG THE GHOST TOWN TRAIL SCENIC DRIVE

✷ Lodging

BED & BREAKFASTS 🐾 **Marie's Engaging Bed and Breakfast** (520-457-3831), 101 N. 4th St. If you want a true (upper-crust) period experience, you've found your room for the night. Originally the John Rock House built in 1906, this is named for its former owner, Marie Detrich, one of the "Ladies of Tombstone" who dressed in full turn-of-the-century regalia. A people lover, she never knew a stranger, and she loved to entertain friends and family in the home. Marie's family, who now owns the house, has decided to keep the same spirit alive. Frilly, fancy, and altogether Victorian, this B&B presents the elegant side of Tombstone with vintage Victorian interiors, antiques, and history. TV for guests in the parlor, and microwave and refrigerator available on patio. Full breakfast included. $70–200. Rates about $30 during events.

✷ Where to Eat

DINING OUT The Longhorn Restaurant (520-457-3405), 501 E. Allen St. Open Mon.–Sat. 7 AM–9 PM, Sun 8 AM–9 PM. Originally the Bucket of Blood Saloon. Virgil Earp (who was shot from the second floor of this building) probably would never believe the establishment has gotten enough respectability to earn repeated awards for their ribs. Specialties include shredded barbecue beef and pork. It's comfort food to the max. Entrées $8.95–18.95, sandwiches $6.50–8.95.

EATING OUT The Patio Restaurant at Big Nose Kate's Saloon (520-457-3107), 417 E. Allen St. Open 11–8. What started as the Grand Hotel, and the place to stay, has evolved into a National Historic Landmark. The bar has an atmosphere that takes you back 125 years. It serves a light menu and is famous for its giant overstuffed Reuben sandwich, huge hamburgers, and tons of legend and lore about the town. $7–8.

✷ Special Events

Contact 520-457-3921 for more information.

April: **Tombstone Old West Founders Days** celebrates the town's founding father, Edward Schieffelin, and his unlikely silver strike with gunslingers, music, mining displays, mucking contest, variety show, and **Rose Festival**. The latter celebrates the bloom of the town's floral mascot, the Lady Banksia rosebush, with a social and parade.

Memorial Day weekend: **Wyatt Earp Days** honors the famous lawman with gunfights, a chili cook-off, mock hangings, an 1880s fashion show, street entertainment, and a Wyatt look-alike contest.

June: **Tombstone Rock & Gem Show** displays gems, jewelry, mineral specimens and fossils. **Tombstone Sweet Onion Festival** features a Taste of Tombstone with music and crowns an Onion Queen.

August: **Vigilante Days** features Tombstone's unique heritage. **Rendezvous of Gunfighters**. Gunfighter groups from around the nation show their talents and costumes.

October: **Corvettes & Ghostriders**. More than 200 Corvettes fill the town for a weekend of fun and festivities. **Helldorado Days** started as the town's golden anniversary in 1929 and has since become a yearly event.

November: **Clanton Days Rendezvous** has a costume contest, historical walking tours, and a ghost tour. **Tombstone Western Music Festival** presents three days of live music on the street and on stage.

PATAGONIA, SONOITA, AND ELGIN

When Arizonans who travel the state talk about their favorite places, the area in the Sonoita Valley (Arizona's premier wine country) and Patagonia Mountains invariably rate high on the list. Folks adore this beautiful countryside of rolling hills with galleries of oaks in a sea of golden or emerald (depending on the season) grasses.

It doesn't take long to experience the classic reaction to open space when you stand in this Empire's countryside, with views so big and far reaching, they swallow you up. At first you feel isolated. Then your soul relaxes into the reality that there are none of the boundaries city folks feel—buildings, privacy fences, strip malls, and sundry responsibilities—restricting you. Highly charismatic with laid-back manners, the place grows on you. Especially if you like to take your days slow and easy, yet fill them with interesting things to do.

The rich grassland landscape bordered by picturesque mountains captured the attention of Hollywood often over the years. More than half a dozen movies were filmed here, as well as two television series. This rich range country sent thousands of head of cattle a day by train to markets in the East decades ago. The cowboy spirit, so attractive to visitors, lingers on the land and just gets more intense when you see it from horseback.

You don't have to be a cowboy, or an equestrian to take to this area. But it helps if you love the outdoors, because there's lots of it. It's a bird watcher's paradise, an oenophile's dream, and an artist's mecca with cutting-edge environmentally sensitive dwellings and organic farming on the rise.

At the end of the day, when thousands of stars seem to swirl in the black ink night sky and the coyote lives up to its nickname of song dog, you can feel as good as the cowboys who ranched here dozens of years ago did—right at home on this classic grassland range.

GUIDANCE **The Patagonia Area Visitor Center** (520-394-0060 or 888-794-0060), 307 McKeown, Patagonia, has a cache of information on this special area, including maps of historic buildings, a vineyard map, area maps, and brochures. The **Nogales Ranger District** (520-281-2296), 303 Old Tucson Rd., Nogales, is open 8–4:30, and can supply information about backcountry use in the Coronado National Forest.

GETTING THERE The only paved highways that approach and travel through the Mountain Empire are AZ 82 and AZ 83.

WHEN TO COME Most visitors wait for winter to travel to this area. However, the land doesn't have its spring–summer verdancy then. Casual visitors should consider traveling during spring through fall: after a wet winter the grasslands are gorgeous, summer rates are attractive, and fall colors turn riparian forests along the creeks golden. If you plan outdoor activities and are from a cooler climate, wait until Oct.–Mar.

MEDICAL EMERGENCY Dial 911.

✷ To See

SCENIC DRIVES This highly romantic landscape begs for a leisurely drive or two. You can travel these routes via sedan, road bicycle, or motorcycle. Just remember to include in your driving time extra moments for gawking; the routes are that scenic: **Patagonia-Sonoita Scenic Byway** (AZ 82: 52 miles from I-10 to Nogales), road to **Parker Canyon Lake** (AZ 83: 32 miles from Sonoita to Parker Canyon Lake), and **San Rafael Valley** (approximately a 50-mile loop on paved and graded gravel roads).

✷ To Do

BIRDING Wherever you are in the area Apr.–Oct., especially the spring and fall migration, you're in for a treat. Located right next to and near flyways where 300 to 400 different species of birds have appeared, the area gives birders a chance to check off a few from their life lists. Your best bet for sightings is to get right into the middle of the action in the **Patagonia-Sonoita Creek Preserve** or one of the area's lakes (see *Wilder Places*).

THERE'S GORGEOUS SCENERY IN THE SAN RAFAEL VALLEY

FISHING **Parker Canyon and Patagonia Lakes** (see *Wilder Places*) get stocked with a variety of fish.

HIKING The nearby **Santa Rita Mountains** have a large network of trails that travel in oak woodlands up to pine forests. Contact the Nogales Ranger District.

Arizona Trail (www.aztrail.org). You only have to travel 3 miles outside Patagonia to access the historic Arizona Trail, which runs from Mexico to Utah.

The **Patagonia-Sonoita Creek Preserve** has a couple of trails that are especially good for bird-watching (see *Wilder Places*).

HISTORIC WALKING TOUR Pick up *A Walk Through Time* map at the **Patagonia Area Business Association Visitor Center** and meander around town to the marked spots of historic interest in Patagonia.

HORSEBACK RIDING **Arizona Horseback Experience** (520-455-5696 or 866-844-7444), 16 Coyote Court, Sonoita. Ron and Marge Izzo have more than 25 years' trail-riding experience and offer trips that last from 3 hours to several days. You won't get a nose-to-tail experience with their horses. These animals are healthy, responsive, and energetic, and they like to move out. People come from around the world to ride with the Izzos. Call for prices and reservations.

Coronado Outfitters (520-394-0187) in Patagonia can take you on hours-long trail rides, day rides, or days-long pack trips. The extended rides are catered and guided. Their **Cherry Creek Campground** can accommodate your horse and tent camping. Call for prices and information.

MOUNTAIN BIKING Residents of Patagonia have moved from Colorado for the scenic quality of the mountain biking in the area. This is comparable to a Napa Valley vintner moving to Elgin (not a bad decision, either). The back roads are exquisite for tour or mountain bike rides that last from several hours to all day. **Patagonia Cyclery** (520-394-2794; patagoniacyclery@theriver.com) offers guided tours Oct.–May and rents bicycles, as well.

ROAD BIKING You can travel the same paved highways listed in "Scenic Drives"; all of the routes if you have a tour bike.

SWIMMING **Patagonia Lake State Park** (see *Wilder Places*) gives you a chance to commune with nature and humanity. It's popular with the locals come summertime, and closures due to capacity crowds are not unusual. Call before heading out at that time.

WINE TOURS Oenophiles will be delighted to know the Sonoita Valley has land perfect for producing award-winning wine. It has the only AVA (American Viticulture Area) designation in the state. The area's fertile soil compares to that in Burgundy, France, with weather akin to that of Mendoza, Argentina. The appellations produce some of the best wines in the country—many served at the White House. A map of the wine country leads you to the area vintners. The area's most consistent and notable producer is **Callaghan Vineyards** (520-455-5322), 336 Elgin Rd., Elgin. Open Fri.–Sun. 11–3. Vintner Kent Callaghan produces wines that have captivated the palate of the single most influential wine critic in the world, Robert Parker, and the consistent attention of the *Wall Street Journal*. Wine aficionados on the lookout for something different wait with interest for Callaghan's next harvest to come of drinking age. $3 for tastings. Check out **Canelo Hills Vineyard and Winery** (520-455-5499), 342 Elgin Rd. open Fri. and Sat. 11–4, makes full-bodied reds. Tastings are $5, which includes a logo glass.

Dos Cabezas Winery & Vineyard (520-455-5141), 3248 AZ 82, Sonoita. Open Fri.–Sun. 10:30–4:30. Originally located near its namesake town along AZ 186, the winery moved here in 2003. The winery has won several awards.

Sonoita Vineyards, Ltd. (520-455-5893), 290 Elgin Canelo Rd., Elgin. Open daily

10–4; closed holidays. Owner Dr. Dutt opened the winery in 1983 and has collected a string of awards through the years. Varieties grown on the estate include Chardonnay, Sauvignon Blanc, Cabernet Sauvignon, Merlot, Pinot Noir, and Mission. The Mission grapes date back to the Spanish missionaries from the 16th century.

✱ Wilder Places

Parker Canyon Lake (520-388-8300), located southeast of Sonoita at the end of AZ 83. The ride to this secluded lake is worth each of the 32 miles it takes to get here from Sonoita for a lakeside picnic. Fishing is the main draw here. You can catch cold- and warm-water species, including stocked rainbow trout and resident bass, sunfish, and catfish, from a boat, the fishing pier, or the lakeside paved area and a graveled path. A country store has last-minute supplies. You can buy a fishing license or rent a boat at the store, too. Free.

Patagonia Lake State Park (520-287-6965), 400 Patagonia Lake Rd., Patagonia. Open daily 4:30 AM–10. Once a canyon through which the Southern Pacific Railroad ran a route from Benson to Nogales, now 2.5-mile-long Patagonia Lake laps against clumps of cattails and masses of smooth bluffs. Formed by the damming of Sonoita Creek to supply water to Nogales, Patagonia Lake makes a picturesque recreation spot in the rolling hills of southern Arizona. The best way to experience the lake is to get in the water. Unsupervised Boulder Beach provides a protected area no more than 6 feet deep from its sandy shore to its corded buoys for swimmers to use; the marina store rents rowboats, paddle boats, and canoes to explore the quiet coves and side canyons along the lake. Water-skiing (prohibited May 1–Sep. 1), fishing, camping (72 developed sites and 12 lakeside boat access sites, 32 hookup sites), picnicking, and hiking trails are available at the park. $10. Lakeside and electric hookup camping $22 per night, tent camping $15 per night.

Patagonia-Sonoita Creek Preserve (520-394-2400), 150 Blue Heaven Rd., Patagonia. From AZ 82 in Patagonia, turn west onto 4th Ave., then turn south onto Pennsylvania; cross the creek and go 1 mile to the entrance. Open Wed.–Sun. 7:30–4; 6:30–4:30 Apr.–Sep. 6:30–4. A rare, streamside habitat along Patagonia-Sonoita Creek presents one of the planet's best birding habitats. About 300 species of birds have been sighted here, including the gray hawk, green kingfisher, thick-billed kingbird, northern beardless tyrannulet, violet-crowned hummingbird, and rose-throated becard. Two and a half miles of hiking paths take you into the world-class bird land. Guided nature walk every Saturday at 9 all year with seasonal birding and natural history programs. $5 admission is good for 7 days from date of purchase; Patagonia residents and under age 16 free. No dogs permitted.

✱ Lodging

The Duquesne House Bed and Breakfast (520-394-2732), 357 Duquesne Ave., Patagonia. More than a century ago this adobe building housed rough-and-tumble miners. Now fixed up with harmonious colors and textures, the rooms make a comfortable and pleasing stay with appointments such as Mexican folk art, hand-stitched samplers, and quilts. Gardens and patios attract avian life. One room has a kitchenette and large shower for handicapped accessibility. Breakfast leans toward healthy gourmet with fresh ingredients made by the owner. Pets are okay with a deposit. $110–130.

An Enchanted Garden Bed & Breakfast (520-604-0070), 136 Forrest Dr., Patagonia. All the native trees, flowers, and birds on this property give it the look and feel of an arboretum. On the rustic Zen side, the outside garden is cozy and secluded and lives up to the property's name. The interiors are simple, clean, and environmentally friendly for allergy-sensitive travelers with a pillow-top bed and your own private porch. Continental breakfast of fruit, fresh-baked breads or muffins from the in-town bakery, and organic coffee and teas. Polite pets are okay with a $15 extra charge. $109.

La Hacienda de Sonoita (520-455-5308), 34 Swanson Rd., Sonoita. Built as a bed & breakfast, so you have the privacy of a hotel but the camaraderie of the hosts and other guests if you like, the hacienda has a warm, laid-back atmosphere. Four themed guest rooms keep the spirit of the West in mind—fully tiled, wooden ceiling beams, and decorated in cowboy legacy. The great room has a library, game table, piano, sitting area, and two fireplaces. All the guest rooms have a private bath: One has a fireplace and full tub and shower; another twin beds; and two have queen beds. A full, delicious breakfast made with local ingredients is included with stay. No pets. Equestrian accommodations available (bring your own feed). $100–115.

Spirit Tree Inn (520-394-0121), 3 Harshaw Creek Rd. Patagonia. Located on a 52-acre inholding right in the Coronado National Forest, you get pretty secluded here, though only a few miles out of town. The property got its name from the majestic 150-year-old cottonwood tree in the front meadow. Its 300-inch girth puts it in the top 10 in the world. Native peoples believed large trees, such as this cottonwood, held the spirits of their ancestors. Originally the Rocking Horse Ranch headquarters, the historic building drips with rustic ranch character—sturdy but unpretentious. The three guest rooms in the home and two casitas have a private bath and WiFi. The casitas have kitchenettes and can accommodate pets. Breakfasts, thanks to Thomas Barholomeaux's career working with some of the world's finest chefs and in five-star restaurants, definitely have gourmet leanings. He also shares his talents in the afternoon social hour with light delights and local wines. Gourmet breakfast included in rates. Dogs are accepted on individual basis; horse facilities for haul-ins. $98–190.

THE SPIRIT TREE INN TAKES ITS NAME FROM THIS HUGE COTTONWOOD

Xanadu Ranch GetAway (520-455-0050 or 800-985-1572), 92 Los Encinos Rd., Sonoita. You get a chance to B or not to B at this guest ranch B&B. This means you can order ingredients to make your own breakfast, bring your own food, or head out with a cup of coffee on the trail. Casitas and rooms decorated in fresh Southwest give you plenty of privacy. Each room has its own bathroom, free high-speed Internet, free satellite TV, refrigerator, microwave, coffee pot, and toaster; some have full kitchens. Guest can use picnic areas with grills. Pets okay with advance notice and $5; horse boarding available ($10–12 per horse per night). $99–129 (discount for cash).

✱ Where to Eat

DINING OUT ♥ **Canela Bistro** (520-455-5873), 3252 AZ 82, Sonoita. Open Thu.–Sun. 4–9. The eclectic spirit of Canela takes from the ranching community and adds south-of-the-border flavors with Seattle freshness. The husband-and-wife team of Joy Vargo and John Hall—both experienced chefs who met at the New England Culinary Institute in Vermont—display their innovative talents through a delicious menu big on local foods and wines. They're into procuring whole animals and using every bit and local produce, making theirs one of the literal farm-to-the-table menus in the state. The menu changes daily, offering a strong variety of meats, a fish dish, and a vegetarian entrée. Joy specializes in fish (a holdover from her Seattle days), which seems to be catching the interest of the local beef eaters. Desserts are house-made and special, from the chocolate truffles to made-to-order sorbet and honey tuilles. The coffee is from Seattle and much of the wine reasonably priced from area vineyards. Entrées $15–28.

THE HUSBAND-AND-WIFE CHEF-OWNERS OF CANELA, JOHN HALL AND JOY VARGO

EATING OUT **Mercedes Mexican Café** (520-394-2331), 328 W. Naugle Ave., Patagonia. Open Tue.–Sat. 7 AM–8 PM, Sun. 7–5; closed Mon. All the food is made from scratch here using local ingredients when possible. Large portions make it hard for temperance. The common comment to this tasty food is, "I ate too much, it was so good." Desserts are homemade. Entrées $7.50–12.99.

Velvet Elvis Pizza Company (520-394-2102), 292 Naugle Ave., Patagonia. Open Thu.–Sun. 11:30–8:30. Owner Cecelia St. Miguel celebrated the opening of this venerated pizza place with a procession to Our Lady of Guadalupe. Since then the restaurant, which serves food made from recipes with 70-year-old roots in a Brooklyn, New York, restaurant, has appeared in international magazines and newspapers. Former Arizona governor Napolitano declared the tiny place filled with paintings of Elvis (on velvet, of course) and our Lady of Guadalupe an Arizona Treasure. You'll find everything from vegetarian soups to organic salads,

calzones to pizza, lemon-herb baked chicken to BBQ back ribs. Freshly blended juices, microbrewed and imported beers, and wines are available. Designer pizzas $22–45, calzones $7.50–10.

✷ The Arts

Patagonia has evolved into an artists' enclave. You'll find all kinds of talent and media, from crafts to collectible pieces, lining the two main streets (Naugle and McKeown). The **Mesquite Grove Gallery** (371 McKeown) opened more than 20 years ago—the town's first gallery—as a local artists' venue. The gallery continues to support the local arts, as well as works from outside the region.

✷ Selective Shopping

The word franchise does not exist in these parts. Terms like *unique*, *one-of-a-kind*, *original*, *independent* are more befitting this land of the self-made man/woman. The gas station in Patagonia declares itself politically incorrect, and the market does not take credit, except for a fee. The dot-on-the-map business area in Sonoita along AZ 83 has a few interesting shops worth checking out. Elgin's heart belongs solely to the vine. Appoint a designated driver, turn wine imbiber, and stock up the cellar.

Nogales, Mexico. Only 20 miles south across the border, you can shop till you drop in Mexican markets. Just remember you need a passport for your return into the states. (See the Tips for Visiting Mexico sidebar on page 238.)

✷ Special Events

April: **Blessing of the Vine Festival** (www.arizonawines.com). Special blessings and celebrations at Sonoita Vineyards.

July: **Fourth of July Celebration** (520-394-0060) in downtown Patagonia and Town Park.

September: **Blessing of the Harvest Festival** (www.arizonawines.com). Special blessings and celebrations at Elgin vineyards. **Sonoita Rodeo** (520-455-5553) is an Old West rodeo along with steak fry and dancing at Santa Cruz County Fairgrounds on Labor Day weekend. **Santa Cruz County Fair** (520-455-5553) features open exhibits, vendors, and entertainment the last weekend of the month.

October: **Patagonia Fall Festival** (520-394-0060 or 888-794-0060). Art and crafts, music, food booths, and a dance in Town Park.

November: **The Arizona Cowboy Symposium** (www.arizonacowboysymposium.org) in Sonoita preserves the traditional music, prose and poetry of the American Cowboy.

Western Arizona

5

ROUTE 66: ASH FORK TO CALIFORNIA

LAKE HAVASU CITY

YUMA

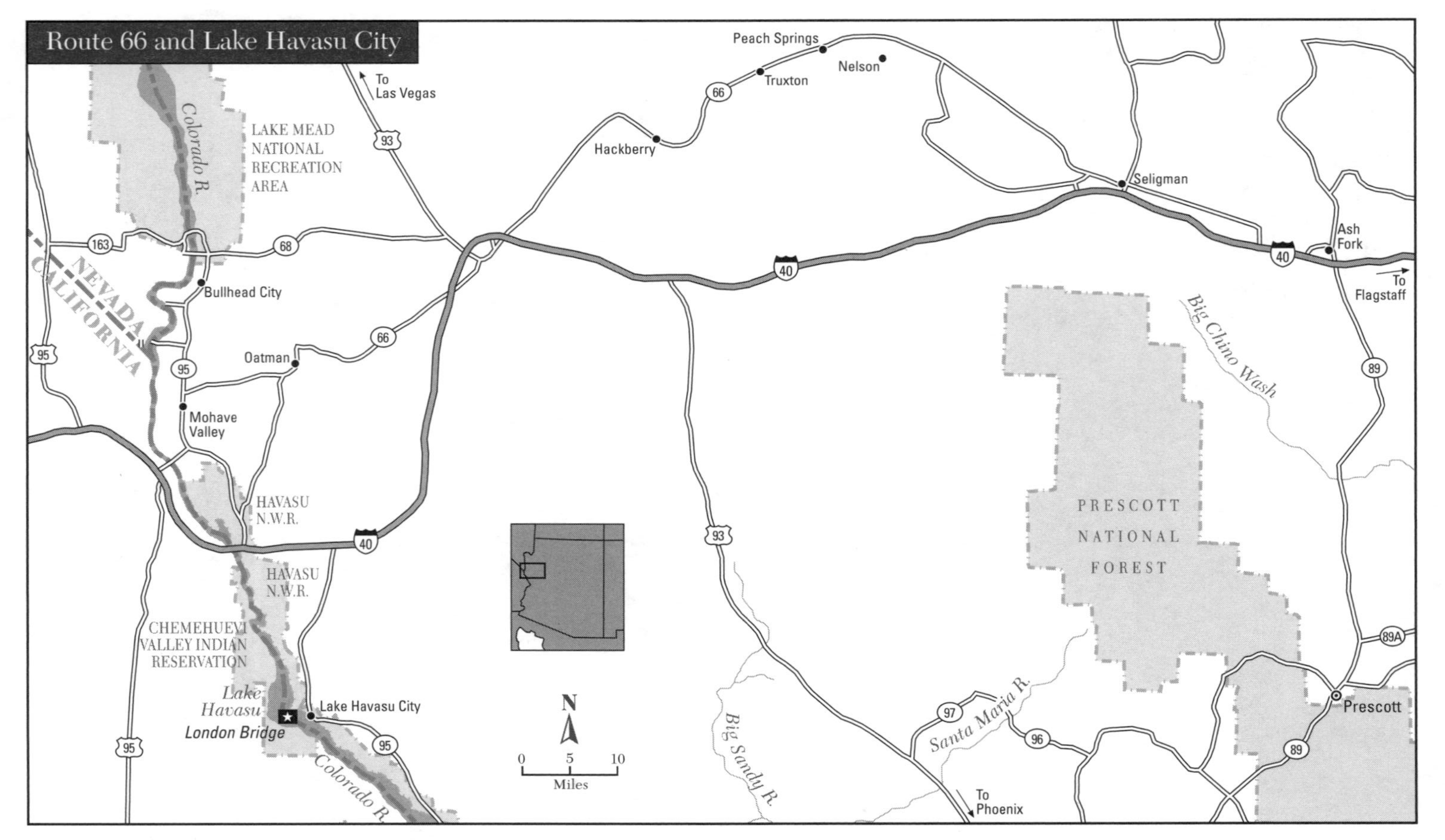
Route 66 and Lake Havasu City
To Las Vegas
LAKE MEAD NATIONAL RECREATION AREA
Colorado R.
NEVADA
CALIFORNIA
Bullhead City
Oatman
Mohave Valley
HAVASU N.W.R.
HAVASU N.W.R.
CHEMEHUEVI VALLEY INDIAN RESERVATION
Lake Havasu
London Bridge
Lake Havasu City
Colorado R.
Hackberry
Peach Springs
Truxton
Nelson
Seligman
Ash Fork
To Flagstaff
Big Chino Wash
PRESCOTT NATIONAL FOREST
Prescott
Santa Maria R.
Big Sandy R.
To Phoenix
N
0 5 10
Miles
163
68
93
95
66
40
89
89A
97
96

ROUTE 66: ASH FORK TO CALIFORNIA

Known as the Mother Road, the Main Street of America, and the Will Rogers Highway, Route 66 has an endearing reputation. The 2,448-mile-long highway, commissioned back in 1926, became the epitome of freedom, linking the strong-shouldered Chicago with the free-spirited Santa Monica. It took more than 10 years to get the whole highway paved, and some of the segments of the route that still exist (not replaced by an interstate) in Arizona feel like they belong right back in the pre-paved days. This western segment that crosses Arizona (dubbed the Heart of Route 66 because it contains the longest original stretch left) starts in Ash Fork and crosses some wide-open spaces with little in the way of luxury. It's the simple life, where extravagance shows up in scenery rather than amenities. The grand finale of Arizona's stretch of Historic Route 66 takes you through the Black Mountains into Oatman, and then on to a segment designated a Scenic Back Country Byway that winds down to Topock at the edge of the Colorado River.

The most scenic stretch lies between Kingman to Oatman, just past the renovated Cool Springs Station, where the road winds trough a most unusual biome of cactus and juniper trees growing on strangely stratified slopes. Check out the "boot hill" burial grounds around milepost 29-30, where you'll wonder if the homespun graves are real or a hoax, especially when you see the one for Jimmy Hoffa.

Oatman looks much the same as it did in its heyday from the early 1900s to its bust in 1942. Boardwalks line storefronts along the mile-long main street. The buildings' blend of wood and corrugated metal, sometimes shaky with age, adds a ramshackle demeanor. Foot-thick old adobe buildings, answers to the 2,700-foot-high town's searing summers, brand Oatman as unmistakably southwestern. The town exudes a cagey twist of mischievous fun and history. West of Oatman, the volcanic tuff peaks take on the otherworldly feel you get the Superstition Mts. east of Phoenix.

The whole highway is the stuff that William Least Heat Moon's classic *Blue Highways: A Journey into America* is about. Here, along Old Route 66, you find out where life really happens. Interestingly, it usually happens to be your own.

GUIDANCE **Powerhouse Visitors Center** (928-753-6106), 120 W. Andy Devine Ave. (Route 66), Kingman. Open daily 8–5; WiFi hot spot. **Oatman Chamber of**

Commerce (928-768-6222). **Hualapai Office of Tourism** (928-769-2230), located in Hualapai Lodge in Peach Springs. Get permits for and information about traveling on the Hualapai tribal lands. Contact the **Havasupai tribe** (928-448-2121), P.O. Box 160, Supai, AZ 86432 for information on Havasu Canyon.

GETTING THERE You can approach Route 66 from Flagstaff via I-40 and exit at Ash Fork; from Prescott, go north on US 89 to Ash Fork; from California, take I-40 east to the Topock exit.

WHEN TO COME Peak season for most of this stretch of high-desert highway runs from Mar.–Nov. However, Oatman, located in a lower desert zone, is flip-flopped: High season is Oct.–Mar.

MEDICAL EMERGENCY Dial 911.

✷ To See

Seligman

Delgadillo's Route 66 Gift Shop and Museum (928-422-3352), 217 E. Route 66. Open daily 8:30–6. The Route 66 Gift Shop hasn't changed a bit since the time it was Angel Delgadillo's barbershop, back when people were getting their kicks on Route 66. Delgadillo, born and raised in Seligman, lobbied the Arizona legislature to designate and preserve Route 66 in Arizona as a historic highway. The unofficial spokesperson that calls himself the "Guardian Angel" for Route 66 loves to talk about his passion. Peruse the memorabilia, add a business card to the collection on the wall, and pick up a Walking Tour Guide to Historic Seligman. If you're lucky, Angel might even give you a haircut.

Peach Springs

Grand Canyon Caverns (928-422-4565), located 2 miles west of Seligman. Open daily; closed Christmas Day. The limestone walls of the natural cavern were formed in prehistoric times by an inland sea. On the 45-minute (0.75-mile) tour, an elevator transports you 210 feet underground. Besides limestone formations, you see fossils and the bones of long-extinct animals. $14.95 adults, $9.95 ages 4–12.

Kingman

Mohave Museum of History and Arts (928-753-3195), 400 W. Beale St. Open Mon.–Fri. 9–5, Sat. 1–5. This collection of historiana from the northwest corner of Arizona features the cultures that played a part in settling the area: Native American tribes, missionaries, miners, ranchers, railroad workers, soldiers, and steamboaters. There are a number of exhibits, murals, and dioramas, plus an outdoor display. If you have time and would like to dig a bit deeper into the area history, check out the museum library and its collection of documents, manuscripts, and photographs centering on Mohave County and the Southwest (open Mon.–Fri. 9–4:30). Call for admission prices. The admission fee also allows access to Route 66 Museum.

Route 66 Museum (928-753-9889), 120 W. Andy Devine Ave. (Route 66). Open daily 9–5. This well-organized museum unfolds the historical evolution of travel along what became Route 66 with murals, dioramas, and photographs about the cultures that traveled the highway from the time it was a trade route for Native peoples, a wagon road for settlers traveling from the East, an escape hatch for the Dust Bowl refugees to the West, and a vacation route. Call for admission prices. The admission fee also allows access to Mohave Museum of History and Art.

Oatman

Oatman's most charming attraction is the group of wild burrows that roam the streets *carte blanche*. Their lineage comes from the mining days when prospectors used them as beasts of burden. Around a dozen of the burros' descendants mosey around town, greeting visitors and chomping carrots—the only legal treat allowed the animals and sold by the bagful by shop owners. The burros basically have a sweet demeanor, but they do have their moody moments, and some may kick or bite if provoked. About 1,500 wild burros hang out in the surrounding mountains.

SCENIC DRIVES Peach Springs Road. From Peach Springs, turn south onto Diamond Creek Road. This is the only place where you can drive down to the Colorado River in the Grand Canyon. The 20-mile drive (high clearance recommended) travels some pretty spectacular countryside, and you can picnic or camp right alongside the river. Purchase a $10-per-person-per-day permit from the Hualapai Nation (see Guidance).

✷ To Do

Hackberry General Store and Visitor Center. Milepost 80 on Route 66 in Hackberry. For more than 25 years Bob Waldmire traveled Old Route 66 like a hippie gypsy in his converted VW bus, a prototype for the van in the film *Cars*. and selling pre-*Genesis* Robert Crumb–style art. Waldmire lived in this former gas station in the 1990s, and the colorful stories about his residence remain even though he sold it in 1998 to John and Kerry Pritchard. Waldmire started the building's folklore, the Pritchards started the visitor center, It took them two years to get the building livable, and they filled it with 1960s and '70s memorabilia they'd collected over the years. What started out as a modest business to tide the Pritchards over in retirement has grown to a summertime tourist hot spot with international infamy where movies are made, commercials are shot, and models pose for European ads. Pritchard's 1956 Corvette parked in front of the building draws a crowd on its own. "The first time I saw a Corvette," said Pritchard, who collects Corvettes, "I was nine years old. I thought it was the most beautiful thing I ever saw; like a beautiful woman. The old '57 Corvette and this gas station are about as American Pie as you can get." Unlike the Pritchards who took to collecting, Waldmire liked to live life free and easy, and wore a T-shirt admonishing readers to LEAVE EARLIER. DRIVE SLOWER. LIVE LONGER. So, slow down and take a little time to peruse the fun collection of Mother Road and American Pie memorabilia. The last weekend in Apr. (Laughlin River Run) and First weekend of May (Route 66 Fun Run) draw hundreds of vintage and modern day cars here. Free.

Peach Springs

HIKING Havasu Canyon (see *Wilder Places*). This classic hike, with pilgrimage status, ends at the hotel in the tiny town of Supai (mile 8) or the campground (mile 10), often drawing repeat visits. From Supai, you can hike another 8 miles to the Colorado River. The hike to the river requires experience with long distances and remote areas. The first 5 miles travel the Havasupai reservation; the last 3 (which has a technical segment), in Grand Canyon National Park. The route must be done as a day hike since the tribe does not allow overnight use on the reservation outside the campground, and the National Park Service does not allow overnight use in that portion of the park. Contact the Havasupai tribe (see *Guidance*) for permits.

Oatman

HORSEBACK RIDING Oatman Stables (928-768-3257). Closed in summer. Head out into the rough-and-ready countryside of the Black Mountains down old cavalry trails on horseback. The rugged desert mountains provide a beautiful Wild West landscape. Guides take you out on 1- ($25) or 2-hour ($45) rides, cookouts, cattle drives, and overnighters. Call for information and reservations.

WILDER PLACES—HAVASU CANYON

✱ Wilder Places

Havasu Canyon. The trailhead is located 60 miles from Peach Springs on Hualapai 18. Sacred to the Havasupai people and so distinctly beautiful, the poetic canyon draws people from around the world. The liquid turquoise flow of Havasu Creek through the red-rock cliffs of Havasu Canyon is the big draw; the waterfalls along the creek's course to the Grand Canyon are some of the most celebrated in the state. The remote town of Supai, 8 miles from the trailhead at Hualapai Hilltop on the bottom of the canyon, has no cars and very little in the way of modern conveniences besides a hotel, small market, and cafeteria restaurant. Two miles downcreek, you can camp. The only ways in to this Edenic piece of nature are hiking, horse, or helicopter—making this a trip to remember. Contact the Havasupai Nation (see *Guidance*) to obtain permits.

Hualapai Mountain Park (928-757-3859). From Kingman, go east on Andy Devine Ave. (Route 66), and turn right onto Hualapai Mountain Rd.; go 14 miles to the signed park entrance. Open daily 5 AM–9 PM. While not a wilderness, the park is a neat little niche in the mountains in which to picnic, camp, and view wildlife, hike, or mountain bike on several multiuse trails.

PARKS AND MONUMENTS Lake Mead National Recreation Area (702-293-8990). When the arch-gravity Hoover Dam was constructed in Black Canyon, the western reaches of the Colorado River bulged into Lake Mead just before it turned into the Lower Colorado. The azure waters that feed desert-hardy animals buzz with human activity. Like the rest of dam-developed lakes along the river, boating, fishing, and swimming is the main draw. The surrounding mountains have unmaintained trails and canyons to explore. The Alan Bible Visitor Center has exhibits, books, brochures, nautical charts, and topographical maps of the area. $5 per car for five days.

✱ Lodging

Seligman

Canyon Lodge (928-422-3255), 114 E. Chino Ave. You can get a comfy and clean room here and watch the world go by on the balcony lounge. Rooms have double or California king beds, refrigerator, microwave, TV, and phone. Continental breakfast included. $42–46.

Peach Springs

Hualapai Lodge (928-769-2230 or 888-255-9550), 900 Route 66, Peach Springs. The Hualapai tribe, owners and operators, have accented the lodge with their culture. The property has a restaurant, gift shop, meeting facilities, laundry, Jacuzzi, pool, and fitness room. Rooms—oversized, comfortable, and clean—have phone and cable TV/movies. $79–109.

Kingman

Hualapai Mountain County Park Cabins (928-681-5700). It's BYO here regarding linens, dishes, food, and the like, but otherwise the cabins (some stone) are fully furnished with beds (double, twin, and/or bunk), table, cooktop stove, refrigerator, heater, electricity, bath and shower, and hot and cold water; some have fireplace or woodstove. Plus, each has a barbecue grill and picnic table outside. Rustic but fun. Three-day holiday minimum. $55–125.

♥ **Hualapai Mountain Resort** (928-757-3545), 4525 Hualapai Rd., Kingman (located 13 miles from US 66 (20 mi. from Kingman). Located in the tall pines up in the Hualapai Mountains where deer and elk herds roam. The lodge has gone through a metamorphosis the last four years with room remodels (wood floors, tongue-and-groove ceilings, river-rock shower, and wood furniture. Each room has access to a communal porch that runs the length of the resort, where you can sit in the wicker chairs and watch the wildlife. Three of the eight guest rooms are suites with a fireplace. Beds are pillow-top and wear flannel sheets in the winter. Property has a restaurant (see *Dining Out*). $79–159.

✱ Where to Eat

Seligman

Snow Cap Drive-In (928-422-3291), 301 E. Route 66. Open daily 9–5; closed Nov. 22–Mar. 1. Owner and general practical joker Juan Delgadillo has a host of gimmicks for the unsuspecting traveler. The drive-in itself looks as zany as the owner's personality. All the food is made to order; the most popular items are the tacos and burritos, but a red chiliburger and soft ice-cream treats make a great meal, too. $2.50–5.25.

Westside Lilo's Café (928-422-5456), 415 W. Route 66, Seligman. The best restaurant in town serves good food at good prices. Breakfast is served all day. Soups are made fresh each day, hamburgers are made of Black Angus chuck, French fries are fresh cut, salads are fresh, and desserts are housemade. All the fried foods are prepared in a low-saturated-fat blend with no cholesterol. *Weinerschnitzel* or *jaegerschnitzel* are dinner favorites. Entrées $4.25–7.25.

Kingman

El Palacio of Kingman (928-718-0018), 401 U.S. 66. Open for lunch and dinner 11–9. Everything's made fresh at this Mexican food favorite. You can get the classics here (red and green chiles are big), plus some unusual fare, such as Mariba Chicken (simmered in wine sauce with *pico de gallo*), Ensalada Del Chef (mixed greens with chunks of warm pork topped with cheddar and Jack cheese, tomato, and avocado), and Shrimp Empanadas. $6–12.

Hualapai Mountain Resort Restaurant (928-757-3545), 4525 Hualapai Rd., Kingman (located 13 miles from US 66). Call for hours. This high-in-the-pines venue draws people from Kingman, 20 miles away. The food—everything from meat loaf to prime rib—is fresh and house-made. The Mountain Lion (blacked prime rib with grilled shrimp and Cajun cream sauce) and Prospector (14 oz. rib-eye steak with Jack Daniel's sauce and shoestring onion attacked atop) are signature dishes. The wild caught salmon (with garlic or pecan crusts or charbroiled) is excellent. Sunday has a breakfast buffet from 8–1. For lunch, the hamburgers and French dip are popular fare. Live music plays on the patio on the summer weekends. $10.95–24.95.

Mr. Dz's Route 66 Diner (928-718-0066), 105 E. Andy Devine Ave. Open daily 7 AM–9 PM. You can't miss the building—turquoise and pink—standing right on the town's main drag. This is soda shop classic, where you order burgers, a "tower" of onion rings, and a root beer float (made from Mr. Dz's own special recipe) to the sounds of the jukebox in the background. Take your meal outside, make yourself at home on one of the benches, and watch motorcycles and vintage cars cruise by. $5.50–12.

Oatman

Oatman Hotel (928-768-4408), 181 Main St. Open daily Mon.–Fri. 10:30–6, Sat. and Sun. 8 AM–9 PM. The hotel, built in 1902, was the happening place during the town's boom. Miners spent much of their off time in the hotel, and the premises hold plenty of memorabilia from the gold-mining past. Thousands of signed and dated dollar bills cover the walls and ceilings of the bar and restaurant (open until 9 PM). The tradition originated with the

THIS IS THE REAL THING ALONG RTE 66 PASSING THROUGH OATMAN

GRAND CANYON SKYWALK

They might have taken more than a decade to complete it, but the Hualapai tribe has the only skyway building over the Grand Canyon. The 1.07 million-pound, $30 million skyway is a U-shaped walkway that juts 70 feet from the rim. Here's the thrilling part—it has a 4-inch glass bottom. If you get a little woozy looking down from the top of the Empire State Building or John Hancock Center, take your required dose of Dramamine before you look down from this attraction. You're 4,000 feet above the canyon floor for the whole 20-plus yards.

Like the Navajo Bridge, the building the Skyway was a masterful feat. To lay it safely in place, engineers perched this bridge at the canyon's edge via a pulley system connected to four tractor-trailers. Hydraulic braces lifted the Skywalk from underneath above a cement track, maneuvered the walkway (balanced by about a half-million pounds of steel cubes at land's end to keep it from forming another set of rapids in the river below) over a web of metal rods, and positioned it onto four steel anchors previously drilled deep into the canyon rock. Workers finished the procedure by welding the walkway onto the anchors.

If you go, you can rest assured the walkway can withstand 100 mph winds and 8.0 earthquakes up to 50 miles away, and shock absorbers should keep it from shaking while you walk. Admission: $43.05 per person.

miners. When they had money, they tacked up a dollar. If they ran out of cash, they knew they could still buy a bottle of beer with their dollar. If you look hard enough, you might see one signed by former president Ronald Reagan. You can get a decent meal here in a historic atmosphere. Entrées $6.95–10.95.

Olive Oatman Restaurant and Ice Cream Saloon (928-768-1891), 171 Main St. Open daily 8:30–4:30. Named for the daughter of a pioneer Illinoisan family sold as a slave to Mojave Indians. Her incredible story is on the back of the menu. You can get a hearty breakfast here and sandwiches for lunch. Specialties include Indian frybread, Navajo taco, and peach frybread (with ice cream). Entrées $4.95–6.50.

✷ Special Events

January: **Polar Bear Dip** (928-757-7919). Start the year off with an icy plunge into Kingman's Downtown Pool.

February: **Wild West Days** (928-768-6222) in Oatman celebrates the town's wild history.

May: **Historic Route 66 Fun Run** (928-753-5001) brings hundreds of classic cars to Seligman to travel Arizona's western stretch of Historic Route 66.

July: **Sidewalk Egg Fry** (928-753-2636) is Oatman's caricature attempt to celebrate the sear of summer by giving participants a chance to fry an egg at high noon.

August: **Hualapai Mountain Arts & Crafts Festival** (928-757-3545) high in the pines at the Hualapai Mountain Resort.

September: **Gold Camp Days** (928-768-6222) is Oatman's Labor Day weekend celebration with a parade, crazy hat contest, beard contest, and fun-filled Burro Biscuit Throwing contest. **Mohave County Fair** (928-753-2636) presents livestock and crafts exhibits, shows, carnival rides, and games. **Andy Devine** Days (928-757-7919) honors the late western actor Andy Devine and Kingman's western heritage all weekend, including a rodeo.

October: **Fall Festival and Parade** (928-692-9599) will have a parade Oktoberfest brats and beer, entertainment, and arts and crafts.

LAKE HAVASU CITY

In summer, when lower desert temperatures run amok, most denizens stay clear of the sun's sizzle. Animals slink into the shadows, and humans head for air-conditioned shelter. This is not true, however, along the lower Colorado River. This near-sea-level segment of the trans-state river passes through some of the hottest spots in the nation, where only 3 inches of rainfall hits the ground each year and temperatures toy with the 120-degree mark.

In this land where record temperatures are more novelty than nuisance, the river becomes the center of attention for man and beast. Where animals depend on the river for sustenance, often stealing sips during the twilight hours, man relies upon it for recreation. When the temperatures rise, the residents of Lake Havasu City simply migrate to the water. They find a cool pocket in the lake, grab a cold drink, don a life jacket, and bob in the refreshing currents.

From springtime (this would be spring break, which you might think was Daytona Beach if you don't have a good sense of direction) to autumn the lower Colorado River around Lake Havasu City roils with activity. With river temperatures hovering in the 80s, the glug-a-lug of racing boats, nasal buzz of personal watercraft, and whoosh of water-skiers prevails through the daylight hours. The hot, humid, and mostly sunny days draw people into the river channel near London Bridge. They wave to the vessels that parade past all day. Once past the no-wake area, these vessels open up to test their mechanical prowess. It's a fast lake with perfect conditions for speed. So many PWCs give it the title of Personal Watercraft Capital of the World.

When temperatures relax back into double digits from autumn through early spring, so does the activity, at least from a human standpoint. From a wildlife point of view the river, a major migratory route, becomes one popular place. Birds travel all the way from the Arctic to winter along the river while resident waterfowl loll along the shore and a variety of mammals become visible. Fishermen take to the quiet lake to catch the trophy fish that might lurk in the blue-green water. At twilight geese honk their way across the sky and great horned owls hoot cross-canyon to each other.

Hot or cold weather, the river stays busy year-round. It just depends what type of migration you're interested in.

GUIDANCE Lake Havasu City Convention and Visitors Bureau (928-453-3444), 314 London Bridge Rd. Open daily 9–4. **Bureau of Land Management**

(928-505-1200 or 888-213-2582), 2610 Sweetwater Ave. **Lake Havasu State Park Windsor Beach** (928-855-2784), 699 London Bridge Rd.

GETTING THERE *By car:* AZ 95 takes you right to the riverside city from either direction (north or south). *By air:* **Lake Havasu City Municipal Airport** (HII) (928-764-3330), 5600 AZ 95.

WHEN TO COME Because of the lure of the water, summertime is high season here. Make sure you have reservations, especially on holidays, when the boats can get so concentrated on the lake that you can walk from one to the other without getting wet.

MEDICAL EMERGENCY **Havasu Regional Medical Center** (928-855-8185), 101 Civic Center Lane.

✷ To See

Lake Havasu Museum of History (928-854-4938), 320 London Bridge Rd. Open Tue.–Sat. 1–4. The museum has a number of interesting exhibits related to the area: mining, steamboats, the London Bridge, and Native peoples. You can even do some research nosing through their collection of old newspapers. Catch a classic film at 1:30 Tue., Thu., or Sat. $4 adults, under age 12 free.

London Bridge. Coined the most expensive antique in the world, England's London Bridge got a new home in Lake Havasu City in 1971. The Brits put the famous bridge up for sale in the early 1960s because the granite span started sinking into the Thames River's clay bed. Lake Havasu City father Robert McCulloch Sr. partnered with C. V. Wood Jr. (the largely unknown brains behind Disneyland) to buy the bridge for $2,460,000. The duo had the bridge dismantled, coded each granite block with a set of numbers, shipped the pieces to the States, and reconstructed the bridge over Lake Havasu by matching the code numbers. The bridge has become Arizona's second biggest tourist draw. In summertime up to 20,000 boats cruise underneath; it's the place to see and be seen.

✷ To Do

BEACHES/SWIMMING If you don't have a boat in which to cruise the river, lounge beside it on one of several beaches in town. **Castle Rock Bay** (760-326-3853) in the Havasu National Wildlife Refuge has a swath of sand and is the put-in of choice for kayakers who want peace and quiet on their paddle. **Cattail Cove State Park** is located 10 miles south on AZ 95. It has camping, a boat launch, picnic area, marina, swimming beach, and hiking trail. $10 per vehicle.

C. V. Wood Family Recreation Center and Aquatic Complex (928-453-8686), 100 Park Ave. Call for hours. You know how serious a lakeside city takes swimming—and kids—when it builds a fabulous aquatic complex like this one with its Olympic-size swimming pool, wave pool, Jacuzzi, whirlpool, water playground and kiddy cove and 257-foot water slide. $5.50 adults, $4.50 kids.

Lake Havasu State Park Windsor Beach, centrally located (near London Bridge) and busy with activities, has camping, a boat launch, swimming beach, nature trail, and events. $15 per vehicle, $3 for an individual on bicycle.

London Bridge Beach. Located along the Bridgewater Channel (access through the public parking lot on the south side of McCulloch Blvd.), this is more a riverside park with picnic ramadas and barbecues, swimming area, playgrounds, and restrooms. It's where everyone not in a boat likes to hang out.

BOAT CAMPING Boat camping is allowed by permit only on a first-come, first-served basis. Arizona State Parks sites located between Red Rock Cove and Cattail Cove cost $14 each night. Sites maintained by the Bureau of Land Management south of Cattail Cove cost $10 for day use and $10 for camping. Rate hikes are on the discussion table. Most boat camps have table, grill, and outhouse, but no drinking water. For more information, contact Lake Havasu State Park or the Bureau of Land Management (see *Guidance*).

BOAT TOURS **BlueWater Jetboat Tour** (928-855-7171), 501 English Village, Lake Havasu City. Sep.–May, the *Starship 2010* cruises at 28 miles per hour northward through Havasu Natural Wildlife Area to a petroglyph site in the Topock Gorge. Along the way a guide narrates natural and cultural history. The jetboat slows down for animal sightings—which, during the cooler months, can be often. Call for tour times and prices.

***Dixie Belle* Tour Boat** (928-855-0888 or 866-332-9231), located in the English Village. Open daily, weather permitting; call for reservations and tours times. For a quick lowdown on Lake Havasu's high points, take an hour-long tour on this paddlewheel boat around the Island, a human-made isle with lodging, restaurants, and London Bridge Beach. As the paddlewheel chugs around the Island, the captain shares fun facts about the lake, the town, and the lower Colorado River while identifying popular places and activities on the lake. $15 per person. Dinner cruises available.

London Bridge Gondolas (928-486-1891), English Village next to Dixie Belle Tours; reservation required. Add serenades to lake scenery on a 20-, 40- or 60-minute gondola tour of the lake for $18, $35, or $45 (respectively) per person.

DOG PARKS 🐾 **Lion's Dog Park** (928-453-8686), 1340 McCulloch. Open 6 AM–10 PM. Lion's Park follows along the Colorado River. Fenced area with a dog fountain.

FISHING **Lake Havasu** has the nation's largest warm-water fisheries program. The lake coves are lined with "crappie condos," "catfish houses" and "bass bungalows" that give fish a place to spawn and hide from predators (except fisherman, of course). The fish housing has created a boom in the small mouth bass and crappie population. Famous for its striped bass, Lake Havasu holds the state Colorado River record for black crappie, green sunfish, and redear sunfish. One of the best times to cast for stripers is in summer when they're actively chasing the shad in the surface waters of the lake. Take a pair of binoculars to spot seagulls. Where seagulls gather (right above schools of shad), stripers aren't far away. Neither are the anglers; they just go from boil to boil. Lakeside hot spots are **Take-Off Point** and **Havasu Springs Resort**. **Site Six** and **Mesquite Bay** have free handicapped-accessible fishing docks.

GAMING—You can hop on the *Kon Tiki* nautical shuttle from London Bridge ($3 round-trip) that takes you across the lake to **Havasu Landing Resort & Casino** on the Chemehuevi Reservation in California. In Parker, the elegant **Blue Water Resort & Casino** (888-243-3360), 11300 Resort Dr., has almost 500 slot, river view rooms, nightly entertainment, fine and casual dining, indoor waterpark, beach, and activity Island.

GOLF **Emerald Canyon Golf Course** (928-667-3366), 7351 Riverside Dr., Parker. The 18-hole, par-72 championship course gets the nod from regional and national golf gurus. Described as raw, rugged, and ravishingly beautiful, it's the site of Southwest Section Senior PGA Championship games. The course has a putting green, driving range, practice green, beverage cart, snack bar, and pro shop. $55.

London Bridge Golf Course (928-855-2719), 2400 Clubhouse Dr. You have two courses to chose from here. Oldé London was the first course built in Lake Havasu City and has a traditional layout rife with water hazards and sand bunkers. Nassau has a number of elevation changes, which means great lake views. But watch out, it's got a narrow fairway and fast greens. $15–49.

KAYAKING If you have your own kayak, you can launch from **Cathedral Rock**, areas along **Windsor Beach**, and **Cattail State Park**. Vendors also rent vessels along the beaches. If you want to go on a guided tour or paddle from Topock Gorge, **WACKO** (Western Arizona Canoe & Kayak Outfitters) (928-855-6414) will outfit and shuttle you. Call for information and prices.

LAND TOURS **Segway of Lake Havasu** (888-422-8198), 2650 Kiowa Blvd. has 1- and 2-hour tours that whir through the Bridgeway Channel to Rotary Park or takes you on a speedy slalom on the bike path. **Sunset Charter Tour Co.** (928-716-8687) takes you by boat to trails in the backcountry to learn about the desert and the area's history. Reservations are recommended.

WALKS **Bridgewater River Walk**. Located on Rotary Park Beach (1400 S. Smoketree). Anytime of year is perfect for a walk along the river. In winter you have your choice of time of day. In summer get out in the cool freshness of the early morning—or wait for sunset, when you see a poetic side to the fast-paced lake. The **Island** (across the London Bridge) has a 4-mile paved walkway.

✷ Wilder Places

Like just about everything else, these wilder places are centered on water, and you will need a boat, canoe, or kayak to travel them. If you don't have your own, see To Do for information on rentals or tours.

Havasu National Wildlife Refuge (760-326-3853). Just over half a dozen decades ago the banks along the lower Colorado River had galleries of cottonwood and willow trees that formed a rich riparian habitat. After Parker Dam tamed this segment of river in 1941, pooling Lake Havasu, the water submerged the cottonwood galleries and formed a waterlog of marshes. The ecosystem transitioned into a waterfowl dream. As one of the best bird-watching spots on the lower Colorado River, the federal government designated the 30 miles between Needles, California, and Lake Havasu City as a wildlife refuge. Clucks, peeps, and chirps continu-

TOPOCK GORGE

ally rise from thickets of tules—8- to 15-foot-high bulrushes—that border the river where you might hear the infamous *kek-kek-kek* of the elusive Yuma clapper rail, one of the four endangered bird species found in the refuge. Southwestern willow flycatcher, peregrine falcon, and southern bald eagle are the others.

Topock Gorge (760-326-3853). Take AZ 95 north to I-40; go west on I-40 to the Golden Shores exit, turn left, and go under the railroad bridge to the marina on the left. If you want to locate the heart of the western Colorado River, you might find it beating in its lower reaches near Yuma, where riverboat commerce had its heyday and colored the history of the river. Its soul, however, would hover in Topock Gorge. At times moody and introspective, then deeply inspirational, the gorge has evoked legends and lore from the different cultures that have passed through it. Rows of needlelike hoodoos, arches, and curious formations carve the gorge's copper ridges leaning pell-mell into one another. In the late 1800s riverboat captains had moments of difficulty and tragedy navigating its midsection, cluttered with serpentine writhes and sandbars, prompting names of landmarks like Devil's Elbow. The jagged ridgelines in the upper gorge inspired the name for Needles, California. Spindly and pinprick-sharp, the hoodoos pocked with arches akin to needles' eyes create a strange beauty. Free.

✷ Lodging

London Bridge Resort & Convention Center (928-855-0888 or 800-624-7939), 1477 Queens Bay. The resort, with its English-castle exterior, has an atmosphere of casual elegance. Walk into the lobby just to see the replica of England's Gold State Coach The property—in the middle of everything at the English Village next to the London Bridge—includes three pools, Jacuzzi, business center, restaurant and nightclub, a golf course, a fitness center, and laundry facilities. Suites have fully equipped kitchenette, coffee service, TV and stereo, multiline cordless phone, robes, and fine linens. The property has a boat launch and an area to store your boats (extra). No pets. Call for rates.

Nautical Inn Resort & Convention Center (928-855-2141 or 800-892-2141), 1000 McCulloch Blvd. The only beachfront accommodation becomes a lively spot when the weather heats up. It's located on an island created by a man-made channel, and boaters cruise right up to the shore and hang out on the patio/bar. Guests can use the 150-foot pool and swim-up bar where there's no shoe, no shirts, but plenty of service, a hot tub, and a conference center. The newly built dry-stack storage and private boat launch are a big draw for boat owners. The inn is the headquarters for the Desert Storm Boat Race in April (where 55-foot vessels top out at 160 mph). At the end of the day, the racers come back to the inn to celebrate their day. Landlubbers head for the multi-use bike path just down the road. Newly remodeled rooms have queen or king beds, TV, refrigerator, private patio, or balcony. Reservations highly recommended during summer. $79–350.

✷ Where to Eat

DINING OUT **Angelina's Italian Kitchen** (928-680-3868), 2137 W. Acoma Blvd. Open for dinner Tue.–Thu. 4–9:30, Fri. and Sat. 4–10. This local favorite, located away from the din of boat motors and tourists, serves up some good Italian classics. It's best to make reservations on weekends. $8–14.

Barley Brothers Brewery & Grill (928-505-7837), 1425 McCulloch Blvd. Open daily 11 AM–1 AM. You can get a decent sandwich or meal here, including dinner salads and pastas, or create your own wood-fired pizza. Plus, they make award-winning microbrews to quench your thirst, from lemon-tinged blond ale to double-espresso stout. Entrées $9.95–24.95.

Cha-Bones (928-854-5554), 112 London Bridge Rd. Open daily 11–10. The name (actually the nickname of one of the owners' son) sounds soul food, but it's more food for the soul: Angus beef, fresh seafood, back ribs, and tapas. Owners Laurie and Tom Moses practically built the whole restaurant, which is based on quality—inside and out of the kitchen. Laurie designed the building, and the family worked together on the interiors to create one of the city's finer spots. In the kitchen, Laurie and her son Cameron use only the freshest and finest foods. Fish are flown in daily and the Angus beef practically melts in your mouth. Twenty tapas go great with the daily half-price Happy Hour (3–6) or as mini meals. The most popular fare is the prime rib French dip at lunch and black eye prime rib (with shrimp and Cajun sauce) for dinner. The ribs are so tender, you can just use a fork, not your hands (so no need for a hand wipe). You can BYOBB (Build Your Own Bones Burger—from hand-formed Angus beef) or BYOB Pizza (handcrafted with pan sauce–infused oils and fresh toppings). Entrées $13.99–38.99.

Javelina Cantina (928-855-8226), 1420 McCulloch Blvd. Open Sun.–Thu. 11–10, Fri. and Sat. 11 AM–11 PM. Grab a beverage (they make specialty margaritas, the newest being pomegranate, from a stash of 90 different tequilas) and find a spot on the back deck, where you can watch boaters and Jet Skiers cruise by. The Sonoran cuisine menu has some excellent fish tacos, fajitas, and *rellenos*. Grilled salmon is a favorite entrée. It's a hot spot on summer weekends; best to make reservations then. Entrées $9.95–18.95.

♥ **Shugrue's** (928-453-1400), 1425 McCulloch Blvd. Open for lunch and dinner from 11–11. Chef Greg Gugliotta's elegant menu has a variety of different flavors and cultures. But don't let the variety put you off. It's all fresh, full of flavor and done well. They're known for their fish and steaks, but the Pork Loin Chop (pretzel crusted and topped with orange-mustard sauce) is tender as a filet mignon and chicken comes four ways. The Ruby Red Ahi (blackened or sesame seared and served with steamed jasmine rice, grilled bok choy, and lemon soy butter) is a favorite. Have your steaks with one of a half-dozen sauces and a number of sides ($4–6). Or try the hamburger of the week (50 Burgers 50 Ways, featuring burgers from each state of the union, a different burger each week). But try to leave room for dessert. The pastry chef creates some great endings, such as Bananas Foster. $14.95–34.95.

EATING OUT ✐ **The Turtle Grill** (928-855-1897), 1000 McCulloch Blvd. Okay, it looks like *Teenage Mutant Ninja Turtles on Vacation*, but somebody back there in the kitchen knows what they're doing. At breakfast, it's Starbucks Coffee and some of the lightest buttermilk pancakes you've tasted, along with some great basics (eggs, bacon, etc.). For lunch or dinner, create your own masterpiece pizza, for which they're known. The pasta is distinctive, such as Island Chicken Penne with cilantro-citrus sauce and Caribbean Shrimp Linguine in a creamy island-spiced rum and garlic sauce; steaks are Angus and seafood a deal (a pound of king crab legs for $24). The World Famous Turtle Buckets is the drink menu from Trader Vic's on hormones. Even if you don't imbibe, have fun reading the menu. Breakfast $4–6, pizza $11–18, dinner $10–26.

Uncle Kenny's Café (928-680-7100), 362 London Bridge Rd. Open 6-ish to 2 PM. "We don't have anything special," Uncle Kenny's cook, Grumpy, remarked when asked what's so special that so many people like the restaurant, "but I wouldn't send anything out I wouldn't eat." Grumpy's right, UK's is a typical diner, but the food is good. It's a hot breakfast spot for the locals that serves up big plates at small prices all the way through lunch. Grumpy uses monster tortillas for the breakfast burrito because, "it's easier for us gringos to roll." They often make things for customers not on the menu, like homemade corn beef hash, or a kid's meal of animal pancakes. A happy face pancake shows up now and again on some of the adults' plates. "We're all a bunch of crazy lunatics here," Grumpy said about the staff, which has all been there "forever." "We can't get fired, so let's have some fun." $2.45–8.80.

✱ Selective Shopping

Stroll the **English Village** next to London Bridge. This shopping area celebrates the bridge's heritage with an English theme. Shops sell souvenirs, food, and specialty items.

✱ Special Events

January: **Polar Bear Ski Run** (928-486-0106) is for all those interested in testing their intestinal fortitude in the cold winter waters.

February: **HavaBBQ** (928-680-3815) starts the Kansas City Barbeque Society's year-long calendar of events with three dozen teams creating quintessential barbeque foods and competing for cash. **Winterfest Festival** (928-855-4115) attracts 40,000 people with its music, vendors, food, kids' activities and off road motor sports. The **Winterblast** (928-855-4115) fireworks display, courtesy of the pyrotechnics convention that meets here annually, puts on a dazzling fireworks show for the common man along the lakefront.

March: **Juried Springs Art Show** (928-855-6340) at the Aquatic Community Center.

July: **Fourth of July Fireworks Display** off the Island at dusk.

October: **London Bridge Days** (928-855-4115) celebrates the dedication of London Bridge with a parade, fun, and festivities. **IJSBA Word Finals** (928-764-2210, ext. 615) shows just how fast and fancy those personal watercraft can get.

December: **Festival of Lights** (928-855-0888) displays more than one million lights under London Bridge. **Boat Parade of Lights** (928-855-8857) presents the Lake Havasu Yacht Club's finest decked out in lights.

YUMA

Since its start in the mid-1800s, Yuma's quiet prominence has popped up throughout the West's history. Yuma's claim to fame grew from an anomalous geological feature that made it the crossing of choice over the impetuous pre-dam Colorado River. Two granite outcroppings—Indian Hill and Prison Hill—forced the river to cut a deep channel, narrowing the flow to 400 yards just south of its confluence with the Gila River.

This passage became known as Yuma Crossing, and over the years it has brought waves of peoples through the city. First came the steamboats and their colorful cargo and crew. When Native peoples saw the first steamboat, they surmised it was the devil approaching with all its fire-and-brimstone glory. Although the steamers always seemed to have a swell of chicanery about them, their payload supplied the growing frontier. Next, fortune seekers made their way via Yuma to gold-rich mountains in California. More than 60,000 gold seekers crossed the Colorado using a rope ferry at the end of the Gila Trail, now Yuma's Main Street. In 1877 the railroad laid tracks on a bridge at the crossing, allowing trains to enter the state for the first time. Decades later the Ocean-to-Ocean Bridge allowed auto traffic to cross the Colorado River, linking San Francisco with New York. The crossing provided a chance for thousands of immigrants to find a new life in California during the Dust Bowl and Great Depression.

Although Yuma's farming foundation started with cotton and citrus, its climate got the attention of Middle Eastern date growers. In 1944, farmers started growing Medjool dates. The signature red box used by Arizona grower Bard Date Company to pack its quality Medjools is the taste standard of excellence used around the world. Since the late 1970s, the farmland around Yuma has produced more than 90 percent of the vegetables sold in a U.S. winter. Practically frost-free and sunny, it's a perfect winter climate for veggies and people, too, not to mention the birds that migrate from points north along the Colorado River. Guinness World Records honors Yuma as the sunniest place on earth, with 339 sunny days and less than 4 inches of rain.

Once World War II ended and the buzz from military personnel at the Yuma Proving Grounds quieted down, Yuma's great winter weather led the whole city into a cyclical rhythm. The city accommodated human and avian snowbirds and crops in winter, and then turned ghost town empty when summer arrived But, since the turn of the 21st century, Yuma has developed in a number of areas.

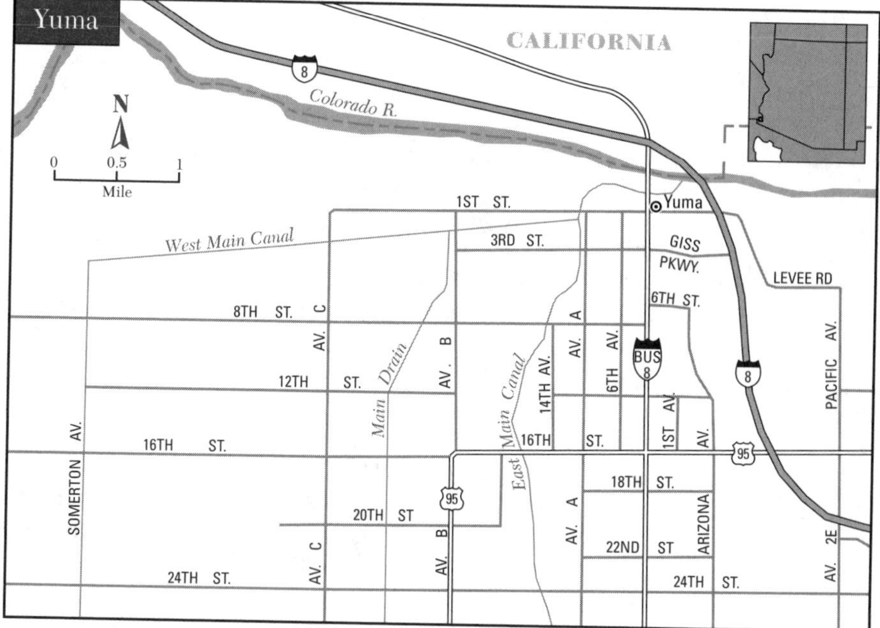

The city has taken on a major restoration project at Yuma Crossing, the historic section of the city along the Colorado River, and it has developed into an international business scene appearing in *Forbes* magazine as one of the Top Ten Up-and-Coming Tech Cities in the U.S. and topping the list in *Inc.* magazine's Boomtowns: Hottest Small Cities. It's also serving up some great food besides the tradition Mexican fare for which it was strictly known. For a city that feeds the nation, is an international hub, and serves as a major wintering spot for avians and humans, Yuma may not get the prominence it deserves, but it sure does have some great winter weather.

GUIDANCE **The Visitors Information Center** (928-783-0071 or 800-293-0071), 201 N. 4th Avenue (inside the historic Yuma Quartermaster Depot State Historic Park), has maps of the historic section and information to get you around town. Open Nov.–Apr., Mon.–Fri. 9–6, Sat. 9–4, Sun. 10–2; Mar.–Oct., Mon.–Fri. 9–5, Sat. 9–2.

GETTING THERE *By car:* Yuma lies at the southern end of AZ 95 and on I-8 on the western border of Arizona. *By bus:* **Greyhound Bus** has a station at 170 E. 17th Place. *By air:* **Yuma International Airport** (928-726-5882) is serviced by United Express and America West Express and can handle any craft up to a 747.

WHEN TO COME With Yuma known as the city with sunshine 95 percent of the year, you can understand why the city's population doubles in winter when temperatures average in the 70s. Summers linger in the triple digits; many businesses take a seasonal siesta.

MEDICAL EMERGENCY Yuma Regional Medical Center (928-344-2000), 2400 S. Avenue A.

✷ To See

The Camel Farm (928-627-7511), Avenue 1E and County 16th St. Open Oct.–May, Mon.–Sat. 9–5. If the romantic silhouettes of palm trees in date gardens against an ice blue or fluorescent sky at twilight aren't enough to make you feel like you're in the Middle East, check out this camel farm with one of the largest camel herds in North America. Livestock includes Arabian camels, Arabian oryx, African pygmy goats, Asian water buffalo, scimitar-horned oryx, and Watusi cattle. $4 adults, $3 seniors, age 3 or under free.

Sanguinetti House Museum (928-782-1841), 240 S. Madison Ave. Open Tue.–Sat. 10–4 year-round. You don't see a lot of old adobe buildings in Yuma because of the propensity of the Colorado River to flood before the river was dammed. Pioneer merchant E. F. Sanguinetti's home, however, still stands and is the headquarters of the Rio Colorado Chapter of the Arizona Historical Society. You can see artifacts, photographs, and furnishings from life during the territorial days. The home features gardens and aviaries with exotic birds. $3 adults, $2 seniors 60-plus and ages 12–18, under age 12 free.

Yuma Crossing State Historic Park (928-329-0471), 201 N. 4th Ave. Open daily Nov.–May 9–5 (call for summer hours); closed Christmas Day. The compelling stories of all the cultures that lived in the sultry riverside heat gets told at the site of the Quartermaster Depot—a compound made up of the commanding officer's quarters, office of the depot quartermaster, quartermaster's storehouse, water reservoir, and corral house. The depot was a clearinghouse for thousands of army supplies shipped by steamers on the Colorado River then disbursed to army installations around the Southwest. Displays feature military and cultural artifacts, pictures, and animated quotes from past residents describing life along the river. $3 age 14 and up.

✷ To Do

BIRDING Located along the Pacific Flyway, Yuma and points along the Colorado River, such as **Imperial National Wildlife Refuge**, **Mittry Lake**, and **Martinez Lake** (all in *Wilder Places*), constitute a major birding area. Waterbirds, waterfowl, and passerines drop in from fall through spring, when more than 200 species of migrating birds travel the flyway. Black-crowned night heron, great blue heron, snowy egret, and osprey make their homes here. Wintering waterfowl—flocks of Canada geese and a variety of northern ducks—start appearing in Dec. and don't leave until late Feb. Also in winter, you'll see a variety of ducks, American white pelican, double-crested cormorant, and northern harrier. You may also sight the yellow-billed cuckoo, summer tanager, southwestern willow flycatcher, Yuma clapper rail, and Virginia rails.

Betty's Kitchen (928-317-3200). Take US 95 to Ave. 7E, turn left, go 9 miles past Laguna Dam, and turn left at the sign. Located just south of Mittry Lake, a 0.5-mile loop trail managed by Bureau of Land Management tunnels inside a forest of trees along the Colorado River near Laguna Dam. Named Betty's Kitchen for a restaurant that once stood in the residential area before getting wiped out in a 1983 flood, now it's a hot spot for birds and wildlife to gather.

YUMA CROSSING NATIONAL HERITAGE AREA
(928-373-5198) Located at 1st St. and 4th Ave., the Heritage Area actually consists of several different projects—some still a work in progress. Pivot Point Interpretative Plaza, next to the Hilton Garden Inn, is an outdoor exhibit built where the first railroad train entered Arizona in 1877. A kiosk gives you the historical lowdown, and the original concrete pivot on which the rail bridge turned to allow steamboats to pass adds a hands-on piece of history to the story. A 1907 Baldwin steam locomotive stands on the exact alignment of the original tracks. Gateway Park, just beyond Pivot Point, got its start in the mid-1990s by the residents of Yuma when they cleared exotic vegetation along the river. This was the beginning of the award-winning restoration project to return the Lower Colorado's path along Yuma to its former pristine vegetative state. The Ocean-to-Ocean Bridge spans the river at this point, and sandy beaches give you a chance to sun and swim. The West Wetlands is a remarkable example of how to turn garbage into something precious. Once the town dump, the 110-acre natural preserve has been transformed into a natural wetlands and nature area. It includes a butterfly garden, burrowing owl apartments, a millennium tree grove, and a children's park designed by kids. The Stewart Vincent Wolfe Creative Playground has a castlelike structure filled with rooms to duck in and out of and slides to zip down, along with swings, teeter-totters, and other amazing amusements. The East Wetlands is one of the projects in process—a 1,400-acre reserve located between the confluence of the Gila and Colorado Rivers and the Ocean-to-Ocean Bridge. Nearly 400 acres of trash and nonnative vegetation have been cleared from the river banks; 50,000 native trees, shrubs, and other plants planted; and more than 220,000 cubic yards of dirt moved to create two miles of side channel and a number of backwater lakes. Several miles of trails wind along the river and lagoons. Backwash filters flush the saline soil to help regenerate it. All this has encouraged the bird population to double and increase diversity of birds, mammals, reptiles, amphibians, and insects. All free.

DATES Since the 1920s, farmers from the Yuma area and Egypt have been visiting one another, swapping farm technology. Like the Nile River Valley, the Coachella and Bard Valleys have date trees. The area is the world's largest producer of Medjool dates. The trees, imported from Middle Eastern countries such as Algeria, Tunisia, and Morocco, created the world's oldest-known cultivated crop of dates. The date stands present a misplaced but exotic scene. You can watch the harvest Sep.–Nov. The produce gets transformed into yummy delights, from dried fruit to date shakes.

Basket Creations and More (928-341-9966), 245 S. Main St. Open 10–5. The retail distributor for Bard Date Company makes it possible for you to enjoy the sumptuous Medjool dates in a variety of ways—shakes, chocolate covered, stuffed, and plain.

Ehrlich's Date Garden (928-783-4778), 868 S, Avenue B. Open daily 9–5 during harvest. This date garden has about 10 different varieties totaling more than 300 trees. Their harvest begins in Aug. and continues through Oct.

Imperial Date Gardens (760-572-0277), 1517 York Rd., Bard, CA. Take 4th Ave. north into California; turn right onto S-24 and go about 6 miles; turn right onto Ross Rd., and continue for about 12 miles to the gardens on your left. Open Mon.–Fri. 9–5; Nov.–Feb., also open Sat. 9–5 and Sun. 10–5.

THE WORLD'S FINEST MEDJOOL DATES GROW IN THE YUMA VALLEY

DOG PARK 🐾 **Bark Park** (928-373-5243), 1705 E. Palo Verde St. Open dawn–9 PM. Let Bowser run to his heart's content in the 3.5-acre off-leash park. The park has double-entry gates, benches, trees, water fountain and doggy waste stations.

FISHING **Martinez Lake Resort** (928-783-9589 or 800-876-7004) rents boats, has a kayak and canoe shuttle, and offers guided fishing. From Yuma, go north on US 95 for 25 miles, turn left (west) onto Martinez Lake Rd. and drive 13 miles to the signs directing the way to the lake. For every mile of river flowing through Martinez Lake, there are five miles of backwater ponds. This is fisherman heaven. One feature Martinez Lake has over most all other waterways in the state is an abundance of private docks. These wooden structures built on underwater stilts make perfect hideouts for bass. Anglers can cast their bait under the docks just as if they were skipping a rock across the water's surface . . . and get a bass surprise. Catfish grow huge here, too—bigger than an ocean fish—requiring tackle fit to fight marlin.

GAMING **Cocopah Resort and Casino** (928-726-8066), US 95 and County 15th St., Somerton. The casino has come a long way from the days (only a couple years ago) when it was a bingo mecca. The casino still boasts award-winning bingo, but it also has table games, 500 slot machines, and video poker. Besides rooms (kids under age 12 stay free) and a restaurant, the expanded walls also include the Wild River Family Fun Center that features bowling and laser tag.

GOLF Because of its sunny weather, Yuma is ranked among the best cities in the country for golf by *Golf Digest*, Yuma might surprise you with its golf options. Especially attractive are the incredibly reasonable prices on well-maintained courses that you can use year-round (just be sure to finish your game by midmorning in summer).

Desert Hills Municipal Golf Course (928-344-4653), 1245 Desert Hills Dr. Open Jan.–Mar., sunrise or 6 AM. Considered one of the best municipal facilities in the state, the par-72 championship course hosts several professional events. The property has a driving range, restaurant, and pro shop. $35–48.

Mesa Del Sol Public Golf Club (928-342-1283), 12213 Calle del Cid. A par-72, 18-hole champion course designed by Arnold Palmer with a number of par-3s to give your game some kick. Driving range, restaurant, and pro shop. $24–46.

HIKING You can take a 1.5-mile loop hike on the **Painted Desert Trail** in Imperial National Wildlife Refuge (see *Wilder Places*). A day trip away up AZ 95 to the north, experienced hikers can get a wilder landscape on the **Kofa Queen Canyon** and **De La Osa Well** routes in the Kofa National Wildlife Refuge (see *Wilder Places*).

MEXICO A 10-minute drive can take you to the Mexican border, where you can park your car and dip into the little village of **Algodones** to shop, refresh yourself at a cantina or restaurant, and visit a pharmacy, doctor, or dentist. Algodones reciprocates the business with two festivals: Welcome Winter Visitors Festival in Dec. and Thank You Festival in Mar. See page 238 for tips on visiting Mexico.

BARD DATES ARE KNOWN AS THE BEST AROUND THE WORLD

HOT-AIR BALLOONING Tranquil Sensations (928-343-2218). Oct.–May. Take a 60- or 75-minute ride at daybreak above the desert floor to see the jigsaw flow of farms and craggy uplifts of volcanic tuft mountains. Once you land back on terra firma, celebrate the flight with a champagne brunch. Call for rates and schedules.

OUTDOOR EVENTS Friday Night Social (928-376-0100), Main Street. Oct.–Mar. If you're in Yuma the last Friday of the month, head to the historic downtown section. Shopkeepers have their doors open for business, car enthusiasts bring their restored numbers and park them up and down the street. Music fills the air and food your stomach. Yumans like to get out and about, so it's a fun time.

RIVER TOURS In a land that only gets about 3 inches of rain a year, a waterway as significant as the lower Colorado River creates a lush contrast with the desert environment. The best way to get to know the Colorado and its wildlife is to travel it by tour boat. **Yuma River Tours** (928-783-4400) offers 2-hour to all-day tours. Tours depart from Fisher's Landing at Martinez Lake (see *Fishing*).

SEGWAY TOURS You can zoom along the river on a Segway provided by **SegwaYUMA Tours** (928-342-1969). Go on a beginner 1-hour tour ($39.95 per person), 1½- hour tour ($59.95) or advanced ($69.95 for 2 hours).

WINE TASTINGS **Market Wine Bar Bistro** (928-373-6574), 1501 S. Redondo Center Dr. Every Mon. 4:30–7:30. Chef Anthony Spinella pairs tapas and wine together. You can order wines by the glass for $5. The **Old Town Wine Cellar** (928-373-0405), 265 Main St. Suite E) has wine tastings every Thu. and Fri. 4–7. Owner Mike Shelhamer grabs bottles from his collection of 500 wines from around the world. $5 for 6 tastings.

✷ Wilder Places

Imperial National Wildlife Refuge (928-783-3371). From Yuma, go north on US 95 for 25 miles; turn west onto Martinez Lake Rd., continue for 13 miles, and follow signs to the visitor center. Open daily. The 25,768-acre Imperial NWR protects and enhances a 30-mile section of the lower Colorado River in Arizona and California, including its associated backwater lakes and wetlands. These marshy areas have given the refuge the nickname of Arizona's Everglades.

Imperial Sand Dunes (760-337-4400) From Yuma, head west on I-8 for about 20 miles. Like a scene from a science-fiction movie, the barren-looking dunes here rise more than 250 feet. Anything but barren, you can find unusual plants and animals unique to this area. The movie-set look worked perfectly for *Star Wars: The Return of the Jedi* and *Stargate*. On winter holidays, starting with Halloween to Easter, the dunes blossom into a small city when tens of thousands of campers with dune buggies gather to buzz around the Sahara-like landscape. The Bureau of Land Management's admission fee of $25 is good for seven days.

Kofa National Wildlife Refuge (928-783-7861), 356 W. 1st St. (office). From Yuma, take US 95 north toward Quartzite, Arizona, to refuge entrance signs. Hot, dry, and rugged, the Kofa National Wildlife Refuge has a surprising native, the California fan palm, flourishing in its mountains. This is one of the few spots in Arizona with native California fan palms, likely descendants from glacial-era palms growing in the area. If you're lucky, you might spot another of the refuge's main attractions: one of the desert bighorn sheep rambling over the refuge's rocky outcrops. The 665,400-acre refuge has a herd of about 800 bighorns, which traipse the area's rugged Kofa and Castle Dome Mountains. These rhyolite peaks have the kind of precipitous landscape sheep like.

Roads and trails are few and far between in this large refuge. You can explore the hillsides further on foot, but not by vehicle. The best time to visit is late fall through early spring, when temperatures remain mild.

Mittry Lake Wildlife Area (602-942-3000). Just downriver from the Imperial National Wildlife Refuge, between Imperial and Laguna Dams, pools a backwater paradise that has become all things to all beings. Fish and fishermen, birds and birders, wildlife and its watchers all find what they're looking for at Mittry Lake Wildlife Area, jointly managed by the Arizona Department of Game and Fish with the U.S. Bureau of Land Management and U.S. Bureau of Reclamation.

While largemouth bass, channel catfish, flathead catfish, crappie, and bluegill lurk in the marshy waters of the dredged lake, a variety of birds take to its labyrinth of bulrushes and cattails. During a winter's visit to the shallow lake, you might see grebes, cormorants, herons, and pelicans, all of which commonly make appearances. Target birds to sight include the western warbler, Crissal thrasher, and Abert's towhee. You might also see, or at least hear, a least bittern or Virginia rail.

✷ Lodging

BED & BREAKFASTS Jenny Kent B&B (928-783-4520), 450 S. Orange Ave. The town's only B&B is located just-inside the historic area. The home, listed on the National Register, was built by schoolteacher Jenny Kent, who taught at the school still standing across the street. The simple interiors get their elegance from wood floors and interesting art on the shelves and walls. Six rooms (king, double, and three with twin beds) have their own baths, Hosts Natalie and John provide a European-style breakfast (yogurt, eggs, cereals, cheeses, and vegetables), but will make a full American-style breakfast upon request. $79.

HOTELS AND INNS 🏵 🐾 ✎ ♿ ((T))
Coronado Hotel (928-783-4453), 233 4th Ave. This Best Western property carries a bit of history: It was the first motor hotel in Yuma. The rooms—large king, queen, or family suites—have a clean, friendly eclectic décor. The property includes two swimming pools and a laundry facility. Rooms have microwave, mini fridge; coffeemaker, safe, free local calls under 30 minutes and free long-distance access. Grounds have a year-round hot tub, two pools, guest laundry facilities, free photocopy and fax services. Your stay includes breakfast at next-door Yuma Landing Restaurant. This eatery, located on the spot where the first airplane landed in Arizona in 1911, has a pictorial transportation museum featuring planes, trains, and automobiles along with quirky memorabilia. Pets are welcome, with no deposit charged. $79.50–89.50.

La Fuente Inn & Suites (928-329-1814), 1513 E. 16th St. The independent hotel has basic rooms, but with personality—color and at bit different furnishing. The mature landscaping on the grounds give is an oasis-like feel. Rooms have a mini fridge, cable, and

YUMA'S POST OFFICE IS IN A HISTORIC BUILDING

include a complimentary full breakfast, *USA Today* newspaper, and complimentary social hour (cocktails and appetizers). Grounds include pool, gas barbeque, fitness room, laundry facilities, $89–119.

♿ "ı" **Hilton Garden Inn at Pivot Point** (928-783-1500), 310 N. Madison Ave. Located right along the riverfront, where all the restoration and cultural things are occurring. The lobby walls read like a newspaper about historic happenings in Yuma. Wall art in the rooms is taken from the heritage area just outside the hotel. The grounds include a pool, laundry/valet service, lounge, restaurant, business center, and fitness center. Rooms have a microwave, mini fridge, coffeemaker, 37-inch flat-panel TV, *USA Today* delivered, clock radio with MP3 connection, oversize desk with laptop pull-out, and in-room printing to the business center. Call for rates.

Radisson Hotel Yuma (928-783-8000), 1501 S. Redondo Center Dr. The owners of this Radisson wanted color in the interior design. And color they got. The designer balanced cobalt blue, fuchsia, and purple in the lobby in a striking, but pleasing, way. The rooms are bright with yellows and red and have a mini fridge, 32-inch flat-screen TV, and down pillows and comforter. Some rooms have Sleep Number beds. Call for rates and specials.

🐾 ✐ ♿ "ı" **Shilo Inn Hotel** (928-782-9511), 1550 S. Castle Dome Ave. You get a great deal here—a basic, clean room with tons of amenities, free high-speed Internet access, free local and long-distance phone calls, a complimentary hot buffet breakfast, two complimentary drinks, an outdoor pool (the largest in Yuma), a fitness center with sauna and steam room, and fresh coffee, fruit, and popcorn in lobby. Kids age 12 and under stay free. Pets are okay with a $10 deposit. $114–134.

✷ Where to Eat

DINING OUT Ciao Bella Ristorante Italiano (928-783-3900), 2255 S. 4th Ave. Open for lunch Mon.–Fri. 11–2 and Mon.–Sat. for dinner 4:30–10; closed Sun. Chef Abel Garcia found his calling with this wonderful Italian menu. The dining area ranges from packed to cozy-cramped; people have been known to feign reservations to slip in without one. All the food is good, from the classic spaghetti and lasagna to True Cod Olivia grilled with olive tapenade over lemon risotto, or signature rack of lamb with berry froth. Several of the desserts are made in-house. You get to choose from more than 100 different labels of wine at reasonable prices. Lunch $7–10, dinner $13–25.

Garden Café & Spice Co. (928-783-1491), 250 S. Madison Ave. Open Tue.–Fri. 9–2:30, Sat. and Sun. 8–2:30; closed May–Oct. Entrepreneur E. F. Sanguinetti once lived in the home where this restaurant is located. Just walking down the brick corridor to the all-outdoor seating area is a treat. The walkway has potted plants, colorful singing birds, and gushes with bougainvillea. Aviaries line the patio—Mr. Sanguinetti loved his birds. It's the place of choice for breakfasts with such fare as specialty quiches, homemade breads and muffins, and pancakes. The Kamman sausage—a spicy Yuma specialty—makes eggs snappy. The breakfast salad combines granola, low-fat yogurt, and fresh fruit, then tops the mixture with raspberry sauce. For lunch, it's sandwiches, homemade soups and their signature strawberry turkey salad. Grilled tri-tip entrées make popular, heartier meals. Save room for rich desserts, especially the

Torture Cake—a family recipe named so because it's torture to stop eating it. Sunday brunch buffet presents a gourmet lineup of egg and meat dishes and sides, fruit, and homemade breads and muffins. Entrées $8.50–9.95.

♿ **Market Wine Bar Bistro** (928-373-6574), 1501 S. Redondo Center Dr. Open for breakfast 6:30–11, lunch 11–3, dinner: 5–10. Walking into this Radisson restaurant is like entering a festival with all its vibrant colors. Chef Anthony Spinella's Mediterranean menu presents some of the freshest food around. The whole idea behind the restaurant was to bring a touch of international sophistication to Yuma. Chef Anthony, who graduated from the French Culinary Institute in New York after externing in St. Tropez, crafts flavors so pleasantly, your meal may end up being one of your more memorable ones. The fish, flown in fresh daily, is a high point on the menu, from the lightly fried calamari to the baked mussels with garlic to the special of the day. The seared Lamb Riblets are a great appetizer and Creekstone Farms Black Angus rib eye or filet mignon makes a tender meat entrée. Pastas come with light, savory sauces. The wine list has interesting labels. Try the Greek red wine. Entrées $15.95–29.25.

Mi Rancho (928-344-6903), 2701 S. 4th Ave. Open Mon.–Thu. 11–9:30, Fri. 10–10, Sat. 8–10, Sun. 8–9:30. Mi Rancho mirrors the flavors and ambience of Old Mexico. You can order classic fare such as enchiladas, tacos, or tortas; or traditional ceviche, *camarones*, *machaca*, *menudo*, and beef tongue—sometime goat. It's all great. A smaller, and cozy-quaint cultural, version—Tacos Mi Rancho—is located just down the street at 188 S. 4th Ave. Entrées $7.99–12.99.

River City Grille (928-782-7988), 600 W. 3rd St. Open for lunch Mon.–Fri. 11:30–2, dinner every night 5–10. The menu leans toward seafood here, flown in fresh from the Pacific Northwest, presented with several different cultural influences East-meets-West style of cooking shows up in the appetizers. Entrées are all over the globe: bouillabaisse, curried shrimp, seafood gumbo, and Jamaican jerked chicken The food's good for you, too—leaning toward low fat and using all-natural beef, wild-river salmon, and Denver lamb. The two outdoor brick patios make pleasant dining alternatives. Entrées $15.95–24.95.

EATING OUT **Brownie's Restaurant** (928-783-7911), 1145 S. 4th Ave. Open Sun.–Thu. 6 AM–3 PM; Fri.–Sat. 6 AM–9 PM. The descriptive statement on the menu explains it all at this local diner where you're likely to see people of all strata—*Good food served right. Where you leave with a full stomach and money in your pocket.* When Brownie's first opened for business in the 1930s, it was the only

THE ENDURANCE FLIGHT

The military had a big influence on the town in World War II. Major Gen. George S. Patton established the Desert Training Center (later known as California-Arizona Maneuver Area) in 1942. More than a million men trained here for combat. In 1943, the army opened the Yuma Test Branch at what is currently the Yuma Proving Ground. When the war ended, the servicemen left and the town quieted down, as in pre–ghost town status. In an attempt to lure the military back, a handful of leaders decided to convince the military that Yuma made a great place for air space, and they did so via the Endurance Flight in 1949. The plan: have an Aeronca Sedan plane named *City of Yuma* circle continuously around Yuma to demonstrate the flight-friendly skies. The *City of Yuma* took off on August 24. To keep the flight continuous, a Buick convertible assisted with refueling the plane. The process required a man to stand on the convertible while it was moving and pass up a gas can (a tall metal creamer can with a strap welded to it, which had a filter and a piece of chamois to make the liquid ultra clean) while the plane flew low enough to track with the auto. The flight could have gone longer than its 1,056 straight hours, but one of the *City of Yuma*'s taillights went out, which forced the pilot to land on October 10. The flight made history as the longest ride at the time in the world.

The U.S. Marine Corps was impressed, and it moved its air station to Yuma. Today, America's allies from around the world test equipment at the Yuma Proving Grounds. Fly Field, named after Col. Benjamin Fly, has the longest runway in the state.

restaurant that would serve the Native peoples, and they remain loyal to this day. You can't beat the breakfast ($5.25–7.25, with specials for $4.95). For lunch, Angus beef hamburgers ($5.95–7.25) are favorites and the dinner steak bonanza draws diners ($9.95–11.95). It's a busy place, but things move fast here and waits are minimal.

The Chili Pepper (928-783-4213), 1030 W. 24th St. Open Mon.–Sat. 8 AM–8 PM. This Yuma staple has locals who have been away for any length of time heading straight for its cafeteria-style dining room to indulge in very basic, very good Mexican food. The smell of homemade tortillas greets you in the parking lot. Breakfast burritos are served until 10 AM. From then on, it's rolled tacos, tortillas, burritos, and a small variety of dinners. Entrées $3.85–4.60.

8th Street Taquerías. In Mexico, some of the tastiest food is available through street vendors. Yuma has its own version of street food on 8th Street, west of 4th Ave. The lineup of *taquerías* starts after El Chorro (a local favorite restaurant) and Elvira's Bakery. These kitchen-in-a-trailer with outdoor seating brings the term *local food* to a new level. Finding them open is hit–or-miss, but definitely worth the try.

Lutes Casino (928-782-2192), 221 S. Main St. Open Mon.–Thu. 10–8, Fri. and Sat. 10–9, Sun. 10–6. The state's oldest pool hall and domino parlor makes an entertaining stop for a hamburger as legendary as the establishment's reputation. Its motto, "Where the Elite Meet," refers to such folks as Clark Gable, who played poker at the now tamed and family-oriented business at a time when pool games lead to wild fights. The wildest thing to happen these days is the Special—an interesting combination of hamburger and hot dog with melted "orange" cheese on a bun said to have been dreamed up when Bobby Lutes imbibed too much tequila. Be sure to douse this half-breed critter with hot sauce. Without a doubt, the hamburgers are king here. Entrées $3.75–5.50.

✷ The Arts

Yuma Art Center & Galleries (928-329-6607), 254 S. Main St. From ongoing art exhibitions in its five galleries to lectures to plays to classes, this art center covers all the bases of artist expression. The center includes an historic 640-seat theater and B&W photography darkroom. Call 928-783-0071 for more information.

January: Old West reenactment groups ride into Yuma during the **Gathering of the Gunfighters at Yuma Territorial Prison State Historic Park** (928-783-4771). **Yuma Lettuce Days** (928-782-5712) celebrates Yuma's status as the country's number two producer of lettuce.

February: **Silver Spur Rodeo** (928-344-5451) at the fairgrounds.

Late February or early March: **The North End Classic** (928-373-0700; www.northendclassic.com) is one of the first pro road biking events of the year and draws more than 400 participants from all over the world.

March: **Midnight at the Oasis** (928-343-1715) classic car show features 1,000 classic cars, regional food, and music concert. **Marine Corps Air Station Yuma Air Show** (928-269-3245) gives viewers a chance to ogle military and civilian aircraft in the air and on the ground at the marine base.

April: The **Yuma Birding and Nature Festival** (928-376-0100) features birding tours, slide shows, and nature tours.

November: **Colorado River Crossing Balloon Festival** (928-343-1715) draws balloonists, by invitation, from all over the world for three days with launches, balloon glow on Saturday night.

YUMA'S ANNUAL BICYCLE RACE DRAWS CYCLISTS FROM AROUND THE WORLD

INDEX

C

D

E

F

G

H

I

J

M

N

O

S

X

Y

Z